Computational Social Sciences

Simulating the Past

This innovative series publishes current international research and instruction on the methodological and theoretical aspects of quantitative and computer simulations in socio-historical contexts. Books published in this series bring together theories, techniques and technologies from backgrounds such as history, ecology, archaeology, anthropology, geography and sociology, combining them with established methodologies from the computational and complex systems sciences in order to promote deeper understanding and collaboration within the study of past human behavior and history.

Situated at one of the most dynamic interfaces of the emerging field of digital humanities and hard sciences, this series covers existing and novel computational approaches in connection with the presentation of case studies from numerous regions of the world and all prehistoric or historic periods. Particular topics of interest include, but are not limited to: have applications of computational modeling in archaeology and history, social organization and change, as well as socio-cultural transmission and evolution.

The audience for all books within this series consists of researchers, professionals and academics.

More information about this series at http://www.springer.com/series/15553

Philip Verhagen • Jamie Joyce
Mark R. Groenhuijzen
Editors

Finding the Limits of the *Limes*

Modelling Demography, Economy and Transport on the Edge of the Roman Empire

OPEN

Springer

Editors
Philip Verhagen
Faculty of Humanities
Vrije Universiteit Amsterdam
Amsterdam
The Netherlands

Jamie Joyce
Faculty of Humanities
Vrije Universiteit Amsterdam
Amsterdam
The Netherlands

Mark R. Groenhuijzen
Faculty of Humanities
Vrije Universiteit Amsterdam
Amsterdam
The Netherlands

ISSN 2509-9574 ISSN 2509-9582 (electronic)
Computational Social Sciences
ISSN 2524-6135 ISSN 2524-6143 (electronic)
Simulating the Past
ISBN 978-3-030-04575-3 ISBN 978-3-030-04576-0 (eBook)
https://doi.org/10.1007/978-3-030-04576-0

Library of Congress Control Number: 2018966816

This Springer imprint is published by the registered company Springer Nature Switzerland AG
The registered company address is: Gewerbestrasse 11, 6330 Cham, Switzerland

Preface

Background

This volume in the series Simulating the Past and in the introduction Computational Social Sciences presents the results of a 5-year research programme titled 'Finding the limits of the *limes*: Using spatial dynamical modelling to reconstruct and understand the development of the cultural landscape in the Dutch part of the Roman *limes*'. The programme, which ran from September 2012 to August 2017 at the Faculty of Humanities of the Vrije Universiteit Amsterdam, was financed by NWO (the Netherlands Organisation for Scientific Research) under the VIDI Innovational Research Incentives Scheme (project number 276-61-005) and aimed to apply spatial dynamical modelling to reconstruct and understand the development of the cultural landscape in the Dutch part of the Roman *limes* zone from 12 BCE to 270 CE. It focused on modelling economic and spatial relations between the Roman army and the local population, in particular the interaction between agriculture, animal husbandry and wood management and the related development of settlement patterns and transport networks in the area.

The project was in essence intended as a testing ground for a number of computer (simulation) modelling approaches that, up to then, had had very little impact on Roman archaeological research in the Netherlands and beyond. The idea for the project originated at a small workshop organised by the University of Basel in January 2011 themed 'Calculations in (bio)-archaeology', where an overview was presented of the state of the art of quantitative approaches to environmental archaeology for the Roman period in NW Europe. While advanced computer simulation models had already been applied to archaeological research questions in many parts of the world and for many time periods (see Van der Leeuw and McGlade 1997; Kohler and Gumerman 2000; Bentley and Maschner 2003; Kohler and Van der Leeuw 2007), Roman archaeology at the time seemed to be largely unaware of the utility of simulation modelling to address archaeological research questions. Also, the adoption of GIS as an analytical and modelling tool seemed, with some exceptions (Vermeulen et al. 2001; Van der Leeuw et al. 2003; Goodchild 2007; Kay and

Witcher 2009), to have been relatively slow. This terra incognita, to use an appropriate Latin phrase, therefore seemed a potentially fertile ground for extending advanced computer modelling approaches. In particular, it was anticipated that the then emerging technologies of agent-based modelling (ABM) and social network analysis (SNA) could contribute to a better understanding of economy, land use and demographic development in the Roman period, especially when combined with more traditional, static and GIS-based models – hence the reference to 'spatial dynamical modelling' in the project title. However, it was also clear that in order to demonstrate and test the utility of this approach, a rich archaeological and palaeo-environmental data set was needed that would cover a substantial geographic space.

Since the Dutch *limes* area ticked both boxes and had also been the subject of extensive previous research by scholars from the Vrije Universiteit Amsterdam and other Dutch universities, it was decided to apply for the project with NWO in October 2011 (Verhagen 2011). The key objectives were defined as follows:

- Producing new perspectives on the development of the cultural landscape in the *limes* area during the Roman period, by translating current theoretical approaches into spatial dynamical models that include the macro-regional scale, the temporal dimension and the interaction between the natural, economic and sociocultural factors shaping the landscape
- Producing a set of procedures and tools (best practices) on how to use spatial dynamical modelling, and in particular ABM, for this purpose

It was the ambition to connect models of subsistence production at the household level to regional and supra-regional trade models, to link models of agricultural production to models of natural vegetation development, to connect models at different scale levels (micro- and macro-regional) and to find suitable methods to confront the model outcomes with the available archaeological and palaeo-environmental data.

The project proposal was positively evaluated in May 2012 and consequently work started in September 2012 by the applicant and two PhD students. Jamie Joyce fully focused on the archaeobotanical and archaeozoological aspects and developed agent-based models of agricultural production and fuel consumption at the settlement level. Mark Groenhuijzen worked on the palaeogeographical reconstruction and developed computer-based analyses of settlement patterns and transport networks at the regional level. Philip Verhagen took care of archaeological data collection, analysis and interpretation and focused on palaeo-demographic and palaeo-economical modelling.

Project Outcomes

Formally, the project was finished in August 2017, but publication of the research findings has taken some more time, with this volume as one of its results together with various articles already published (Groenhuijzen and Verhagen 2015, 2016,

2017; Joyce and Verhagen 2016, Verhagen et al. 2016a, b) and two PhD dissertations (Joyce 2019; Groenhuijzen 2018). As indicated in the proposal, the methodological approach was completely new for the area and time period addressed and aimed to integrate different geographical, temporal and thematic scales of analysis. Apart from developing new methods and tools in simulation modelling, network analysis and GIS, we have also compiled a new, comprehensive database of archaeological records of the area, prepared a detailed palaeogeographical reconstruction and performed the first macro-regional analysis of the development of land use and settlement in the area.

It is, however, important to stress that the research done in this project has not only focused on modelling as a methodological improvement but also to evaluate archaeological research questions of a larger scope and geographical scale than many of its predecessors. Our approach proved to be most valuable for two aspects of the research. First of all, it integrated models of agriculture, animal husbandry and wood production and investigated their interdependency. The models of agricultural production (see Chap. 7; Joyce) are, as far as we are aware, the first to achieve this kind of integration. Second, it contributed to understanding the spatial effects of changes in economic and settlement systems. The question of distribution of goods and interaction between Roman and local settlements was tackled using network construction and analysis techniques that can be integrated into simulation modelling approaches (see Chap. 12; Groenhuijzen).

A major challenge for the agricultural production models was the translation of 'expert judgement' models into formal simulation models, since the assumptions underlying expert judgement models have varying degrees of certainty. Simulation modelling offers an environment to experiment with different scenarios, so this can be seen as a strong point of the chosen approach: uncertainties can be made (more) explicit, and their consequences for the behaviour of the system under consideration can be explored. However, the sometimes anecdotal evidence and contradictory archaeological interpretations available implies that the level of detail of the individual model components is not the same. This implies a large degree of freedom in experimenting and a wide array of possible conclusions on the interplay of the factors involved, highlighting the crucial importance of sensitivity analysis. It has also become clear that scaling up of the agricultural production models from the level of the individual household to the full study region is a task that is at the limits of the capabilities of currently available, off-the-shelf modelling solutions. Experiments carried out by De Kleijn et al. (2018) with our data sets show that other spatial modelling techniques may be helpful for this.

For the transport network modelling, we had to deal with uncertainties in the interpretation of archaeological information and its spatial distribution. In particular, the (lack of) chronological accuracy of find spots can potentially play havoc with the network reconstructions for specific time periods, and simulations of many potential networks were therefore necessary to assess the robustness of the reconstructions and analyses. Furthermore, the development of tools to reconstruct and analyse potential transport and communication networks needed much work to refine existing techniques and making these operational for use with spatial data.

Apart from these methodological results, the project has tried to address two major archaeological research questions. The first one is the question of surplus agricultural production for the Roman army in the study area, based on the hypothesis of Van Dinter et al. (2014) that (partial) provisioning of the soldiers with food must have been possible. From our modelling, it is concluded that the major limitation to agricultural production must have been the availability of workforce, as the area must have posed few limitations to the expansion of settlement and growth of agricultural production, with the exception of the marshlands in the west of the Netherlands. Specialised production, while evidenced to some extent in the archaeological record, does not seem to have been a necessary condition to produce the required surplus, but the models do not rule out the possibility either. Also, scaling up from subsistence-only to surplus production must have been relatively easy given the available land and workforce, even when the exact amount of possible surplus is hard to gauge given the uncertainties surrounding population densities and demographic development (see Chap. 3; Verhagen). However, the low availability of woodland in most of the region may have had long-term effects on the possibility to collect fuel and building material in the immediate vicinity of settlements. Also, the gathering of wood for fuel may have had a significant effect on the availability of workforce.

Secondly, the transport network modelling has resulted in new insights regarding the possible transport and distribution of goods. Local transport networks were thus far mostly neglected in studies on the Dutch *limes*. Our research shows that the position of sites within local networks can explain some of their characteristics, such as stone-built architecture, the presence of grain storages and their (assumed) function as a redistribution site. These results lend support to earlier assumptions on the existence of a system of collection and redistribution through local centres. However, the precise mechanisms responsible for the growth of certain sites still need to be explored. Social and economic interaction between the military and local population also remains a somewhat underexplored modelling theme, with at the moment only tentative interpretations possible of, for example, the negative effects of army recruitment on available workforce and the balance between taxation or forced requisition and market-based trade.

The impact of the project is currently mostly visible in the community of archaeologists involved in simulation and network modelling. Some of our approaches were never applied before, in particular the integrated agricultural production model developed by Jamie Joyce and the transport network reconstruction techniques by Mark Groenhuijzen, and we are confident that these will be useful tools for future research in other contexts. The impact on the archaeological discipline at large and Roman archaeology in particular is harder to gauge at this moment. Simulation modelling is not yet very well established in archaeological research, and the final results from our studies, while pointing indeed to novel explanations for observed settlement patterns, also raise a number of new questions, in particular where it concerns the economic and social theories underpinning the interpretative frameworks used to understand the development of the Roman *limes*. This implies that further research should focus even more on finding ways to translate expert judgement and incomplete evidence into formal models and to investigate socio-economic issues at larger scales than the settlement level.

Setup of This Volume

Importantly, this volume is not just a final report of our project. In January 2017, we organised a project conference in Amsterdam to present our preliminary results (https://limeslimits.wordpress.com/project-conference-2017/) and invited various other researchers to present case studies and reflect on the application of computer (simulation) modelling to the four most important themes we focused upon: subsistence economy, demography, transport and mobility, and socio-economic networks in the Roman period. The papers presented at this conference form the core of this book, with most of the presenters having submitted a chapter.

In this volume, we do not present a general theoretical framework and introduction to the modelling approaches used. Several good introductions exist on how to use ABM (Premo 2010; Kohler 2012), SNA (Collar et al. 2015) and GIS (Conolly and Lake 2006; Verhagen and Whitley 2012) to tackle archaeological research questions, and numerous case studies have appeared over the last two decades where these are used and sometimes even combined to good effect.

The volume is roughly subdivided into three sections: demography and settlement (Chaps. 2, 3, 4, and 5), economy (Chaps. 6, 7, 8, 9, and 10) and transport and movement (Chaps. 11, 12, 13, 14, and 15), although some papers also make connections between the subjects. After a general introduction to the Dutch *limes* zone (Chap. 2; Verhagen, Joyce & Groenhuijzen), Section 1 starts with a chapter by Isabelle Séguy, who provides backgrounds and thoughts on the demography of the *limes* zone, highlighting the special character of the region as an immigration zone. This is followed by a discussion of the demographic model we developed (Chap. 3; Verhagen) to better understand the mechanisms of population growth and decline in the area, which highlights the importance of social and economic factors when trying to project demographic developments and to estimate population sizes from generalised demographic assumptions. Tyler Franconi and Chris Green (Chap. 4) then demonstrate how 'broad-brush' approaches based on large datasets can provide valuable information on large-area population and settlement dynamics, especially when considered over longer time spans than just the Roman period. Antonin Nüsslein (Chap. 5), on the other hand, shows how the detailed study of the development trajectories of excavated settlements in NE France was used to understand the characteristics and diversity of survey data and thus could be applied to study the development of settlement patterns in larger areas.

Section 2 starts with a discussion by Willem Jongman of the macro-economic setting of the *limes* zone (Chap. 6). Jamie Joyce then summarises the set-up and outcomes of the agricultural production model for the *limes* zone (Chap. 7). Antoni Martín i Oliveras and Víctor Revilla Calvo (Chap. 8) then take us to Spain in a study on modelling the economy of wine in the Roman period. Eli Weaverdyck (Chap. 9) stays close to home, with a GIS-based statistical model of the distribution of settlements with regard to possible markets in the Dutch *limes*, applying an approach that he developed earlier for the Lower Danube *limes*. Stefano Bertoldi, Gabriele Castiglia and Angelo Castrorao Barba (Chap. 10) then bring us to the Ombrone Valley in the heart of the Roman Empire, where they show how combining spatial and network analysis and the study of diagnostic find categories can shed light on the spatial and economic organisation of hierarchical settlement systems.

The last section starts with an extensive overview of modelling of routes and transport networks (Chap. 11; Verhagen, Nuninger & Groenhuijzen). Mark Groenhuijzen then presents his work on reconstructing the local transport network of the Dutch *limes* (Chap. 12) and its implications for the interpretation of the settlement pattern. After that, Pau de Soto (Chap. 13) shows that network analytical approaches can be used to understand connectivity over the large scale, by analysing the Roman road network of the Iberian peninsula. Another Spanish case study is then presented on modelling and understanding the development of the Roman road network in the northwestern Iberian peninsula (Chap. 14; Parcero-Oubiña et al.). Katherine Crawford (Chap. 15), finally, takes us to the micro-scale with her analysis of movement in the city of Ostia.

Acknowledgements

A special word of thanks goes to Dr. Alžběta Danielisová at the Czech Academy of Sciences (Prague) for her help with and peer review of the simulation models developed by Jamie Joyce. We also want to thank Dr. Laure Nuninger (UMR 6249 Chrono-Environnement, Besançon) for stimulating Mark Groenhuijzen to pursue the comparison of spatial network reconstruction and analysis techniques and for her hospitality on four separate occasions, which in the end also allowed us to finish this volume. Special thanks also go to Prof. Nico Roymans at the Faculty of Humanities, Vrije Universiteit Amsterdam, who, as formal PhD supervisor, has been very supportive of the project and on various occasions supplied us with perspectives from the non-modelling side that made us rethink our model assumptions. Also, a word of thanks to Dr. Willem Jongman (Department of History, University of Groningen) for his enthusiasm and advice to pursue this book.

A large number of colleagues in and outside the Netherlands have participated in discussions in conference sessions and workshops, have given us solicited and unsolicited advice and provided us with data. In particular, we want to thank the members of the *Werkgroep Nederrijnse Limes* ('Working Group for the Lower Rhine *Limes*') for sharing their profound knowledge of the Dutch Roman *limes* with us, Ivo Vossen (Antea Group Archeologie, Oosterhout) for giving us access to his database of archaeological sites, Dr. Marieke van Dinter (ADC Archeoprojecten, Amersfoort) for sharing her data and knowledge of the palaeogeography of the *limes* zone, Dr. Maurice De Kleijn (SpinLab, Vrije Universiteit Amsterdam) for fruitful discussions on past land use modelling, Dr. Stijn Heeren (Faculty of

Humanities, Vrije Universiteit Amsterdam) for commenting on paper drafts and sharing his data on Roman *fibulae*, Dr. Iza Romanowska (Barcelona Supercomputing Centre) and Dr. Tom Brughmans (University of Oxford) for preventing us from falling into the pitfalls of simulation model programming and Dr. Matthias Lang (eScience Centre, University of Tübingen) for his advice on database issues.

Of course, we are also very grateful to the invited authors of this volume, who agreed to contribute their chapters to this book and who have provided us with new perspectives on many issues. We hope that the publication process has been smooth and that you will find the book to your liking. Finally, we want to thank the reviewers of the chapters of this book, who provided their feedback enthusiastically and on time. We hope that the final result matches your expectations.

Amsterdam, The Netherlands

Philip Verhagen
Jamie Joyce
Mark R. Groenhuijzen

References

Bentley RA, Maschner HDG (eds) (2003) Complex systems and archaeology. Empirical and theoretical applications. University of Utah Press, Salt Lake City

Collar A, Coward F, Brughmans T, Mills BJ (2015) Networks in archaeology: phenomena, abstraction, representation. J Archaeol Method Theory 22:1–32. https://doi.org/10.1007/s10816-014-9235-6

Conolly J, Lake M (2006) Geographical information systems in archaeology. Cambridge University Press, Cambridge

De Kleijn M, Beijaard F, Koomen E, Van Lanen RJ (2018) Simulating past land use patterns; the impact of Romans on the Lower Rhine delta in the first century AD. In: De Kleijn M (ed) Innovating landscape research through Geographic Information Science. Implications and opportunities of the digital revolution in science for the research of the archaeology, history and heritage of the landscape from a GIScience perspective. Vrije Universiteit Amsterdam, Amsterdam, pp 125–148. Available at http://dare.ubvu.vu.nl/handle/1871/55517. Accessed on 7 June 2018

Goodchild H (2007) Modelling Roman agricultural production in the middle Tiber valley, Central Italy. University of Birmingham, Birmingham

Groenhuijzen MR (2018) Palaeogeographic analysis of the Dutch part of the Roman limes and its hinterland. Vrije Universiteit Amsterdam, Amsterdam

Groenhuijzen MR, Verhagen P (2015) Exploring the dynamics of transport in the Dutch limes. eTopoi J Anc Stud Special Volume 4:25–47. Available at http://journal.topoi.org/index.php/etopoi/article/view/203. Accessed on 5 July 2018

Groenhuijzen MR, Verhagen P (2016) Testing the robustness of local network metrics in research on archeological local transport networks. Front Digit Humanit 3(6). https://doi.org/10.3389/fdigh.2016.00006

Groenhuijzen MR, Verhagen P (2017) Comparing network construction techniques in the context of local transport networks in the Dutch part of the Roman limes. J Archaeol Sci Rep 15:235–251. https://doi.org/10.1016/j.jasrep.2017.07.024

Joyce J (2019) Farming along the limes. Using agent-based modelling to investigate possibilities for subsistence and surplus-based agricultural production in the Lower Rhine delta between 12 BCE and 270 CE. Vrije Universiteit Amsterdam, Amsterdam

Joyce J, Verhagen P (2016) Simulating the farm: computational modelling of cattle and sheep herd dynamics for the analysis of past animal husbandry practices. In: Multi-, inter- and transdisciplinary research in landscape archaeology. Proceedings of LAC 2014 Conference, Rome, 19–20 September 2014. Vrije Universiteit Amsterdam, Amsterdam. https://doi.org/10.5463/lac.2014.59

Kay SJ, Witcher RE (2009) Predictive modelling of Roman settlement in the middle Tiber valley. Archeologia e calcolatori 20:277–290. Available at http://www.archcalc.cnr.it/indice/PDF20/21_Kay.pdf. Accessed on 14 May 2018

Kohler TA (2012) Complex systems and archaeology. In: Hodder I (ed) Archaeological theory today. Polity Press, Cambridge, pp 93–123

Kohler TA, Gumerman GJ (eds) (2000) Dynamics in human and primate societies: agent-based modeling of social and spatial processes. Oxford University Press, New York

Kohler TA, Van der Leeuw SE (eds) (2007) The model-based archaeology of socionatural systems. SAR Press, Santa Fe

Premo LS (2010) Equifinality and explanation: the role of agent-based modeling in postpositivist archaeology. In: Costopoulos A, Lake M (eds) Simulating change. Archaeology into the twenty-first century. University of Utah Press, Salt Lake City, pp 28–37

Van der Leeuw SE, McGlade J (eds) (1997) Time, process and structured transformation in archaeology. Routledge, London

Van der Leeuw S, Favory F, Fiches J-L (2003) Archéologie et systèmes socio-environnementaux. Études multiscalaires sur la vallée du Rhône dans le programme Archaeomedes. CNRS Éditions, Paris

Van Dinter M, Kooistra LI, Dütting MK, Van Rijn P, Cavallo C (2014) Could the local population of the Lower Rhine delta supply the Roman army? Part 2: modelling the carrying capacity using archaeological, palaeo-ecological and geomorphological data. J Archaeol Low Ctries 5:5–50

Verhagen P (2011) Finding the limits of the limes. Using spatial dynamical modelling to reconstruct and understand the development of the cultural landscape in the Dutch part of the Roman limes. Vrije Universiteit Amsterdam, Amsterdam. Available at https://limeslimits.wordpress.com/full-project-proposal. Accessed on 6 July 2018

Verhagen P, Whitley TG (2012) Integrating archaeological theory and predictive modelling. A live report from the scene. J Archaeol Method Theory 19(1):49–100. https://doi.org/10.1007/s10816-011-9102-7

Verhagen P, Joyce J, Groenhuijzen M (2016a) Modelling the dynamics of demography in the Dutch Roman limes zone. In: Multi-, inter- and transdisciplinary research in landscape archaeology. Proceedings of LAC 2014 Conference, Rome, 19–20 September 2014. Vrije Universiteit Amsterdam, Amsterdam. https://doi.org/10.5463/lac.2014.62

Verhagen P, Vossen I, Groenhuijzen MR, Joyce J (2016b) Now you see them, now you don't: defining and using a flexible chronology of sites for spatial analysis of Roman settlement in the Dutch river area. J Archaeol Sci Rep 10:309–321. https://doi.org/10.1016/j.jasrep.2016.10.006

Vermeulen F, Antrop M, Hageman B, Wiedemann T (2001) Ancient roads and fields in Northwestern Gaul – a GIS-based analysis. In: Stančič Z, Veljanovski T (eds) Computing archaeology for understanding the past. CAA 2000. Computer applications and quantitative methods in archaeology. Proceedings of the 28th conference, Ljubljana, April 2000. Archaeopress, Oxford, pp 187–196. Available at https://proceedings.caaconference.org/paper/27_vermeulen_et_al_caa_2000. Accessed on 26 July 2018

Contents

1 **Finding the Limits of the Limes: Setting the Scene** 1
Philip Verhagen, Jamie Joyce, and Mark R. Groenhuijzen

Part I Demography and Settlement

2 **Current Trends in Roman Demography and Empirical Approaches to the Dynamics of the *Limes* Populations** 23
Isabelle Séguy

3 **Modelling the Dynamics of Demography in the Dutch Roman *Limes* Zone: A Revised Model** 43
Philip Verhagen

4 **Broad and Coarse: Modelling Demography, Subsistence and Transportation in Roman England** 61
Tyler Franconi and Chris Green

5 **A Different Vision of Ancient Settlement Dynamics: Creation and Application of a Model of Evolution of Roman Settlement of the Plateau Lorrain (France)** 77
Antonin Nüsslein

Part II Economy

6 **The Economic Archaeology of Roman Economic Performance** 95
Willem M. Jongman

7 **Modelling Agricultural Strategies in the Dutch Roman *Limes* via Agent-Based Modelling (ROMFARMS)** 109
Jamie Joyce

8 **The Economy of Laetanian Wine: A Conceptual Framework to Analyse an Intensive/Specialized Winegrowing Production System and Trade (First Century BC to Third Century AD)** 129
Antoni Martín i Oliveras and Víctor Revilla Calvo

9 The Role of Forts in the Local Market System in the Lower Rhine: Towards a Method of Multiple Hypothesis Testing Through Comparative Modelling 165
Eli J. S. Weaverdyck

10 A Multi-scalar Approach to Long-Term Dynamics, Spatial Relations and Economic Networks of Roman Secondary Settlements in Italy and the Ombrone Valley System (Southern Tuscany): Towards a Model? 191
Stefano Bertoldi, Gabriele Castiglia, and Angelo Castrorao Barba

Part III Transport and Movement

11 Modelling of Pathways and Movement Networks in Archaeology: An Overview of Current Approaches 217
Philip Verhagen, Laure Nuninger, and Mark R. Groenhuijzen

12 Palaeogeographic-Analysis Approaches to Transport and Settlement in the Dutch Part of the Roman *Limes* 251
Mark R. Groenhuijzen

13 Network Analysis to Model and Analyse Roman Transport and Mobility 271
Pau de Soto

14 Footprints and Cartwheels on a Pixel Road: On the Applicability of GIS for the Modelling of Ancient (Roman) Routes 291
César Parcero-Oubiña, Alejandro Güimil-Fariña, João Fonte, and José Manuel Costa-García

15 Rethinking Approaches for the Study of Urban Movement at Ostia 313
Katherine A. Crawford

Index 329

Chapter 1
Finding the Limits of the Limes: Setting the Scene

Philip Verhagen, Jamie Joyce, and Mark R. Groenhuijzen

Abstract The Dutch Roman *limes* zone has a rich history of archaeological and historical research. In this paper, we present an overview of the current state of knowledge as an introduction to other chapters in this volume dealing with the area's demography, economy and transport system (Chaps. 2, 3, 7, 9 and 12). The main historical developments are sketched against the background of ongoing archaeological research in the area, and the main hypotheses concerning the development of settlement and the rural economy are discussed.

Keywords Limes · Roman period · The Netherlands · Archaeology · Rural economy

1.1 Introduction

In this chapter, we sketch the geographical and historical setting of the Dutch Roman *limes*, together with background on the research history in the area and an overview of the main hypotheses on economic and demographic developments in the region. It serves to set the scene for the chapters dealing with modelling of the demographic development, subsistence economy and transport networks (Chaps. 2, 3, 7, 9 and 12). Inevitably, however, it can only touch the surface of a substantial and lively debate in Dutch Roman archaeology and should therefore be considered as a basic introduction. We have provided numerous relevant references to more in-depth studies for those wishing to know more about the details of specific research projects and the theoretical debate.

P. Verhagen (✉) · J. Joyce · M. R. Groenhuijzen
Faculty of Humanities, Vrije Universiteit Amsterdam, Amsterdam, The Netherlands
e-mail: j.w.h.p.verhagen@vu.nl; m.r.groenhuijzen@vu.nl

P. Verhagen et al. (eds.), *Finding the Limits of the Limes*, Computational Social Sciences, https://doi.org/10.1007/978-3-030-04576-0_1

1.2 The Geographical Space

The Dutch *limes* zone roughly comprises a 50 km wide strip in the middle of the Netherlands, stretching from the North Sea until Germany over a distance of approximately 150 km from west to east. To the north, the zone is bordered by the course of the Rhine, which was established as the northern frontier of the Roman Empire around the middle of the first century CE. The Romans never clearly demarcated the geographical extent of the *limes*, but it may have meant as much as a zone of hundreds of kilometres wide (Whittaker 1997). For all practical purposes, however, the Dutch '*limes* zone' can be defined as the extent of the two *civitates*, or allied states, of the Batavians and Cananefates immediately south of the Rhine. The exact extent of these *civitates* remains somewhat speculative, but it is thought that the Batavian *civitas* covered the zone roughly to the east of the current town of Woerden up into current Germany, and to the south it would have reached a few kilometres inland from the Meuse (*Maas*) river (Vossen 2003; Vos 2009). The Cananefatian *civitas* occupied the western half of the *limes* zone, roughly delimited to the south by the current provincial borders of Zuid-Holland (Fig. 1.1).

This region has undergone considerable environmental and anthropogenic change over the past 2000 years, leading to substantial changes in river courses, coastline, vegetation and land use. The Rhine diverted its main branch to the south in the course of the Early Middle Ages, and the current coastline dates from the Late Medieval period. Peat reclamation in the Late Middle Ages and Early Modern period created the current polder landscape, and large-scale urbanization in the

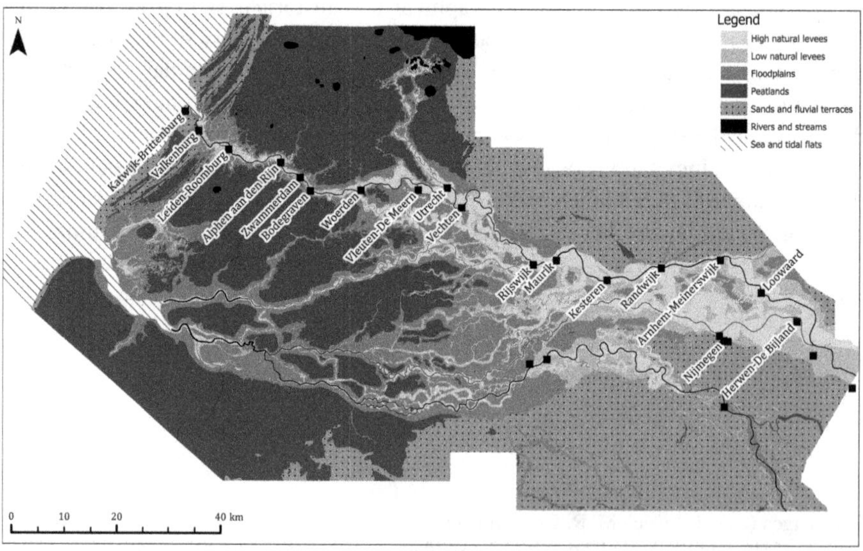

Fig. 1.1 Overview map of the Dutch limes zone, with reconstructed palaeogeography. (From Groenhuijzen 2018)

nineteenth and twentieth centuries further altered the rural landscape. All in all, the current region would be almost unrecognizable to the inhabitants of the Roman period. This means that no meaningful historical and archaeological analysis of the Dutch *limes* zone can be undertaken without a reconstruction of its palaeogeography. Fortunately, a palaeogeographical map of the north-western part of the *limes* zone was already assembled by Van Dinter (2013) on the basis of an extensive database of geological bore holes collected by the University of Utrecht, and of detailed LiDAR-based elevation data. We have followed her methodology to complete this reconstruction for the remaining area of the study region. A detailed description of the data sources used and the methodology applied is given in Groenhuijzen (2018).

On the basis of this reconstruction, we can broadly distinguish three major landscape zones in the Roman period from east to west. To the east of the current city of Utrecht, the landscape was dominated by fluvial landforms: river beds, levees and flood basins. These areas were mostly suitable for all kind of agricultural activities and posed no serious challenges for settlement and transport apart from the major river crossings. In a few places, glacial moraines form more pronounced hills; the city of Nijmegen was founded on one such outcrop. To the west of Utrecht up to the coastal dune area, the landscape was much wetter. Here, the levees only occupied narrow strips of land surrounded by vast areas of marshland and peat. Opportunities for settlement and agriculture were much more limited here. Finally, the coastal dune area formed a narrow strip of more elevated terrain that was eminently suitable for human occupation. Palaeobotanical evidence indicates that the *limes* zone was already largely deforested before the Roman period (Kooistra et al. 2013). More detail on the suitability of the landscape for human settlement and agriculture is given in Chap. 7 (Joyce).

1.3 History of Research

The interest in Roman frontier forts in the Netherlands has a long history and received its first impetus by the discovery of remains of the Brittenburg fort on the seaside near Katwijk in the sixteenth and seventeenth centuries (Dijkstra 2011). However, more focused research on the presence of the Romans in this part of the Netherlands only started with the excavations on the site of Arentsburg near current Voorburg by Casper Reuvens in the early 1800s, where the remains of the Cananefatian *civitas* capital Forum Hadriani were unearthed (Reuvens 1829). By the early twentieth century, Dutch archaeologists, operating from the State Museum of Antiquities (RMO) and the University of Leiden, had established the location of a number of Roman forts in the area and partly excavated a few of them, in particular the fort at Vechten (Fectio; see Polak and Wynia 1991). However, the structure and development of the *limes* forts remained rather obscure until the 1940s, when excavations by the University of Groningen at Valkenburg (Praetorium Agrippinae) yielded masses of new information (Van Giffen 1948, 1955), in particular since organic materials were very well preserved in the waterlogged conditions along the

Rhine. The Valkenburg fort therefore remains one of the best known examples of a Roman *castellum*. From then on, the number of known forts steadily increased through research by the State Service for Archaeological Research (ROB), universities and amateur archaeologists. A spectacular find was the discovery of six Roman shipwrecks in Zwammerdam between 1971 and 1974 (De Weerd and Haalebos 1973; De Weerd 1988), again pointing to the importance of the Dutch *limes* zone for the preservation of organic remains.

In the eastern river area, the course of the Rhine has shifted considerably since the Roman period, having obliterated many traces of occupation along the river. Consequently, very little new data on military sites in the eastern region has been added to the information that was available in the early 1990s (Bechert and Willems 1995). To the contrary, the western river area, where no substantial erosion has taken place, has yielded large amounts of new information over the past 20 years. This was spurred on by the new system for heritage management in the Netherlands which allowed for commercial excavations from 1998 onwards, and included more finds of Roman shipwrecks at Vleuten-De Meern (Van der Kamp 2007, 2009; Langeveld et al. 2010), and hitherto unknown smaller forts at Bodegraven (Van der Kooij et al. 2005; Vos et al. 2016) and The Hague-Ockenburgh (Waasdorp 2012). The position of the Roman forts west of Wijk bij Duurstede is therefore now well established, with the exception of the Brittenburg fort which is thought to have been eroded by the North Sea. A good overview of the development of the military infrastructure in the Dutch *limes* zone before 37 CE is given by Polak and Kooistra (2013). For the later period, however, a comprehensive synthesis is still lacking, even when the investigations of the individual forts have been published in much detail. Most of these are in Dutch, making them less accessible to the outside academic world.

The hinterland of the *limes* was traditionally less intensively studied, even though the city of Nijmegen (Noviomagus) has been a focus of investigation since the 1970s, since it is the only major Roman town and military centre in the Netherlands (Willems 1990; Willems and Van Enckevort 2009; Van Enckevort and Heirbaut 2010). The first regional analyses of the rural areas were published by Tom Bloemers (1978) and Willem Willems (1986) as part of their PhD research. Bloemers' study focused on the site of Rijswijk-De Bult, and he took great efforts to use the excavation results to understand the development of rural settlement of the Cananefatian area. Willems, on the other hand, worked on an overall inventory of settlement for the Batavian area, and produced one of the first truly regional archaeological studies in the Netherlands. The problem that both had to confront was that the excavation evidence and survey data were difficult to reconcile. The number of excavations at the time was limited and concentrated on the larger sites, so many of their conclusions have now been challenged, even when their work is still valuable for its broad overview.

Since then, the rural areas have become the focus of intensive academic and heritage management driven research with large surveys and extensive excavations carried out in the Kromme Rijn region (Vos 2009), the area around Tiel (Vossen 2003; Groot 2008; Heeren 2009), the Midden-Delfland region (Van Londen 2006) and the

Maaskant region (Jansen and Fokkens 1999). A relatively recent research focus is the military road connecting the forts, which has become the subject of detailed investigation since the early 2000s (Luksen-IJtsma 2010; Van der Heijden 2016).

1.4 Historical Setting

1.4.1 Early Roman Involvement (20 BCE–39 CE)

The region that would become the *limes* zone in the Netherlands is mentioned first in the historical record by Julius Caesar (BG 4.10). While Caesar's campaigns brought him to the Rhine in 55 BCE, possibly even fighting a battle at the bifurcation of Rhine and Waal, he had no great interest in the region (Willems 1986). Roman interference at first remained restricted: the Roman policy seems to have been to repopulate the area with allied tribes and control it in that way. In 16 BCE, this strategy proved unsuccessful when Germanic tribes raided into the Roman-controlled areas to the west and south of the Rhine. Possibly, these raids were triggered by the building of a legionary camp (*castra*) housing two legions at Nijmegen-Hunerberg in 19/20 BCE (Driessen 2007). In response, emperor Augustus dispatched his general Drusus, who, within a few years' time, launched three major campaigns into Germanic territory. Legions were stationed in Nijmegen, Xanten and Mainz in 15 BCE, and in 12 BCE the Roman fleet sailed into the North Sea to fight the Frisians and *Chauci* on the north coast of Germany. The operation included digging one or more canals and the construction of a dam in the river Waal to provide better access to Lake Flevo. There is no archaeological evidence of other military camps associated with this campaign, and the Nijmegen *castra* was abandoned in 12 BCE. By this time, the native peoples in the Lower Rhine region could already be divided into the Cananefates of the western region and the larger tribe of the Batavians in the east (Willems 1986).

The military base of operation was evidently thought to be effective, since the first Roman fort on Dutch territory was constructed in Vechten, probably between 5 BCE and 0 CE, at the entrance to the Vecht river (Zandstra and Polak 2012). During Germanicus' campaigns in 14–16 CE, two more *castella* were founded, at Velsen (Bosman and De Weerd 2004) and Arnhem-Meinerswijk (Willems 1980). The *limes* at that point in time did not exist as a military or political concept: Velsen is located to the west of Amsterdam, where the Oer-IJ river flowed into the North Sea. Nijmegen remained the centre of military operations, even when the military camp was much reduced in size after Drusus' campaigns. The town of Oppidum Batavorum developed alongside it from approx. 10 CE onwards and served as the Roman administrative and economic centre. It is doubtful whether the *limes* was, in this period, a well-organized infrastructure (as it clearly is in later periods) or rather a set of loosely connected key points. In 28 CE the supposedly pacified Frisians rebelled against Roman taxations and laid siege to the Velsen *castellum*. After this, the Romans withdrew their troops to the south of the Rhine.

1.4.2 The Development of the Limes as a Frontier Zone (39–70 CE)

Emperor Caligula took up the plan for the invasion of Britannia in 39 CE, leading to a new phase of military activity in the area. A fort was erected at Valkenburg, a new one built at Velsen, smaller fortifications were constructed in Alphen aan den Rijn and Vleuten-De Meern, and a first road may have been built to connect the forts along the Rhine. After the death of Caligula, emperor Claudius decided that it would be impossible to maintain two offensive armies stationed in the Lower Rhine area, one to fight in Britain, and one to fight in Germany. Instead, the Rhine was fixed as the northern boundary of the Roman Empire. During Claudius' reign, the number of forts expanded quickly. With the exception of Leiden-Roomburg, all known forts to the west of Vechten date from before 50 CE. These forts are assumed to initially have been built to protect shipping on the Rhine (Graafstal 2002). In addition, a new *castra* was developed at Nijmegen and numerous watchtowers were erected between the fortifications. General Corbulo, who oversaw the operation, also had a canal constructed that connected the Rhine to the Meuse estuary via an inland waterway. This makes clear that the Lower Rhine *limes* was designed as a transportation infrastructure more than anything else.

Where archaeological evidence is available, it is observed that the first forts were somewhat makeshift constructions made from earth and wood, which were already extended and repaired within a few years' time. The exact occupation strength of the forts is unknown, and it is doubtful whether they were at all times fully occupied. Each fort could station one cohort (technically 480 soldiers); the one at Vechten was built to house a double cohort. It is considered plausible that the forts were initially manned with local (Batavian) auxiliaries (Haalebos 1997), although nothing is certain in this respect (De Weerd 2006).

In this early period of Roman occupation, local and new groups were encouraged to settle in the region, leading to both economic development and population increase. Continuity of settlement from the pre-Roman Late Iron Age is likely with the rural population living in small settlements engaging in mixed agriculture with a focus on pastoralism that was characteristic of the Germanic tribes of the region (see Roymans 1996). A treaty between the Romans and Batavians (and perhaps also the Cananefates) is inferred from Tacitus (Germ. 29) in which the local population was exempt from taxation and instead supplied manpower for the army. In fact, 'no other population group within the empire was as intensively exploited for recruitment purposes' (Derks and Roymans 2006, 122). The actual number of recruited individuals has been discussed in a number of studies (e.g. Alföldy 1968; Bloemers 1978; Willems 1986; Vossen 2003). Verhagen et al. (2016a) demonstrated the negative impact on population growth that removal of young adult males from the marriage pool could have. Recruitment could also have had a negative impact on the availability of labour. The impact of incomplete households on agricultural productivity in the study region was discussed briefly by Van Dinter et al. (2014), but there remains scope for further discussion (see Chap. 2, Séguy and Chap. 3, Verhagen).

1.4.3 Integration in the Roman Empire (70–275 CE)

In 69/70 CE, a revolt among the tribes of the Dutch *limes* zone is attested in the historical sources (Tac. Hist. 4), connected to a much wider Gallic uprising related to the struggle for power in Rome after emperor Nero's death. Archaeological evidence shows that almost all forts along the Rhine were burned down, but they were rebuilt quickly. In order to keep better control of the region, the Romans built a new *castra* in Nijmegen and stationed the 10th Legion there. Oppidum Batavorum was deserted, and the population moved to the site of Nijmegen-Waterkwartier, where Ulpia Noviomagus, as the *civitas* capital of the Batavians, eventually developed into the only major Roman town on Dutch territory (Willems and Van Enckevort 2009). The policy of stationing local troops in the forts was changed. Auxiliary troops were now recruited from different parts of the empire, and included plain infantry, cavalry and naval units, although the emphasis is on infantry. Only Vechten and Vleuten-De Meern have yielded evidence for the existence of a civilian settlement before 70 CE, in all other cases the *vici* seem to date from after the Batavian revolt.

It is probable that from then on taxation was imposed on the local population (Groot 2008; Aarts 2013) and the area became formally incorporated into the empire as part of the province of Germania Inferior. From this point on, the Cananefatian *civitas* capital of Forum Hadriani started to grow into a small town (Driessen and Besselsen 2014). The *limes* became the formalized frontier of the Roman empire, and the linear system of forts seems to have been quite stable for a long time. Even when the military occupation strength in Germania Inferior was considerably reduced under emperor Trajan in 103/104 CE, there is little indication that this also led to a reduction in occupation of the *limes* forts (Polak 2009). In cases where we have sufficient evidence, it is clear that the forts and the connecting *limes* road were repaired, extended and improved on several occasions (Graafstal 2002; Van Rijn 2011). The major building activities are associated with the reigns of Hadrian, Marcus Aurelius and Septimius Severus. In the late second century, all forts were rebuilt in stone (tuff). Recently, it has also become plausible that a coastal defence system was established after approximately 150 CE (Dhaeze 2011).

Recent studies (Roymans 2004; Van Londen 2006; Groot 2008; Vos 2009; Heeren 2009; De Bruin 2017) have abundantly made clear that, despite the incorporation into the province of Germania Inferior, developments in the Lower Rhine region remained specific to the area and do not fit very well to generalized models of Roman 'colonization'. Even when Roman material culture and customs were gradually more and more adopted, both the Batavians and Cananefates continued to emphasize their own cultural identity throughout the Roman period, as is clear from inscriptions, building types, material culture, religion and subsistence economy. In particular, rural settlements consisting of byre houses remain abundant in the zones surrounding the *limes* forts.

1.4.4 The End of the Dutch Limes (~ 275 CE)

The end of the occupation of the *limes* forts is debated but is generally put around 275 CE, after the collapse of the short-lived Gallic empire, although Heeren (2017) argues that discontinuity cannot be proven and that some forts were garrisoned until 293 CE. It seems, however, that already in the mid-third century occupation was not maintained at the intended level, although there is no clear sign of abandonment of forts in this period. The prolonged political and economic crisis within the Roman Empire must have placed an enormous stress on the military system, and the general paucity of archaeological finds (notably coins) from that period may well point to an intermittent rather than permanent occupation. A tell-tale sign in that respect is that some *vici* already seem to have been deserted around 240 CE, and many rural sites come to an end or are dramatically reduced in size in this period. However, the collapse of the *limes* was not the end of the Roman involvement in the region: the defence system was eventually restored in the 290s (Heeren 2017), albeit in a different form. Even when certain forts were completely abandoned, several others seem to be have been used intermittently in Late Roman times.

1.4.5 Settlement Development and Population Size

Rural settlement densities in the Late Iron Age are thought to have been relatively low. A significant rise in the number and size of settlements has been extensively documented in the Early Roman B and Middle Roman A periods (25–150 CE; see Table 1.1 for the periodization used in Dutch archaeology). This is followed by a drastic decline in settlement density in the second half of the third century CE, which is usually linked to the collapse of the Dutch *limes* as a frontier. In fact, recent research suggests that the whole area was almost completely depopulated by the end of the third century (Heeren 2015; De Bruin 2017), before new settlers arrived in the late fourth century.

The site inventories for the study region suffer from poor dating, making it difficult to be specific about the precise development of settlement numbers and inhabitants in the region (see also Chap. 2, Séguy and Chap. 3, Verhagen). The method we

Table 1.1 Periodization of the Roman period used in Dutch archaeology

Period	Calendar years	Code (Dutch)	Code (English)
Late Iron Age	250 BCE–12 BCE	IJZL	LIA
Early Roman A	12 BCE–25 CE	ROMVA	ERA
Early Roman B	25–70 CE	ROMVB	ERB
Middle Roman A	70–150 CE	ROMMA	MRA
Middle Roman B	150–270 CE	ROMMB	MRB
Late Roman A	270–350 CE	ROMLA	LRA
Late Roman B	350–450 CE	ROMLB	LRB

developed (Verhagen et al. 2016b) to take into account ambiguity and uncertainty of dating, using the principles of aoristic analysis, largely corroborated earlier assessments, although our results suggest previous underestimates of Early Roman Period settlements (see also Vos 2009) and overestimates of Late Roman site numbers. The development of settlement numbers in the *limes* zone throughout the Roman period using this method is presented in Fig. 1.2. The study undertaken by Van Lanen et al. (2018) of demographic patterns in the eastern part of the *limes* region confirms this general pattern, even when the exact numbers are different because of a different approach to using poorly dated evidence.

Apart from the rural settlements, non-rural settlements started to appear in the area during the Early and Middle Roman period. The forts, associated *vici* and the urban centres were all installed by the Romans, and there is no clear evidence of rural settlements developing independently into real villages during the Roman period, even when some of them grew into larger sites with multiple farmsteads like Oss-Westerveld (Jansen and Fokkens 1999) and Wijk bij Duurstede-De Horden (Hessing and Steenbeek 1990). The only exception may have been the site of

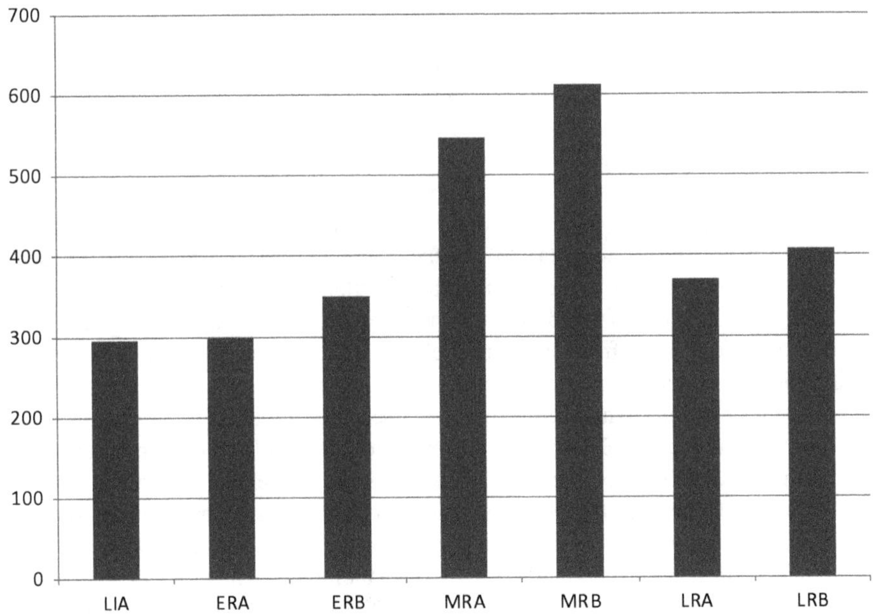

	LIA	ERA	ERB	MRA	MRB	LRA	LRB
Number of settlements	296	298	350	547	612	370	407

Fig. 1.2 Development of observed rural settlement numbers during the Roman period (After Verhagen et al. 2016b). The numbers are estimated taking into account uncertainty of dating, and refer to settlements that have a 0.5 or higher probability of having 10 or more artefacts from the period considered

Rossum (Grinnes) which was already a larger settlement in the Late Iron Age (Roymans 2004).

Growth of the 'urban' population is therefore closely tied to the military occupation of the area, with *vici* appearing alongside the forts mainly from 70 CE onwards. The number of forts is thought to have been between 16 and 21 with 350 soldiers each, bringing the total occupational strength to 5950–7700 soldiers (Van Dinter et al. 2014), and a similar number of non-military inhabitants in the *vici*, although not all forts have yielded evidence for an associated civil settlement. Apart from the troops needed to maintain the *limes*, the stationing of the 10th Legion in Noviomagus in the Flavian period implied an extra military force of 5000 soldiers plus approximately 2500 non-military inhabitants (Buijtendorp 2010) in the period 70–104 CE.

The development of Noviomagus, Forum Hadriani and also Ceuclum (Cuijk) into urban settlements was a gradual process, but even at the peak of its expansion, the town of Noviomagus may not have had more than 3000 inhabitants (Buijtendorp 2010). For Forum Hadriani and Ceuclum, these figures may have been close to 1000 (Buijtendorp 2010) and 750 respectively (Haalebos et al. 2002). All non-rural settlements were deserted after the collapse of the *limes* in 275 CE, with only Noviomagus and Ceuclum being re-occupied in the Late Roman Period.

Estimating the number of households, and thus the population per rural settlement is hard to gauge given that many of the settlements are known only from surface finds (Vossen 2003). Bloemers (1978) was the first to try to estimate rural population sizes in the Cananefatian *civitas* from settlement data, assuming that in the Early Roman period settlements on average consisted of one or two households with five to eight inhabitants. The size of the investigated settlements then increased in the Middle Roman period to an average of three to four households, an estimate that was repeated by Willems (1986) for the Batavian area. Vossen (2003) revised this average down to three and noted that large settlements of five or six households were exceptional. He also noted that settlements in the eastern part of the *limes* zone showed a range of sizes from single households to much larger settlements, which is also clear from our own data. Counting the number of registered house plans in our own dataset points to an average of 2.7 per settlement with 15.7% of sites showing more than five plans. These may, however, not all have been contemporaneous. Van Dinter et al. (2014), on the other hand, assumed an average for the west of the *limes* region of only one to two households per settlement. Extrapolations on the basis of these assumptions have led to population estimates for the second century CE ranging from 8000 to 16,800 for the Cananefatian *civitas* (Bloemers 1978; Buijtendorp 2010) and from 13,500 to 117,800 for the Batavian area (Willems 1986; Vossen 2003; Van Lanen et al. 2018). This large range is mainly due to lack of information on the actual site density, and our own estimates (see Table 1.2) suffer from the same problem. We will discuss the implications of these estimates in more detail in Chap. 3 (Verhagen), but it should be noted that, whatever the estimate used, the proportion of non-rural population in the area, in particular during the first part of the Middle Roman period, must have been substantial.

Table 1.2 Estimated population numbers in the Dutch *limes* zone during the Middle Roman A period

Site type	No. of sites	No. of inhabitants
Rural settlement, post-built	1048	13,660–26,447
Rural settlement, stone-built	39	
Burial site without associated settlement	82	1030–1993
Castellum	16–21	5950–7700
Military *vicus*	10–12	3850–4550
Castra	1	5000
Cannabae	1	2500
Civil settlement	3	1500
Town	3	4750
Total		*38,240–54,440*

Population sizes of rural settlements are based on the number of house plans found in our inventory, but have not been corrected for uncertainty of dating. For the number of inhabitants of the *castella*, *vici* and towns we have followed Buijtendorp (2010) and Van Dinter et al. (2014). Actual population numbers for the rural settlements may have been higher because of the uneven recovery of sites (see also Van Lanen et al. 2018)

1.5 The Rural Economy

1.5.1 The Surplus Question

Before the Romans arrived, it is supposed that the local population engaged in subsistence production only. A modest surplus of cereals could be achieved (see Chap. 7, Joyce) but was probably not actively pursued. The arrival of the Romans implied a fundamental change. A new and substantial demand for (forced) agricultural surplus production was created because of the deployment of troops in the region and the associated immigration of dependents, officials, craftsmen and others not involved in agricultural production, and because of taxation.

Evidence for surplus agricultural production in the Dutch *limes* zone has been mounting for some time (Vos 2009; Groot et al. 2009; Heeren 2009; Van Dinter et al. 2014), and since the study region did not see the widespread development of specialized *villa* settlements, surplus production of in particular cereals and meat must have been achieved by the local communities.

However, switching to a more 'rational' system of surplus production may not have been an easy transition. According to Erdkamp (2005), the 'workers' in pre-modern European small peasant households were chronically underemployed, and thus a large potential of unused labour was available. Part of this hidden labour surplus would have been used to meet the Roman demand for non-agricultural occupations, in particular military service (Roymans 1996, 2004). The remaining labour surplus may in theory have been used for increasing agricultural production. However, maximum productivity is ultimately limited by the availability of labour during harvest time. Without the possibility to hire extra (temporary) labour, the households' production capacity can therefore never have exceeded what could have been harvested by the available workforce.

According to Aarts (2013) there is no evidence of surplus production of grain or other crops in the pre-Flavian period, and surplus production of cattle and horses only seems to have started in the second half of the first century CE as well (Vos 2009; Heeren 2009). This would point to a connection of surplus production with the closer integration of the area with the rest of the Roman Empire after the Batavian revolt. Indeed, there is ample evidence for increased material exchange after 70 CE, and from that point on money is found all over the eastern part of the *limes* zone. This inflow of imported goods and money can be linked to the massive military presence during the Flavian period and the associated expansion of Noviomagus as Batavian *civitas* capital (Aarts 2013). It seems evident that the Romans started to trade extensively with the local population, although money must also have been introduced by returning veteran soldiers.

The introduction of a monetary economy by the Romans would have made it possible to break through the economically inefficient system. With money, goods and labour can be traded more easily, supply and demand can be better balanced, and as a consequence economic growth becomes possible; it fundamentally changes the rules of the game. However, such a monetized, market-oriented system would work best in cases where a large non-farming population needed to be supplied, so it may not be the best suitable model for all of the Dutch *limes* area.

The site of Rijswijk-De Bult (Bloemers 1978) shows interesting patterns in this respect. The settlement started as a single farm in the early first century CE, comparable to most other settlements in the region. In the second half of the first century, it grew into a small hamlet of four farms. The character and size of the buildings changed and gradually took on features of a Roman *villa*. The site was much bigger than most of the other settlements in the area. Van Londen (2006) therefore assumed that a limited number of larger farms supplied the town of Forum Hadriani with the necessary grain, meat and vegetables, and these farms were found close to the market. Further away, the farms would have been simpler, and may not have produced for the market.

1.5.2 Taxation and Landownership

A poorly understood aspect of the economic system in the area is the role of taxation. It is estimated that the tax on land (*tributum solis*) accounted for about two-thirds of the income of the Roman state (Boek 2008). It was only applied in the provinces, not in Italy. In some areas tax was paid in crops, in others in cash. The basis for taxation was the valuation of the land. In the words of the second-century writer Hyginus Gromaticus (De Limitibus 205 L)[1]:

[1] Translation by Boek (2008).

> *In some provinces they pay part of the crop, in some a fifth, in others a seventh; in still others a money payment. The amount is assessed by a valuation of the land itself. Set values are established for types of land, as in Pannonia, where the categories are: first and second class arable; meadow-land; first- and second-class woodland; fruit-bearing trees and pasture. For all these different land types a rate is established on a per iugerum*[2] *basis according to its productiveness.*

Hyginus goes on to state that the lands of the *Frisii* and *Batavi* were among those who paid their tax in kind. Hopkins (1980) estimates that the proportion of tax to be paid was in the order of 10% of the gross produce. As we know from historical sources, however, the taxes levied on the Batavians and Frisians before 70 CE were of a different kind. The Batavians were formally exempt from taxes because they were a valued ally of Rome, but in return they had to supply the army with soldiers. The Frisians revolted in 28 CE because of the taxation regime they had been subjected to: their tax was to be paid in cowhides.

The land valuation system described by Hyginus depends on the existence of a land registration service. We do not know how landownership was organized before the Romans came, but we can suppose that in the pre-Roman period land was not sold, but redistributed mainly through inheritance and dowry. It can even be questioned whether there was such a thing as individual ownership of land. Once the Romans conquered an area, it was common practice to confiscate all territory and redistribute this in one of the following ways: return it to the original owners, assign it to colonists (mostly veterans), sell it to big landowners (from the senatorial order) or keep it as public land (as imperial estates with tenants).

Given the initial exemption of tax for the Batavians, it seems plausible that the Romans simply assigned all the land to the local population and allowed them to manage it in the traditional way. After 70 CE, however, the introduction of taxation on the basis of a land valuation system seems probable (Groot 2008; Aarts 2013). It is assumed that this implied and is reflected in changes in parcellation. Roman surveyors would have registered and demarcated the land, and the boundaries would have been fixed physically, generally by digging ditches (Heeren 2009, 241–250).

There is ample evidence that the Midden-Delfland area was newly parcelled out in the first half of the second century CE (Van Londen 2006). Road connections were improved, and the area was better drained to allow for more settlements. The Midden-Delfland landscape made it impossible to set out a standard rectangular centuriation pattern of parcels, so regular patterns perpendicular and parallel to local water courses were set out instead. This would have been coupled to changes in the practices of landownership, tenancy and taxation, and it may also have served to increase the general productivity of the region, possibly connected to the elevation of Forum Hadriani to the status of *municipium*. There is however no evidence that farms were relocated, which suggests that the inhabitants were given the right to remain on their lands after the restructuring of the landscape. In the Kromme Rijn area (Vos 2009), to the contrary, there are no indications for large-scale restructuring and reclamation of land. However, there is evidence for a different parcellation

[2] The *iugerum* is a Roman area unit corresponding approximately to 0.25 ha.

from Flavian times onwards, as is also observed elsewhere in the Batavian area (Heeren 2009, 241–250).

Concluding, before 70 CE, the Batavians did not have to pay taxes and only supplied manpower to the Roman army. For the Cananefates the tax may (partly) have been in the form of cattle, just like for the Frisians. The restructuring of the Midden-Delfland area suggests that a formal land valuation system was only implemented in the early second century CE. The provisioning of the forts, which became a necessity after approximately 47 CE can therefore not have been part of a taxation scheme, which implies that the Roman military initially had to import their foodstuffs and/or buy them locally.

After the Batavian revolt, we find indications that the area was subjected to land tax, even when some authors have denied this possibility (Willems and Van Enckevort 2009). In any case, it should be assumed that the frontier provinces were net importers of tax revenues (Hopkins 1980), since the upkeep of the military infrastructure was too expensive to be borne by those provinces themselves. This means that local taxation would not be based on what the army in the province needed, but on what the province could produce that could be used by the army all over the empire, or that could be easily transferred into money, since it would be too cumbersome to transport all goods over long distances. Since it is stated by Hyginus that the Batavians paid their taxes in kind, it seems most plausible to assume that the revenues from their lands were mostly used to directly supply the local army units and bureaucracy. The Batavians are thought to have paid part of their taxes in horses (Groot 2008), and these can be transported easily to the army units needing them. Such a system of course does not exclude the possibility of selling produce for cash, but most probably this will then have been sold on the free market.

1.5.3 Boom and Bust?

Since local taxation will not have been enough to supply the army with all it needed, tax income must have flowed into the area from other regions allowing the army to acquire labour and goods from the local population. This economic growth, however, was not sustainable without a continued military presence. The significant reduction of troops in the Lower Rhine region under Trajan in 103/104 CE (Alföldy 1968, 149–152) to about 60% of its previous strength would have had adverse effects on the local economy, which is reflected in a decrease in coin supply. The Roman authorities may have recognized the problem, and therefore have extended *municipium* rights to Noviomagus to counteract the economic downturn. However, since similar rights were extended to Forum Hadriani as capital of the Cananefatian *civitas*, where no large military encampment is found, this may not have been the only reason.

Already from around 160 CE a decline of Roman settlement in the eastern river area has been signalled. Most probably, a number of interconnected events contributed to this (Vos 2009), including the assumed gradual reduction of Batavian recruitment for the Roman army (Van Driel-Murray 2003; Van Rossum 2004), which led to a further decrease in money supply, the Antonine Plague that ravaged the empire between 165 and 189 CE, and coastal raids by Chaucian pirates around 170–180 CE. Furthermore, a fire which ravaged Noviomagus around 170 CE significantly reduced the town's size. Jongman (Chap. 6) provides more background on the negative economic effects on the Roman Empire of epidemics and its prolonged political crisis in the third century. In particular, the population decline following the epidemics was coupled to an overall decrease in productivity and living standards.

There is little concrete information on economic developments in the region after the mid-second century. The fortification of Forum Hadriani and Noviomagus with city walls, the replacement of wooden by stone-built forts, and the establishment of a coastal defence system in the late second century all suggest that serious investments were made to protect the area from outside invaders. Under the Severan emperors in the early third century efforts were undertaken to restore Forum Hadriani and to repair the *castella*. De Bruin (2017) notes that the material culture of the Cananefatian area in this period is becoming more and more comparable to that of the rest of the Lower Rhine area, indicating increased exchange within the province of Germania Inferior. After ca. 240 CE, however, there are no longer any clear signs of building activities and repairs, pointing to a withdrawal of imperial investments in the region. The last reported building activity in the Cananefatian *civitas* is the erection of a milestone in 250 CE at the site of Wateringse Veld (Waasdorp 2003), and this was paid for by the local community.

It is not very evident how these developments influenced the rural economy in the region. Some changes in settlement pattern are already visible in the first half of the third century: most settlements in the Midden-Delfland area do not last beyond 210 CE (Van Londen 2006), but this may be due to the specific environmental characteristics of this area that was confronted with rising water tables. Vos (2009) also observes a decline in settlement density in the Kromme Rijn area starting in the first half of the third century. As long as the forts, *vici* and 'urban' centres were inhabited, however, there would have been a market for agricultural surplus production. In fact, the site of Rijswijk-De Bult seems to have been inhabited right up to 270 CE (Bloemers 1978). Heeren (2017) also confirms the continuation of habitation in much of the area until the end of the third century, albeit in smaller-sized settlements. The collapse of the *limes*, however, also must have signified the end of the 'urban' economy. The rapid and almost complete depopulation of the area after 275 CE (Heeren 2015) may therefore have been a consequence of the surviving urban population relocating to safer areas, with the rural population having no other choice than to follow. It has even been suggested (De Bruin 2017) that this move was forced upon the population by the Roman authorities.

References

Aarts J (2013) A frog's eye view of the Roman market: the Batavian casus. In: Van der Spek RJ, Van Leeuwen B, Van Zanden JL (eds) A history of market performance. From Ancient Babylonia to the modern world. Routledge, London, pp 394–409

Alföldy G (1968) Die Hilfstruppen der römischen Provinz Germania Inferior. Rheinland-Verlag, Düsseldorf

Bechert T, Willems WJH (eds) (1995) De Romeinse Rijksgrens tussen Moezel en Noordzeekust. Matrijs, Utrecht

Boek JA (2008) Taxation in the later Roman Empire. A study on the character of the late antique economy. Leiden University, Leiden. Available at http://hdl.handle.net/1887/18524. Accessed on 3 May 2018

Bosman A, De Weerd M (2004) Velsen: the 1997 Excavations in the Early Roman Base and a Reappraisal of the Post-Kalkriese Velsen/Vechten Dating Evidence. In: Vermeulen F, Sas K, Dhaeze W (eds) Archaeology in confrontation. Aspects of Roman military presence in the Northwest, Studies in Honour of Prof. Em. Hugo Thoen. Academia Press, Ghent, pp 31–62

Buijtendorp T (2010) Forum Hadriani. De vergeten stad van Hadrianus: Ontwikkeling, uiterlijk en betekenis van het 'Nederlands Pompeji'. Vrije Universiteit Amsterdam, Amsterdam

Bloemers JHF (1978) Rijswijk (Z.H.), 'De Bult' Eine Siedlung der Cananefaten. Rijksdienst voor het Oudheidkundig Bodemonderzoek, Amersfoort

De Bruin J (2017) Rurale gemeenschappen in de Civitas Cananefatium 50–300 na Christus. Universiteit Leiden, Leiden

De Weerd MD (1988) Schepen voor Zwammerdam. University of Amsterdam, Amsterdam

De Weerd MD (2006) Repressie op afstand in een voorland zonder grenzen. De Romeinse limes in Nederland voor de opstand van de Bataven. Westerheem 55:5–26

De Weerd MD, Haalebos JK (1973) Schepen voor het opscheppen. Spiegel Historiael 8(7/8):386–397

Derks T, Roymans N (2006) Returning auxiliary veterans: some methodological considerations. J Roman Archaeol 19:121–135. https://doi.org/10.1017/s1047759400006292

Dhaeze W (2011) De Romeinse kustverdediging langs de Noordzee en het Kanaal van 120 tot 410 na Chr. Ghent University, Ghent. Available at http://hdl.handle.net/1854/LU-8505147. Accessed on 3 May 2018

Dijkstra MFP (2011) Rondom de mondingen van Rijn en Maas. Landschap en bewoning tussen de 3e en 9e eeuw in Zuid-Holland, in het bijzonder de Oude Rijnstreek. Sidestone Press, Leiden. Available at http://hdl.handle.net/11245/1.352527. Accessed on 15 May 2018

Driessen MJ (2007) Bouwen om te blijven: de topografie, bewoningscontinuïteit en monumentaliteit van Romeins Nijmegen. Rijksdienst voor Archeologie, Cultuurlandschap en Monumenten, Amersfoort. Available at http://hdl.handle.net/11245/1.274189. Accessed on 3 May 2018

Driessen MJ, Besselsen E (2014) Voorburg-Arentsburg: Een Romeinse handelsstad tussen Rijn en Maas. University of Amsterdam, Amsterdam

Erdkamp P (2005) The grain market in the Roman Empire. A social, political and economic study. Cambridge University Press, Cambridge. https://doi.org/10.1017/CBO9780511482755

Graafstal EP (2002) Logistiek, communicatie en watermanagement. Over de uitrusting van de Romeinse rijksgrens in Nederland. Westerheem 51:2–27

Groenhuijzen (2018) Palaeogeographic analysis of the Dutch part of the Roman limes and its hinterland. Vrije Universiteit Amsterdam, Amsterdam

Groot M (2008) Animals in ritual and economy in a Roman frontier community. Excavations in Tiel-Passewaaij. Vrije Universiteit Amsterdam, Amsterdam

Groot M, Heeren S, Kooistra LI, Vos WK (2009) Surplus production for the market? The agrarian economy in the non villa landscapes of Germania inferior. J Roman Archaeol 22:231–252. https://doi.org/10.1017/S1047759400020687

Haalebos JK (1997) Van Nijmegen naar Utrecht. De limes in Nederland. In: Jaarboek Oud-Utrecht. Vereniging Oud-Utrecht, Utrecht, pp 35–66

Haalebos JK, Van Enckevort H, Thijssen J, Van der Heijden P (2002) De Romeinen in Cuijk. In: Van Enckevort H, Thijssen J (eds) Cuijk, een regionaal centrum in de Romeinse tijd. Matrijs, Utrecht, pp 20–47

Heeren S (2009) Romanisering van rurale gemeenschappen in de Civitas Batavorum: de casus Tiel-Passewaaij. Rijksdienst voor het Cultureel Erfgoed, Amersfoort

Heeren S (2015) The depopulation of the Lower Rhine region in the 3rd century. An archaeological perspective. In: Roymans N, Derks T, Hiddink H (eds) The Roman villa of Hoogeloon and the archaeology of the periphery. Amsterdam University Press, Amsterdam, pp 269–292

Heeren S (2017) Social dynamics in the Northwest Frontiers of the Late Roman empire. Beyond decline or transformation. In: Roymans N, Heeren S, De Clercq W (eds) From Germania Inferior to Germania Secunda and beyond. A case study of migration, transformation and decline. Amsterdam University Press, Amsterdam, pp 149–178

Hessing WAM, Steenbeek R (1990) Landscape and habitation history of 'De Horden' at Wijk bij Duurstede, an overview. Berichten van de Rijksdienst voor het. Oudheidkundig Bodemonderzoek 40:9–28

Hopkins K (1980) Taxes and trade in the Roman Empire (200 B.C.–A.D. 400). J Roman Stud 70:101–125. https://doi.org/10.2307/299558

Jansen R, Fokkens H (1999) Bouwen aan een verleden, 25 jaar archeologisch onderzoek in de gemeente Oss. Leiden University, Leiden. Available at http://hdl.handle.net/1887/9846. Accessed on 3 May 2018

Kooistra LI, Van Dinter M, Dütting MK, Van Rijn P, Cavallo C (2013) Could the local population of the Lower Rhine delta supply the Roman army? Part 1: The archaeological and historical framework. J Archaeol Low Ctries 4(2):5–23

Langeveld M, Luksen-IJtsma A, Weterings P (2010) Een goede buur? LR46 en LR49: definitief archeologisch onderzoek naar de vicus, grafvelden, infrastructuur en een inheemse nederzetting in de omgeving van het Romeinse castellum in De Meern, deelgebied "De Woerd" (Gemeente Utrecht). Cultuurhistorie gemeente Utrecht, Utrecht. Available at https://erfgoed.utrecht.nl/publicaties/onderzoeksrapporten-archeologie/. Accessed on 3 May 2018

Luksen-IJtsma A (2010) De limesweg in West-Nederland. Inventarisatie, analyse en synthese van archeologisch onderzoek naar de Romeinse weg tussen Vechten en Katwijk. Cultuurhistorie gemeente Utrecht, Utrecht. Available at https://erfgoed.utrecht.nl/publicaties/onderzoeksrapporten-archeologie/. Accessed on 3 May 2018

Polak M (2009) The Roman military presence in the Rhine delta c. AD 40–140. In: Morillo Á, Hanel N, Martín E (eds) Limes XX. Roman Frontier Studies. Consejo Superior de Investigaciones Científicas, Madrid, pp 945–953

Polak M, Kooistra LI (2013) A sustainable frontier? The establishment of the Roman frontier in the Rhine delta, Part 1: From the end of the Iron Age to the death of Tiberius (c. 50 BC-AD 37). Jahrbuch des Römisch-Germanischen Zentralmuseums 60:355–458. https://doi.org/10.11588/jrgzm.2013.2.20315

Polak M, Wynia SL (1991) The Roman forts at Vechten. A survey of the excavations 1829–1989. Oudheidkundige Mededelingen uit het Rijksmuseum van Oudheden te Leiden 71:125–156

Reuvens CJC (1829) Korte Beschrijving en plan der Romeinsche Bouwvallen gevonden ter waarschijnlijke plaatse van het Forum Hadriani, op de hofstede Arentsburg, bij 's Gravenhage. S. en J. Luchtmans, Leiden

Roymans N (1996) From the sword to the plough. Three studies on the earliest Romanisation of northern Gaul. Amsterdam University Press, Amsterdam

Roymans N (2004) Ethnic identity and imperial power. The Batavians in the early Roman empire. Amsterdam University Press, Amsterdam

Van der Kamp JS (2007) Vroege wacht. LR31 Zandweg: archeologisch onderzoek van twee eerste-eeuwse houten wachttorens in Leidsche Rijn. Sectie Cultuurhistorie gemeente Utrecht, Utrecht. Available at https://erfgoed.utrecht.nl/publicaties/onderzoeksrapporten-archeologie/. Accessed on 3 May 2018

Van der Kamp JS (2009) Werk aan de weg. LR 31 Zandweg: Archeologisch onderzoek aan een verspoelde sectie van de limesweg. Cultuurhistorie gemeente Utrecht, Utrecht. Available at https://erfgoed.utrecht.nl/publicaties/onderzoeksrapporten-archeologie/. Accessed on 3 May 2018

Van der Kooij D, Sprey S, Dijkstra M, Postma H (2005) Romeinen in Bodegraven. AWN-opgravingen in de periode van 1995–2002. Westerheem 54:275–306

Van der Heijden P (ed) (2016) Romeinse wegen in Nederland. Matrijs, Utrecht

Van Dinter M (2013) The Roman Limes in the Netherlands: how a delta landscape determined the location of the military structures. Neth J Geosci 92(1):11–32. https://doi.org/10.1017/S0016774600000251

Van Dinter M, Kooistra LI, Dütting MK, Van Rijn P, Cavallo C (2014) Could the local population of the Lower Rhine delta supply the Roman army? Part 2: Modelling the carrying capacity using archaeological, palaeo-ecological and geomorphological data. J Archaeol Low Ctries 5(1):5–50

Van Driel-Murray C (2003) Ethnic soldiers: the experience of the Lower Rhine tribes. In: Grünewald T, Seibel S (eds) Kontinuität und diskontinuität. Germania inferior am Beginn und am Ende der römischen Herrschaft. Beiträge des deutsch-niederländischen Kolloquiums in der Katholieke Universiteit Nijmegen (27. bis 30.06.2001). Walter de Gruyter, Berlin, pp 200–217. https://doi.org/10.1515/9783110900903.200

Van Enckevort H, Heirbaut E (2010) De zoektocht naar de betekenis van Oppidum Batavorum. In: Van Enckevort H, Heirbaut E (eds) Opkomst en ondergang van Oppidum Batavorum, hoofdplaats van de Bataven. Gemeente Nijmegen, Nijmegen, pp 45–54

Van Giffen AE (1948) De Romeinsche Castella in den Dorpsheuvel te Valkenburg aan den Rijn (Z.H.) (Praetorium Agrippinae). I. De Opgravingen in 1941. J.B. Wolters, Groningen

Van Giffen AE (1955) De Romeinsche castella in de dorpsheuvel te Valkenburg aan den Rijn (Z.H.) (Praetorium Agrippinae), II. De opgravingen in 1942-‘43 en 1946–1950. In: Jaarverslag van de vereniging voor Terpenonderzoek, pp 33–37

Van Lanen R, De Kleijn M, Gouw-Bouwman M, Pierik HJ (2018) Exploring Roman and early-medieval habitation of the Rhine-Meuse delta: modelling large-scale demographic changes and corresponding land-use impact. In: De Kleijn M (ed) Innovating Landscape Research through Geographic Information Science: Implications and opportunities of the digital revolution in science for the research of the archaeology, history and heritage of the landscape from a GIScience perspective. Vrije Universiteit Amsterdam, Amsterdam, pp 149–201. Available at http://dare.ubvu.vu.nl/handle/1871/55517. Accessed on 7 June 2018

Van Londen H (2006) Midden-Delfland: the Roman native landscape past and present. University of Amsterdam, Amsterdam. Available at http://hdl.handle.net/11245/1.260370. Accessed on 3 May 2018

Van Rijn P (2011) Wood supply for the Roman army and reconstruction of the woodlands from c. AD 40-140 in the Lower Rhine delta of the Netherlands. In: Scherrer P (ed) Lignum: Holz in der Antike. Karl-Franzens-Universität, Graz, pp 29–40

Van Rossum JA (2004) The end of the Batavian auxiliaries as “national” units. In: De Ligt L, Hemelrijk EA, Singor HW (eds) Roman rule and civic life: local and regional perspectives. Proceedings of the fourth workshop of the international network impact of empire (Roman Empire, c. 200 B.C.-A.D. 476). Leiden, June 25–28, 2003. J.C. Gieben, Amsterdam, pp 113–131

Verhagen P, Joyce J, Groenhuijzen MR (2016a) Modelling the dynamics of demography in the Dutch limes zone. In: Multi-, inter- and transdisciplinary research in landscape archaeology. Proceedings of LAC 2014 Conference, Rome, 19–20 September 2014. Vrije Universiteit Amsterdam, Amsterdam. https://doi.org/10.5463/lac.2014.62

Verhagen P, Vossen I, Groenhuijzen MR, Joyce J (2016b) Now you see them now you don’t: defining and using a flexible chronology of sites for spatial analysis of Roman settlement in the Dutch river area. J Archaeol Sci Rep 10:309–321. https://doi.org/10.1016/j.jasrep.2016.10.006

Vos WK (2009) Bataafs platteland. In: Het Romeinse nederzettingslandschap in het Nederlandse Kromme-Rijngebied. Rijksdienst voor het Cultureel Erfgoed, Amersfoort

Vos WK, Lanzing JJ, Siemons H (2016) Romeinse Bodegraven. Een overzicht van en visie op de archeologische bewoningsresten. Vos Archeo, Oosterbeek. Available at http://vosarcheo.nl/publicaties/. Accessed on 3 May 2018

Vossen I (2003) The possibilities and limitations of demographic calculations in the Batavian area. In: Grünewald T, Seibel S (eds) Kontinuität und Diskontinuität. Germania inferior am Beginn und am Ende der römischen Herrschaft. Beiträge des deutsch-niederländischen Kolloquiums in der Katholieke Universiteit Nijmegen (27. bis 30.06. 2001). Walter De Gruyter, Berlin, pp 414–435

Waasdorp JA (2003) IIII M.P. naar M.A.C. Romeinse mijlpalen en wegen. Gemeente Den Haag, The Hague

Waasdorp JA (ed) (2012) Den Haag Ockenburgh: een fortificatie als onderdeel van de Romeinse kustverdediging. Gemeente Den Haag, The Hague

Willems WJH (1980) Arnhem-Meinerswijk: een nieuw castellum aan de Rijn. Westerheem XXIX:334–348

Willems WJH (1986) Romans and Batavians. A Regional Study in the Dutch Eastern River Area. University of Amsterdam, Amsterdam

Willems WJH (1990) Romeins Nijmegen. Vier eeuwen stad en centrum aan de Waal. Matrijs, Utrecht

Willems WJH, Van Enckevort H (2009) Ulpia Noviomagus. Roman Nijmegen, the Batavian capital at the imperial frontier. Journal of Roman Archaeology, Portsmouth

Whittaker CR (1997). Frontiers of the Roman Empire: A Social and Economic Study. Johns Hopkins University Press, Baltimore

Zandstra MJM, Polak M (2012) De Romeinse versterkingen in Vechten-Fectio. In: Het archeologisch onderzoek in 1946–1947. Auxilia, Nijmegen. Available at http://repository.ubn.ru.nl/handle/2066/100578. Accessed on 3 May 2018

Part I
Demography and Settlement

Chapter 2
Current Trends in Roman Demography and Empirical Approaches to the Dynamics of the *Limes* Populations

Isabelle Séguy

Abstract Based on the three principal and inevitably incomplete information sources on ancient historical demography, and taking into account the particularities of the populations living around the *Limes Germanicus*, a largely male population of soldiers and migrants, this chapter examines the factors that may have influenced their dynamics over the short, medium and long term. It also looks at the possible consequences of increased pressure on the environment, heightened risk of epidemics linked to the rise in population concentration, long-distance communication and adverse climate changes observed from the second half of the second century AD. The proposed empirical approach aims to shed light on the factors that shaped the dynamics of these very specific populations over the long term.

Keywords Migration · Border populations · Environmental crises · Reconstruction of population dynamics

2.1 Introduction

The creation of a frontier region at the northern boundary of the Roman Empire and its survival over three centuries were highly dependent upon the living conditions and demographic behaviours of the populations who lived there or in neighbouring areas, be it temporarily or permanently. The stationing of a military population with specific socio-demographic characteristics and material needs in a populated zone, even if sparsely inhabited, necessarily gave rise to confrontation, change and adaptation in all areas of life (economic, social, cultural, technical, demographic, etc.).

What can we learn about the demographic behaviours of the populations of Ancient Rome, and to what extent can we reconstruct the dynamics of the peoples of the *Limes Germanicus* with a reasonable level of confidence? What sources do

I. Séguy (✉)
French Institute for Demographic Studies (INED), Paris, France
e-mail: seguy@ined.fr

P. Verhagen et al. (eds.), *Finding the Limits of the Limes*, Computational Social Sciences, https://doi.org/10.1007/978-3-030-04576-0_2

we have for studying ancient populations? Among the main findings of the various disciplinary approaches, which ones might be relevant to the populations of the *limes*? Last, which specific demographic features should be taken into account when modelling the history of populations in a frontier region over a dozen generations? We will address these three points successively, after recalling several key concepts of historical demography, considered in the broadest sense. This discipline has the same objectives and uses the same vocabulary as the demography of contemporary populations; only the sources and the associated analysis methods are different. Historical demography studies the structures (age-sex distributions)[1] and behaviours (fertility, mortality and migration) of past populations as defined at specific moments in time and space.

Demographic analysis also seeks to identify changes in these populations in a dynamic perspective and to explain the causes and consequences of these changes. Interactions between the age-sex structure of a population and its demographic laws (fertility, mortality and migration) govern its evolution over time. Changes in these attributes (size, structure, dynamics and density) can be predicted for a particular population if its fertility, mortality and migration rates are known (projection to forecast its future or retro-projection to reconstruct a part of its past) or inferred (by means of modelling).

As these are historical populations, we must apply the parameters specific to preindustrial populations, defined as largely rural and with no access to modern healthcare. These populations predate the demographic and epidemiological transitions[2] that began in Europe (France) at the end of the eighteenth century and which led to a sharp rise in life expectancy at birth, notably thanks to a spectacular reduction in infant mortality. By adding extra years to the mean length of life, these transitions also modified other key parameters of demographic dynamics, i.e. mortality, fertility and population age structure. To model the survival probabilities of preindustrial populations, and all associated behaviours, the variables of current demographic models must be adapted accordingly or specific new models developed.

[1]The population age-sex distribution – also known as the "population pyramid" – describes the composition of a population at a precise moment, like a snapshot. But it is also a memory of its past events and a strong predictor of its future.

[2]"Demographic transition: shift in a population from a traditional demographic regime marked by high fertility and mortality to a modern demographic regime in which fertility and mortality are low". https://www.ined.fr/en/glossary/demographic-transition/

"Epidemiological transition or health transition: the period of mortality decline which accompanies the demographic transition. It is characterized by improved health, nutrition and organization of health services and a change in the causes of death, with mortality from infectious diseases progressively being replaced by mortality from chronic and degenerative diseases and accidents". https://www.ined.fr/en/glossary/epidemiological-transition/

2.2 A Brief Review of Sources and Methods to Study Roman Demography

For Roman times (and later periods), three main categories of data are available for demographic approaches, each with its own biases and modes of analysis and each offering a fragment of the history of populations and their demographic behaviour.

Historical demography uses written sources, like ancient censuses, epigraphs, gravestones or literary sources, to reconstruct the size, spatial distribution, composition (by sex, age, marital status and household) of populations and to track their evolution over time. Certain demographic parameters, in terms of mortality, fertility and migration, can then be calculated by applying equations that link these different variables. As these written sources are often limited and fragmentary, quantitative results give limited insights, but can be complemented by qualitative approaches. The available documents generally concern very specific, mainly urban, populations from the southern part of the Roman Empire. Of course, while this approach provides useful information about demographic behaviour in ancient times, its results cannot be directly transposed to other populations living in the Roman Empire. Numerous academic publications concern the demography of ancient times, offering us a good overview of the Roman family and the demography of Mediterranean part of the Roman Empire. Good syntheses are given by Holleran and Pudsey (2011), De Ligt and Northwood (2008), De Ligt (2012), Pelgrom (2012) and Hin (2015).

Archaeological demography is based solely on material evidence, considered in time and space. Using traces of human activity, such as artefacts and habitats, it determines the spatial distribution and density of populations at different moments in time, giving a dynamic picture of settlement patterns in the areas under study. This research field is mainly that of archaeologists and geographers who apply specific qualitative models, developed in the fields of ecology, resource availability (carrying capacity) and economics, to quantitative data in order to track the evolution of populations, often observed over very long periods (especially in prehistory). Andrew Chamberlain (2006, 2009) proposes an interesting overview on the possibilities and the limits of archaeological demography. However, even when it can be established that population size is proportional to the quantity of material evidence uncovered, it is not easy to convert this evidence of resource usage into actual population numbers. This approach is, therefore, better suited to analysis of changes over time in relative rather than absolute population size. The recent work of Palmisano et al. (2017), for example, using a multi-proxy approach, compares several different archaeological indices to assess the extent to which they corroborate or diverge from one another to model the population dynamics in central Italy from Neolithic times to the fall of the Roman Empire.

Palaeodemography, based on the analysis of buried or cremated human remains, aims to reconstruct the age-sex distributions of one or more sets of individuals at the time of death, based on the assumption of human biological uniformity (see Buchet and Séguy 2002; Hoppa and Vaupel 2002a; Bocquet-Appel 2008; Séguy and Buchet

2013). Attempts to understand fertility behaviours have not been so successful, but the recent study by McFadden and Oxenham (2017) offers some promise. Bones and teeth provide information that can be used by demographers to determine sex and age at death or, more precisely, to indicate the stage of growth or ageing reached by individuals when they died. This biological material also provides information on health status, activities, pathologies, nutrition, breastfeeding patterns, genetic relationships and migratory behaviours of buried populations. The palaeodemographic approach borrows from forensic medicine (even if its goals are fundamentally different) and demography.

Although written sources and material evidence are often studied separately, they also can be used jointly in a holistic approach (Fig. 2.1).

2.3 A Brief Overview of Roman Demographic Behaviours

2.3.1 Roman Population Size and Structures

Apart from the ongoing scholarly debate about population numbers in Roman Italy (see Hin 2008, 2015, with an intermediate position between Brunt 1987 and Lo Cascio 1994), there appear to be no estimates of local or regional population size, except for Roman Egypt (see, e.g. Lo Cascio 1997, Storey 1997 and Morley 2013 on the size of the population of Rome, in connection with the estimation of the

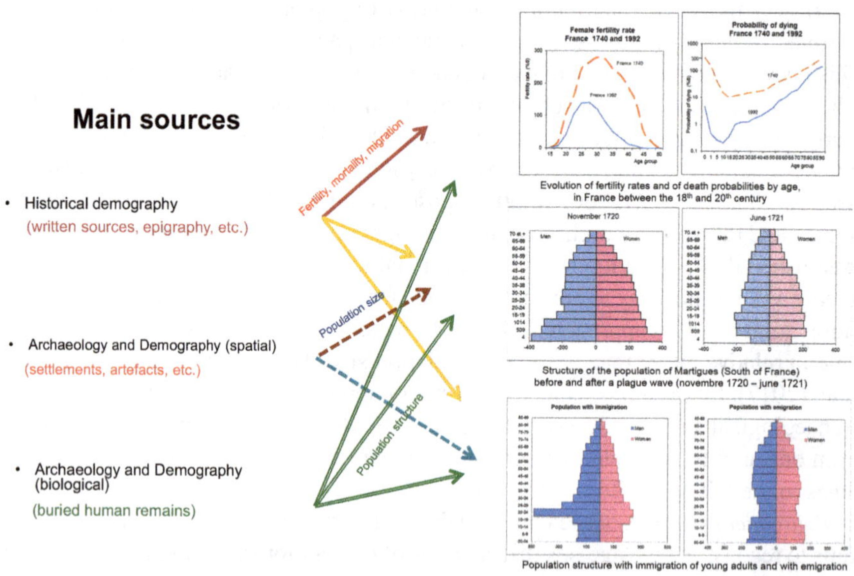

Fig. 2.1 Contributions of the different sources to demographic parameters. (Source: author's previous work)

population of Roman Italy; see also Launaro 2011 focusing on the rural population of Roman Italy, McIntyre 2015 estimating the size of the population of Roman York from human skeletal remains and the recent methodological proposition of Hanson and Ortman 2017).

Although numerous censuses were conducted throughout the Roman Empire to "identify taxpayers and recruit soldiers" (Le Teuff 2012), no estimates of provincial or urban populations can be given. The *Brevarium totius imperii*, requested by Emperor Augustus to provide an inventory of the Empire's material and human resources, has totally disappeared (Le Teuff 2014, 87–88). We have already pointed out the difficulties inherent to archaeological approaches. For villages, towns and city-scale settlements, no single constant can be employed to convert settlement area into population size, as there are wide inter-regional variations in the spatial density of human settlement. But a regular relationship between the area of Roman military camps and the size of the forces that occupied them has been proposed by Richardson (2000) who calculated a density of 127 persons/ha for these camps.

Very little is also known about the age-sex structures of Roman populations. Moreover, these structures may have differed widely from one group to another, and from one place to another, particularly in the context of large-scale immigration or emigration (Fig. 2.1c). The Roman population was a preindustrial one, probably with high infant mortality and high fertility; so one might expect to find a triangular population pyramid with a wide base that tapers inwards towards the top. However, exceptional levels of urbanization, as was the case in Rome, were liable to modify the population structure and the demographic parameters of mortality and fertility.

2.3.2 *Fertility*

Fertility is usually considered in relation to marital status, but while we have some information about the nuptiality of Roman elites (e.g. see Grubbs 1995; George 2005; Bodel and Olyan 2008; Hübner and Ratzan 2009; Rawson 2011; Harlow and Larsson Lovén 2012; Hübner and Nathan 2017), we know quite nothing about nuptiality patterns for other social categories or about concubinage practices (see, e.g. Phang 2001 and Scheidel 2005 on the varied conjugal relationships of soldiers in the Roman Empire). So, the simplest option is to calculate the mean number of children per women (total fertility rate) necessary to ensure population replacement, regardless of marital status. According to demographic models, a population with low life expectancy at birth[3] needs four to six children per woman to maintain replacement levels under these conditions of mortality and many more, of course, to achieve a positive growth rate. Reproductive behaviours are highly variable in time and space and across socio-economic groups; they are also affected by mortality

[3] Generally estimated to be between 20 and 30 years, signifying that one in two children died before adulthood.

levels, especially at reproductive ages. That is true both under normal conditions and in times of crisis.

Bruce Frier (1994) calculated a natural fertility pattern (theoretical number of children a woman can bear during her reproductive life) and compared it with the marital fertility of Egyptian women during Roman domination. The difference between the observed and the expected rates reflects the influence of factors limiting natural fertility, both biological factors such as female mortality before or during reproductive life, frequent divorce, widowhood and sterility and cultural behaviours such as prolonged breastfeeding, sexual taboos and birth control within families.

Using osteological data, Jean-Pierre Bocquet-Appel revealed changes in fertility following the transition from a nomadic hunter-gatherer lifestyle to the sedentary lifestyle of the first farmers; or more exactly, the consequences of this change in terms of child mortality (Bocquet-Appel 2002; Bocquet-Appel and Bar Yosef 2008). By observing the proportion of juvenile skeletons in cemeteries from Mesolithic and Neolithic times, i.e. the Juvenility index (the ratio of 5- to19-year-old skeletons to all skeletons 5 or more years old), and by using a relative chronology to fix the starting point (t_0) of the transition from foragers to farmers in each place, regardless of the precise date when it actually occurred, he demonstrates that throughout the world, the transition from foragers to farmers was characterized by an abrupt increase in the proportion of juvenile skeletons, which expresses a corresponding increase in the parameter values for entry into the population age pyramid (birth, growth and fertility rate). He named this starting point the "Neolithic Demographic Transition" in reference to the Contemporary Demographic Transition, described for industrialized societies, when the decline in mortality was followed by a decline in fertility.

Adopting a different approach, Pennington (1996) showed that the transition from nomadic to sedentary lifestyles could substantially increase young children's chances of survival. A very small mortality gain is sufficient to create the conditions for substantial population growth without any increase in birth rates.

2.3.3 *Mortality*

Few sources can be used to study mortality by sex and age. Funerary inscriptions provide information about age at death, but these statistics are not reliable indicators of mortality rates and life expectancy (Henry 1959). The same arguments apply with respect to documentary evidence about members of the Roman elites. Census records from Roman Egypt give an idea of the life expectancy of ordinary citizens (Bagnall and Frier 2006), but most of the mortality data are empirically based on model life tables for low-life-expectancy populations derived from contemporary model life tables (see Parkin 1992; Scheidel 1996, 2001; Bagnall and Frier 2006; Woods 2007; Hin 2013). Thus, distributions by age at death, age-specific mortality rates and low life expectancies (between 20 and 30 years) are extrapolations.

Because infant mortality data are missing in historical sources, these researchers all used Coale and Demeny's model life Tables (1983), which are based on observed life tables, mostly from developed countries (overwhelmingly European), some dating from the nineteenth century. None of these populations had a life expectancy at birth of less than 30 years; the parameters for populations with a lower life expectancy at birth are extrapolated. Considering this fact and the huge change in mortality pattern in the last two centuries, Séguy et al. developed a set of mortality models for preindustrial populations, taking into account theoretical growth rates which can be applied in palaeodemographic approaches (Séguy et al. 2008; Séguy and Buchet 2013), as well as in other fields of research. These statistical and pre-statistical life tables characterizing the mortality of preindustrial populations are called the "pre-industrial standard".

Moreover, these parameters doubtless varied considerably across the Roman Empire, depending on environmental conditions, socio-economic status and gender. See, for example, Sallares (2002) and Scheidel (2015) on malaria in ancient Rome, Lo Cascio (2012) on the "Antonine Plague" of 165–190 AD which affected some places but spared neighbouring ones and Harper (2014) on epidemics of the third century AD.

Archaeo-osteological data can provide evidence of demographic perturbations that were sufficiently intense to leave long-term traces. Using the method proposed by Henri Caussinus and Daniel Courgeau (2010, 2013),[4] a recent study on a buried population in Normandy revealed that demographic conditions in Merovingian times were less favourable than in Gallo-Roman times (Buchet et al. 2017). Significant differences in the age distribution of death from one period to another were noted: the age distribution was very close to the preindustrial standard during the Gallo-Roman period, while mortality was higher, particularly at young ages, during Merovingian times. These differences may be due to a variation in the age mortality distribution or to differences in the population structure (by sex and age) to which the same age-at-death distribution is applied (or both). Both hypotheses are plausible in light of the available archaeological evidence. A forthcoming paper confirms this point for a sample of cemeteries in northern France (Séguy et al. 2017, forthcoming).

2.3.4 Migration

Migration, the third component of population dynamics, is rather difficult to evaluate and tends to be the "poor cousin" of historical demographic analysis (it is much easier to analyse populations with no migration), especially since historians long believed that rural populations were immobile.

---

[4] This method, called *Bayesian Inference Procedure*, is based on the principle of Bayesian inference and uses a parametric formulation of the problem, as recommended by the Rostock Manifesto (Hoppa and Vaupel 2002b).

Migration refers to the process whereby individuals enter or leave a population other than through birth or death. It is a special instance of spatial mobility, distinct from the regular movements within a territory that are undertaken by nomadic peoples, itinerant workers and traders (in these cases, the more appropriate term is "circulation"; see Pressat 1985). People migrate for different reasons (Coleman 2004, 36):

- Mobility (e.g. short distance movements for trade, work or marriage)
- Conquest (migration of a small number of people who impose their laws and their organization upon another population, despite their numerical inferiority)
- Mass migration (*Völkerwanderung*) (movements of entire peoples, with their hierarchies and their livelihoods, in search of new lands or expelled by other peoples)
- Forced migration
- Infiltration ("infiltration" of foreigners unopposed by the local population, with no change of governing class nor allegiance to an outside power; ex-missionaries, refugees)
- Deportation (different from the forced migration in the sense that it consists in capturing individuals or whole communities, extracting them from their territories of origin and selling them as slaves either for hard labour or for army enlistment, e.g. slave trade)
- Invitation to immigrate (when a state or a city invites individuals or groups to immigrate in order to increase its own population and revive its economy, for example, after the heavy losses of the Black Death).

Of course, to analyse migration, the population concerned must have recognizable boundaries, usually defined for human populations in terms of the individuals' places of permanent residence. Migration also implies the existence of two populations (donor and recipient); but as migrants' mortality and fertility characteristics may differ from those of both donor and recipient populations, they constitute a third population group.

In demography, studying migration is complex because, unlike birth and death which are singular and irreversible events, an individual can participate in more than one migration event. Human migration is also difficult to model and predict because it depends on individual decision-making,[5] and on fluctuating demographic, economic and political circumstances, both in donor and recipient populations. From a socio-economic point of view, migration can influence a society's culture and economy (crafts, agriculture, fishing, trade and so on), its environment and carrying capacity. It may also accelerate the spread of infectious diseases, or generate insecurity and the destruction of harvests (leading to famine and malnutrition) in case of war or conquest. Last but not the least, it also modifies population genetics.

These questions are now widely studied by historians, archaeologists and bioanthropologists whose findings, sometimes presented in multidisciplinary collective

[5] Migration incentives include work opportunities, improved living conditions, and the desire to escape from objective hazards such as conflict and epidemics.

works (see, e.g. Eckardt 2010; De Ligt and Tacoma 2016; Yoo and Zerbini 2018), show the importance of mobility and migration in the Roman world and examine how differences were expressed in both the host and migrant communities and how identities were maintained and evolved over time (see Noy 2000; Roymans 2004; Derks and Roymans 2009). Material artefacts allow the identification of migrants, at least for the first generations, while human remains provide individual information, mainly derived from isotopic (see, e.g. Killgrove and Montgomery 2016; Gowland 2017) and DNA (MtDNA or nuclear DNA) analyses.

2.4 Demographic Dynamics of *Limes* Populations over the Long Term: An Empirical Approach

2.4.1 One Border Zone, But Very Diverse Populations

The *Limes Germanicus*, a border zone between the Roman Empire and the peoples of Northern Europe, has some highly specific features: (1) a very large military presence, (2) major population movements (migrations) that took different forms over time, (3) a colonization process resulting from the settlement of demobilized soldiers and (4) small-scale urbanization or, more precisely, population concentration in camps or small towns, in sparsely populated territories.

Analysis of demographic behaviours, over both the short and long term, must therefore be conducted with considerable flexibility. Studies of immigrant populations reveal differences in behaviour between the recipient and donor countries and between immigrants and natives; they also show a relatively rapid convergence between the demographic behaviours of immigrants' and natives' children or grandchildren. Other studies on the demography of frontier populations[6] highlight the interpenetration of their cultural behaviours (Renard 1992). These studies are certainly helpful for shedding light on the demographic dynamics of the *limes*. However, it is not sufficient to simply describe the particularities of this population, or of the historical period in question.

The *limes*[7] was not a clearly demarcated area, despite its fortifications, but probably an area of mixing and intercommunication, where population groups of very

[6]Contemporary frontiers separate two distinct spaces characterized by different population, health policies and different levels of economic development.

[7]Lively debate among historians on the notion of "frontier" – a clear boundary between two territories or a "no man's land" with no clear demarcation? – has led to a new perception of the limits of the Roman Empire. The *limes* was not so much a frontier, as defined today, but a "patrol route" as suggested by the etymology of the word. Often following natural barriers, the role of the line of fortifications was less to separate the Romans from the Barbarians than, in military terms, to establish major bridgeheads and an effective surveillance system and, in political economic terms, to create mandatory points of passage to control population movements and levy taxes on traded goods. The importance of the different functions varied according to the level of tension or harmony in relations with neighbouring (Germanic) populations.

different origins and statuses intermingled (Morin 2011a). Not only did the garrisons include foreign soldiers from throughout the Empire (see Roselaar 2016), but the busy trade generated by their presence attracted merchants and artisans from both southern and northern Europe. All these "foreigners" lived side by side with local populations, sometimes in close contact, given that the legion auxiliaries were recruited from among native people or married local women and that the legionnaires settled beyond the boundaries of the *limes*.

In demographic terms, this mixing gave rise to dynamics and behaviours that must have varied considerably between the Roman or Romanized populations, the inhabitants originating from Germania Magna and the mosaic of people's native to the *limes*, a region of "convergence", to use the expression coined by Mélissa Morin (2011b), and of acculturation (Bloemers 1983, 1989; Blagg and Millett 2016).

2.4.2 A Migrant Population with a Skewed Sex Ratio

The demography of the *limes* was thus characterized by intense and varied forms of migration (cf. supra) which also varied over time. For the first generations, the demographic dynamics were probably shaped less by natural population change than by migration. In the early days of the *limes*, despite the massive influx of soldiers and forced population displacement, the conditions probably did not favour natural population growth. On the contrary, the departure of inhabitants who fled the region or were sent away as slaves and the increased mortality and lower fertility associated with insecure living conditions must have reduced the size of populations and modified their age-sex structure (cf. Fig. 2.1). By comparison with other historical situations, it is reasonable to imagine that the massive influx of men, but also of women and young adolescents in the context of military conquest, produced a psychological shock (and perhaps an epidemiological shock, cf. infra) with physiological repercussions. Though covering a different region, a statistical comparison of pre- and post-colonial skeletal remains by Kyle et al. (2016) revealed the physical stigmata of the stresses inflicted upon the population of Apollonia (in present-day Albania) after the Greek colonization in the sixth century BC. The authors attribute this physiological stress to a reduction in locally available resources and the adverse health impact of urbanization (insalubrity and propagation of disease).

Apart from the negative effects on population growth of war, forced migration and constant insecurity, the unprecedented concentration of people living in camps and towns also created conditions for radical demographic regime changes, potentially masked by the spectacular increase in numbers of inhabitants. In the same way as the sedentarization of Neolithic populations profoundly modified their fertility and the mortality of their young children, the rapid "urbanization" of previously scattered populations may have produced new fertility behaviours and mortality patterns. In addition, the assignment by Rome of officials to one town rather than another may also have modified the appeal of certain territories over time. This is suggested in a study by Ouriachi and Nuninger (2011) who cross-linked a spatial model of the settlement system in a region of southern France and an analysis of the local gentry's social networks, revealing the existence of competition, not only between individuals for administrative positions but also between towns wishing to attract the most influential officials and thereby raise their prestige. The spatial distribution of the population and its density thus depend not only on the numbers of migrants, but also on the quality of the most high-ranking ones.

In more peaceful times, the age-sex structure of the population around the *limes* was highly favourable for positive demographic dynamics and population growth. The predominant presence of young, affluent men clearly oriented the marriage market in favour of soldiers and legion auxiliaries. Phang (2001) draws upon funerary epitaphs to show the types of relationships that existed among soldiers. Soldiers who married did so later, in their mid-thirties, and their wives were usually from the families of military comrades. Soldiers could find a partner, live with her and have offspring in a union not legally recognized under Roman law. Penelope Allison (2008) investigated the presence, activities and status of women and children in Roman military forts on the German frontier during the first and second centuries AD. She concluded that women played a greater role in military life in the early Roman Empire than has previously been acknowledged (see also Allison 2011, 2013). Elisabeth Greene (2011) provides evidence for the presence of women and children within military garrisons during the earliest periods of military conquest and during consolidation in the first and second centuries AD. In the first century AD, the auxiliary units stationed on the frontiers of the western provinces were legally allowed to cohabit with women during their period of service; soldiers were later granted the same right. A comparison can be made with the soldiers present in the same zone some centuries later (see the doctoral work by Dana Rus 2010, 2016 on Roman border guards in the late eighteenth and nineteenth centuries).

Such marriages created new ties on other side of the "border", or rather consolidated existing ones, since other practices had the same purpose (recruitment of local auxiliaries, allocation of land behind the *limes* to legionnaires, reception of hostages, etc.), thus forming a sort of giant human shield (e.g. Picard 2014 and Boatwright 2015 on forced displacements; Foubert 2011 on migration of high-ranking women; Moatti 2017a and b on legal evidence and categorization of migrants; and Lo Cascio and Tacoma 2017 on the impact of mobility and migration). The establishment of human populations in the *limes* doubtless owes much to these marriage migrations and to higher fertility (and better child survival) made possible by material wealth and better health conditions.

2.4.3 Demographic Crises Were Inevitable

Generally stemming from insecurity and social and economic difficulties, recurrent demographic crises are a characteristic of preindustrial population dynamics. These brief, but intense, episodes of excess mortality (often accompanied by fewer marriages and births) most likely affected the populations of the *limes*, and the general curve of population growth doubtless includes a number of sudden dips.

While mortality is correlated with advancing age as much as with the perils of early childhood, it is also highly sensitive to random events that may modify its intensity and selectivity. When the *limes* was established, a road network was built that facilitated troop movements, food transport and trade, but also the circulation of infectious diseases. And the large migrant inflows inevitably brought in new diseases that produced epidemics which were especially severe if the populations had no prior exposure and, therefore, no immunity to the pathogen. One such example was the epidemic of smallpox, known as "Antonine Plague", that swept across the Roman Empire between 165 and 190 AD, spread by soldiers returning from campaigns in the Near East (Lo Cascio 2012). It was described in detail by Galen of Pergamon, a contemporary physician, enabling historians (Littman and Littman 1973) to recognize it as haemorrhagic smallpox, a virulent and highly lethal form of the disease. They agree that the epidemic hit a previously unaffected population, resulting in higher mortality than in subsequent outbreaks.

Living close to major communication routes or in crowded towns or military camps greatly increased the risk of contagion, with consequences in terms of excess mortality. In demographic, economic and geopolitical terms, the actual impact of Antonine Plague across the Empire remains uncertain (estimated mortality rates range from 7–10%, following Littman and Littman 1973, to 25–33%, according to Duncan-Jones 1996 and Zelener 2003). More certain is the series of epidemics that struck the Roman world between the second and the sixth centuries AD, causing a significant population decrease and contributing, along with many other factors, to the decline of the Roman Empire (see Little 2007; Harper 2014).

Indeed, after a long period of climatic stability and limited volcanic activity between 100 BCE and 150 AD (McCormick et al. 2012), climate conditions worsened. Some scientists have postulated that major volcanic eruptions produced severe weather disturbances, which destroyed crops and led to famine and disease. The scale of these climatic repercussions is still a topic of debate. However, as northern Europe was particularly exposed to the after-effects of Icelandic volcanic eruptions, it is reasonable to imagine that it endured several years of poor harvests. Between 150 and 200 AD, when climatic conditions began to deteriorate, the Empire was confronting a major economic and political crisis and a number of military challenges (McCormick et al. 2012, 203).

Given the close correlation between climate and food resources (cf., e.g. Bevan et al. 2017), such change is generally accompanied by episodes of food shortage or famine, which adversely affect the populations and increase their susceptibility to disease and epidemics. The populations of the *limes* must have been severely exposed to such risks, first because of the high population density (and the absolute priority given to supplying the garrisons) and, second, because the region was unable, even under normal conditions, to meet the population's food needs and relied on imports, themselves in short supply when the producer regions no longer had a surplus (see, e.g. the calculation models proposed by Van Dinter et al. 2014 and Chap. 7, Joyce, to estimate the local carrying capacity).

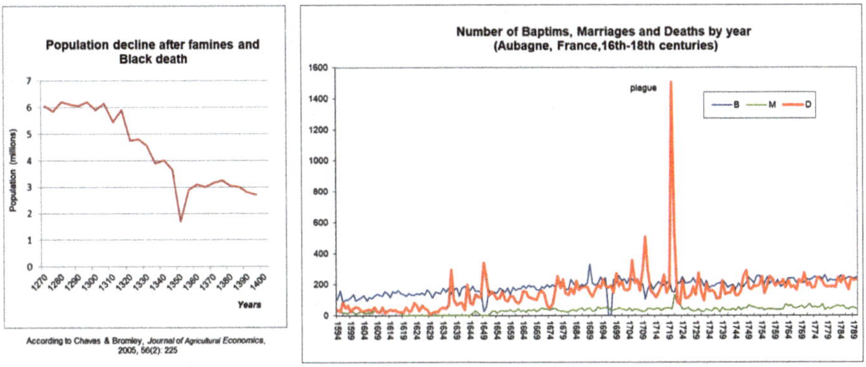

Fig. 2.2 Short- and long-term impact of demographic crises (detection of excess mortality crises in the vital records of Aubagne, English population decline up to the arrival of the Black Death). (Sources: author's previous studies and Chavas and Bromley (2005))

Chronic and acute malnutrition (famine) and the accompanying disease and epidemics caused by wars or poor climatic conditions give rise to excess mortality, but also result in a deficit of births that is proportional to the severity of the famine and its duration. Famines also encourage migration and can lead to local population decline. Recurrent severe demographic crises can hinder demographic recovery.

2.4.4 A Faltering Demographic Recovery

Demographic crises that decimate young adults (such as the plague or influenza) often have a more pronounced long-term impact; the population size and structure are such that the population cannot immediately renew itself despite the generally observed increase in birth rates (Fig. 2.2). Most often, it is regenerated through the arrival of new immigrants but only if neighbouring regions have not themselves been severely affected. Populations are more resilient over the short term when difficulties are short-lived or only affect young children. Yet repeated food shortages and cyclical epidemics of childhood diseases may hinder demographic growth, with population size remaining practically constant over the long term. Preindustrial populations were confronted by these regulatory mechanisms, which are linked to epidemic thresholds[8] and to environmental carrying capacity.[9]

The worsening environmental conditions in the second half of the third century, and mainly the cooling that affected the north-western provinces of the Empire (McCormick et al. 2012), could have severely disrupted food production and slowed

[8] i.e. the number or density of receptive individuals required for an epidemic to take hold.

[9] i.e. at the prevailing levels of technological development, the maximum population size that can be sustained indefinitely, in terms of food, water, living space, energy, etc., by a given environment.

down the recovery capacities of populations. Economic difficulties often encourage those who have nothing (or nothing left) to migrate. If emigration occurs on a large scale, such movements can hinder demographic recovery and lead to a significant decline in local settlement.

2.5 Conclusions

In demographic terms, the *limes* was a specific and complex territory where different populations intermingled and where trade was conducted on a large scale. A remarkable instrument of acculturation but also an ideal environment for the propagation of new contagious diseases, the *limes* doubtless exhibited very specific demographic structures and behaviours which evolved in response to the levels of security or insecurity experienced by its populations. It is difficult to model demographic behaviours in a region such as this, as Verhagen et al. (2016) can confirm. The "migration" parameter is of key importance, yet difficult to quantify or predict. Apart from migration linked to militarization and forced population displacements, migration behaviours, like those of fertility and mortality, are governed as much by individual and family decisions as by parameters of well-being and security.

This rapid overview of historically attested demographic situations does not take account of data provided by the documents and archaeology of the *limes*. Its sole purpose is to suggest some avenues for future research to better understand the factors underlying the long-term population dynamics of the region.

Acknowledgements The author thanks Catriona Dutreuilh (INED) for the English version of her text.

References

Allison PM (2008) Measuring Women's Influence on Roman Military Life: using GIS on published excavation reports from the German frontier. Internet Archaeology 24. https://doi.org/10.11141/ia.24.5

Allison PM (2011) Soldiers' families in the early Roman Empire. In: Rawson B (ed) A companion to families in the Greek and Roman worlds. Blackwell Publishing, Oxford, pp 161–182. https://doi.org/10.1002/9781444390766.ch10

Allison PM (2013) People and spaces in Roman military bases. Cambridge University Press, Cambridge. https://doi.org/10.1017/CBO9781139600248

Bagnall RS, Frier BW (2006) The demography of Roman Egypt, 2nd edn. Cambridge University Press, Cambridge

Bevan A, Colledge S, Fuller D, Fyfe R, Shennan S, Stevens C (2017) Holocene population, food production, and climate. PNAS 14(49):E10524-E10531. https://doi.org/10.1073/pnas.1709190114

Blagg TFC, Millett M (2016) The early Roman empire in the west. Oxbow, Oxford

Bloemers JHF (1983) Acculturation in the Rhine/Meuse Basin in the Roman Period: a preliminary survey. In: Brandt RW, Slofstra J (eds) Roman and Native in the Low Countries, Spheres of interaction. BAR, Oxford, pp 159–209

Bloemers JHF (1989) Acculturation in the Rhine/Meuse Basin in the Roman Period: some demographical considerations. In: Barrett JC, Fitzpatrick AP, MacInnes L (eds) Barbarians and Romans in North-West Europe from the later Republic to late Antiquity. BAR, Oxford, pp 175–234

Boatwright MT (2015) Acceptance and approval: Romans' Non-Roman population transfers, 180 BCE-ca 70 CE. Phoenix 69(1/2):122–146. https://doi.org/10.7834/phoenix.69.1-2.0122

Bocquet-Appel J-P (2002) Paleoanthropological traces of Neolithic demographic transition. Curr Anthropol 43:638–650. https://doi.org/10.1086/342429

Bocquet-Appel J-P (ed) (2008) Recent advances in paleodemography: data, techniques, patterns. Springer, Dordrecht. https://doi.org/10.1007/978-1-4020-6424-1

Bocquet-Appel J-P, Bar Yosef O (eds) (2008) The Neolithic demographic transition and its consequences. Springer, Dordrecht. https://doi.org/10.1007/978-1-4020-8539-0

Bodel JM, Olyan S (eds) (2008) Household and family religion in antiquity. Blackwell, Oxford. https://doi.org/10.1002/9781444302974

Brunt PA (1987) Italian manpower 225 B.C. – A.D. 14, 2nd edn. Oxford University Press, Oxford

Buchet L, Séguy I (2002) La paléodémographie aujourd'hui: bilan et perspectives. Annales de démographie historique 1:161–212. https://doi.org/10.3917/adh.103.0161

Buchet L, Caussinus H, Courgeau D, Séguy I (2017) Atouts d'une procédure récente d'inférence bayésienne pour l'étude de l'impact des crises démographiques. Application à trois sites médiévaux bas-normands. Bull Mém Soc Anthropol Paris 29(1):70–84. https://doi.org/10.1007/s13219-016-0175-4

Caussinus H, Courgeau D (2010) Estimating age without measuring it: a new method in paleodemography. Population-E 65(1):117–144. https://doi.org/10.3917/pope.1001.0117

Caussinus H, Courgeau D (2013) A new method for estimating age-at-death structure. In: Séguy I, Buchet L (eds) Handbook of palaeodemography. Springer, Dordrecht, pp 255–286. https://doi.org/10.1007/978-3-319-01553-8_13

Chamberlain AT (2006) Demography in archaeology. Cambridge University Press, Cambridge. https://doi.org/10.1017/CBO9780511607165

Chamberlain AT (2009) Archaeological demography. Hum Biol 81(2–3):275–286. https://doi.org/10.3378/027.081.0309

Chavas J-P, Bromley D (2005) Modelling population and resource scarcity in fourteenth-century England. J Agric Econ 56(2):217–237. https://doi.org/10.1111/j.1477-9552.2005.00001

Coale AJ, Demeny P (1983) Regional model life tables and stable populations, 2nd edn. Academic Press, New York

Coleman DA (2004) Le rôle majeur de la migration dans les processus démographiques. In: Caselli G, Vallin J, Wunsch G (eds) Traité de démographie. Démographie. Analyse et synthèse, tome V: Histoire du peuplement et des prévisions. INED, Paris, pp 33–69

De Ligt L, Northwood S (eds) (2008) People, land, and politics: demographic developments and the transformation of Roman Italy, 300 BC-AD 14. Brill, Leiden. https://doi.org/10.1163/ej.9789004171183.i-656

De Ligt L (2012) Peasants, citizens and soldiers: studies in the demographic history of Roman Italy 225 BC-AD 10. Cambridge University Press, Cambridge. https://doi.org/10.1017/CBO9781139003834

De Ligt L, Tacoma LE (2016) Migration and mobility in the early Roman Empire. Brill, Leiden

Derks T, Roymans N (eds) (2009) Ethnic constructs in antiquity: the role of power and tradition. Amsterdam University Press, Amsterdam. https://doi.org/10.5117/9789089640789

Duncan-Jones RP (1996) The impact of the Antonine plague. J Roman Archaeol 9:108–136. https://doi.org/10.1017/S1047759400016524

Eckardt H (ed) (2010) Roman Diasporas: archaeological approaches to mobility and diversity in the Roman Empire. Journal of Roman Archaeology, Portsmouth

Foubert L (2011) The impact of women's travels on military imagery in the Julio-Claudian period. In: Hekster O, Kaizer T (eds) Frontiers in the Roman World. Proceedings of the Ninth Workshop of the International Network Impact of Empire (Durham, 16–19 April 2009). Brill, Leiden, pp 349–362. https://doi.org/10.1163/ej.9789004201194.i-378.78

Frier BW (1994) Natural fertility and family limitation in Roman marriage. Class Philol 89(4):318–333. https://doi.org/10.1086/367430

George M (2005) The Roman family in the empire: Rome, Italy, and beyond. Oxford University Press, Oxford. https://doi.org/10.1093/acprof:oso/9780199268412.001.0001

Gowland RL (2017) Embodied identities in Roman Britain: a bioarchaeological approach. Britannia 48:175–119. https://doi.org/10.1017/S0068113X17000125

Grubbs JE (1995) Family and law in late antiquity: the emperor Constantine's marriage legislation. Oxford University Press, Oxford

Greene EM (2011) Women and families in the auxiliary military communities of the Roman west in the first and second centuries AD. University of North Carolina, Chapel Hill

Hanson JW, Ortman SG (2017) A systematic method for estimating the populations of Greek and Roman settlements. J Roman Archaeol 30:301–324. https://doi.org/10.1017/S1047759400074134

Harlow M, Larsson Lovén L (eds) (2012) Families in the Roman and late antique world. Continuum, London/New York

Harper K (2014) Pandemics and passages to late antiquity: rethinking the plague of c.249–270. J Roman Archaeol 28:223–260. https://doi.org/10.1017/S1047759415002470

Henry L (1959) L'âge au décès d'après les inscriptions funéraires. Population 14(2):327–329. https://doi.org/10.2307/1526414

Hin S (2008) Counting Romans. In: De Ligt L, Northwood S (eds) People, land, and politics: demographic developments and the transformation of Roman Italy, 300 BC-AD 14. Brill, Leiden, pp 187–238

Hin S (2013) The demography of Roman Italy: population dynamics in an ancient conquest society, 201 BCE-14 CE. Cambridge University Press, Cambridge. https://doi.org/10.1017/CBO9780511782305

Hin S (2015) Ancient demography. In: Clayman DL (ed) Oxford bibliographies in classics. Oxford University Press, Oxford. https://doi.org/10.1093/obo/9780195389661-0208

Holleran C, Pudsey A (2011) Introduction: studies in ancient historical demography. In: Holleran C, Pudsey A (eds) Demography and the Graeco-Roman world: new insights and approaches. Cambridge University Press, Cambridge, pp 1–13. https://doi.org/10.1017/CBO9780511863295.001

Hoppa RD, Vaupel JW (2002a) Paleodemography: age distributions from skeletal samples. Cambridge University Press, Cambridge. https://doi.org/10.1017/CBO9780511542428

Hoppa RD, Vaupel JW (2002b) The Rostock Manifesto for paleodemography: the way from stage to age. In: Hoppa RD, Vaupel JW (eds) Paleodemography: age distributions from skeletal samples. Cambridge University Press, Cambridge. https://doi.org/10.1017/CBO9780511542428.001

Hübner SR, Ratzan DM (eds) (2009) Growing up fatherless in antiquity. Cambridge University Press, Cambridge. https://doi.org/10.1017/CBO9780511575594

Hübner SR, Nathan G (eds) (2017) Mediterranean families in antiquity: house-holds, extended families, and domestic space. John Wiley & Sons, Oxford

Killgrove K, Montgomery J (2016) All roads lead to Rome: exploring human migration to the Eternal City through biochemistry of skeletons from two imperial-era cemeteries (1st–3rd c AD). PLoS ONE 11(2):e0147585. https://doi.org/10.1371/journal.pone.0147585

Kyle B, Schepartz LA, Larsen CS (2016) Mother city and colony: bioarchaeological evidence of stress and impacts of Corinthian Colonisation at Apollonia. Int J Osteoarchaeol 26:1067–1077. https://doi.org/10.1002/oa.2519

Launaro A (2011) Peasants and slaves: the rural population of Roman Italy (200 BC to AD 100). Cambridge University Press, Cambridge

Le Teuff B (2012) Census: les recensements dans l'empire romain d'Auguste à Diocletien. Université Michel de Montaigne – Bordeaux III, Bordeaux

Le Teuff B (2014) Les recensements augustéens aux origines de l'Empire. Pallas (96):75–90. https://doi.org/10.4000/pallas.1179

Little LK (ed) (2007) Plague and the end of antiquity: the pandemic of 541–750. Cambridge University Press, Cambridge

Littman RJ, Littman ML (1973) Galen and the Antonine Plague. Am J Philol 94(3):243–255. https://doi.org/10.2307/293979

Lo Cascio E (1994) La dinamica della popolazione in Italia da Augusto al III secolo. Publications de l'École française de. Rome 198(1):91–125

Lo Cascio E (1997) Le procedure di recensus dalla tarda repubblica al tardo antico e il calcolo della popolazione di Roma. In: La Rome impériale: démographie et logistique. Actes de la table ronde de Rome, 25 mars 1994. Publications de l'École française de Rome 230, pp 3–76

Lo Cascio E (ed) (2012) L'impatto della "Peste Antonina". Edipuglia, Bari

Lo Cascio E, Tacoma LE (eds) (2017) The impact of mobility and migration in the Roman Empire. Brill, Leiden

McCormick M, Büntgen U, Cane MA, Cook ER, Harper K, Huybers P, Litt T, Manning SW, Mayewski PA, More AFM, Nicolussi K, Tegel W (2012) Climate change during and after the Roman Empire: reconstructing the past from scientific and historical evidence. J Interdiscip Hist 43(2):169–220. https://doi.org/10.1162/JINH_a_00379

McFadden C, Oxenham MF (2017) The D0-14/D ratio: a new paleodemographic index and equation for estimating total fertility rates. Am J Phys Anthropol 165(3):471–479. https://doi.org/10.1002/ajpa.23365

McIntyre LJ (2015) Reconstructing population size in a Romano-British Colonia: the case of Eboracum. J Roman Archaeol 28:413–429. https://doi.org/10.1017/S1047759415002561

Moatti C (2017a) Les paradoxes de l'immigration dans l'Empire romain. In: Garcia D, Le Bras H (eds) Archéologie des migrations. La Découverte (Recherches/INRAP), Paris, pp 197–210

Moatti C (2017b) Migration et droit dans l'Empire romain: Catégories, contrôles et integration. In: Lo Cascio E, Tacoma LE (eds) The impact of mobility and migration in the Roman Empire. Brill, Leiden, pp 222–245

Morin MS (2011a) Pour une étude des contacts culturels en zone frontalière à l'époque romaine: quelques réflexions conceptuelles. Dialogues d'histoire ancienne 37(2):63–88

Morin MS (2011b) Convergence à la frontière rhénane: les modes de contacts entre les populations frontalières (Ier s. de n. è.). Gerión 29(1):149–168

Morley N (2013) Population size and social structure. In: Erdkamp P (ed) The Cambridge companion to ancient Rome. Cambridge University Press, Cambridge, pp 29–44

Noy D (2000) Foreigners at Rome: citizens and strangers. Duckworth, London

Ouriachi M-J, Nuninger L (2011) Trajectoires des hommes et des établissements: contribution à la modélisation du système de peuplement antique en Languedoc oriental. Revue archéologique de Narbonnaise 44:99–116. https://doi.org/10.3406/ran.2011.1822

Palmisano A, Bevan A, Shennan S (2017) Comparing archaeological proxies for long-term population patterns: an example from Central Italy. J Archaeol Sci 87:59–72. https://doi.org/10.1016/j.jas.2017.10.001

Parkin TG (1992) Demography and Roman Society. Johns Hopkins University Press, Baltimore

Pelgrom J (2012) Colonial Landscapes. Demography, Settlement Organization and Impact of Colonies founded by Rome (4th- 2nd centuries BC). University of Leiden, Leiden

Pennington RL (1996) Causes of early human growth. Am J Phys Anthropol 99:259–274. https://doi.org/10.1002/(SICI)1096-8644(199602)99:2<259::AID-AJPA4>3.0.CO;2-U

Phang SE (2001) The marriage of Roman soldiers (13 B.C.-A.D. 235): law and family in the Imperial Army. Brill, Leiden

Picard J-B (2014) Les déplacements contraints de part et d'autre du Danube romain d'Auguste à Trajan. Hypothèses 17(1):197–206. https://doi.org/10.3917/hyp.131.0197

Pressat R (1985) Manuel d'analyse de la mortalité. INED, Paris

Rawson B (ed) (2011) A companion to families in the Greek and Roman worlds. Wiley-Blackwell, Malden/Oxford

Renard J-P (1992) Populations et frontières: problématiques et méthodes. Espace, populations, sociétés 2:167–184. https://doi.org/10.3406/espos.1992.1523

Richardson A (2000) The numerical basis of Roman camps. Oxf J Archaeol 19(4):425–437. https://doi.org/10.1111/1468-0092.00119

Roselaar ST (2016) State-organised mobility in the Roman Empire: legionaries and auxiliaries. In: De Ligt L, Tacoma LE (eds) Migration and mobility in the early Roman Empire. Brill, Leiden, pp 138–157. https://doi.org/10.1163/9789004307377_008

Roymans N (2004) Ethnic identity and Imperial power. The Batavians in the early Roman Empire. Amsterdam University Press, Amsterdam. https://doi.org/10.5117/9789053567050

Rus D (2010) Mariages et remariages sur le territoire du Deuxième Régiment roumain de frontière à l'époque moderne: perspectives démographiques et anthropologiques. Université de Nantes, Nantes

Rus D (2016) La militarisation de la frontière et les mutations des mentalités en Transylvanie roumaine (1750–1850). In: Catala M (ed) Frontières oubliées, frontières retrouvées: Marches et limites anciennes en France et en Europe. Presses universitaires de Rennes, Rennes p

Sallares R (2002) Malaria and Rome: a history of malaria in antiquity. Oxford University Press, Oxford. https://doi.org/10.1093/acprof:oso/9780199248506.001.0001

Scheidel W (1996) Measuring sex, age and death in the Roman Empire: explorations in ancient demography. Journal of Roman Archaeology, Portsmouth

Scheidel W (2001) Death on the Nile: disease and the demography of Roman Egypt. Brill, Leiden. https://doi.org/10.1163/9789004350946

Scheidel W (2005) Marriage, families, and survival in the Roman imperial army: demographic aspects. Stanford University, Stanford. Available at https://www.princeton.edu/~pswpc/pdfs/scheidel/110509.pdf. Accessed on 21 June 2018

Scheidel W (2015) Death and the City: ancient Rome and beyond. Soc Hist eJ, mai 2015. https://doi.org/10.2139/ssrn.2609651

Séguy I, Buchet L, Bringé A (2008) Model life tables for preindustrial populations. First applications in paleodemography. In: Bocquet-Appel J-P (ed) Recent advances in paleodemography: data, techniques, patterns. Springer, Dordrecht, pp 109–141. https://doi.org/10.1007/978-1-4020-6424-1_4

Séguy I, Buchet L (2013) Handbook of paleodemography. Springer, Dordrecht. https://doi.org/10.1007/978-3-319-01553-8

Séguy I, Caussinus H, Buchet L, Courgeau D, Le Forestier C, Paresys C, Richard I (2017) Indirect detection of major demographic events with no written sources (France – 6th–7th centuries). Poster presented at the XXVIIIth IUSSP International Population Conference (Capetown, South Africa, 29 October - 4 November 2017). doi:https://doi.org/10.13140/RG.2.2.36331.23843

Séguy I, Caussinus H, Buchet L, Courgeau D, Le Forestier C, Paresys C, Richard I (forthcoming) Détection indirecte d'événements démographiques majeurs en l'absence de sources écrites (France VIe -VIIe siècles). In: Manuel de statistiques à l'usage des archéologues

Storey GR (1997) The population of ancient Rome. Antiquity 71(274):966–978. https://doi.org/10.1017/S0003598X00085859

Van Dinter M, Kooistra LI, Dütting MK, Van Rijn P, Cavallo C (2014) Could the local population of the Lower Rhine delta supply the Roman army? Part 2: Modelling the carrying capacity using archaeological, palaeo-ecological and geomorphological data. J Archaeol Low Ctries 5(1):5–50

Verhagen P, Joyce J, Groenhuijzen MR (2016) Modelling the dynamics of demography in the Dutch limes zone. In: Multi-, inter- and transdisciplinary research in landscape archaeology. Proceedings of LAC 2014 Conference, Rome, 19–20 September 2014. Vrije Universiteit Amsterdam, Amsterdam. https://doi.org/10.5463/lac.2014.62

Woods R (2007) Ancient and early modern mortality: experience and understanding. Econ Hist Rev 60(2):373–399. https://doi.org/10.1111/j.1468-0289.2006.00367.x

Yoo J, Zerbini A (eds) (2018) Migration and migrant identities in the Middle East from antiquity to the Middle Ages. Routledge, Milton

Zelener Y (2003) Smallpox and the disintegration of the Roman economy after 165 A.D. Ph.D. thesis Columbia University

Chapter 3
Modelling the Dynamics of Demography in the Dutch Roman *Limes* Zone: A Revised Model

Philip Verhagen

Abstract In this chapter, a simulation model for better understanding the population dynamics of the *limes* zone is presented, building on our earlier study on the possible effects of recruitment of soldiers for the Roman army (Verhagen et al., Modelling the dynamics of demography in the Dutch limes zone. In: Multi-, inter- and transdisciplinary research in landscape archaeology. Proceedings of LAC 2014 Conference, Rome, 19–20 September 2014. Vrije Universiteit Amsterdam, Amsterdam. https://doi.org/10.5463/lac.2014.62, 2016a). In this earlier study, a number of questions were raised concerning the realism of using estimates from historical demographical sources for understanding the population dynamics of the region. In the current paper, the available data sets, approaches and hypotheses regarding fertility and mortality in the Roman period are re-assessed, together with the available archaeological evidence on the population dynamics of the region. A revised model is then presented that allows for more refined experimenting with various demographic scenarios, showing that a much larger number of parameters can be responsible for changes in population growth than is often assumed in archaeological studies. In particular, marriage strategies would seem to play an important role in regulating the number of births. The model remains a work in progress that can be further refined and linked to models of settlement and land use development.

Keywords Roman demography · Simulation modelling · Population dynamics · Fertility · Mortality

---

P. Verhagen (✉)
Faculty of Humanities, Vrije Universiteit Amsterdam, Amsterdam, The Netherlands
e-mail: j.w.h.p.verhagen@vu.nl

P. Verhagen et al. (eds.), *Finding the Limits of the Limes*, Computational Social Sciences, https://doi.org/10.1007/978-3-030-04576-0_3

3.1 Introduction: Demographic Modelling in the Roman Period

3.1.1 Available Data Sets

In order to better understand population growth dynamics, base data on mortality, fertility and migration are needed. For the periods before the introduction of parish records in Europe from the fifteenth century onwards, however, this information is almost completely lacking. This has led palaeo-demographers to employ datasets from the recent past instead. These datasets, collected from the 1950s onwards for modern population studies, can be used to study premodern populations as long as we are aware of the difficulties of obtaining reliable data on ancient population structures (see Chap. 2, Séguy).

In palaeo-demographic studies, it has often been assumed that prehistoric populations were stable, i.e. that the fertility and mortality patterns did not change over time and that net migration was zero (Lotka 1934, 1939). Under these conditions, a population will grow at a constant rate. Furthermore, it has often been assumed that population growth rates in premodern times were close to zero, following Acsádi and Nemeskéri (1970). This is partly because of the Malthusian principle that populations will not grow beyond carrying capacity but also because all the available evidence seems to point to very low growth rates throughout the premodern period of at most 0.2% per year. Even in cases where higher population growth is observed, like at the onset of the Neolithic, the growth pattern seems to quickly stabilize to near-equilibrium again (Bocquet-Appel 2008). Nevertheless, this does not mean that short-term population growth patterns need to be very stable (Séguy and Buchet 2013).

The generally low population growth rates observed in the past can mostly be attributed to devastatingly high (infant) mortality, but were also the consequence of (conscious) birth control. Most studies, however, have focused on mortality since it can be estimated with relative ease from the age structure of a population. If we can reconstruct a population's age structure, then we can also estimate its mortality very precisely.

The empirical data on mortality for the Roman period stem from epigraphic evidence on tombstones, skeletal material and a limited number of written sources, in particular census records from Egypt (Frier 1982; Parkin 1992; Bagnall and Frier 1994). On fertility and migration there is hardly any data at all. However, the available information is usually thought to support the assumption that the average life span in the Roman period was approximately 25 years and that Roman mortality patterns were very close to those of modern non-industrialised societies. The use of demographic data from 'non-industrialised' societies (Séguy and Buchet 2013) has therefore become a widely accepted approach to obtain demographic estimates for the Roman period (e.g. Parkin 1992; Bagnall and Frier 1994; Woods 2007; Hin 2013).

Life tables (Box 3.1) present the relationship between mortality and population age structure and have, therefore, been used extensively for Roman demographic studies. Since they only provide population age structure, but not growth rates, we also need to estimate birth rates in order to understand population dynamics in the Roman period. Henry (1961) and Coale and Trussell (1974, 1978) presented *natural fertility* schedules on the basis of historical demographic data that approach the situation when there is no form of birth control (Boxes 3.2 and 3.3).

Using these figures, the net reproduction rate (*NRR*) under the often used Model West 3 Female life table equals 2.1, corresponding to an annual growth rate (r) of 2.8% for the whole of the childbearing period of females. This is substantially higher than what can be inferred from historical and archaeological data (Wrigley and Schofield 1981; Bagnall and Frier 1994). Therefore, natural fertility rates do not reflect the true patterns of fertility in premodern times, and methods of birth control must have been applied extensively in the past, unless mortality really was much higher than is assumed.

Box 3.1 Life tables

A life table is a table of survivorship of people in an age group, usually starting with a population of 10,000 or 100,000 at age 0. Depending on the *mortality rate* per age group (usually denoted as $\boldsymbol{q_x}$), the number of people in subsequent age groups will decline by a figure $\boldsymbol{d_x}$ until reaching 0 at the maximum age. The number of survivors at age x is denoted $\boldsymbol{l_x}$, although this is also used sometimes to indicate the proportion of survivors, or survivorship, $\boldsymbol{l_x/l_0}$.

Usually, the age groups are presented as 5-year cohorts, with the exception of the first life year that is often included separately, since infant mortality is high in non-industrialised societies. In the case of cohort life tables, l_x refers to survivorship at the end age of the age group, not to the start. Note, however, that mortality rates for an age cohort are often given as ${}_nq_{x-n}$, with n denoting the number of years in the age cohort.

From life tables, a number of additional statistics can be obtained, including the *life expectancy* ($\boldsymbol{e_x}$) at a specific age.

Model life tables were first constructed on the basis of census data by the United Nations (1955) as idealised representations of the population age structure in various parts of the world. The more detailed model life tables published by Coale and Demeny (1966) are frequently used in palaeo-demographic studies since they include tables for life expectancies at birth ($\boldsymbol{e_0}$) that are supposed to reflect pre-industrial mortality regimes. The often cited *Model West 3 Female* life table, for example, is based on reliable historical census data from predominantly Western countries for females with $e_0 = 25$ years.

Box 3.2 Natural and true fertility

The concept of *natural fertility* was introduced by Henry (1961) to refer to the situation in which a population will make no conscious effort to limit the number of children born, such as was the case in many pre-industrial societies. Since Henry only studied historical data of fertility among married couples, the concept is also referred to as *marital fertility*. Natural fertility is only dependent on the physiological factors that influence *fecundity* during the reproductive period of females, usually taken as the age interval between 15 and 50 years. From his analysis, Henry concluded that natural fertility was remarkably similar throughout the cases studied.

True fertility on the other hand, refers to a situation where birth control is applied. This can be a highly variable figure, depending on the socio-cultural and historical context.

A *fertility schedule* (either natural or true) lists the *age-specific fertility rate (ASFR)* or the average number of births per female per age group; $\boldsymbol{m_x}$ then denotes the average number of daughters born.

Note that fertility schedules are always based on the assumption that a female survives all her childbearing years from age 15 to 50.

Box 3.3 Reproduction and growth rates

The *gross reproduction rate* (*GRR;* Kuczynski 1935) is a hypothetical figure denoting the number of daughters born to a woman that survives all her childbearing years from age 15 to 50, and it is calculated as the sum of m_x over all age groups. The *total fertility rate* (*TFR*) then is the number of children, male and female, born to this same woman.

The *net reproduction rate* (*NRR;* Kuczynski 1935) is equal to *GRR*, corrected for mortality of the females. It is also known as the *reproductive rate* (R_0). If *NRR* is larger than one, then the population will grow; if it is lower, it will decline.

NRR can be easily calculated on the basis of a life table and a fertility schedule, and equates to $\boldsymbol{\Sigma\, l_x/m_x}$. When using age cohorts, however, the value of l_x should be calculated based on the survivorship at the mid-point of the age group; so, at $x - 0.5n$ (see Caswell 2001:24–25).

The annual population *growth rate* ($\boldsymbol{r}$) is slightly more difficult to calculate and equals $\mathbf{ln}(\boldsymbol{NRR})/\boldsymbol{t}$, where $\boldsymbol{t}$ is the average length in years of a generation and equates to $(\boldsymbol{\Sigma\, x\, l_x/m_x})/\boldsymbol{NRR}$. When working with age cohorts this becomes $(\Sigma\, (x - 0.5n)\, l_{x-0.5n}/m_x)/NRR$.

3.1.2 Birth Control in the Roman Period

Bocquet-Appel (2008) states that regulating the birth interval was the most important factor influencing fertility in most prehistoric societies through post-partum abstinence and/or an extended lactation period. Extension of the lactation period was a well-known strategy of birth control in the Roman period (Bagnall and Frier 1994), and one that could have been applied quite easily—although it should be noted that in the upper classes, wet-nursing was common (Caldwell 2004). Bagnall and Frier (1994) also suggest that family size may have been effectively limited by 'stopping behaviour', meaning that once the desired number of children was born, couples no longer had intercourse. In the Roman Empire, divorce was quite common and therefore also constituted an effective way of reducing the duration of the childbearing period.

However, there are a number of other socio-cultural factors that can influence birth rates, in particular, where it concerns the rules around marriage. Increasing the (first) marriage age (or better said, the age at which females become sexually active) has a substantial reducing effect on birth rate. It is also known from historical data that the proportion of never-married females could be substantial (Wrigley and Schofield 1981), but there is little evidence for this in the Roman period. In the case of the Dutch *limes*, this would seem an unrealistic assumption anyway because of the male surplus created by the influx of immigrants (see Chap. 2, Séguy).

When raising the female first marriage age from 20 to 25 years under the Model West 3 Female life table, for example, the number of births will be reduced by about 23%, *NRR* will go down from 1.7 to 1.2 and *r* from 1.7% to 0.5%. Marrying of females to older males will also have an effect on population growth, especially if females are not allowed to remarry, since the average duration of the union will then be shorter because of the higher mortality among males (Caldwell 2004). The net effect however under the Model West 3 Female life table of females marrying a 5-year older male is only a 0.2–0.4% reduction in *r*.

Contraception, abortion and infanticide may have played a role as well in regulating the number of births. Evidence for contraception and abortion in the Roman period, however, is limited, and its effectiveness can be doubted (Caldwell 2004). Infanticide, though often suggested, seems not to have been practiced very widely, although 'exposure' of new-born children was quite common (Caldwell 2004), which could either mean the death of the child, or, more probably, its adoption as a foundling.

All in all, a number of effective strategies were available to premodern societies to limit the number of births, although their actual application will have been highly tied to social and possibly religious norms. For this reason, modelling ancient birth rates remains challenging, since it will be hard to identify the precise causes for reduced or increased birth rates. In an earlier study (Verhagen et al. 2016a), we demonstrated that removing a sufficiently large number of males from the marriage pool because of army recruitment will in the end lead to population collapse, since the number of unmarried females will then become too large. The figures presented there were compared to a base scenario of natural fertility. However, since the population in the Dutch *limes* zone does not show signs of substantial growth before the arrival of the Romans, its inhabitants may already have applied one or more of the birth control strategies mentioned. This also implies that there was at least a theoretical opportunity to increase the number of births per female and thus to provide the Roman army with more men by 'breeding soldiers'.

3.1.3 Mortality Crises in the Roman Period

A factor usually not addressed in ancient population modelling studies is the influence of mortality crises on population size and structure. This is probably because these can be poorly linked to modern-day equivalents. However, the ancient world was full of diseases, famine and warfare that could wipe out substantial portions of the population over a short period of time (see also Chap. 2, Séguy and Chap. 6, Jongman). Quantitative data on these aspects is scarce, however, especially where it concerns the effects of famine. Furthermore, ancient written sources often seem to exaggerate the effects of these crises.

3.1.3.1 Epidemics

Some estimates are available of the effects of epidemics in the Roman period, in particular those of the Antonine Plague that struck the Empire in the years between 165 and 189 CE with outbreaks of varying severity. Littman and Littmann (1973) estimated that 7–10% of the population died during the major outbreaks and suggested that contemporary reports of 25% to one-third of the population are unlikely. Duncan-Jones (1996) indicates that epidemics were a common occurrence but that the Antonine 'plague' (presumably smallpox) was likely an especially devastating case since it was so often mentioned in later sources and at the same time led to a decrease in written sources in general (see also Chap. 6, Jongman). The available quantitative evidence is mainly from Egypt and Rome. Egyptian sources would seem to point to a mortality of over one-third of the population. These effects could however be (very) localised, and the spread of the plague is thought to have occurred mainly through the main communication arteries and the army. A side effect of epidemics was also an increased animal mortality, leading to a reduction in the availability of animals for both food consumption and agricultural work.

3.1.3.2 Warfare

Where it concerns warfare, Rosenstein (2004) provides detailed figures of soldier mortality in the Roman Republican army in the period 200–168 BCE. Combat losses would amount to 2.6% of the soldiers per year. During major battles, however, these figures would be much higher (around 5.6%), especially in the case of defeats, although it is noted that mortality rates were not as high as in the nineteenth-century mass warfare. In major documented battles, some 15–30% of the soldiers would die, but these are exceptional events.[1] In the study region, the only major battles were fought during the Batavian revolt (69–70 CE), but of course the recruited Batavian soldiers were also involved in other military campaigns, especially in the conquest of Britain (43–66 CE).

Estimates on the loss of civilian life during wartime are unavailable, although it should be borne in mind that the killing of civilians was relatively rare and mainly affected non-Roman enemies, like in the case of Julius Caesar's campaign against the Eburones. However, prolonged military campaigns might have had a negative effect on the availability of food, as well as carry diseases with them and lead to an exodus of population fleeing from the advancing armies.

3.2 The Settlement Evidence

As part of our research, we have collected and evaluated all the publicly available information on Roman period settlements in the Dutch *limes* (Verhagen et al. 2016b) in order to analyse patterns of settlement distribution in the region through time. Of course, all settlement inventories can be criticised for their level of detail and accuracy, and ours is no exception. The main problems associated with large-scale settlement databases are found in their uneven geographic and temporal representation, and in their lack of detail on the number of inhabitants of individual settlements that can be inferred from the number of house plans, cemetery sizes and other indicators. The problem of estimating population sizes on the basis of settlement inventories has been discussed in various studies on the Dutch *limes* (Bloemers 1978; Willems 1986; Vossen 2003; Buijtendorp 2010; Van Lanen et al. 2018) and has led to a large range of estimates (see Chap. 1, Verhagen, Joyce & Groenhuijzen). However, reliable information on the development of rural settlements throughout the Roman period is limited to a few studies (e.g. Hessing and Steenbeek 1990; Jansen and Fokkens 1999; Van Londen 2006; Heeren 2009; Vos 2009) and has not been fully synthesised. A study like the one presented by Nüsslein in Chap. 5 could therefore be very useful to better understand the development trajectories of settlements beyond the major studied ones, but so far this has not been undertaken.

The general trends, however, can be easily identified. First of all, as was already pointed out in Chap. 1 (Verhagen, Joyce and Groenhuijzen), the growth in settlement numbers during the Early and Middle Roman period is well attested, although the exact growth rate remains open to debate. From our own data, we estimated an approximate 70% increase in rural settlement numbers in the period between 25 CE and 150 CE. Also, there is sufficient evidence that many existing settlements grew in size, so the actual increase in population will have been more than that. For this

[1] https://www.quora.com/How-has-mortality-rate-per-battle-changed-throughout-history

reason, Van Lanen et al. (2018) postulated a population increase of more than 260% from the Early Roman to the Middle Roman period. These are clear indications of a population growth increase that goes well beyond the supposed maximum of 0.2% per year for pre-industrial societies, and it is in sync with observed larger trends in the Roman empire (see Chap. 6, Jongman). The rural population growth is most probably linked to increased economic productivity and urbanisation, following the arrival of a substantial Roman military and civilian population (possibly in the order of 20–30%).

Natural population growth (without immigration) needs to come from a decrease in mortality, an increase in fertility, or a combination of the two. Jongman points out that economic growth must have led to higher living standards and thus to a higher life expectancy and the possibility to raise more children, but the fact remains that we have no reliable evidence for this. Cremation burial evidence from the cemetery of Tiel-Passewaaij (Heeren 2009, 81–93) does not reveal significant changes in life expectancy from the mid-first century until the third century CE even when evidence for pathologies decreases somewhat. For the whole cemetery, the life expectancy of the buried individuals was estimated at 29.4 years, which is clearly higher than the usually assumed life expectancy for the Roman period, but it is assumed that the high infant mortality is not reflected correctly in the burial evidence. Furthermore, an increase in the site's population in the Early Roman B and Middle Roman A periods is evident with a demographic peak suggested for the period 90–120 CE.

An open question remains on how the economic growth and urbanisation in the Roman empire may have influenced the local population dynamics. On the one hand, immigrants will have moved into the region, possibly bringing spouses with them, but it is conceivable that they sought and found local marriage partners as well. On the other hand, there also was a strong pressure on the inhabitants to supply the Roman army with soldiers, leading to (temporary) emigration of men from the region. There is, however, ample evidence for family life of soldiers and the maintenance of contacts with the homeland in the form of army diplomas and military finds in rural settlements. It is therefore assumed that the legal ban on marriage for soldiers only applied to Roman citizens and was probably not enforced. Saller and Shaw (1984) point out that the phenomenon of *dilectus* (family separation) is well known from historical evidence and was much resented. This led Van Driel-Murray (2008) to hypothesise that a large proportion of the females was left behind in the rural settlements. She suggested that extended leave would have allowed soldiers to maintain families in their homeland, but as Heeren (2009, 251–252) points out, it is also plausible that women accompanied their men. Also, spouses from different corners of the empire may have been taken back to the homeland after the service term.

The evidence from the Tiel-Passewaaij cemetery suggests that, at least for this site, there was only a small surplus of females in the period between 40–150 AD, although no statistical test was performed on the data set. This relative lack of a female surplus is attributed to the practice of Batavian soldiers to take local spouses with them to their place of deployment. Emigration could therefore have affected the population size as a whole, but may not have had a significant effect on the biological reproductive capacity of the ones left behind. However, emigration would then suppose an even stronger natural population growth than can be deduced from the settlement and cemetery evidence alone.

The available settlement data then suggest a strong population decline starting in the Middle Roman B period, again following general trends in the Roman empire. The number of rural settlements in the area decreases by at least 40% from the Middle Roman B to the Late Roman A period, but the situation may have been much more serious than that, given the almost complete disappearance of indicators for occupation from excavated settlements in the period 275–300 CE (Heeren 2015; De Bruin 2017), coupled to clear evidence for incoming new settlers in the late fourth century. Van Lanen et al. (2018) assume a reduction to about 20% of the population size in the Late Roman period. An almost complete depopulation of the area in the late third century therefore seems plausible, possibly forced by the Roman authorities but certainly triggered by the abandonment of the forts and the disappearance of the urban settlements. Several authors have suggested that the population decline may already have started by the end of the second century and have linked this to the compound effects of diseases, economic downturn and raids by Germanic tribes (De Jonge 2006; Vos 2009). While these all seem plausible explanations, a good understanding of the effects of these events on the local population is lacking, since the decline does not seem to be equally severe for all settlements and micro-regions. Again, the evidence from the Tiel-Passewaaij cemetery does not indicate any changes in life expectancy, but shows a clear reduction in population size from approximately 150 CE onwards (Heeren 2009, 81–93).

3.3 Towards a Dynamical Model of Human Reproduction

In our earlier study (Verhagen et al. 2016a), we presented a preliminary demographic simulation model to understand the possible effects of recruitment on population growth in the Dutch *limes* region, prompted by the long-standing debate on the problem for the local population to sustain the Roman army with men without jeopardizing agricultural production capacity (Bloemers 1978; Willems 1986; Vossen 2003; Van Driel-Murray 2008). This model, written in NetLogo 5.1.0 (Wilensky 1999; http://modelingcommons.org/browse/one_model/4678), was kept as simple as possible in order to come to grips with the main factors influencing population growth. It only allowed for experimentation with the mortality regime and recruitment rate, and the resulting scenarios pointed to a potentially precarious balance between recruitment rate and viability of the population over the longer term.

The main problem with the model was that it was difficult to judge the realism of its outcomes, partly because of the simplification of the factors involved and the small modelled population size, but also because of the lack of any reliable data or well-defined hypotheses on marriage strategies, mortality regimes, recruitment rates and actual population size. This is all the more relevant since relatively small changes in fertility and mortality can lead to large differences in outcomes, provided the time period considered is long enough.

For the current paper, the original model was therefore extended to address the following questions:

1. What is the effect of marriage strategies on population growth?
2. What is the effect of birth control strategies?
3. What is the effect of mortality crises on long-term population viability?

The extended model was written in NetLogo 6.0.4 and can be accessed at http://modelingcommons.org/browse/one_model/5764.

3.3.1 Marriage Strategies

In the original model, high annual population growth rates of 0.95–2.15% were obtained, depending on the mortality regime chosen. This high growth rate was achieved because almost all females in the model would get first married at age 18, remarriage was allowed, and no birth control options were included. The males were not allowed to get married under the age of 26. These marriage rules were assumed to be broadly valid for the Roman period (Verhagen et al. 2016a). By contrast, however, the census data from Egypt (Bagnall and Frier 1994) point to different patterns, with only 60% of females married at age 20 and no remarriage allowed.

The new model therefore allows to experiment with more scenarios by manipulating the allowed age difference between spouses, adding an option to prevent remarriage, and by introducing a 'first marriage probability' factor for females, reflecting the fact that they would not all be first married at the same age and following the 'standard schedule of the risk of first marriage' described by Coale (1971). Coale's model departs from two basic parameters: the allowed first age of marriage and the time span it takes for all females to become first married:

$$r(a) = (0.174k)e^{-4.411e^{-\left(\frac{0.309}{k}\right)(a-a_0)}}$$

where

a = age of female

$r(a)$ = risk of getting married at age a

a_0 = allowed first age of marriage

k = time span reduction factor; the lower the k, the shorter the time span until all females will be married and thus the higher the number of births

A separate option for non-marriage of females has not been added in this stage since it is not supposed to be a realistic assumption for the Roman period, but it can easily be implemented as an extra option. In practice, this was already experimented with: when modelling the effects of recruitment (Verhagen et al. 2016a), the number of unmarried females increased with increasing recruitment rates, leading to long-term negative effects on population growth.

Lastly, the original model had no limitation to the number of available marriage partners. Interaction between any member of the population was allowed. In reality, the rural population lived in settlements with only one or a few households (see also Chap. 7, Joyce), potentially limiting the number of available partners because of distance and/or kinship relations. We have, however, not aimed to model these more complex effects in this stage.

3.3.2 Birth Control

The original model only had one fertility schedule based on the natural fertility regime as defined by Coale and Trussell (1978). As discussed in Sect. 3.1.2, this schedule is not realistic for most pre-industrial societies. The census data from Egypt, for example, points to an average gap of 45 months between the birth of children (Bagnall and Frier 1994). Experimenting with the fertility schedule in the model can now be achieved in two ways: either by setting a fertility reduction factor that will lead to a lower number of births in general (simulating a longer birth spacing), and/or by allowing for stopping behaviour after a certain number of children is born and surviving, as suggested by Bagnall and Frier (1994).

3.3.3 Mortality Crises

Lastly, a 'mortality crisis' option was introduced in the model, with the possibility to explore two parameters: frequency and severity. Severity is modelled by adding a mortality multiplier, and frequency by specifying a return period of the mortality crisis.

In practice, mortality will have fluctuated from year to year, selective diseases might have targeted the elderly and or young disproportionately, and diseases, famine and warfare may have varied geographically as well. More specific mortality crisis scenarios should therefore be included in the model, but for the moment these have not been implemented.

3.4 Results

3.4.1 Marriage Strategies

While many combinations of marriage strategies can be explored in the new model setup, the major effects on population growth are found when manipulating the first marriage probabilities. The revised model runs suggest that the most effective strategy for increasing population growth is reducing the first marriage age and time span for females. The effects of changing the marriage age difference and allowing remarriage are limited compared to this.

The models were run with the 'Woods South 25' high mortality schedule and a natural fertility regime (Table 3.1). Under these conditions, applying very long first marriage time spans will lead to population decline, especially when combined with higher first marriage ages. Coale (1971) compared data from early twentieth-century Taiwan with those from Sweden, with k values of, respectively, 0.48 and 0.89. Even applying the 'Taiwanese' model already leads to a low mean population growth of only 0.2% if the first marriage age is set at 18 years with no minimum age difference between spouses; the 'Swedish' scenario is not viable. However, lowering the first marriage age to 15 dramatically increases the number of births, with a mean population growth of 1.2% for the 'Taiwanese' model.

3.4.2 *Birth Control*

Applying birth control is highly effective to reduce population growth. A reduction of the natural fertility rate to 80% is already sufficient to reduce population growth from 0.9% to 0.1% in a scenario with a_0 = 15 years and k = 0.5 (Table 3.2).

Table 3.1 Effects of first marriage age (a_0; columns) and first marriage time span (k; rows) on annual population growth

	15 years	18 years
0.1	1.9%	1.3%
0.3	1.5%	0.7%
0.5	1.2%	0.2%
0.7	0.7%	−0.3%
0.9	0.0%	−0.9%

Averages based on 100 model runs over 100 years per scenario with 'Woods South 25' mortality schedule and natural fertility

Table 3.2 Effects of fertility reduction (left) and stopping behaviour (right) on annual population growth

Fertility reduction factor		Stopping behaviour	
1.0	0.9%	8	0.9%
0.9	0.5%	7	0.9%
0.8	0.1%	6	0.8%
0.7	−0.5%	5	0.8%
0.6	−1.2%	4	0.5%

Averages based on 100 model runs over 100 years per scenario with 'Woods South 25' mortality schedule, natural fertility regime and first marriage span with a_0 = 15 years and k = 0.5

Manipulating stopping behaviour will only have a major effect on population growth when the limit on the number of children is substantially below the average number of children born under the natural fertility regime. When set at seven or eight children there is no discernible difference, but setting the stopping behaviour at four surviving children reduces population growth from 0.9% to 0.5%.

Averages based on 100 model runs over 100 years per scenario with 'Woods South 25' mortality schedule, natural fertility regime and first marriage span with $a_0 = 15$ years and $k = 0.5$

3.4.3 Mortality Crises

Annual average mortality rates based on the 'Woods South 25' high mortality schedule (Woods 2007) are in the order of 4%. Adding a mortality multiplier to the model results in clear temporary population declines, but the return rate is a very important factor for determining whether mortality crises will have a long-term effect. For example, when departing from the same scenario as above (natural fertility regime and first marriage span with $a_0 = 15$ years and $k = 0.5$), a 50% increase in mortality will not have a significant long-term effect on population growth when the return rate is only 20 years: average population growth will then decrease from 0.9% to 0.8% (Table 3.3). With faster return rates, however, it will quickly start to have a larger negative effect. For higher mortality rates, this is even more evident. A fivefold increase (so from 4% to 20%) will clearly reduce population growth with longer return rates as well, but it is important to note that even severe mortality crises will not be sufficient to bring the population in decline when they occur in isolation. It is only when the crises return more regularly that the long-term survival of the population will be in danger.

Table 3.3 Effects of mortality crises on annual population growth for different mortality multipliers (rows) and return rates (columns)

	20 years	10 years	5 years	2 years
1.5	0.8%	0.7%	0.5%	0.1%
2	0.7%	0.5%	0.2%	−0.8%
3	0.5%	0.1%	−0.9%	−2.4
4	0.3%	−0.3%	−1.9	X
5	0.1%	−0.6%	−2.2	X

Averages based on 100 model runs over 100 years per scenario with 'Woods South 25' mortality schedule, natural fertility regime and first marriage span with $a_0 = 15$ years and $k = 0.5$. X = populations did not survive over model run

3.5 Conclusions

The model runs demonstrate that relatively small changes in some of the parameters used may greatly influence long-term population dynamics. These results are not all completely new or surprising, but the advantage of modelling population dynamics in the NetLogo environment is the ease of manipulation of scenarios to help us understand the contribution of various factors to population growth and decline that are suggested in historical and archaeological studies.

Of course, we do not know whether the *limes* population was aware of the modelled effects and adapted their reproductive behaviour accordingly. However, while mortality patterns were largely outside the influence of conscious human behaviour in the Roman period, marriage and birth control strategies could be effectively manipulated to regulate reproduction. In practice, a combination of strategies may have been consciously or unconsciously applied that would increase population growth, driven by the Roman demand for armed forces and the improved economic prospects in the first half of the Roman period. For example, restrictions on early marriage might have been more relaxed in times of economic prosperity, when it would be easier for couples to achieve economic independence. Stopping behaviour, while not the most effective birth control strategy at the macro-level, may have been very effective at the household level to make sure that the number of children would not exceed the settlements' carrying capacity.

The models also suggest that mortality crises in themselves are not sufficient to cause long-term population decline, but when the return rate increases their negative effects will be clearly felt. This confirms the assumption that diseases like the Antonine Plague, which returned at irregular intervals, must have kept a prolonged pressure on the population (see Chap. 2, Séguy). This may have been exacerbated by the effects of economic decline (see Chap. 6, Jongman) which may have led to changes in marriage and birth control strategies as well. In the end, however, the strong depopulation of the area in the Late Roman period may have been the consequence of (forced) emigration rather than of internal population dynamics.

The models presented in this paper remain a work in progress. The main difficulty is to set up a dynamical model that does not become too complex to handle while still producing meaningful results. While general conclusions on the causes and effects of changes in reproductive behaviour can be obtained relatively easily with the current models, fully understanding the interplay of various factors for the *limes* zone and judging the realism of the modelled outcomes is a much more difficult task. Especially the rules for finding marriage partners, based on socio-economic status, distance and/or kinship would seem a fertile ground for further experimentation, but this would also involve finding realistic approximations of marriage probabilities that are not based on the generalised model that has been used now. Also, questions about the limitations to the growth of rural settlements into settlements with multiple households are currently not addressed, nor were the questions of rural-urban relationships and the effects of migration included in the model. For this, we would also need to couple the demographic model to socio-economic simulation models such as the ROMFARMS model developed by Jamie Joyce (Chap. 7) or land use simulation models (De Kleijn et al. 2018).

References

Acsádi G, Nemeskéri J (1970) History of human life span and mortality. Akadémiai Kiadó, Budapest

Bagnall RS, Frier BW (1994) The demography of Roman Egypt. Cambridge University Press, Cambridge

Bocquet-Appel JP (2008) Explaining the Neolithic demographic transition. In: Bocquet-Appel JP, Bar-Yosef O (eds) The Neolithic demographic transition and its consequences. Springer, Dordrecht, pp 35–55

Bloemers JHF (1978) Rijswijk (Z.H.), 'De Bult', Eine Siedlung der Cananefaten. Rijksdienst voor het Oudheidkundig Bodemonderzoek, Amersfoort

Buijtendorp T (2010) Forum Hadriani. De vergeten stad van Hadrianus: Ontwikkeling, uiterlijk en betekenis van het 'Nederlands Pompeji'. Vrije Universiteit Amsterdam, Amsterdam

Caldwell JC (2004) Fertility control in the classical world: was there an ancient fertility transition? J Popul Res 21(1):1–17. https://doi.org/10.1007/BF03032208

Caswell H (2001) Matrix population models: construction, analysis and interpretation, 2nd edn. Sinauer Associates, Sunderland, MA

Coale AJ (1971) Age patterns of marriage. Popul Stud 25(2):193–214

Coale AJ, Demeny P (1966) Regional model life tables and stable populations. Princeton University Press, Princeton

Coale AJ, Trussell TJ (1974) Model fertility schedules: variations in the age structure of childbearing in human populations. Popul Index 40:185–258

Coale AJ, Trussell TJ (1978) Technical note: finding the two parameters that specify a model schedule of marital fertility. Popul Index 44:203–213. https://doi.org/10.2307/2733910

De Bruin J (2017) Rurale gemeenschappen in de Civitas Cananefatium 50–300 na Christus. University of Leiden, Leiden

De Kleijn M, Beijaard F, Koomen E, Van Lanen RJ (2018) Simulating past land use patterns; the impact of the Romans on the Lower-Rhine delta in the first century AD. In: De Kleijn M (ed) Innovating landscape research through geographic information science: implications and opportunities of the digital revolution in science for the research of the archaeology, history and heritage of the landscape from a GIScience perspective. Vrije Universiteit Amsterdam, Amsterdam, pp 125–148. Available at http://dare.ubvu.vu.nl/handle/1871/55517. Accessed on 7 June 2018

De Jonge W (2006) Ondergang. De crisis in het rijk en de teloorgang van Forum Hadriani. In: De Jonge W, Bazelmans J, De Jager D (eds) Forum Hadriani. Van Romeinse Stad Tot Monument. Matrijs, Utrecht, pp 146–159

Duncan-Jones RP (1996) The impact of the Antonine plague. J Roman Archaeol 9:108–136. https://doi.org/10.1017/S1047759400016524

Frier B (1982) Roman life expectancy: Ulpian's evidence. Harv Stud Class Philol 86:213–251

Heeren S (2009) Romanisering van rurale gemeenschappen in de Civitas Batavorum: de casus Tiel-Passewaaij. Rijksdienst voor het Cultureel Erfgoed, Amersfoort

Heeren S (2015) The depopulation of the lower Rhine region in the 3rd century. An archaeological perspective. In: Roymans N, Derks T, Hiddink H (eds) The Roman villa of Hoogeloon and the archaeology of the periphery. Amsterdam University Press, Amsterdam, pp 269–292

Henry L (1961) Some data on natural fertility. Eugen Q 8:81–91

Hessing WAM, Steenbeek R (1990) Landscape and habitation history of 'De Horden' at Wijk bij Duurstede, an overview. Berichten van de Rijksdienst voor het Oudheidkundig Bodemonderzoek 40:9–28

Hin S (2013) The demography of Roman Italy. Population dynamics in an ancient conquest society 201 BCE–14 CE. Cambridge University Press, Cambridge

Jansen R, Fokkens H (1999) Bouwen aan een verleden, 25 jaar archeologisch onderzoek in de gemeente Oss. Leiden University, Leiden. Available at http://hdl.handle.net/1887/9846. Accessed on 3 May 2018

Kuczynski RR (1935) The measurement of population growth: methods and results. Sidgwick and Jackson Ltd, London

Littman RJ, Littmann ML (1973) Galen and the Antonine plague. Am J Philol 94:245–255

Lotka A (1934) Théorie analytique des associations biologiques. Première partie: principes. Hermann & Cie., Paris

Lotka A (1939) Théorie analytique des associations biologiques. Deuxième partie: analyse démographique avec application particulière à l'espèce humaine. Hermann & Cie., Paris

Parkin TG (1992) Demography and Roman society. The Johns Hopkins University Press, Baltimore

Rosenstein N (2004) Rome at war. Farms, families, and death in the Middle republic. University of North Carolina Press, Chapel Hill

Saller RP, Shaw BD (1984) Tombstones and Roman family relations in the Principate: civilians, soldiers and slaves. J Roman Studies 74:124–156. https://doi.org/10.2307/299012

Séguy I, Buchet L (2013) Handbook of Palaeodemography. Springer, Cham

United Nations (1955) Age and sex patterns of mortality: model life tables for under-developed countries. United Nations, New York

Van Driel-Murray C (2008) Those who wait at home: the effect of recruitment on women in the Lower Rhine area. In: Brandl U (ed) Frauen und römisches Militär: Beiträge eines Runden Tisches in Xanten vom 7. bis 9. Juli 2005. BAR, Oxford, pp 82–91

Van Lanen R, De Kleijn M, Gouw-Bouwman M, Pierik HJ (2018) Exploring Roman and early-medieval habitation of the Rhine-Meuse delta: modelling large-scale demographic changes and corresponding land-use impact. In: De Kleijn M (ed) Innovating landscape research through geographic information science: implications and opportunities of the digital revolution in science for the research of the archaeology, history and heritage of the landscape from a GIScience perspective. Vrije Universiteit Amsterdam, Amsterdam, pp 149–201. Available at http://dare.ubvu.vu.nl/handle/1871/55517. Accessed on 7 June 2018

Van Londen H (2006) Midden-Delfland: the Roman native landscape past and present. University of Amsterdam, Amsterdam. Available at http://hdl.handle.net/11245/1.260370. Accessed on 3 May 2018

Verhagen P, Joyce J, Groenhuijzen MR (2016a) Modelling the dynamics of demography in the Dutch limes zone. In: Multi-, inter- and transdisciplinary research in landscape archaeology. Proceedings of LAC 2014 Conference, Rome, 19–20 September 2014. Vrije Universiteit Amsterdam, Amsterdam. https://doi.org/10.5463/lac.2014.62

Verhagen P, Vossen I, Groenhuijzen MR, Joyce J (2016b) Now you see them now you don't: defining and using a flexible chronology of sites for spatial analysis of Roman settlement in the Dutch river area. J Archaeol Sci Rep 10:309–321. https://doi.org/10.1016/j.jasrep.2016.10.006

Vos WK (2009) Bataafs platteland. Het Romeinse nederzettingslandschap in het Nederlandse Kromme-Rijngebied. Rijksdienst voor het Cultureel Erfgoed, Amersfoort

Vossen I (2003) The possibilities and limitations of demographic calculations in the Batavian area. In: Grünewald T, Seibel S (eds) Kontinuität und Diskontinuität. Germania inferior am Beginn und am Ende der römischen Herrschaft. Beiträge des deutsch-niederländischen Kolloquiums in der Katholieke Universiteit Nijmegen (27. bis 30.06. 2001). Walter De Gruyter, Berlin, pp 414–435

Wilensky U (1999) NetLogo (and NetLogo user manual). Northwestern University, Evanston, IL

Willems WJH (1986) Romans and Batavians. A regional study in the Dutch Eastern River area. University of Amsterdam, Amsterdam

Woods R (2007) Ancient and early modern mortality: experience and understanding. Econ Hist Rev 60:373–399. https://doi.org/10.1111/j.1468-0289.2006.00367.x

Wrigley EA, Schofield RS (1981) The population history of England 1541–1871. A Reconstruction. Edward Arnold, London

Chapter 4
Broad and Coarse: Modelling Demography, Subsistence and Transportation in Roman England

Tyler Franconi and Chris Green

Abstract The English Landscape and Identities project (EngLaId), which ran from 2011 to 2016 (ERC grant number 269797), was designed to take a long-term perspective on English archaeology from the Middle Bronze Age (c. 1500 BCE) to the Domesday survey (1086 CE). It was a legacy data project that collated an immense number of records of English archaeology from a large number of different public and academic sources. Within this mountain of material, the Roman period (43 to 410/411 CE) stood out as being particularly fecund, accounting for 40% of the data (by record count) coming from only 15% of the total timespan of the project. This paper examines the ways in which the EngLaId project approached the modelling and analysis of its data for Roman England. We focus here on the three themes of demography, subsistence economy and transportation. Overall, EngLaId provides an interesting contrast to the possibilities and limitations of the other projects presented in this volume because of its large spatiotemporal scale and its (thus necessary) broad-brush approaches to data analysis and modelling. It is also this large spatiotemporal scale that helps situate the Roman period within a much longer span of history, making evident what was unique to this time period and what was constant across multiple periods.

Keywords England · Roman · Landscape archaeology · Big data · GIS

T. Franconi (✉)
Department of History and Classics, University of Alberta, Edmonton, AB, Canada
e-mail: franconi@ualberta.ca

C. Green
School of Archaeology, University of Oxford, Oxford, UK
e-mail: christopher.green@arch.ox.ac.uk

P. Verhagen et al. (eds.), *Finding the Limits of the Limes*, Computational Social Sciences, https://doi.org/10.1007/978-3-030-04576-0_4

4.1 Introduction

The English Landscapes and Identities project (EngLaId) ran from 2011 until 2016 and was funded by the European Research Council. It was in essence a legacy data project that collected a very large amount of material on the archaeology of England covering the timespan from the Middle Bronze Age (c. 1500 BCE) to the Domesday survey of 1086 CE. The team gathered a database of over 900,000 records of archaeological sites (including find-spots and also uncertainly dated material) from a large number of sources. These included almost all of the local government/national park-based Historic Environment Records (HERs), Historic England (HE), the Portable Antiquities Scheme (PAS) and a number of other smaller datasets collated by individuals or other bodies. The team also gathered various ancillary datasets including the results of HE's National Mapping Programme, the grey literature library held by the Archaeology Data Service (ADS), and HE's Index of Excavations (also curated by the ADS). This mass of material was complex and rich in detail but was mostly rather high level: in other words, the data could describe English archaeology at the scale of sites and landscapes but could answer few questions on an intra-site or contextual basis, simply due to lack of consistent recording of archaeology at greater levels of detail than the site. All told, the archaeological records contained in the EngLaId database cover a range of site types that were simplified down to 119 defined types and grouped into 8 categories: agriculture and subsistence; religious, ritual and funerary; domestic and civil settlements; architectural forms; industry; communication and transportation; defensive structures; and a final catch-all for 'other' (Green et al. 2017, 246–247; https://englaid.arch.ox.ac.uk/). In addition, find types ranging from coins to weapons were also included, but these are not relevant to the discussion herein.

As such, the datasets gathered by the project could be best put to use in the exploration of questions and themes at a rather broad-brush scale/resolution. Although more detailed case studies were undertaken, at a national level there was little possibility for manual cleaning of our data, and so the data was resampled using spatial bins (see Green 2013 for more detail) to minimize problems caused by imprecise spatial coordinates and double (or more) counting of the same objects across multiple datasets (see Cooper and Green 2016). The national-level models presented here have thus passed through a stage of being binned into 1-by-1-kilometre cells before any analysis was undertaken, with the presence/absence of each type of site defined (e.g. 'cremation cemetery', 'villa', 'hillfort', etc.) recorded for each cell. Although this process will have removed some level of detail on a high-resolution spatial scale, this should not have unduly affected models created at low-resolution spatial scales, such as investigations carried out at the national level.

Obviously, England is not an entity that existed until perhaps the very end of our time period of interest and certainly did not exist during the Roman period that is the focus of this particular paper. However, one must set limits to any analysis and using the bounds of modern-day England allowed a reasonable degree of consistency to exist across most of the original data sources gathered, as almost all of the bodies from whom we collected data are governed by guidelines set by HE (the HERs and HE itself at least). If we had included data from Wales or Scotland, or from Ireland or the near continent, then that would have increased the time taken both to gather and to rationalize the data, which was already not insignificant. As such, although 'England' remains an anachronous construct for the majority of our time period, it is a convenient construct nevertheless.

Throughout the approximately 2500-year time period covered by the EngLaId project, the approximately 400 years of the Roman period stands out as particularly significant in terms of the amount of data. Around 40% of the records in our main database are of Roman date, despite the period only representing around 15% of the Bronze Age to early medieval time period as a whole. Demonstrably, the Romano-British left a lot more evidence of their existence in (and above) the ground for archaeologists (and others) to discover than their prehistoric predecessors or (early) medieval successors did. This could be explained in a number of ways: there may have been more people (the demographic explanation), there may have been more intensive exploitation of resources (the subsistence economy explanation) or there may have been stronger links between different places both within and outside England (the transportation explanation). Almost certainly, the answer will be a mixture of these explanations and others (including the modern factors that partially structure the recovered archaeological record, as discussed in Green et al. 2017, 253–256; Cooper and Green 2016), but these three themes will be the subject of the rest of this paper, also aligning well as they do with the topics of the other papers presented in this volume.

4.2 Demography

The massive amount of data from the Roman period led us to first re-examine an age-old archaeological question: how does the distribution of sites and artefacts relate to the numbers of people that left them behind? The demography of the Roman Empire has recently been the subject of a number of studies that range from regional (Marzano 2011; Hanson 2011) to Empire-wide studies (Scheidel 2007; Wilson 2011; Hanson 2016). These studies have generally relied on estimates of urban populations based on hypothetical settlement densities within defined city spaces that are then extrapolated to estimate the (much larger) rural population. Exact methodologies and outcomes vary widely, from low estimates of 54 million (Beloch 1886, 501–507) to high estimates of 122 million (Hanson 2016, 72) in the middle of the second century CE. Within this Empire-wide uncertainty, regional estimates of provincial populations reflect the same orders of variation. For the province of Britannia, estimates range from 2 to 2.5 million (Frere 1987, 311; Jones 2004; Mattingly 2006) to as high as 5–6 million (Salway 1981, 544). There is, therefore, much said about Roman demography, but very little proven. Outside of pure numbers, there are significant obstacles in understanding both geographical and chronological fluctuations in demographics as well, as the situation of the early Roman Empire would undoubtedly be very different from that of 200 or 400 CE.

Because of these difficulties and others, the EngLaId team did not attempt to model actual population numbers within its study region, as it seemed unlikely that any accurate measures could be derived from the data to hand, especially considering the amount of work already done inconclusively on the subject. Instead, we sought out proxies that ought to relate on some level to relative population density in the past. After some experimentation, we settled on a rough proxy based upon the complexity of information for each time period in each 1 by 1 kilometre cell, averaged out across space using Kernel Density Estimate (KDE) modelling (see O'Sullivan and Unwin 2010, 68–71). The complexity measure was essentially the number of different types of site within each cell based upon the terms defined in our site type simplification thesaurus (which contained 119 different potential

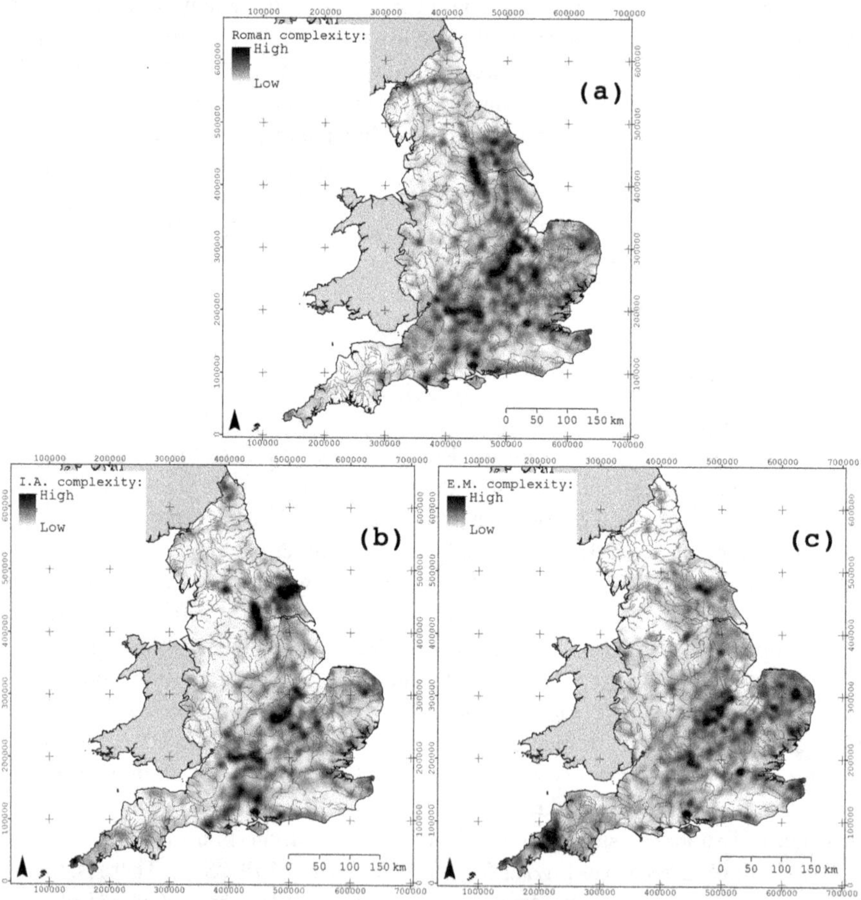

Fig. 4.1 Models of relative complexity of archaeology for the (**a**) Roman, (**b**) Iron Age, and (**c**) early medieval periods

types). The methodology has been explained and its merits/problems have been discussed in detail elsewhere (Green et al. 2017), but essentially we argue that these models must relate on some level to variation in population density across England, as more people ought to mean more archaeological remains and more variety of archaeological remains, at least if we are dealing with relatively settled lifeways. The models were normalized for cross comparison using *z*-scores (i.e. subtracting the mean and dividing by the standard deviation).

The model of relative data complexity for the Roman period (Fig. 4.1a) shows a large and partially discontinuous peak that covers most of south eastern England, with some smaller peaks in the north and west which are mostly associated with military landscapes (e.g. Hadrian's Wall). Particular peaks within the zone of higher general complexity include the Thames and Nene river valleys and a swathe of countryside to the south and west of the legionary fortress and colony of York. The area of the Weald of Kent and Sussex shows a clearly lower density, as an area known mostly for iron working in the Roman period and which is generally of low complexity throughout the total time period studied by the EngLaId project. When compared against the preceding Iron Age (Fig. 4.1b) and succeeding early medieval periods (Fig. 4.1c), the earlier period shows a similar overall pattern but with a more restricted zone of higher complexity, alongside a notable peak in North Yorkshire that is reduced in the Roman period. The later period shows a generally lower value but also generally similar overall pattern, albeit with a much stronger peak of high complexity in the Cornwall/Devon peninsular. East Anglia also shows a much broader peak of high complexity, which is of little surprise as this region is traditionally characterized as one of the heartlands of Anglo-Saxon migratory settlement.

Although clearly not direct models of variation in past population density, the results presented here do suggest that the south eastern half of England must have seen relatively greater densities of settled (i.e. archaeologically visible) peoples throughout the Iron Age to early medieval periods. It is unfortunate that the coarseness of dating evidence for the majority of our data does not allow modelling at finer temporal resolutions, as it seems inevitable that the patterns presented must also have varied within each time period, whether due to changing economic circumstances, migration or plague (among other factors). Nevertheless, we would hope that these relatively simple models will help provide background context for more detailed work on the past demography of Roman Britain in the future, especially in comparison to earlier and later periods.

4.3 Subsistence Economy and Landscape Change

These regionally and chronologically varied patterns of settlement across Roman England had similarly varied impacts on the landscape, especially through agricultural exploitation. The EngLaId project was broadly interested in the relationship between society and environment through all periods, investigating how human development resulted in environmental change and, conversely, how environmental dynamism caused societal change, and agricultural exploitation of the English landscape formed a central area of investigation. England, especially the southeast, had been at least partially cleared since the Neolithic period and farmed in a settled way since at least the middle Bronze Age, and thus significant portions of the territory were already ancient farmland by the time of the Roman invasion (Fyfe et al. 2013; Edwards et al. 2015). The Roman period saw similar spatial patterns of exploitation in the southeast, and they increased the amount of land under cultivation in wetlands (Rippon 2007; Van de Noort 2011) as well as in the north and west (more on this expansion below). Some regions show remarkable continuity into the early medieval period, especially in the southeast (Rippon et al. 2015), as farmers in this period continued to exploit Roman-era field systems.

The agricultural exploitation of the English landscape through time left noticeable markers in environmental archives, including pollen (Dark 2006; Fyfe et al. 2013; Edwards et al. 2015) and fluvial sequences (Brown 1997; Macklin et al. 2014). Both of these datasets suggest significant environmental change through time, often corresponding to shifts in human activity, such as new technologies (e.g. the introduction of the ard plough c. 1500 BCE) or new settlement patterns (e.g. the establishment of a permanent garrison along the Hadrian's Wall corridor c. 122 CE). The Roman period left its mark in these environmental records in different ways, but fluvial sequences show a repeated pattern of rivers entering into periods of hydrological crises during the later first and second centuries CE. These crisis periods are marked by an increase in floods and alluviation and, in some cases, by an accompanying rise in groundwater level. While climatic change could have played some role in these hydrological processes (see Franconi 2017a for an overview of this relationship), the chronology of fluvial change in Britain seems to predate the onset of significantly different patterns in temperature or precipitation fluctuation, indicating a different, anthropogenic driver.

While the Roman Empire did not necessarily introduce new agricultural methods to Britain (both arable agriculture and animal husbandry already had a long history by 43 CE), it certainly introduced a new scale of exploitation, visible in the increased extent of field systems and rural settlement (Smith et al. 2016; Allen et al. 2017). The necessity for farmers to produce income to pay taxes to the Roman State, either through cash or products in kind, helped drive an agricultural revolution that saw an increase in both the amount of land under cultivation and the intensity with which this land was worked. The fiscal necessity was augmented by substantial growth in both urban and military populations throughout the new province, increasing the need for farmers to produce a surplus that could be sold on to non-agricultural populations. Thus, while significant amounts of the English landscape were already given over to agriculture at the end of the Iron Age, the Romans dramatically increased the demands on the landscape. This legacy is perhaps most archaeologically visible in the creation of *villa* landscapes.

This increased demand on agricultural land came with an environmental price. By clearing more land for agriculture (as well as for timber for construction and fuel), and by continuing to plough existing fields year after year, the Roman agricultural economy increased surface erosion of soils across the country. As soils were exposed and loosened by Roman farming, they were washed away by rainfall, travelling via surface flow into river systems where the sediment was then carried downstream to floodplains where it was subsequently re-deposited as alluvium during floods. It is this alluvium that we find preserved on archaeological sites today, and its frequency of appearance during the middle- and late-Roman periods on riverside sites certainly suggests an increasingly changed hydrological system.

Sites with these sorts of environmental archives are relatively well known in Britain, especially within the Thames River basin (Robinson and Lambrick 1984; Robinson 1992; Booth et al. 2007; Lambrick et al. 2009; Powell et al. 2010). These site-based chronologies give solid evidence of hydrological change, but their anecdotal nature requires a model-based approach to extrapolate their societal context to larger scales.

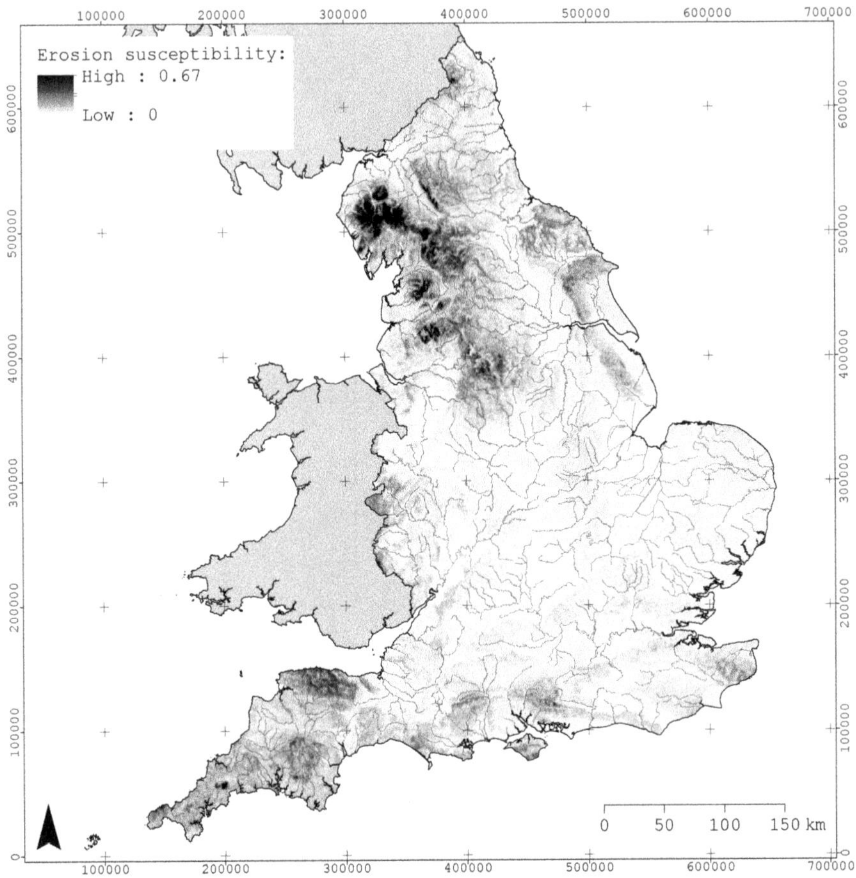

Fig. 4.2 Erosion susceptibility in England

The EngLaId project thus created a model of soil erosion susceptibility for England, based on a variety of pedological, climatic and topographic qualities, such as soil erodibility, slope angle and length, rainfall erosivity and wind erosivity that were compiled by the European Soil Data Centre and made available online (https://esdac.jrc.ec.europa.eu/). These raster data were combined using GIS and normalized, resulting in a range of values from 0 to 1, and then subjected to kriging to interpolate between the known values (O'Sullivan and Unwin 2010, 293–311). The resulting model of erosion susceptibility (Fig. 4.2) shows significant regional variation, with the Thames Basin actually showing relatively low susceptibility while regions like the Pennines and the Lake District Fells in the northwest, the Yorkshire Dales and Cheviots in the northeast, and Dartmoor, Exmoor and Cornwall in the southwest show much higher levels of erosion susceptibility.

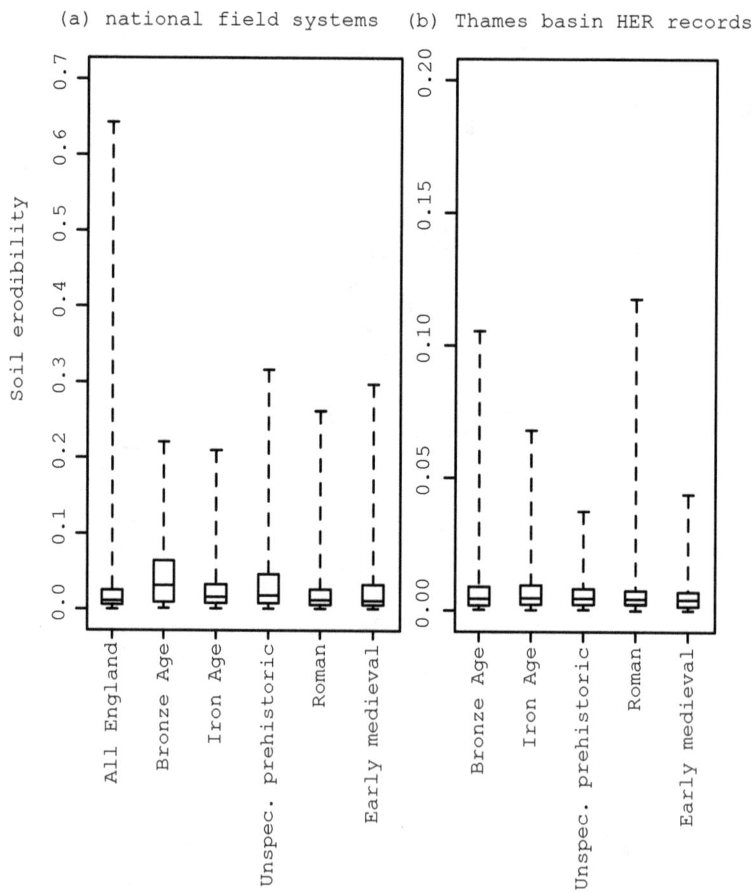

Fig. 4.3 Erosion susceptibility of (**a**) field systems by period at national level and (**b**) all records in the Thames Basin

Using this model, we were able to extract the erosive values of field systems throughout all EngLaId periods and gauge the relative impact of Bronze Age, Iron Age, Roman and early medieval agriculture on erosive activity nationwide. The resulting boxplots (Fig. 4.3a) by period did not show a significantly varied temporal pattern in the overall range of soil erodibility, and this can be explained by the relative homogeneity of a low erosive susceptibility across most flat, low-lying agricultural land in the south and east of the country: the exception to this is the Bronze Age, where upland field systems do show greater levels of potential soil erosion. We recognized, however, that this nationwide pattern obscured significant local variation, and so a second step of analysis was performed at the scale of river catchment basins.

The Thames Basin was chosen as a detailed case study, in part to look at the systemic patterns that helped create the archaeologically visible pattern of hydrological change discussed above. Within the Thames Basin (Fig. 4.3b) and looking only at HER records to avoid issues regarding overlapping datasets, we see a decrease in activity on more erosive land from the Bronze Age to the Iron Age, followed by an increase again in the Roman period, albeit with the majority of activity in less erosive areas according to the model. This change can be explained through an increase in Roman activity on slopes, especially the Berkshire Downs, Chilterns and North Downs, each part of the chalk ridgeways that crosses the basin on a southwest-northeast orientation. The higher susceptibility of erosion on these slopes meant that more sediment entered the Thames Basin during this time, leading to the increased deposition of alluvium on the floodplains of the river in the second and third centuries. Medieval activity closely followed this same spatial pattern, but we do not see similar peaks in hydrological crisis periods at this time. We can perhaps attribute this return to environmental normalcy to the removal of state impetus to produce a massive surplus, which ended with the removal of Roman fiscal control in the early fifth century CE (Rippon et al. 2015, 337–338), lessening the intensity with which the landscapes of the Thames Basin were worked.

We can see, therefore, that the Roman period in England had a relatively brief, but nonetheless substantial, impact on the environment of the province of Britannia. This pattern of increased strain on the landscape is seen elsewhere in the Roman Empire (Franconi 2017a, b), but has yet to be explored at the system level made possible by the extensive archaeological data compiled by the EngLaId project. The resulting national and regional models discussed here are, then, a step towards understanding the ways in which the Roman Empire exercised a significant influence over its environment.

4.4 Transportation

The increasingly developed and connected landscape of Roman England required a commensurate level of infrastructural development that could link rural settlement, towns, cities and military sites together into a system of easy communication and exchange. The rapid development of this system in the first century CE has been referred to as Britain's 'first information revolution' (Haynes 2000, 112–113) that mainly centred on the creation of the provincial road network (Margary 1973) but also important river and sea hubs that helped link Britannia to the rest of the Empire (Blair 2007; Morris 2010).

The EngLaId team was interested in the long-term development of connections both within England and without, as we wished to know how movement, transportation and communication changed through time. It was clear, however, that the Roman period saw such a dramatic increase in route ways and connective hubs that the earlier periods were dwarfed in comparison. The differences in scale between the Bronze and Iron ages and the Roman and early Medieval periods were so striking that it became clear that in order to understand the relative contributions of each period, a different approach was needed rather than just counting roads or something similar.

As with demography, the EngLaId team built a series of proxy models for potential transportation cost rather than attempting to model movement in a more formalized manner. As with population, density of archaeological data was used as a proxy for how connected people living in different regions of England were in the past, on the assumption that greater connectivity implies greater access to goods and to economic enrichment, and that travel costs ought to be lower in areas of dense, well-connected settlement. In these models, the density measures were converted into cost allocation surfaces and used to produce a series of cost surfaces (see Herzog 2014 for detailed discussion of cost modelling) from a large number of points. These were then summed together to build a combined model of cumulative cost across the country, and normalized (to remove edge effects) by dividing by a similar cumulative cost model constructed using a cost allocation surface of constant cost: if this were not done then the only visible pattern would be a radiating zone of increasing cost out from the low cost centre of England. Again, the models were normalized for cross comparison using *z*-scores (see above).

It is very clear that the model of travel cost for the Roman period (Fig. 4.4a) shows notably lower costs in the areas of higher complexity seen in the demographic proxy model for the same period (Fig. 4.1a). As the two models are derived from the same dataset and the transport model based upon an assumption of 'more people equals lower cost', clearly this should be expected. The appearance of clear road lines within the travel model is a pleasing result, alongside routes that appear to travel along river valleys in some regions. As Roman roads were part of the dataset used to create the model, again this is somewhat expected. When compared against the preceding Iron Age (Fig. 4.4c) and succeeding early medieval periods (Fig. 4.4d), however, the continuing appearance of some of the road lines (particularly in the later period) is of particular note as the Roman roads were not themselves built into these datasets (due to being dated to the Roman period). Of particular importance appears to be the communication corridor that runs north through the eastern central part of England, as this appears as a clear route of low cost in all three models. This is approximately equivalent to the modern A1 road,

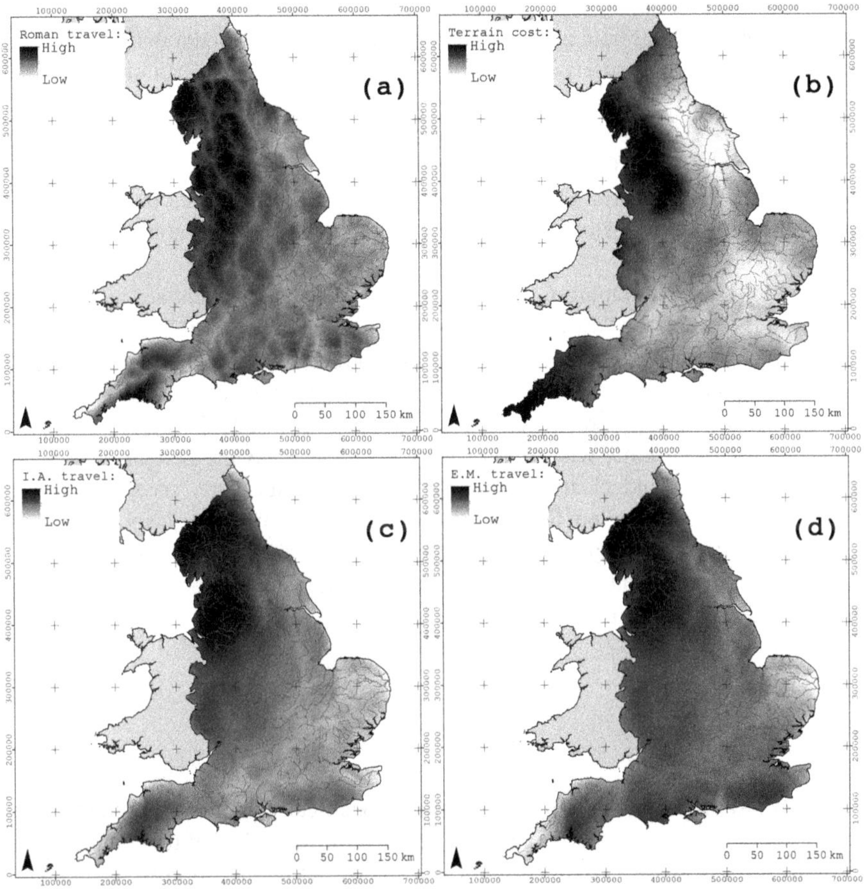

Fig. 4.4 Model of relative transportation cost (proxy) for the (**a**) Roman, (**c**) Iron Age, (**d**) early medieval periods, and (**b**) based on terrain character

which, as its numeric designation suggests, is one of the most important non-motorway arterial transport routes in modern day England.

A somewhat more conventional transportation cost model was also constructed for England using the same cumulative cost surface method (Fig. 4.4b). This was based upon terrain ruggedness (double-weighted to give it prime importance), a model of terrain wetness (based upon flow accumulation, modern wet and seasonally wet soils and modern precipitation) and a model of visual prominence of the landscape (on the assumption that travel through visually prominent locations would be desirable for people travelling on non-nefarious business). This combined transport cost model shows a very clear divide between the rugged and wet western half of England (where most rainfall falls due to the elevated ground causing weather systems travelling inland from the Atlantic to deposit their moisture as precipitation) showing much higher relative travel costs that the drier and less rugged (albeit less visually open due to lack of elevated areas) landscape of the eastern half of England. Of particular note is the broad concordance of this model with the models presented above using purely archaeological data. This is again particularly notable for the communication corridor running north through eastern central England, but also for the area represented approximately by the modern counties of Northamptonshire and Cambridgeshire. The way in which these models derived from different datasets all generally support one another suggests that these may form relatively strong proxies for the degree of transport connectivity present in Roman period England.

As with the demographic models, these transportation models are also clearly rather rough proxies for how movement of people and goods might have taken place in the past, and finer chronological resolution would also undoubtedly pick out further subtle change over time. However, it is apparent that again the southeastern half of England was more interconnected and communicative than the other half of the country throughout time, with major routeways clearly having their origins in the pre-Roman period and clearly surviving in part into the early medieval period (indeed, as many so-called Roman roads still survive in the transport network today). As with the demographic models, we would also hope that these transportation models provide context and inspiration for further study of transport and communication (and trade) in Roman Britain.

4.5 Conclusions

The EngLaId project was not designed with a specifically Roman-centred research agenda, but it was clear that no matter what question was asked of the longue durée of English history, the Roman period had a significant contribution to its archaeological appearance. The case studies of demography, the environmental impact of agriculture and the transportation infrastructure were three of the main foci of the project's investigation of Roman England, though there were others in resource management, ritual activity, systems of enclosure, literacy and material consumption that cannot be discussed in the space available here. The examples of demography, agriculture and transportation show that the Roman period was a substantially different beast in the long-term history of the English landscape. The years between the conquest of 43 CE and the provincial abandonment of 410/411 CE left a remarkable and lasting imprint on England that was both distinct from what came before and prescriptive of what would come later. Future scholarly narratives of change and continuity in Britain must be written with an awareness of the scale of these changes that are visible at the macro level.

These case studies also help demonstrate the incredible value of being able to interrogate national datasets of Roman archaeology. While other countries in Europe may have similarly strong datasets (see Bradley et al. 2015 for an overview of the prehistoric data on both sides of the English Channel or Demján and Dreslerová 2016 on Bohemia), few have been able to be brought to bear on major questions in

Roman archaeology, and thus the EngLaId project offers a particular insight into the problems and possibilities that lay ahead in the creation of a more complete (national or international) dataset of Roman archaeology, and the types of questions that can or cannot be addressed at these scales. The future of the discipline lies in being able to marshal increasingly large and international datasets to address important historical issues, and we hope that the EngLaId project will help focus these research agendas as they develop.

Acknowledgements The English Landscape and Identities project (EngLaId), which ran from 2011 to 2016, was funded by the European Research Council (Grant number 269797). We would like to thank them alongside all of the various people and organizations who provided us with data and also alongside our colleagues for providing a rich and rewarding research environment. At the time of writing, a simplified version of the EngLaId dataset can be explored at https://englaid.arch.ox.ac.uk.

References

Allen M, Lodwick L, Brindle T, Fulford M, Smith A (2017) The rural economy of Roman Britain: new visions of the countryside of Roman Britain, vol 2. Society for the Promotion of Roman Studies, London

Beloch KJ (1886) Die Bevölkerung der griechisch-römischen Welt. Duncker & Humbolt, Leipzig

Blair J (ed) (2007) Waterways and canal-building in medieval England. Oxford University Press, Oxford

Booth P, Dodd A, Robinson M, Smith A (2007) The Thames through time: the archaeology of the gravel terraces of the upper and middle Thames: the early historical period, AD 1–1000. Oxford Archaeology, Oxford

Bradley R, Haselgrove C, Vander Linden M, Webley L (2015) The later prehistory of north-West Europe: the evidence of development-led fieldwork. Oxford University Press, Oxford

Brown AG (1997) Alluvial geoarchaeology: floodplain archaeology and environmental change. Cambridge University Press, Cambridge. https://doi.org/10.1017/CBO9780511607820

Cooper A, Green C (2016) Embracing the complexities of 'big data' in archaeology: the case of the English Landscape and Identities project. J Archaeol Method Theory 23:271–304. https://doi.org/10.1007/s10816-015-9240-4

Demján P, Dreslerová D (2016) Modelling distribution of archaeological settlement evidence based on heterogeneous spatial and temporal data. J Archaeol Sci 69:100–109. https://doi.org/10.1016/j.jas.2016.04.003

Dark P (2006) Climate deterioration and land-use change in the first millennium BC: perspectives from the British palynological record. J Archaeol Sci 33:1381–1395. https://doi.org/10.1016/j.jas.2006.01.009

Edwards KJ, Fyfe RM, Hunt CO, Schofield JE (2015) Moving forwards? Palynology and the human dimension. J Archaeol Sci 56:117–132. https://doi.org/10.1016/j.jas.2015.02.010

Franconi TV (2017a) Studying rivers in the Roman world. In: Franconi TV (ed) Fluvial landscapes in the Roman world. Journal of Roman Archaeology, Portsmouth, RI, pp 7–22

Franconi TV (2017b) Pater Rhenus: the hydrological history of Rome's German frontier. In: Franconi TV (ed) Fluvial landscapes in the Roman world. Journal of Roman Archaeology, Portsmouth, RI, pp 85–96

Frere SS (1987) Britannia: a history of Roman Britain. 2nd Edition. Routledge and Kegan Paul, London
Fyfe RM, Twiddle C, Sugita S, Gaillard M-J, Barratt P, Caseldine CJ, Dodson J, Edwards KJ, Farrell M, Froyd C, Grant MJ, Huckerby E, Innes JB, Shaw H, Waller M (2013) The Holocene vegetation cover of Britain and Ireland: overcoming problems of scale and discerning patterns of openness. Quat Sci Rev 73:132–148. https://doi.org/10.1016/j.quascirev.2013.05.014
Green C (2013) Archaeology in broad strokes: collating data for England from 1500 BC to AD 1086. In: Chrysanthi A, Wheatley D, Romanowska I, Papadopoulos C, Murrieta-Flores P, Sly T, Earl G (eds) Archaeology in the digital era: Papers from the 40th Annual Conference of Computer Applications and Quantitative Methods in Archaeology (CAA), Southampton, 26–29 March 2012. Amsterdam University Press, Amsterdam, pp 307–312 Available at http://arno.uva.nl/cgi/arno/show.cgi?fid=516092. Accessed on 10 May 2018
Green C, Gosden C, Cooper A, Franconi T, Ten Harkel L, Kamash Z, Lowerre A (2017) Understanding the spatial patterning of English archaeology: modelling mass data from England, 1500 BC to AD 1086. Archaeol J 174:244–280. https://doi.org/10.1080/00665983.2016.1230436
Hanson JW (2011) The urban system of Roman Asia Minor and wider urban connectivity. In: Bowman AK, Wilson A (eds) Settlement, urbanization, and population. Oxford University Press, Oxford, pp 229–275. https://doi.org/10.1093/acprof:oso/9780199602353.003.0009
Hanson JW (2016) An urban geography of the Roman world, 100 BC to AD 300. Archaeopress, Oxford
Haynes IP (2000) Britian's first information revolution; the Roman army and the transformation of economic life. In: Erdkamp P (ed) The Roman army and the economy. Gieben, Amsterdam, pp 111–126
Herzog I (2014) Least-cost paths – some methodological issues. Internet Archaeol 36. https://doi.org/10.11141/ia.36.5
Jones MJ (2004) Cities and urban life. In: Todd M (ed) A companion to Roman Britain. Blackwell, Oxford, pp 162–192. https://doi.org/10.1002/9780470998861.ch10
Lambrick G, Robinson M, Dodd A (2009) The Thames through time: the archaeology of the gravel terraces of the upper and middle Thames: the Thames Valley in late prehistory, 1500 BC-AD 50. Oxford University School of Archaeology, Oxford
Macklin MG, Lewin J, Jones AF (2014) Anthropogenic alluvium: an evidence-based meta-analysis for the UK Holocene. Anthropocene 6:26–38. https://doi.org/10.1016/j.ancene.2014.03.003
Margary ID (1973) Roman roads in Britain, 3rd edn. J. Baker, London
Marzano A (2011) Rank-size analysis and the Roman cities of the Iberian Peninsula and Britain: some considerations. In: Bowman AK, Wilson A (eds) Settlement, urbanization, and population. Oxford University Press, Oxford, pp 196–228. https://doi.org/10.1093/acprof:oso/9780199602353.003.0008
Mattingly DJ (2006) An imperial possession: Britain in the Roman empire, 54 BC-AD 409. Allen Lane, London/New York
Morris FM (2010) North Sea and channel connectivity during the late Iron Age and Roman period (175/150 BC - AD 409). Archaeopress, Oxford
O'Sullivan D, Unwin D (2010) Geographic information analysis, 2nd edn. John Wiley & Sons, Hoboken. https://doi.org/10.1002/9780470549094
Powell K, Smith A, Laws G, Allen L (2010) Evolution of a farming community in the upper Thames Valley: excavation of prehistoric, Roman and post-Roman landscape at Cotswold Community, Gloucestershire and Wiltshire. Oxford Archaeology, Oxford
Rippon S (2007) Focus or frontier? The significance of estuaries in the landscape of southern Britain. Landscape 8(1):23–38. https://doi.org/10.1179/lan.2007.8.1.23
Rippon S, Smart C, Pears B (2015) The fields of Britannia. Oxford University Press, Oxford.
Robinson MA, Lambrick GH (1984) Holocene alluviation and hydrology in the upper Thames basin. Nature 308(5962):809–814. https://doi.org/10.1038/308809a0

Robinson MA (1992) Environment, archaeology, and alluvium on the river gravels of the South Midlands. In: Needham S, Macklin MG (eds) Archaeology under alluvium. Oxbow, Oxford, pp 197–208

Scheidel W (2007) Demography. In: Scheidel W, Morris I, Saller RP (eds) The Cambridge economic history of the Greco-Roman world. Cambridge University Press, Cambridge, pp 38–86. https://doi.org/10.1017/CHOL9780521780537.004

Salway P (1981) Roman Britain. Clarendon Press/Oxford University Press, Oxford/New York

Smith A, Allen M, Brindle T, Fulford M (2016) The rural settlement of Roman Britain: new visions of the countryside of Roman Britain. Society for the Promotion of Roman Studies, London

Van de Noort RV (2011) North Sea archaeologies: a maritime biography, 10,000 BC - AD 1500. Oxford University Press, Oxford

Wilson A (2011) City sizes and urbanization in the Roman Empire. In: Bowman AK, Wilson A (eds) Settlement, urbanization, and population. Oxford University Press, Oxford, pp 161–195. https://doi.org/10.1093/acprof:oso/9780199602353.003.0007

Chapter 5
A Different Vision of Ancient Settlement Dynamics: Creation and Application of a Model of Evolution of Roman Settlement of the Plateau Lorrain (France)

Antonin Nüsslein

Abstract Research concerning settlement dynamics is mainly based on data from archaeological field survey. This method of investigation provides researchers with a lot of information that can help to identify trends and to model the evolution of settlement structure at different scales. Nonetheless, field survey data is sometimes incomplete and only shows a snapshot of the settlements. This static information lacks a certain number of parameters (evolution of architectural, economic, social features, etc.) which are essential to perceive the inherent evolution of the settlements and therefore to visualize their own evolution within the dynamics of settlement trajectory networks. On the other hand, data from archaeological excavations enable us to detect those phenomena. This paper aims to propose a methodological approach to try to resolve this lack of parameters: the creation of an evolutionary model of the settlements from the information collected during excavations. Applied to the sites discovered by field survey, and combined with other analytical tools, the model allows for a better understanding of the diversification phenomena and the processes of spatial development of the settlement pattern. This method, which offers solutions to enhance the static information provided by survey data, was designed for the study of Roman settlement of the Plateau Lorrain (France), but it can be applied to other periods and to other regions as well.

Keywords Field survey · Temporal dimension · Archaeological excavation · Modelling · Settlement study

---

A. Nüsslein (✉)
UMR 7044 'Archimède', University of Strasbourg, Strasbourg, France
e-mail: antonin.nusslein@archeologie.alsace

P. Verhagen et al. (eds.), *Finding the Limits of the Limes*, Computational Social Sciences, https://doi.org/10.1007/978-3-030-04576-0_5

5.1 Introduction[1]

Archaeological field survey allows archaeologists to discover structures and artefacts of all kinds betraying the presence of settlement or other ancient human activity at the surface. It is then possible, after study, to gather information on the function, the spatial organization and the chronology of the archaeological sites investigated. If the survey is carried out in a systematic and spatially continuous way, archaeologists can visualize the number of settlements, their function, their size and their dating throughout a territory, in order to perceive the organization and the settlement dynamics of an area at a given moment or over the long term (see for a few examples of this type of studies in Roman Gaul: Favory et al. 1987–1988; Durand-Dastès et al. 1998; Trément 1999; Van der Leeuw et al. 2003; Gandini 2008).

Beside the fact that survey data quality is highly conditioned by post-depositional processes (erosion, overlap, soil acidity, etc.) or the uneven exposure of artefacts linked to tillage conditions that can alter their distribution on the surface and thus bias the perception of a settlement (see Alcock and Cherry 2004; Dabas et al. 2006), they can also present a major problem due to the nature of this method of investigation. The observation of structures and collection of surface artefacts does not always allow us to understand the internal history of the settlements, which could sometimes present several phases of evolution. This has implications for the visualization and the understanding of ancient settlements. As we shall see, part of the research questions then cannot be addressed and problems can arise in spatial analysis.

Therefore, this contribution proposes solutions to qualify and improve the study of settlement systems based on archaeological field survey data. To this end, information from archaeological excavations—which reveals the intrinsic history of settlements—was used. The investigation of the Roman settlement system of the Plateau Lorrain (France) provides keys to improve and evaluate analyses based on results from archaeological field survey.

5.2 The Temporal Dimension of Data from Archaeological Field Surveys

In order to understand the origin and the nature of the problem posed by these data, let us first consider the specific signal given by the results of archaeological field surveys.

[1] A French version of this chapter was published in 2016 (Nüsslein 2016b). Some adjustments have been made following the suggestions of the reviewers of this chapter.

5.2.1 Results of Archaeological Field Surveys: A Linear Signal

While archaeological field survey offers many advantages, such as the possibility of exploring large areas and listing numerous deposits while gathering a large amount of data, this method presents a major problem. Prospecting only allows for the collection of the artefacts found on the ground. The building materials and objects stemming from different phases of the explored settlement are thus mixed. Stratigraphic information, provided only by excavations, which allows for the reconstruction of the evolution of a settlement, is absent. The remains collected during archaeological field survey give information on the building materials used, the artefacts present and the surface area, but they are compressed into a flattened assemblage detached from the chronological evolution, and thus from the different phases of the settlement.

In many cases, especially because of lack of artefacts, limited study of artefacts and/or poor preservation of sites, data from archaeological field surveys only offer three chronological elements: date of appearance, date of disappearance and duration of existence (Durand-Dastès et al. 1998). Therefore, this method of investigation will often only provide a summary and a fixed image of the settlement. Consequently, since these data do not give a true temporal dimension, the results of archaeological field survey produce a linear signal (Fig. 5.1). Without excavations or detailed artefact study from field survey, it is not possible to trace the different stages of the history of a settlement: creation, expansion, peak, various functions over time, architectural evolution, decline, abandonment, etc. From an ontological point of view, an excavated settlement and a prospected site could also be regarded as different entities referring to their own concepts (Favory et al. 2012). Grenon and Smith (2004) proposed to distinguish, on one hand, 'Snap' entities, which have a chronological depth and which exist at each time step, and 'Span' entities which constitute events and processes that require a temporal extent. These two entities are entwined: a Roman *villa*, for example, is a 'Snap' entity, but its evolutionary process, measurable by its increase in size or changes in architectural and decorative features, is a 'Span' entity. Similarly, a settlement that is known only from archaeological field survey and whose date of establishment and abandonment are known along with its main characteristics could be considered as a 'Snap' entity, but an excavated settlement, for which evolutionary mechanisms are known may be perceived as a 'Span' entity.

5.2.2 Consequences for the Study of Settlement Patterns

In some cases, the temporal information from survey data can be best exploited by extensive field analyses or advanced artefact studies (e.g. Trément 2000; Moreau et al. 2011; Tol 2012). Sometimes, even the temporal evolution of the surface of a settlement may be reconstructed. For example, on the site of Dachstein (Bruche

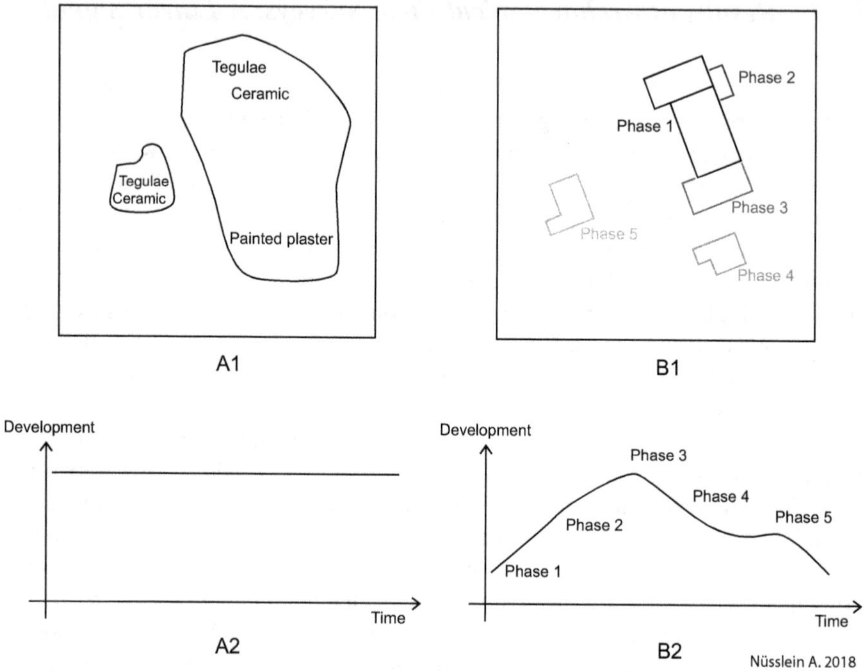

Fig. 5.1 The difference in information content between archaeological field survey and excavation. The same settlement was discovered in an archaeological field survey (A1) and in an excavation (B1). After analysis of the artefacts, this settlement did not show the same evolution configuration depending on the mode of investigation employed. The survey data revealed a linear development (A2) located at its 'optimal' level throughout its existence, while the excavation data showed a complex evolution of the settlement with phases of enlargement or decline (B2)

Valley, Alsace, France) it was possible, thanks to the study of ceramics, to determine the spatial and economic evolution of the settlement (Baudoux 2012). However, the realization of this type of study is often complicated, time-consuming and cannot be applied over large regions. So, there is information missing for many sites in most study regions. This has consequences for the study of settlement patterns in two respects.

First, as was already pointed out, at the level of the temporal dynamics of the settlement system, it is often impossible to retrace the history of a settlement and to relate its various characteristics to a specific phase of its existence in order to follow its architectural, economic and social evolution. Without knowing what is going on at the level of the settlements during their different phases of evolution, the understanding of the evolution of a number of settlements is not complete.

Secondly, at the level of spatiotemporal dynamics of a (regional) settlement system, it is necessary to characterize the sites present in the study area and to classify them in relation to each other, period by period, in order to analyse their organization and evolution. For this, the ideal is to have information on the characteristics of each phase for all settlements. The ideal situation is therefore to have data that form a three-dimensional cube, such as Berry's 'geographical information matrix' (Berry 1964; Favory et al. 2012), where settlements, their attributes and time intersect. However, this ideal configuration can only be provided by excavation information or very advanced artefact studies. Without this, archaeologists are therefore often obliged to work on a 'snap' summary of the settlements' characteristics.

To illustrate this point, let us take the example of a site discovered in archaeological field survey, occupied from the first to the fourth century CE. When creating the typology, a status (small farm, *villa*, etc.) is typically assigned according to its general characteristics. The settlement will thus be assigned the same status over the whole of its existence, whereas in reality it did not necessarily hold the same status from its creation to its abandonment. The typological classification carried out on settlements discovered in archaeological field survey here finds its limit (Gandini 2008). Subsequently, during spatiotemporal analysis, if the study is done on a fine timescale—per century, for example—this phenomenon can cause errors in the modelling of settlement networks. For example, a site with a hierarchically high status will appear in the first century CE as an important pole compared to its neighbours, when in reality it may not have had this importance in the structure of the settlement network at that time. However, researchers have tried to address these problems:

- By formulating the hypothesis that the data collected on an settlement constitute a description of the 'optimal' state of the site (Durand-Dastès et al. 1998).
- By working quantitatively on the evolution of the number of settlements and their area over time (Durand-Dastès et al. 1998).
- By treating temporal data as descriptors in the formation of typologies (date of creation, duration of occupation, previous occupation, etc.) as much as the variables materials, surface area, artefacts, etc. This is to create interrelationships between the different characteristics of settlements and in particular to improve the characterization of occupation phases (Durand-Dastès et al. 1998; Favory et al. 2012).
- By analysing sets of settlements existing in the same periods in order to characterize each epoch (Durand-Dastès et al. 1998).
- By making comparisons and associations between the typological classes of settlements discovered in archaeological field surveys and the excavated settlements (Van der Leeuw et al. 2003).
- By modifying the character of the 'duration of occupation' descriptor when classifying settlements by period. Thus, it is not the duration of the whole occupation which is taken into account in the calculation, but the duration of existence of a settlement at the end of each century. However, this approach was not conclusive and did not allow the researchers to obtain the desired results (ARCHAEDYN 2013).

Although these studies managed to adapt, with varying degrees of success, to the limitations of survey data, important elements were still missing for a good understanding of the dynamics and spatiotemporal organization of settlement systems. To reduce these problems and to refine analyses carried out on ancient settlement patterns, it is here proposed to make a wider use of the results of excavations.

5.3 Survey Data Versus Excavation: How to Improve the Understanding of the Ancient Settlement System of the Plateau Lorrain

In some studies dealing with the evolution of ancient societies based on field survey data, the settlement system dynamics can only be studied quantitatively. The nature of the archaeological data limits the visualization of temporal dynamics to displaying the evolution of the number of settlements and a series of quantitative observations (rate of increase, rate of decline, number of creations, abandonments, etc.).

From excavation data, a different approach can be proposed to analyse the characteristics of the settlements and, by extension, to study their temporal evolution. This is possible by studying the dynamics, not in a quantitative way, but in a qualitative way by looking at the internal settlement trajectory. This approach is used to achieve two objectives.

First, the aim is to study the internal dynamics of the settlements in order to weigh the quantitative evolution curves of the settlement system and to perceive the evolution of the hierarchical relations (in a large and functional sense) that the settlements maintain with each other over time (Nuninger and Favory 2011). The second objective is to create a model for the evolution of settlements. This model, established over several stages, allows us to provide solutions to problems induced by survey data and thus to improve our analysis of temporal and spatial dynamics.

5.3.1 The Roman Settlement System in Two Micro-Regions of the Plateau Lorrain

The proposed approaches were used in the study of the Roman settlement system of two micro-regions located on the Plateau Lorrain (Grand-Est region, France): Alsace Bossue (zone 1), and the sector located between the Seille river and the Nied river (zone 2). These two micro-regions are situated in a hilly landscape formed by a limestone substratum. These areas are very well known by archaeological field surveys. Indeed, the ancient occupation of these areas is widely recognized thanks to the many campaigns carried out since the 1980s (to mention only the main ones, see Laffite 1998; Thomann and Nüsslein 2000, 2001). As a result, several syntheses deal with the evolution of the settlement pattern in the Roman period in these micro-regions (Laffite 2004; Nüsslein 2016a; Nüsslein 2018). Nevertheless, the sites have not been the object of advanced artefact studies that would have made it possible to follow their chronological evolution in the details.

A typology of settlements at the time of their apogee was made according to various criteria and from statistical methods (for more details see Nüsslein 2016a; Nüsslein et al. in press). This classification is composed of six types of settlements. The agglomerations (small towns) are at the top of the hierarchy. They are very big settlements that host artisanal activities and have a long life span (class A). The very large *villae* correspond to the second level of the typology (class B). They are built in stone with mortar and display a very high level of wealth and comfort. The medium-sized *villae* (class C) are just below. They are smaller than the large *villae* but are richly ornamented. Small *villae* are even smaller and sometimes consist of buildings built of perishable materials (class D). Finally, farms and small farms are small settlements, formed by one to three buildings, which are not very rich and have a relatively short lifetime (classes E and F).

From this classification, based essentially on survey data, the dynamics of the settlement system in these sectors, which were almost similar, had been studied. During the first century CE, the first Roman settlements are gradually implanted on occupations from the La Tène period: they constituted the basis of the ancient settlement system. In addition to this phenomenon, new settlements were created. During the second century, the settlement network was completed by the small and medium-sized settlements which increase the number of sites. The settlement pattern extends. During the High Empire, poles of attraction structured the network of settlements by organizing and attracting sites on their periphery. Around these centres (road nodes and agglomerations), small local networks expanded. Large and medium-sized *villae* were at the head of these networks, around which the other smaller settlements were set up. Throughout the High Empire, the space was strongly polarized and hierarchized and the settlement system extended over all available space at the time of its peak. During Late Antiquity, the organization of the settlement network gradually changed: the number of sites decreases, the system refocused on the large settlements of the High Empire and lower status sites disappeared. At the end of the fourth century and at the beginning of the fifth century, the last traces of known Roman settlements disappeared.

5.3.2 *Methodology*

5.3.2.1 Choice of Data: Conditions and Modalities

The first step is to select and compile the excavation data that we possess.[2] This information can be unequal and it is necessary to only select reliable data: archaeological materials studied after excavation (to understand the evolution and phasing of the site), well-preserved settlements (to avoid any taphonomic bias) and size of site properly explored (in order to have the most complete information possible).

[2] For references to the excavation reports used, see Nüsslein (2016a).

Although data for the sector between Seille and Nied (zone 2) was sufficient, few excavated settlements were known for the sector Alsace Bossue (zone 1).

In order to overcome this problem, we selected sites outside the micro-region. For example, settlements within a radius of less than 20 km around the study area were chosen. The choice to use external data can of course be debatable. However, the selected settlements were located near the study area, in a similar geographical (same landscape unit) and historical (the territory of the Mediomatrices tribe) context. The settlements selected, 22 in total, represent, at their peak, relatively equally, all the classes of settlements of our typology (Fig. 5.2).

5.3.2.2 From the Settlement Trajectory

Once the excavated sites are chosen, their trajectory is visualized and analysed. This provides information on the complexity of the evolution of settlement while placing these dynamics in a larger context. By extension, the goal is to lay the foundation

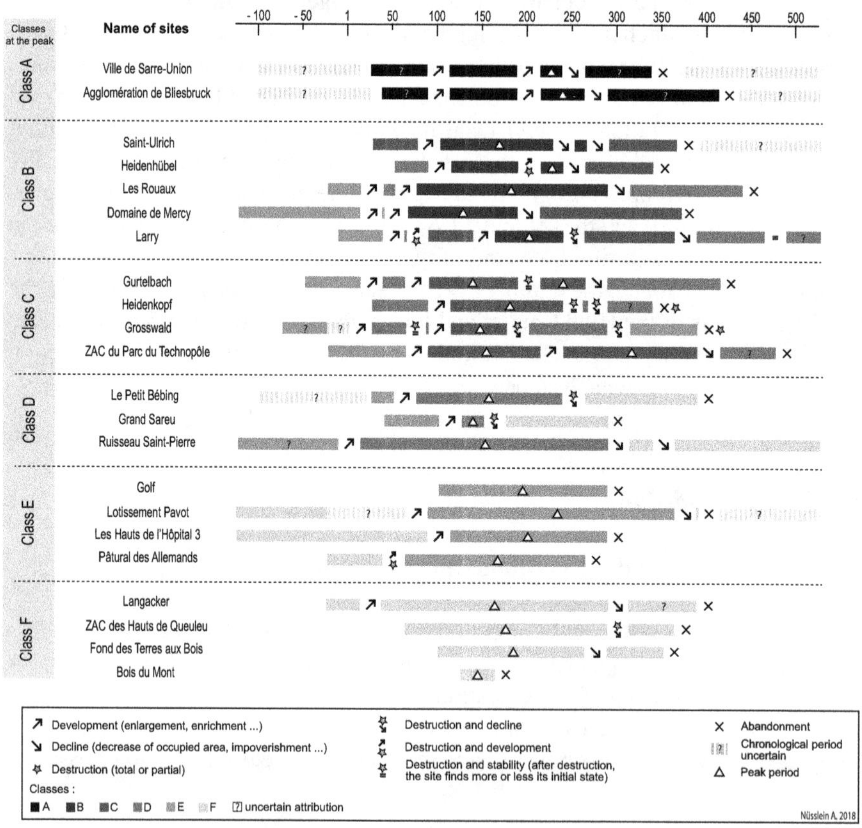

Fig. 5.2 Matrix of the typological trajectories of settlements

for a development analysis to perceive and understand how and why settlements evolve in one way or another. We want to understand how a site moves from one status to another and when. In this context, we relied on their morphological evolution and on their hierarchical trajectory, in other words on their evolution within the different classes of our typology over time. To carry out this study, it is first necessary to compare the criteria of each class of our typology with those of the phases of the excavated settlements. Thus, one of the categories of the typology is assigned to each period of the selected sites according to their characteristics. For example, if during its second phase of evolution, that began around the year 75 and ended around the year 125, a settlement displayed the characteristics of the class D profile, this status was attributed during this period. Note, however, that for its peak phase, a settlement has the status assigned to it during the creation of the typology since the characteristics of the site during this period were used for its ranking.

The results make it possible to create a matrix in which the typological trajectory of each settlement was placed on the same timescale (Fig. 5.2). The 'story' of each settlement is represented by a line whose length represents its lifetime, punctuated by events (development, decline, destruction, etc.) that marked the beginning and the end of the different internal states for which a typological class was assigned. Settlements were ordered according to their class at the time of their peak (the class assigned when creating the typology). We can observe that the development is reflected by an extension of the occupied area or by an enrichment illustrated by new elements of comfort and decor (hypocaust, bath, painted plaster, etc.). On the other hand, a decline is characterized by a smaller occupied area and/or an impoverishment. Finally, the peak phase corresponds to the moment where the site displays its largest size and highest degree of wealth, and its highest hierarchical status.

5.3.2.3 … to the Creation of a Model of Evolution

As we have seen, the traditional typological approach reduces the reality of settlements discovered in archaeological field surveys to a single function throughout their existence. The matrix shows that in each of their phases, sites have a different status. Moreover, within each class, virtually all settlements follow the same typological trajectory. It is then possible to create a hierarchical evolution model for each class of our typology. Thus, in order to break this fixed vision of the prospected sites and to improve our vision of the temporal and spatial evolution of the settlement system, an evolution model that allows to follow the typological evolution of each type of site was created and applied to the sites discovered in pedestrian surveys.

To establish the model, we chose a 100-year time step, despite the good chronological resolution of the excavation data (Fig. 5.3). This is for reasons of convenience related to its development and its application to field surveyed settlements that are often poorly dated. Thus, from the information contained in the evolution matrix (Fig. 5.2), we assigned for each century a class to each of the groups. The

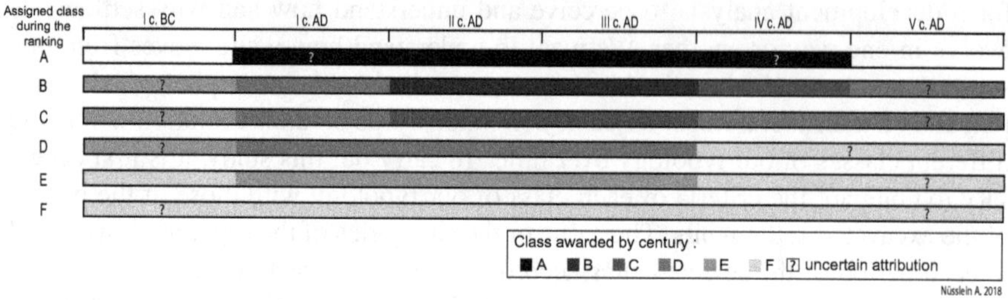

Fig. 5.3 Model of evolution of settlements

attribution was made according to the similarity of the status of the settlements within the century in question. Some attributions are uncertain, particularly at the end of the period studied, because of the presence of too few sites.

Despite this pitfall, it was possible to progressively build a model that corresponds to a functional evolution reference system for almost all types of settlements (Fig. 5.3). Thus, for each of the classes treated, the typological trajectory could be followed of the settlements classified in this group during the creation of the typology. For example, we can see that the settlements classified during the realization of the typology in class C corresponded to class E during the first century BCE, to settlements from Class D during the first century CE, to settlements of Class C throughout the second and third centuries and finally to class D settlements throughout the fourth and fifth centuries.

5.4 Results

5.4.1 Composition and Evolution of the Settlement System

Using the matrix, many observations on the temporal evolution rate and the typological settlement trajectory can be established (Fig. 5.2). Let's quickly review the main ones. First, it was clear that all settlements followed, sometimes long, processes leading them, in a first instance, to their peak and, in a second instance, to their disappearance: indeed, except for class F settlements, no site had its highest status at the time of its creation and no sudden disappearance was observed directly after a peak phase. Settlements follow the same evolution curve, which is divided into three major periods, but the rate of change may be different depending on the site. The development phase at the beginning of the first millennium was sudden and took place in less than a century, while the period of decline and abandonment during Late Antiquity took over two centuries. Between these two periods, from 100 to 250 CE, the peak phase was shared by all settlements. Within these periods of evolution, a settlement could grow faster or more slowly than the whole system. Sites, similar in status at the beginning of the Roman period, thus took different development trajectories. For example, very large *villae* had the same status as medium-sized *villae* at the beginning of the Roman period. Similarly, during Late Antiquity, some settlements were declining faster than others.

Meanwhile, other results were produced by comparing this matrix with the quantitative evolution of the settlement pattern from field survey data (sites dated to the

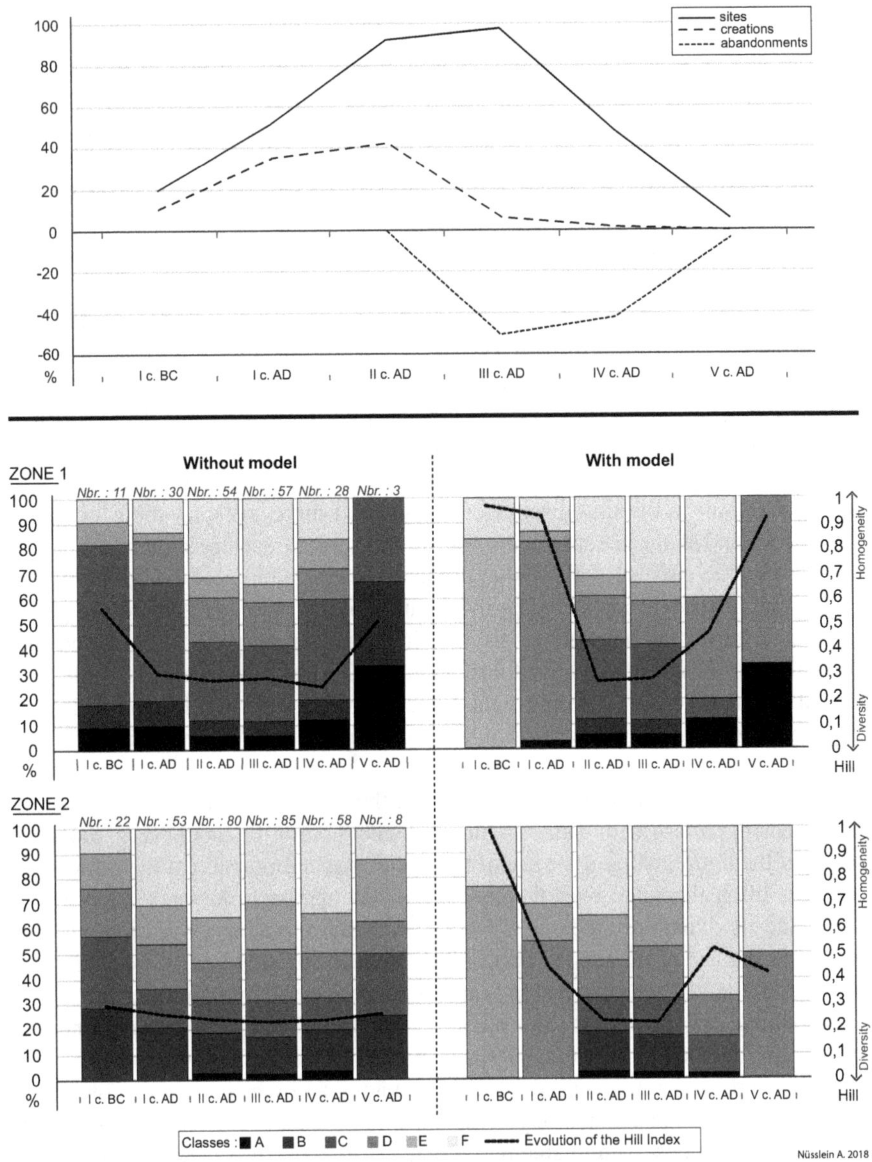

Fig. 5.4 Above: Relative evolution in the number of settlements, creation and discontinuations in the two micro-regions. Below: Relative evolution of the size of classes and evolution of Hill's index

century) (Fig. 5.4). Thus, quantitative data was confronted with qualitative data. Two observations are in order. First, when looking at the chronology of the excavated settlements, there are slight offsets within the curves. They are obviously due to the difference in chronological resolution between these two types of information, but not only. For example, the excavated settlements almost all still exist in the fourth century, whereas the curve of the number of sites discovered during surveys drops at that time. This is probably due to the characteristics of the settlements dating from this century because few visible traces were discovered in the surveys (because of wooden constructions, fewer ceramics, etc.). It is, then, necessary to qualify this collapse of the number of settlements during the fourth century. Secondly, we can see that the quantitative dynamics of the number of settlements is similar to the qualitative evolution of the settlements in term of development, stability and decline by comparing what is happening within the sites themselves and with the profile of the curves made from the results of surveys. When the settlement network becomes denser in the first and second centuries, the excavated sites are developing: they are getting bigger and better equipped, for some even with elements of comfort (hypocaust, bath, etc.). At the peak and at the end of the wave of creation, the excavated settlements stabilize. During the third century, when the curves are reversed, the settlements progressively collapse: their area decreases and they become, over time, mostly small sites.

Following this first analysis step, the model is then applied to the field surveyed settlements. Thus, if the sites discovered during field surveys display their 'optimal' state (peak) and if these settlements follow the same trajectory as the excavated sites, we can reconstruct, with all due prudence, their typological evolution. A settlement classified in group B during the creation of the typology is therefore given the status E during the first century BCE, D in the first century CE, B in second and third century CE and finally C in fourth century CE. Once the model is applied to all settlements discovered during field surveys, the static vision is modified: it is now changing. This allows us to visualize settlement pattern dynamics in a different way.

In order to demonstrate this, we compared the evolution of the composition of the settlement pattern with and without the application of the model (Fig. 5.4). On the left of the figure, without the use of the model, the composition of the settlement pattern is often the same over the centuries. This approach does not allow us to understand its dynamics since we do not understand the actual evolution. On the right, with the use of the model, appears a complete different image. In particular, we can note that the settlement shows another aspect in the two centuries that mark the beginning and the end of the studied period. In order to better understand the changes, we decided to measure and quantify the diversity of the settlements.

To this end, we applied an index used in ecology and which, to our knowledge, has never been used in archaeology: Hill's index. It is usually applied to measure the variety of species observed in an environment (Hill 1973). It is calculated from the Shannon index and the Simpson index, which make it possible to analyse the specific diversity of an environment by integrating the changes in the numbers of the rarest species, for the first one, and the most abundant for the latter. By combining these two indices, the Hill index, applied to our field of study, thus provides a synthetic value revealing the diversity of a stand by taking into account both the number of categories of settlements and the distribution of individuals within the classes. The Hill index is expressed as: $(1/\lambda)/eH'$, where $1/\lambda$ corresponds to the inverse of the Simpson index and eH' to the exponential of the Shannon index. The closer the result of the calculation is to 0, the higher the diversity, and the closer it gets to 1, the more homogeneous is the settlement system. With the application of the model and the use of Hill's index, we can see that in the first century BCE, the settlement in the two micro-regions was little developed and only small farms existed. In the first century CE, with the development of farms, the first small villae appear and settlement begins to diversify as shown by the evolution of Hill's index. In the second and third centuries, the settlement system is more diversified. We can even see a society with a pyramidal structure. In the fourth century, because of the abandonment of many settlements and the loss of the status of certain sites (e.g. large *villae* become small settlements), the settlement system becomes more homogeneous again.

From this analysis, we can thus see that the transition between the La Tène period and the Roman period generated a strong diversification of the settlement system in which certain sites become very important. At the end of the Roman period, with the decline of sites, the settlement system became more homogeneous. As can be seen, the application of the model, in addition to Hill's index, therefore makes it possible to better visualize phenomena of diversification or homogenization of the regional settlement structure.

5.4.2 Structuring and Spatial Evolution of the Settlement Pattern

In parallel, the model also allows to understand the spatial dynamics in another way. For the evolution of the settlement systems of zones 1 and 2, it is clear that in the first century CE, the settlement is morphologically different with the application of the model: the areas seem less layered, and the poles of the networks (the principal sites) do not yet seem to have this status. The area is thus relatively homogeneous. In the second and third centuries, the settlement pattern is more layered with the presence of several small local networks represented by *villae* and small farms. In the fourth century, new scenarios can be drawn. With the application of the model, the main settlements of the previous phase no longer have the same hierarchical importance and the shape of the networks changes radically. The areas now seem less structured.

Thanks to the model, we can see that the main sites do not have the same role throughout the Roman period and their effect on the area may thus vary significantly. For example, a class C *villa* is at the head of a small network only in the second and third centuries. In reality, we see that the spatial configuration, just like the internal trajectory of the sites, follows a bell-shaped evolution. It becomes layered and progressively more complex at the beginning of the Roman period and then becomes more homogeneous and less structured again during Late Antiquity.

Thus, with the application of this model, spatial analysis and the perception of settlement networks are no longer based on fixed data—settlements without phasing—but on dynamic information, settlements with (hypothetical) phases. They can thus provide results that are a little closer to the evolutionary reality of the settlement pattern. In this way, this approach makes it possible to reduce to a certain extent the uncertainties related to prospecting data and, above all, to propose improvements in the modelling of spatial dynamics.

5.5 Conclusion

Using field survey data for the study of regional settlement dynamics can have limitations because of the difficulty of precisely dating the evolutionary phases of sites. However, when excavation data are available in a study region, solutions can be considered to break down the static information provided by surface surveys into more dynamic chronological attributions of site development.

The study of the hierarchical trajectory of the sites and the comparison between the quantitative curves and the qualitative information resulting from excavations allow us to improve the understanding of the evolution of the settlement. In addition, the construction of an evolution model makes it possible to attribute hypothetical trajectories to the settlements discovered in surveys: this helps us to refine our perception of the temporal and spatial dynamics of the settlement system. In addition, Hill's index is a useful tool that allows us to follow the processes of homogenization or heterogeneity of the settlement pattern and thus to show the changes from a different angle.

From a methodological point of view, it is also important to note that the different analyses presented here show that, starting from a typology established on the basis of archaeological field surveys data, it is possible, with the addition of excavation data, to create models of evolution and to generalize information. In the end, the field survey data constitute a solid documentation base for the creation and the use of complex tools. However, the established model has a low value in terms of its representativeness: the number of settlements that were used to develop it is not very large. It is therefore advisable to remain cautious in its use and not to take this model as a finished piece of work but as an exploratory tool—destined to be refined—representing the main features of the typological evolution of the settlements.

It is hoped that this paper has shown the importance of using excavated data, when available, in studies based mainly on information collected in field surveys. Excavation data can provide many elements for a better understanding of settlement systems. They should not only serve to illustrate the results of the analyses, but especially be used in connection with field survey data.

References

Alcock SE, Cherry JF (eds) (2004) Side-by-side survey: comparative regional studies in the Mediterranean world. Oxbow Books, Oxford

ARCHAEDYN (2013) ARCHAEDYN. Dynamique spatiale des territoires de la Préhistoire au Moyen Âge, Compte rendu final. MSHE, Besançon. Available at https://mshe.univ-fcomte.fr/documents/poles/pole1/P1_A1_ArchaeDyn_Compte-rendu-final_130228.pdf. Accessed on 10 May 2018

Baudoux J (2012) Analyse des grandes étapes chronologiques du peuplement et des échanges économiques sur les sites du piémont des Vosges et de la vallée de la Bruche à l'époque gallo-romaine. In: Oswald G, Triantafillidis G (eds) Rapport intermédiaire 2012, Projet Collectif de Recherche "Occupation du sol dans la vallée de la Bruche de la Préhistoire au Haut Moyen Âge". Service Régional de l'Archéologie Alsace, Strasbourg, pp 10–70

Berry BJL (1964) Approaches to regional analysis : a synthesis. Annals of the Association of American Geographers 54-1:2–11

Dabas J, Delétang H, Ferdière A, Jung C, Zimmermann HW (2006.) La prospection. Errance, Paris

Durand-Dastès F, Favory F, Fiches J-L, Mathian H, Pumain D, Raynaud C, Sanders L, Van der Leeuw S (1998) Des oppida aux métropoles. Economica Anthropos, Paris

Favory F, Fiches J-L, Girardot J-J (1987-1988) L'analyse des données appliquée à la typologie des sites gallo-romains dans le Beaucairois (Gard): matériel de prospection et environnement paysager, essai méthodologique. Gallia 45:67–85. Available at https://www.persee.fr/doc/galia_0016-4119_1987_num_45_1_2880. Accessed on 10 May 2018

Favory F, Nuninger L, Sanders L (2012) Intégration de concepts de géographie et d'archéologie spatiale pour l'étude des systèmes de peuplement. L'espace géographique 41:295–309. https://doi.org/10.3917/eg.414.0295

Gandini C (2008) Des campagnes gauloises aux campagnes de l'antiquité tardive. La dynamique de l'habitat rural dans la cité des Bituriges Cubi. Supplément à la Revue Archéologique du Centre de la France, Tours

Grenon P, Smith B (2004) SNAP and SPAN: towards dynamic spatial ontology. Spatial Cognition and Computation: An Interdisciplinary Journal 4(12):69–104. https://doi.org/10.1207/s15427633scc0401_5

Hill MO (1973) Diversity and evenness: a unifying notation and its consequences. Ecology 54:427–432. https://doi.org/10.2307/1934352

Laffite J-D (1998) L'occupation du sol en milieu rural à l'époque gallo-romaine entre la Seille et la Nied française, DFS de prospection. Service Régional de l'Archéologie Lorraine, Metz

Laffite J-D (2004) Occupation du sol et structures agraires à l'époque antique sur le Plateau Lorrain entre la Seille et la Nied française. In: Flotté P, Fuchs M (eds) La Moselle, Carte archéologique de la Gaule. Académie des Inscriptions et Belles-Lettres, Paris, pp 147–155

Moreau A, Morice S, Salvador-Blanes S, Bourenname H (2011) Distribution spatiale des objets archéologiques et mouvements de matière à l'échelle des versants cultivés: le cas de Mougon (Indre-et-Loire, France). ArchéoSciences 35:103–116. https://doi.org/10.4000/archeosciences.2987

Nuninger L, Favory F (2011) Romanisation et mutations des établissements ruraux dans l'Est des Gaules. Questions et mise en perspective. In: Reddé M, Barral P, Favory F, Guillaumet J-C, Joly M, Marc J-Y, Nouvel P, Nuninger L, Petit C (eds) Aspect de la Romanisation dans l'est de la Gaule, Bibracte, Glux-en-Glenne, pp 487–495

Nüsslein A (2016a) Les campagnes entre Moselle et Rhin dans l'Antiquité. Analyse comparative des dynamiques spatiales et temporelles du peuplement de quatre micro-régions du Ier s. av. J.-C. au Ve s. ap. J.-C. University of Strasbourg, Strasbourg

Nüsslein A (2016b) Nuancer et améliorer l'analyse des systèmes de peuplement basée sur les données de prospection pédestres: l'étude de la dynamique d'occupation antique du Plateau Lorrain. Archeologia e Calcolatori 27:47–64. https://doi.org/10.19282/AC.27.2016.03

Nüsslein A (2018) Les campagnes entre Moselle et Rhin dans l'Antiquité. Dynamiques du peuplement du Ier s. av. J.-C. au Ve s. ap. J.-C., AVAGE, Strasbourg, 2018 (Monographie d'Archéologie du Grand-Est, 2)

Nüsslein A, Nuninger L, Verhagen P (in press) To boldly go where no one has gone before: integrating social factors in site location analysis and predictive modelling, the hierarchical types map. In: Proceedings of CAA2018, Atlanta

Thomann E, Nüsslein P (2000) Occupation de la frange orientale du territoire Médiomatrique de la conquête au IVe siècle, rapport de prospection thématique 2000: les cantons de Sarre-Union et Drulingen. Société de Recherche Archéologique en Alsace Bossue, Service Régional de l'Archéologie Alsace, Strasbourg

Thomann E, Nüsslein P (2001) Occupation de la frange orientale du territoire Médiomatrique de la conquête au IVe siècle, rapport de prospection thématique 2001: le canton de Rohrbach-lès-Bitche. Société de Recherche Archéologique en Alsace Bossue, Service Régional de l'Archéologie Lorraine, Metz

Tol G (2012) A methodological and artefactual approach to the study of ancient settlement in the territories of Satricum and Antium. Barkhuis, Eelde

Trément F (1999) Archéologie d'un paysage: Les étangs de Saint-Blaise. Maison des Sciences de l'Homme, Paris

Trément F (2000) Prospection et chronologie: de la quantification du temps au modèle de peuplement. Méthodes appliquées au secteur des étangs de Saint-Blaise (Bouches-du-Rhônes, France). In: Francovich R, Patterson H (eds) Extracting meaning from Ploughsoil assemblages. Oxbow Books, Oxford, pp 77–91

Van der Leeuw S, Favory F, Fiches J-L (2003) Archéologie et systèmes socio-environnementaux. Etudes multiscalaires sur la vallée du Rhône dans le programme Archaeomedes. CNRS Éditions, Paris

Part II
Economy

Chapter 6
The Economic Archaeology of Roman Economic Performance

Willem M. Jongman

Abstract Recent years have witnessed a paradigm shift in the study of the Roman economy. Methodologically modern economic analysis is now far more acceptable than it once was, and archaeology has become the major source of empirical data for many questions. On the substantive side there is now a far clearer appreciation of the major changes that the Roman economy underwent, with substantial growth of population and aggregate production and even some improvements in standard of living, but followed by equally dramatic decline. This economic success was not limited to the imperial core, but also extended to the provinces.

Keywords Economic analysis · Roman Empire · Demography · Living standards

6.1 Introduction

'What did the Romans ever do for us'? Few have nailed the fundamental question of Roman provincial history and archaeology with greater precision than the Monty Python team in their 'Life of Brian'. To put it more academically, the question of Roman economic performance should indeed be the core of research on the Roman economy: how well did the Roman economy succeed in providing scarce goods and services to its population, and how does that performance compare with earlier and later periods of preindustrial economic history, or in other regions of the world, such as beyond the frontiers of the Empire, or with a faraway Empire such as China?

For decades, however, this fundamental question has been ignored by ancient historians and to a lesser extent by archaeologists. Until the mid-1960s the dominant paradigms in ancient history had been that of the philological tradition that isolated the study of Greco-Roman society from the dominant narratives and methodological advances in other periods. Ancient history was a backwater taken less and less seriously by more modern historians, or by society at large, and quite rightly so.

W. M. Jongman (✉)
Department of History, Rijksuniversiteit Groningen, Groningen, The Netherlands
e-mail: w.m.jongman@rug.nl

P. Verhagen et al. (eds.), *Finding the Limits of the Limes*, Computational Social Sciences, https://doi.org/10.1007/978-3-030-04576-0_6

This started to change in the 1960s, and that change owed much to the towering eminence of the late Sir Moses Finley. Educated in America, and principally as a social scientist, he began to ask fundamental questions about the nature of ancient society, about antiquity's place in world history, and about our methodologies (Finley 1985). Introduced to his work by my teachers, for me as a young student it was a breath of fresh air and at the first opportunity I moved to Cambridge to work with him.

Yet, for all its uniquely innovative qualities his work was also a very particular take on comparative social history, steeped as he was in a very personal mix of neo-Marxist thought, substantivist economic anthropology, and later also Weberian sociology. As a result, Classical Antiquity was reduced to a relatively primitive forerunner of the Medieval and Early Modern economy, without integrated markets, with only small-scale trade and manufacturing, and with a low standard of living for the mass of the population (Jongman 1988). His explanation was a cultural one: the Greco-Roman elite disdained involvement in trade and manufacturing, and hence these potentially innovative sectors of the economy remained small and underdeveloped. The wealth that no one could deny that there was, given the splendour of elite residences in, for example, Pompeii, or the impressive public buildings of many Roman towns, was ultimately the product of rent extraction by the elite and of provincial exploitation. So altogether the picture of the Roman economy was a quite pessimistic one, unless you were rich. Standard of living of the mass of the population was and remained barely above minimum subsistence, there was little or no economic growth, and for many provinces inclusion into the Empire meant plunder and hardship. In contrast, and in a kind of post-colonial discourse, pre-Roman society was often viewed as successful. The resulting picture was necessarily a static one, and also implies that Late Antique decline was vastly exaggerated by earlier scholars. With Peter Brown, the world of Late Antiquity was one of transformation rather than decline (Brown 1971).

Methodologically, in Finley's view, and in line with his earlier mentor Karl Polanyi, the alleged absence of economic growth and innovation and of a market economy implied that modern economic analysis was useless as a tool: Antiquity was different. The gap between this and what other innovative social science historians were doing at the time was enormous, and as a result ancient history remained intellectually separate from mainstream historiography—it still remained what Finley himself once critically called 'a funny kind of history'.

Recent years have seen a major paradigm shift, however. That shift has happened along two lines. The first was theoretical and methodological. The aversion to modern economic theory had created an unholy alliance between modern substantivist social science historians, traditional philologists who abhorred having to learn the mathematics of economics, and fashionable neo-Marxist demands for an alternative economic theory. I guess my book on the economy and society of Pompeii was the first explicit critique of all this, and the first example by a professional ancient historian of how one might apply the logic of the dismal science of economics (Jongman 1988). I tried to show that using modern economics does not immediately make Antiquity into the mirror of the modern world. In fact, I used it to unravel the logic of Roman economic stagnation and underdeveloped such as I perceived it at the time. The book was widely reviewed, but the shift in the theoretical paradigm was hardly noticed, even if not criticized either. However, all this did change in more recent years. The turning point was the work for the Cambridge economic history of the Greco-Roman world, and its publication in 2007 (Scheidel et al. 2007). It reflected the two lines of the paradigm shift: the use of economics, even if of the neo-institutionalist kind, and the second more substantive of the introduction of archaeological data into the debate on a scale not seen before (best examples in Greene 1986 and Brun 2012). And indeed, the inclusion of the vastly increased corpus of archaeological data has critically changed the content of recent debate, from one that was mostly concerned with the paucity of data, to one that needs to harness an unheard-of quantity of data in a systematic way.[1] Not surprisingly, therefore, aggregate statistical analysis has become a highly productive tool, changing both ancient historians' apprehension about statistics, and challenging archaeologists' post-processual dislike for generalization, and their insistence on the unique and individual. In short, I think we, ancient historians and archaeologists, have finally become grown-up numbers of the historical discipline.

6.2 How Can We Understand the Roman Economy?

6.2.1 Estimating Population Numbers and Demographic Trends

So how can we understand the Roman economy? What are the most important variables that an economist wants to know about an economy, how can we know about them, and what have we learned about them and what not (yet)? The most important variable in human history is that of population numbers. How many people were there, and how does that relate to resources and to aggregate output in particular? Remember: per capita income, the most common measure of personal prosperity, equals total production/consumption divided by the number of people. The long-term trend in human population history has been decidedly upwards, and increasingly so. Data are highly speculative, but what all estimates have in common is that for a long time the planet was pretty empty. The most commonly quoted estimates are from McEvedy and Jones (1978), who estimated that at the beginning of the Neolithic world population was only four million. This slowly began to increase in the Bronze Age, and from then on at an increasingly rapid rate as well, particularly since the Industrial Revolution. Their estimate for world population at the beginning of the first millennium is 170 million, and this is a very low estimate. It implies that roughly a third of world population lived in the Roman Empire, another third, or a bit less, in Han China, and yet another third in the rest of the world. For the Roman

[1] The Oxford Roman Economy Project is the best example of this trend.

Empire, this is based on the relatively low estimates by Beloch, about a century ago (see Scheidel 2007 for an overview). These, however, are increasingly criticized, with alternative estimates up to about 90–100 million for the Roman Empire. In the end, these estimates are little more than wild guesses, without much in the way of hard empirical data. Also, they tend to be quite static, pretending to be valid for long periods of time.

Recent archaeological research has begun to address both problems, using field survey data. The method is to assign hypothetical population numbers to particular site types, and multiply these by the number of sites of that type. For long-term population history Andreas Zimmermann and his team have produced an impressively robust population reconstruction from the early Neolithic to the Early Modern period for the Rhineland, using unique data from the lignite mining region (Zimmermann et al. 2009). Apart from the rapid rise in the modern period, what really stands out is the dramatic peak in the Roman period, with populations some eight times higher than in the pre-Roman Iron Age, and some 13 times higher than in the subsequent Merovingian period. What these Rhineland data lack is sufficient chronological resolution (but more precision is easily possible). What they have in their favour is the exceptionally long timeframe. And it is precisely this long timeframe that shows that the Roman period is indeed extraordinary, even in relatively remote provincial areas: for northern Gaul (north eastern France, Luxembourg and Western Germany) Xavier Deru (2017) has recently demonstrated a similar trend of rapidly rising site numbers followed by a steep Late Antique decline for a multitude of regions, this time with much greater chronological resolution and smartly using index numbers rather than absolute numbers for the site numbers to make them comparable. The weakness is of course that these are site numbers and not people.

To move from site numbers to numbers of people, Lisa Fentress (2009) has pioneered assigning putative numbers of inhabitants to the different site categories, and then multiply these for the number of sites in that category. Since then, archaeologists from the University of Groningen team have applied the same methodology for the Nettuno data of their survey in the Pontine region (De Haas et al. 2011; Fig. 6.1).

The absolute numbers are of course guesses that depend on many unknowns, but it is important to note that the trends in relative change over time are far more secure. And the trend that we see is pretty clear: a dramatic rise in population, particularly from the late fourth and early third century BCE onwards. This growth probably reached its peak in the late second century CE, to then move in pretty dramatic reverse: decline and fall were steep. The second thing that can be seen in this graph is that population trends in these two regions roughly moved in sync, and resemble the trends in site numbers for northern Gaul. A few years ago, Alessandro Launaro already observed the same for many of the Italian surveys, even if not using these more sophisticated methods (Launaro 2011). I am quite sure that many, though probably not all parts of the Empire, will show similar trends of considerable population growth, followed by equally dramatic decline, even if that decline may well be later in, for example, the Roman East.

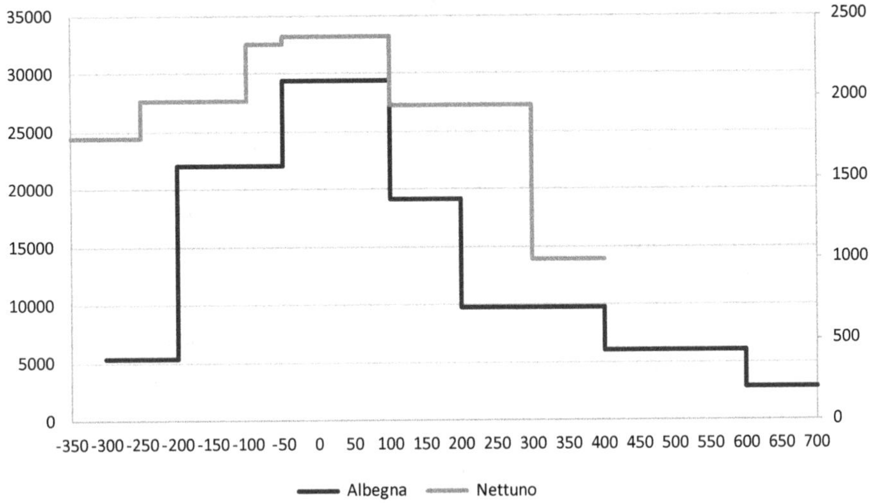

Fig. 6.1 Population estimates for Albenga and Nettuno. (Sources: Fentress 2009 and De Haas et al. 2011)

Conceptually this is a wake-up call to abandon the tradition to avoid generalization, only looking for local differences in what I like to call the 'my-valley-is-different-syndrome'. Of course, regional differences matter, but primarily in relation to a general trend. If we do not identify that larger trend, we cannot even identify what is locally specific.

Therefore, three survey teams working around Rome, the British School at Rome's Tiber Valley Project, the Suburbium Project at La Sapienza, and the Groningen Pontine Region Project, have joined forces and have recently succeeded to integrate their datasets, mostly down to the level of individual sherds. Doing so was a big job, and many said it was impossible, but we are pleased that we have succeeded, and have solved many thorny issues of pottery and site classification, and chronology. The ambition of the consortium is to use our concepts and methods to extend this integrated dataset first to some other parts of Italy where conditions are likely to be quite similar to what we experienced thus far, and then to other parts of the Empire, where as yet unpredictable conditions will probably pose new challenges for which our methods may or may not provide solutions. The analytical ambition is of course to have good empirical data to reconstruct the big story of Roman population trends, rural social relations and material culture, if possible for the empire as a whole, but also regionally, to differentiate the local from the global.

This population boom and the subsequent decline that we see in so many surveys are perhaps the most important things one can say about the Roman economy, but their identification is really quite a recent thing. I think it represents the complete refutation of the old static paradigm of a preindustrial Roman economy without any change. And it is reflected in many other data, of course, such as pollen diagrams that show a receding forest and its return in Late Antiquity.

6.2.2 The Economic Effects of Population Increase

The next question is, of course, what such a population boom meant for the economy. As I said earlier, per capita income is the result of dividing aggregate production and consumption by the number of people. If aggregate production and consumption went up to the same degree as population, per capita income would obviously remain the same. But that is not necessarily the case. In the modern world, population growth is usually outstripped by the growth of production, and as a result in Western society per capita incomes have typically grown by about 2% per annum, roughly doubling standard of living every generation.

For many preindustrial economies, however, the story was often a more depressing one: population pressure resulted in a declining standard of living for the mass of the population.

The graph in Fig. 6.2 by Bob Allen gives what he calls the welfare ratio, i.e. the extent to which incomes of ordinary families exceeded bare subsistence (Allen et al. 2005; Allen 2009). There are a few important things to note. The first is that after the Black Death of the fourteenth century people were quite prosperous, but this declined under the population growth of subsequent centuries. The second observation is that the Netherlands and later also England were an exception to this grim scenario, and were already far more prosperous than other countries. And a final observation is that at least in Late Antiquity, by the time of Diocletian's price edict, life does not seem to have been very cheerful (Allen 2009).

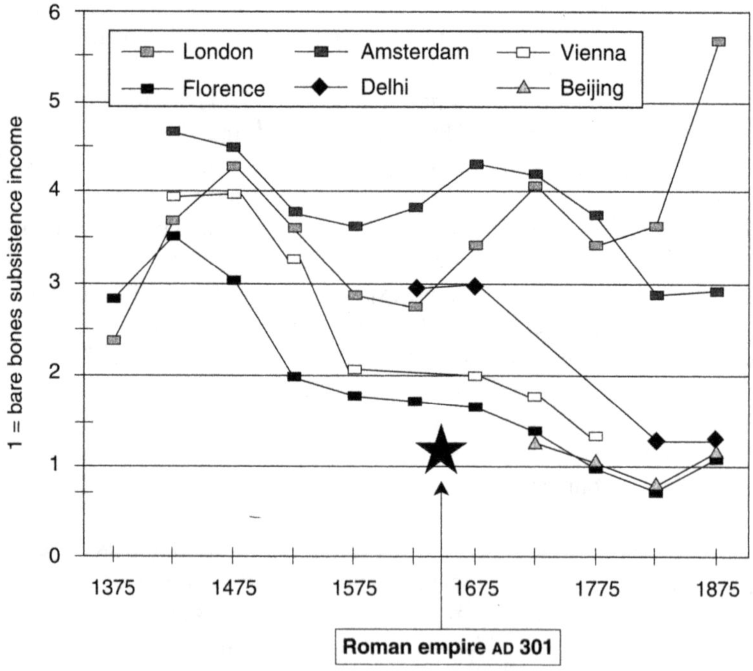

Fig. 6.2 Preindustrial welfare ratios. (Reprinted with permission from Allen (2009, 342))

Theoretically, it is not surprising that population growth depressed the standard of living. A preindustrial economy is essentially a system with two factors of production: land and labour. Of the two, land is in more or less inelastic supply, so population growth changes the land/labour ratio. Technically, this means a move along the production function. If nothing else happens, the economy will suffer from decreasing marginal labour productivity. In normal words: if you double the labour force on a given plot of land you will increase output, but you will not double it. Such lower marginal labour productivity inevitably implies lower labour incomes. So if nothing else happens, population pressure depresses the standard of living. The only escape is technological change of one kind or another, meaning that the movement along the production function is compensated by a shift of the production function. And that increased efficiency is why we have become so much more prosperous, and continue to do so. Such increased efficiency can originate in technology in the narrow sense of the word, such as using watermills, but also in the wider sense of using different crops, more division of labour and trade, better management or better institutions. The list is a long one. So, once we have established that the Roman Empire experienced a population boom, the first challenge is to reconstruct incomes and standard of living for the mass of the population. Did they deteriorate under population pressure, or not? What is the true answer to the Monty Python team's question?

Unfortunately, the normal wage data to answer this question are few and far between. For the Roman Republican period we have the extensive set of slave prices from the Delphi manumission inscriptions (Jongman 2007a; Hopkins 2018). These show that slave prices went up significantly, suggesting that during the last two centuries BC real wages for free labour did as well. Roman slaves were expensive because free labour cost quite a bit more than the cost of subsistence. For the subsequent Imperial period we have a fair number of wages and prices from Roman Egypt, and these have recently been studied extensively by Kyle Harper (2016; Fig. 6.3).

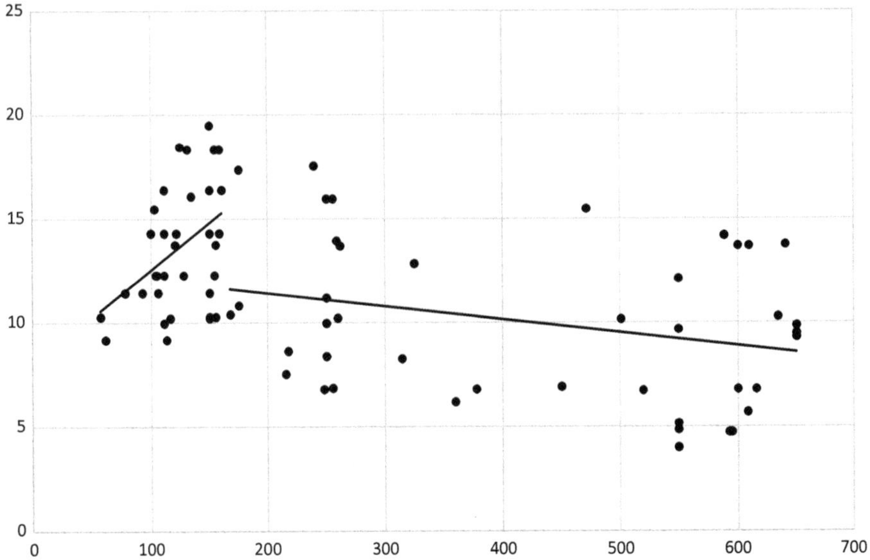

Fig. 6.3 Wages (in wheat) in Roman Egypt. (Source: Harper 2016)

Clearly, the Antonine plague marks a turning point, not only in the amount of written documentation but also in wage levels (Jongman 2012). Population pressure had eased, and yet this did not improve labour productivity and standard of living, on the contrary. Therefore, and unlike Harper, who included one linear regression for the entire date range, my version of the graph includes separate regression lines for the period before and after the Antonine Plague. The last set of wage data is from Diocletian's price edict of 301 CE. As we have seen from Bob Allen's analysis, by that time, standard of living was barely above subsistence (Allen 2009). To summarize these pretty meagre wage data, the standard of living seems to have moved with population rather than against it, and theoretically that is quite unusual for a preindustrial society.

However, these data are not very good. Fortunately, archaeology now offers far better data on material culture and lifestyle. If you cannot measure income, these archaeological datasets measure what is done with that income. A first example is a dataset on animal bones from archaeological sites, using bones as a proxy for trends in meat consumption (Jongman 2007b, 2014b; Fig. 6.4).

This graph represents animal bones from provincial sites, and as can be seen, not only is the number of assemblages enormous, but there is also a very clear trend. Other data on food consumption trends show a similar pattern, from wine and olive oil,

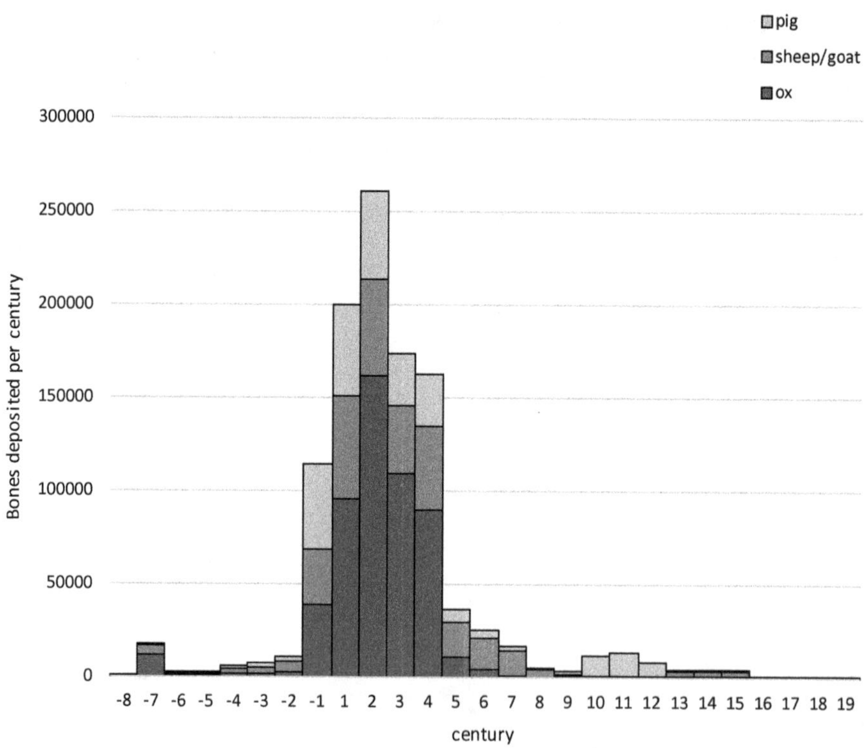

Fig. 6.4 Animal bones from Roman provinces as a proxy for meat consumption

fruits and vegetables to fish salting installations (Bakels and Jacomet 2003; Wilson 2006; Van der Veen 2016). And the consumption boom was not restricted to food: housing quality also improved, with larger and more comfortable dwellings, with even some window glass. That trend is also visible in the quantities of wood for building from Western Germany (Holstein 1980).

What all these types of consumer expenditure have in common is that they are not bare bones subsistence goods: they are not the cheapest calories, but the icing on the cake. In economic language, they are high income elasticity goods, i.e. goods that are consumed more than what you would expect just from income growth. So if incomes grow by, for example, 10%, consumption of these goods increases by more than 10%. As such they represent the qualitative change in consumption patterns that comes with greater prosperity.

6.2.3 *Why Did Roman Population Growth and Wealth Go Together?*

So all in all, I want to claim that Roman population growth did not produce a deterioration of standard of living, on the contrary. Similarly, Roman population decline in Late Antiquity did not improve standard of living like it would do after the Black Death of the fourteenth century (Borsch 2005; Campbell 2016). Therefore, the pessimistic Malthusian model did not apply. Instead the period of population growth went hand-in-hand with greater labour productivity. This leaves us with the final question: how could this be? I think there are three possible answers, and they probably all apply.

The first is that of market integration and increased division of labour. The Roman Empire had created an enormous more or less integrated market, connected by cheap water transport, and enjoying more or less uniform and effective institutions, ranging from military security to a stable monetary system, good laws and pretty good government. The high urbanization rate was where all these processes came together (Hanson 2016).

Secondly, however, none of this would have been possible without growth in agricultural productivity. New crops managed attentively catered for a taste for better and more expensive food, but also produced much higher returns, as long as people were prosperous enough to afford them. The prime examples would be wine and olive oil. In the end, farmers can choose from a wide range of crops and a wide range of strategies. The prevailing carrying capacity modelling fatally ignores alternative and more intensive strategies. For example, in the Italian context, producing wine and oil could generate perhaps five times more calories per hectare, and 10–20 times more revenue, but it was labour-intensive, and presupposed a prosperous market for these far more expensive calories (Jongman 2016). They presuppose an escape from life at the bare subsistence. And that, of course, also made the system unstable. When things went wrong, they would go badly wrong.

The third possible explanation is that these few happy centuries also experienced favourable climatic conditions. Economically, that is of course the same as technological improvement: the same quantities of land and labour began to produce more. All this started to go wrong from the mid second century CE, with a deteriorating climate, bad harvests, followed by the first in a series of epidemics, which in turn was followed by urban decline, social disintegration, and political and military upheaval (Manning 2013; Harper 2017). In the West at least the Empire did not really recover, even if in the East it did, at least for a while, until another round of bad weather and epidemics and the Justinian Plague in particular put an end to much of the eastern Empire as well.

6.3 Conclusions

These tentative and provisional conclusions require a far larger and more detailed empirical basis, to validate the broad contours, to extricate regional and temporal differences and to provide potential explanations. So what do we need for that, and what can we do?

First, to create the right analytical framework, I think historians and archaeologists of the ancient economy should involve themselves with proper economic theory, just like historians of medieval or early modern Europe have done (Jongman 1988). There is no reason to be on a different planet. And they should do so in a comparative framework: where does Antiquity stand in comparison to the modern world, and perhaps more usefully, in comparison to other preindustrial societies?

Second, they should follow the example of those same Medieval and Early Modern historians and the paradigm shift of exhaustive empirical data collection exemplified by French *Annales* historiography and American New Economic History. The choice is not between on the one hand big histories based on generalizations from secondary literature and on the other hand deeply factual microhistories. Modern economic historians have shown that it is possible to write big history from large aggregate datasets (e.g. Fogel 2004; Broadberry et al. 2015). For the Roman world, the written documentation will never give us those datasets, but archaeology can. Over the last few decades archaeology has moved from a subject of few and isolated data to one where the biggest concern should be to develop methodologies and practices that explore the current abundance of data. The challenge is to develop methods and concepts to serialize those data (the *mise en série* of the *Annales*) and harness them as proxies for economic variables. A famous early example was Keith Hopkins' use of Parker's catalogue of Mediterranean shipwrecks as proxies for long distance shipping (Hopkins 2018). Since then, many other examples have followed (Jongman 2014a, b, 2018).

Third, it is time we (and Medieval and Early Modern historians as well) pay more attention to the rapid progress made in scientific archaeology (e.g. McConnell et al. 2018). Apart from progress in established fields of archaeological science such as archaeobotany and archaeozoology, biological standard of living (human body length) or scientific dating methods, we now have more and more stable isotope analyses of skeletal material to the extent that for the first time statistically meaningful datasets are becoming available to reconstruct diet or patterns of migration. Dental plaque is revealing past infectious disease, and DNA studies show our genetic origins. Climate reconstructions are rapidly becoming more realistic and uncontroversial. There is no doubt that here we are at the threshold of completely new fields of historical knowledge, bringing us closer than ever to our ancestors and their quality of life.

Finally, we need more experimental archaeology to reconstruct the logic of many ancient practices. What were the opportunity costs of choosing one process over another, in terms of labour productivity, total output or risk? If and when agriculture is the dominant productive activity, this is something that has to be done within constraints and mechanisms from nature, and hence it should be relatively easy to model. What strategic alternatives did our ancestors have, and how successful were their choices? In short, I am convinced we are witnessing the end of traditional histories of the Roman economy, both substantially and methodologically.

References

Allen R (2009) How prosperous were the Romans? Evidence from Diocletian's price Edict (AD 301). In: Bowman BA, Wilson A (eds) Quantifying the Roman economy: methods and problems. Oxford University Press, Oxford, pp 327–345. https://doi.org/10.1093/acprof:oso/9780199562596.003.0016

Allen RC, Bengtsson T, Dribe M (eds) (2005) Living standards in the past: new perspectives on well-being in Asia and Europe. Oxford University Press, Oxford. https://doi.org/10.1093/0199280681.001.0001

Bakels CC, Jacomet S (2003) Access to luxury foods in Central Europe during the Roman period. World Archaeol 34:542–557. https://doi.org/10.1080/0043824021000026503

Borsch SJ (2005) The Black Death in Egypt and England. A comparative study. University of Texas Press, Austin

Broadberry S, Campbell BMS, Klein A, Overton M, Van Leeuwen B (2015) British economic growth 1270–1870. Cambridge University Press, Cambridge

Brown PRL (1971) The world of late antiquity: from Marcus Aurelius to Muhammad. Thames and Hudson, London

Brun JP (2012) Techniques and economies in the ancient Mediteranean. Inaugural lecture Collège de France, 5 April 2012. Collège de France, Paris. Available at http://books.openedition.org/cdf/2999. Accessed at 18 June 2018

Campbell B (2016) The great transition: climate, disease and society in the late-medieval world. Cambridge University Press, Cambridge

De Haas T, Tol G, Attema P (2011) Investing in the colonia and ager of Antium. Facta 5:111–144

Deru X (2017) Croissance et crise dans le nord de la Gaule romaine. Proceedings of Crisis Auxesis. Crise et croissance dans les économies des mondes anciens. Lyon, 11-12 Octobre 2013. Topoi 21:217–232

Fentress E (2009) Peopling the countryside: Roman demography in the Albegna valley and Jerba. In: Bowman BA, Wilson A (eds) Quantifying the Roman economy: methods and problems. Oxford University Press, Oxford, pp 127–161. https://doi.org/10.1093/acprof:oso/9780199562596.003.0005

Finley MI (1985) The ancient economy, 2nd edn. Chatto and Windus, London
Fogel RW (2004) The escape from hunger and premature death, 1700–2100: Europe, America and the Third World. Cambridge University Press, Cambridge
Greene K (1986) The archaeology of the Roman economy. Batsford, London
Hanson JW (2016) An urban geography of the Roman world, 100 B.C. to A.D. 300. Archaeopress, Oxford
Harper K (2016) People, plagues, and prices in the Roman world: the evidence from Egypt. J Econ Hist 76:803–839. https://doi.org/10.1017/S0022050716000826
Harper K (2017) The fate of Rome. Climate, disease and the end of an empire. Princeton University Press, Princeton
Holstein E (1980) Mitteleuropäische Eichenchronologie. Philipp Von Zabern, Mainz
Hopkins K (2018) Taxes and trade in the Roman empire (200 BC-AD 400). In: Kelly C (ed) Keith Hopkins: sociological studies in Roman history. Cambridge University Press, Cambridge, pp 213–259. https://doi.org/10.1017/CBO9781139093552.008
Jongman WM (1988) The economy and society of Pompeii. J.C. Gieben, Amsterdam
Jongman WM (2007a) The early Roman Empire: consumption. In: Scheidel W, Morris I, Saller RP (eds) The Cambridge economic history of the Greco-Roman world. Cambridge University Press, Cambridge, pp 592–618. https://doi.org/10.1017/CHOL9780521780537.023
Jongman WM (2007b) Gibbon was right: the decline and fall of the Roman economy. In: Hekster O, De Kleijn G, Slootjes D (eds) Crises and the Roman Empire. Proceedings of the Seventh Workshop of the International Network Impact of Empire (Nijmegen, June 20–24, 2006). Martinus Nijhoff/Brill, Leiden, pp 183–199. https://doi.org/10.1163/ej.9789004160507.i-448.38
Jongman WM (2012) Roman economic change and the Antonine Plague: endogenous, exogenous or what? In: Lo Cascio E (ed) L'impatto della "peste Antonina". Edipuglia, Bari, pp 253–263
Jongman WM (2014a) The new economic history of the Roman Empire. In: De Callatay F (ed) Quantifying the Greco-Roman economy and beyond. Edipuglia, Bari, pp 153–168
Jongman WM (2014b) Re-constructing the Roman economy. In: Neal L, Williamson J (eds) The Cambridge history of capitalism, vol 1. Cambridge University Press, Cambridge, pp 75–100
Jongman WM (2016) Italian urbanization and Roman economic growth. In: Capogrossi Colognesi L, Lo Cascio E, Tassi Scandone E (eds) L'Italia dei Flavi. Atti del Convegno, Roma, 4–5 Ottobre 2012. L'Erma di Bretschneider, Rome, pp 105–117
Jongman WM (2018) Afterword to "Taxes and trade in the Roman empire (200 BC-AD 400)". In: Kelly C (ed) Keith Hopkins: sociological studies in Roman history. Cambridge University Press, Cambridge, pp 260–268
Launaro A (2011) Peasants and slaves: the rural population of Italy (200 B.C. to A.D. 100). Cambridge University Press, Cambridge
Manning S (2013) The Roman world and climate: context, relevance of climate change, and some issues. In: Harris WV (ed) The ancient Mediterranean environment between science and history. Brill, Leiden, pp 103–170. https://doi.org/10.1163/9789004254053_007
McConnell JR, Wilson AI, Stohl A, Arienzo MM, Chellman NJ, Eckhardt S, Thompson EM, Pollard AM, Steffensen JP (2018) Lead pollution recorded in Greenland ice indicates European emissions tracked plagues, wars, and imperial expansion during antiquity. PNAS 115(22):5726–5731. https://doi.org/10.1073/pnas.1721818115
McEvedy C, Jones R (1978) Atlas of world population history. Penguin, Harmondsworth
Scheidel W (2007) Demography. In: Scheidel W, Morris I, Saller RP (eds) The Cambridge economic history of the Greco-Roman world. Cambridge University Press, Cambridge, pp 38–86. https://doi.org/10.1017/CHOL9780521780537.004
Scheidel W, Morris I, Saller R (eds) (2007) The Cambridge economic history of the Greco-Roman world. Cambridge University Press, Cambridge. https://doi.org/10.1017/CHOL9780521780537
Van der Veen M (2016) Arable farming, horticulture and food: expansion, innovation, and diversity. In: Millet M, Revelle L, Moore A (eds) The Oxford handbook of Roman Britain. Oxford University Press, Oxford. https://doi.org/10.1093/oxfordhb/9780199697731.013.046

Wilson A (2006) Fishy business: Roman exploitation of marine resources. J Roman Archaeol 19:525–537. https://doi.org/10.1017/S1047759400006760

Zimmermann A, Hilpert J, Wendt KP (2009) Estimates of population density for selected periods between the Neolithic and A.D. 1800. Hum Biol 81(2–3):357–380. https://doi.org/10.3378/027.081.0313

Chapter 7
Modelling Agricultural Strategies in the Dutch Roman *Limes* via Agent-Based Modelling (ROMFARMS)

Jamie Joyce

Abstract This chapter presents an agent-based model developed to investigate the impact on land and labour costs of different agricultural strategies that could have been undertaken in the Early and Middle Roman periods (12 BCE to 270 CE) in the Lower Rhine delta. A short description of the sub-processes in ROMFARMS to simulate settlement population dynamics, arable farming, animal husbandry and wood acquisition is provided. The results show that settlements in the Dutch *limes* zone during the Roman period were mostly limited by the relatively small labour pool available. Whilst not prevented outright by the availability of labour, the results show that only a small proportion of the total quantity of grain demanded by to military settlements, towns and *vici* can be supplied by local settlements. Two different possible scales of supply were envisaged with the results indicating that a macro-regional supply network was more feasible in which all settlements in the Lower Rhine delta were involved in the supply of consumer-only settlements. Whilst several methodological issues were noted, ROMFARMS is presented as an innovative tool for Dutch Roman archaeology with good potential for further development.

Keywords Agent-based modelling · Agriculture · Roman archaeology · Dutch *limes* · Surplus production

7.1 Introduction

ROMFARMS is an agent-based model developed in NetLogo (v. 6.0.2; Wilensky 1999) to investigate different possible agricultural strategies undertaken during the Early and Middle Roman periods (12 BCE to 270 CE) in the Lower Rhine region. ROMFARMS produces results on the land and labour costs of agriculture under the conditions of different scenarios. These have been used to assess the relative limiting impact of these factors of production on agricultural productivity to better understand the impact of different agricultural behaviours and the feasibility of

J. Joyce (✉)
Faculty of Humanities, Vrije Universiteit Amsterdam, Amsterdam, The Netherlands

P. Verhagen et al. (eds.), *Finding the Limits of the Limes*, Computational Social Sciences, https://doi.org/10.1007/978-3-030-04576-0_7

different strategies of subsistence-based and surplus arable farming and animal husbandry.

7.1.1 *The Surplus Debate in Dutch Roman Archaeology*

Whether rural agrarian settlements in the Dutch Roman *limes* zone were capable of supplying *castella*, *castra*, *vici* and towns that developed from the Early Roman period (12 BCE onwards) has been the subject of significant debate within Dutch archaeology. Initial assessments of the agricultural economy of the Lower Rhine delta before and during the Roman period cited literary sources, the limitations of the natural landscape and the local spectra of cereals cultivated locally as evidence against local supply of grain or animal products (Van Es 1981; Bloemers 1983; Willems 1986; Whittaker 2004). In contrast, archaeobotanical, zooarchaeological and other archaeological evidence points to the strong likelihood of at least partial supply by native agrarian settlements in the Lower Rhine region (see Kooistra et al. 2013, 5–7).

Recent research undertaken by Van Dinter et al. (2014) and De Kleijn et al. (2016, 2018) have used detailed landscape capacity models to develop further theories regarding the extent of possible supply by local agrarian settlements. Neither study excluded local supply of either grain or meat outright. Rather, they both calculated that the full quantity demanded by military settlements, towns and *vici* could not be fulfilled by local supply. Both landscape capacity approaches assume agricultural extensification as the mechanism undertaken for surplus production of grain and animal products. In contrast, previous studies have also posited arable intensification and different herd management strategies aimed to exploit cattle or sheep for different products (e.g. Groot 2008; see Sect. 7.2.3). This paper adds further results to the surplus production debate in Dutch Roman archaeology. It uses spatial dynamic modelling techniques to simulate the various processes of the agricultural economy as well as fundamental underlying processes such as settlement population dynamics.

7.2 Overview of Sub-models and Processes

7.2.1 *Initialization*

ROMFARMS is a discrete patch model comprising of cells each representing 1 hectare. Distances between cells are calculated from the centre of each cell. Both randomly generated and reconstructed landscapes are used in the simulation depending on the tested scenario. Each cell possesses a value for the variable *landscape-type* which determines whether a cell contains flood-basin, levee or neither.

Settlements are located on levee cells which are also used for arable land. Flood-basin is used for animal husbandry by settlements. These land-use assumptions are derived from Groot and Kooistra's (2009) assessment of land use at Tiel-Passewaaij. In randomly generated landscapes, areas of flood-basin and levee are generated with the number of cells for each landscape element determined by the value for parameters *area-levee* and *area-floodbasin*. In reconstructed landscapes, the GIS extension is used to provide values to cells from 32 rasters which cover the majority of the inhabited Lower Rhine delta during the end of the pre-Roman Iron Age and Roman period. Whilst all cells are coloured in reconstructed landscapes according to the landscape element they contain, only raster values corresponding to levees or flood-basin update the value for *landscape-type*. Levees or flood-basins remain the only landscape element used by settlements for arable farming or animal husbandry.

Settlements in ROMFARMS vary from small settlements comprising one household to larger settlements comprising two, three or five households. A household in ROMFARMS is considered one couple with any dependent children, elderly or unmarried adults. Within one step of the simulation, settlements undertake arable farming, animal husbandry and fuel acquisition. One step of the simulation represents one calendar year. Timber collection for construction wood is undertaken by the settlement's inhabitants once per 20 years. The number of households each settlement comprises is the maximum number of households. During a simulation, the number of married couples with dependents in each settlement may drop below the maximum number of households but cannot exceed it (see Sect. 7.2.2). At the start of each simulation, settlements are inhabited by one adult male and female per household and four individuals between 0 and 15 per household, with ages of children generated randomly. Settlements are provided with herds of livestock at the beginning of each simulation. Settlements start each simulation with 1 herd of sheep, cattle or horse containing 30 adult animals. In addition, each settlement is provided with a catchment area containing all cells within a 10 km round trip from the settlement. A settlement's catchment area contains all arable land and woodland on levees that a settlement has access to. Whether the arable land and woodland remains available for use depends on whether other agents have already made use of it.

ROMFARMS is described in more detail in Joyce (2019) and can be accessed from http://modelingcommons.org/browse/one_model/5687#model_tabs_browse_info.

7.2.2 Population Dynamics

The agricultural production unit in ROMFARMS is the settlement. Each settlement is comprised of one or multiple households. A system dynamics model of settlement demography was combined with a further sub-model which simulated marriage, establishment of new settlements and migration. Mortality was determined by probability values for death per age of individual which are derived from Coal and Demeny's Model West Level 3 Female life table (1966). Fertility rates were taken from Coale and Trussell's (1978) estimates. This sub-model simulates changes in settlement populations each step from which settlements derive their individual labour supply. Labour supply is divided into "weak" and "strong" forces (after Danielisová and Štekerová 2015). The latter can undertake all agricultural tasks; the former can only undertake fuel collection. Children under 10 years have no labour value. Unmarried or widowed individuals will remarry provided there is another individual of the opposite sex between 16 and 49. Marriages are patrilocal unless the number of households in the male spouse' settlement has reached the maximum. If the female spouse' settlement has also reached the maximum number of permitted households, a new settlement is established. If the maximum settlement density of the landscape has been reached, the settlement is established outside of the simulation and the new couple is removed.

In each step, the population of each settlement is calculated, and the total calories required by the inhabitants are estimated using demands from Gregg (1988) and FAO (2004). The quantity of fuel required is also calculated.

7.2.3 *Arable Farming*

A sub-model simulating arable farming was included in ROMFARMS. In this sub-model, settlements cultivate grain using different behaviours based on three agricultural strategies: subsistence-based, extensification and intensification. Under subsistence-based arable farming, settlements seek to cultivate only enough land to produce grain for their own consumption needs and sowing seed for the following year. Harvests fluctuate each year, with grain yields per hectare of cultivated land fluctuating ±20% around a mean 1000 kg/ha. In addition, settlements can cultivate a small surplus each year to serve as a buffer against exogenous forces such as disease, adverse weather, pests and socio-political factors. Settlements undertaking arable extensification seek to cultivate extra land provided there is sufficient labour, arable land and sowing seed to do so. Settlements undertaking arable intensification cultivate no more land than they would under subsistence-based farming. However, they will incorporate manure into arable land to boost grain yields and remove the need for fallowing each year. ROMFARMS does not simulate nutrient cycles in the soil but settlements undertaking either subsistence-based arable farming or arable extensification must leave land cultivated 1 year, fallow in subsequent years.

In each step, the land costs and labour expenditure for the various tasks associated with arable farming are calculated for each settlement. Arable tasks that require labour expenditure are sowing, ploughing, harvesting and manuring. The yield of grain is also calculated. Any grain not required by settlements for their own consumption or for sowing seed is considered surplus.

Arable extensification and intensification are the two strategies of surplus arable production simulated in ROMFARMS. The two strategies are distinguished by the land use and resource input (Ellis 1993, 206). The two strategies simulated in ROMFARMS follow the two proposed by De Hingh (2000, 43). Extensification increases the area of land used, but the labour input per unit of land does not increase from subsistence-based farming. Intensification increases the labour input per unit of land but does not increase the overall area of land that is cultivated. Although the investment of labour and capital has defined the concept of agricultural intensification (Bieleman 2010), manure as a valuable commodity can be seen as a form of capital (Ellis 1993; De Hingh 2000).

7.2.4 Animal Husbandry

To simulate animal husbandry, a system dynamics model of herd population dynamics was included in ROMFARMS. This sub-model simulates the herd dynamics of three major livestock species: cattle, sheep and horse. Each year, livestock reproduce, die of natural causes and are slaughtered. Death due to natural causes of livestock is simulated using the method developed by Galic (2014). Slaughter rates are expressed as the probability of an individual animal dying. They were developed from an earlier study of animal husbandry for the "Finding the limits of the *limes*" project (Joyce and Verhagen 2016). Horse herds are simulated differently, as settlements in ROMFARMS exploit these animals to maximise the number of immature animals that can be removed as a surplus commodity. Horses are therefore not slaughtered but are removed from the herd.

Settlements can exploit sheep and cattle for different products resulting in different slaughter rates per age cohort of animals. Accordingly, settlements can exploit cattle for meat, milk or manure/traction, and they can exploit sheep for meat, milk or wool. Exploitation strategies reflect behaviour of settlements to maximise the potential output of a particular product from a herd but simultaneously maintaining the viability of the herd and preventing its extinction.

In each step, the yields of potential products are estimated from cattle and sheep herds as is the potential number of immature horses that can be removed from the horse herd kept by a settlement as a surplus commodity. In addition, the area of land needed to pasture animals and the area of grassland needed to produce hay for winter fodder for 4 months are calculated. The labour expenditure required to produce this fodder is also estimated.

7.2.5 Wood Collection

The collection of fuel and timber from the local environment was probably a major task of the agricultural economy in the past. ROMFARMS simulates this task by combining a patch choice and central place foraging model (after Shaw 2008). Settlements collect wood from the landscape with the resource spread heterogeneously. Settlements will seek a patch containing wood that is the nearest patch containing more wood than the average per patch in that year. Settlements will stay in a patch until either sufficient wood has been collected or the quantity of wood falls below the average per patch. In the case of the latter, settlements will look for a new patch to collect wood from. Once sufficient wood has been collected, or the maximum quantity of wood that can be collected by the foraging party has been reached or there is no more wood left in the landscape, collected wood is returned to the settlement. This approach avoided using the Principle of Least Effort as the sole behavioural rule for wood acquisition (see Shackleton and Prins 1992; Shaw 2008; see also Brouwer et al. 1997). Unless a patch is used as arable land, wood regenerates in the patch.

Settlements will collect wood for fuel multiple times in a year. The number of times is determined by the user-defined parameter collection-frequency. To minimise the number of foragers required per collection, the "strong" workforce (see Sect. 7.2.2) is used primarily with the "weak" workforce only used when the quantity of wood that can be collected by the "strong" workforce is less than the quantity required by all the settlement's inhabitants.

In each step, the combined time required to travel by the foraging party from the settlement to each patch foraged from and back to the settlement is calculated. In addition, the time spent in each patch to process wood to be returned to the settlement is calculated. The combined time is the labour expenditure per settlement for wood acquisition.

7.2.6 Description of Experiments

Whilst ROMFARMS has been used to simulate a large number of scenarios, they cannot all be discussed here. The experiments included in this study concern surplus production in randomly generated and reconstructed landscapes. The values for user-defined parameters for these scenarios are provided in Appendix Table 7.4. Scenarios were simulated using NetLogo's inbuilt BehaviourSpace function. This allowed for a model to be run multiple times, automatically recording outputs and iterating over different parameter values.

The experiments discussed in this chapter concern only surplus arable farming and animal husbandry. Firstly, surplus strategies of arable farming and different exploitation strategies of livestock were simulated in randomly generated landscapes to identify their key limiting factors and to identify cause and effect chains of agricultural decisions in optimum conditions. Subsequently, the same strategies were simulated in reconstructed landscapes of the 32 sub-regions to gauge the relative impact of the natural landscape as well as generate new results related to supply and demand of food in each sub-region.

7.3 Discussion

7.3.1 Arable Extensification and Intensification

7.3.1.1 Limiting Factors for Arable Intensification and Extensification

Experiments with subsistence-based arable farming identified a number of limiting factors that impact settlements' abilities to undertake arable farming successfully. The availability of land, labour and sowing seed were identified as possible limiting factors. These same factors also have a limiting impact on the ability for settlements to undertake arable intensification and extensification. For the former, a further limiting factor was expected. Without access to manure, settlements would be unable to boost yields. The differences in the two strategies of surplus arable farming resulted in differences in the relative impact of the limiting factors.

Settlements undertaking extensification require larger quantities of sowing seed than required under subsistence-based arable farming or arable intensification. Without extra sowing seed, the area of land that can be cultivated cannot increase. In randomly generated landscapes, the principal limiting factor for settlements undertaking arable extensification was the availability of labour. Provided that the proportion of grain removed as surplus for external consumers did not exceed 70%, settlements had access to more sowing seed than needed. The availability of labour placed a maximum limit on the area of land that could be cultivated that was lower than the area that could be sown or the area that settlements had access to in randomly generated landscapes (see Table 7.1).

The ability for settlements to produce surplus grain when undertaking arable intensification is dependent on the availability of manure. Settlements must manage cattle herds to undertake arable intensification and therefore are limited by the number of cattle that can be managed. The workforce available to settlements enabled enough cattle to be managed to supply sufficient manure for an optimal application on the arable land to be cultivated. The availability of manure is therefore limited by the cattle exploitation strategy employed by settlements.

Table 7.1 Maximum area of land (ha) that can be cultivated by settlements per limiting factor when surplus takeoff is 70%

No. of households	Availability of labour	Availability of sowing seed
1	6.83	24.08
2	9.03	34.54
3	12.27	49.22
5	18.99	78.15

7.3.1.2 Cost-Effectiveness of Strategies

A calculation of the cost-effectiveness of intensification and extensification was made to compare the increased labour and land costs for surplus grain produce. Costs for extensification incorporated only the area of extra land cultivated and labour to cultivate this extra land. Costs for intensification incorporated the labour costs to produce the manure required in addition to the labour costs for sowing, ploughing, harvesting and the incorporation of manure into cultivated land.

The results showed that the two surplus arable strategies provided different advantages to settlements depending on the availability of land and labour (see Table 7.2). Under intensification, the land cost per ton of surplus grain is lower than under extensification. This indicates that intensification is a more advantageous strategy when the availability of arable land is reduced. For per ton of surplus grain, extensification uses less labour than intensification. Accordingly, despite overall higher absolute labour costs under extensification, it would be a more beneficial strategy should the availability of labour be restricted.

7.3.2 *Surplus Animal Husbandry in Randomly Generated Landscapes*

In ROMFARMS, the available workforce for each settlement permits the management of herds larger than the herd sizes that emerge via the system dynamics submodel of animal husbandry. A small surplus of meat and milk is already available from the cattle herds simulated in ROMFARMS, with more meat and milk available from smaller settlements as their consumption requirements are smaller. If settlements managed larger herds, the quantity of surplus meat and milk would increase although more pasture and meadow land would be required as well as a greater expenditure of labour. Settlements can manage more cattle than required for their own needs with the labour available to them.

The availability of surplus meat and milk is dependent on the exploitation strategy employed. Cattle exploited for meat and milk produce larger quantities of meat and milk each year than herds exploited for manure (see Table 7.3). Slaughter rates for cattle exploited for manure result in fewer adult animals slaughtered, reducing meat yields. Furthermore, the size of herds exploited for manure is smaller, which also reduces the quantity of milk available. The likelihood of sheep husbandry being a viable mechanism for surplus production of meat and milk is slim. The number of sheep needed to be kept by settlements is not reflected in the zooarchaeological evi-

Table 7.2 Extra land and labour costs per ton of surplus grain under different arable farming strategies

Strategy	Hours per ton surplus grain	Hectares per ton surplus grain
Extensification	74.68	1.34
Intensification	127.74	0.00

Table 7.3 Mean annual yield output per herd of cattle and sheep as simulated in ROMFARMS

Species	Strategy	Milk (l)	Meat (kg)	Wool (kg)	Manure (kg)
Cattle	Milk	5313.28	632.13	–	81078.76
Cattle	Meat	3488.94	688.27	–	62329.22
Cattle	Manure/traction	1966.92	459.58	–	30972.12
Sheep	Meat	160.51	19.38	51.40	–
Sheep	Milk	300.80	14.88	59.89	–
Sheep	Wool	242.97	31.02	66.86	–

dence available from the study region. If sheep husbandry did play a role in surplus farming in the Lower Rhine delta, it is likely it was small-scale or even specialised, such as the surplus production of wool (see Groot 2008; Van Dijk & Groot 2013).

The results from ROMFARMS show that the possible yield of milk from cattle herds regardless of the exploitation strategy employed outstrips the possible yield of meat. The supply of raw milk from rural agrarian settlements to military settlements, towns or *vici* in the region is unlikely. Instead, a small-scale and specialised way of market participation in the Roman period could have been through the production of cheese (van Driel-Murray 2003, 2008).

Specialised horse-breeding in the region to supply surplus horses, primarily to the army, has been argued in many studies of the ancient economy in the Dutch *limes* zone (see Kooistra 1996; Nicolay 2008; Vossen and Groot 2009). Horse bones in rural zooarchaeological assemblages are almost ubiquitous with some assemblages containing up to 30% horse remains (see Lauwerier and Robeerst 2001, Table 1). Vossen and Groot (2009) calculated an annual demand of 373 horses from military settlements in the Early Roman period and 413 in the Middle Roman period for the eastern part of the Dutch *limes* zone alone. Potentially seven immature horses can be removed from horse herds simulated by ROMFARMS without causing the extinction of the herd. To fulfil the total demand of horses for the Roman army in the Lower Rhine delta, not every rural settlement would need to specialise in horse-breeding therefore. The near ubiquity of horse bones in rural settlements indicates there was a distinction between specialised horse-breeders who managed herds like those simulated in ROMFARMS and small-scale breeders who supplied an animal on an ad hoc basis.

7.3.3 Surplus Production in Reconstructed Landscapes

Simulating agriculture using landscapes reconstructed from palaeogeographic data enabled an analysis of land as a limiting factor. Owing to restrictions in computer processing power, the whole Lower Rhine delta was divided into 32 equal sized sub-regions of 100 km^2 (see Fig. 7.1). The natural landscape of each of these sub-regions presented different possibilities and challenges (see Kooistra et al. 2013).

In addition to reconstructing the natural landscape, settlement densities for each sub-region were calculated from a data-set of find-spots. A data-set of military settlements, towns and *vici* was also compiled from available evidence to estimate

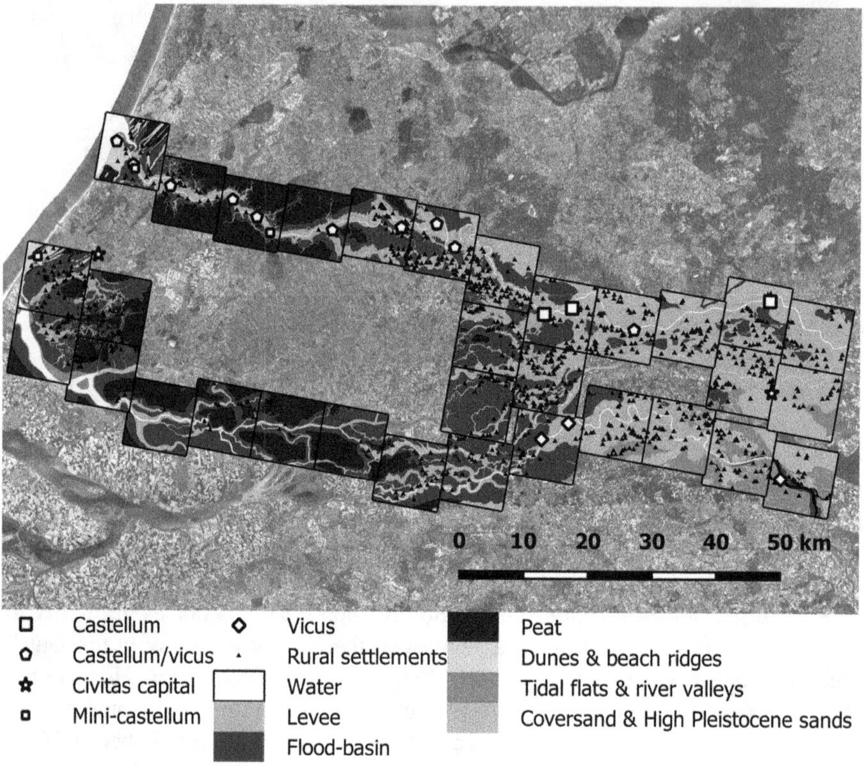

Fig. 7.1 Palaeogeographic reconstruction of the Lower Rhine delta showing the location of 32 sub-regions used in ROMFARMS. Base map = PDOK Luchtfoto Beeldmateriaal 25 cm

possible demand in each of the sub-regions in the Early and Middle Roman periods. This is one of only a few formal estimates of demand in the study region for this period and uses data-sets produced from new methods developed by Verhagen et al. (2016a, b). As such it is subject to significant uncertainties. Nevertheless, this formal estimate of demand has helped to identify the data necessary to establish more accurate and robust estimates.

7.3.4 *Land Use in Reconstructed Landscapes*

Despite uncertainties in the data-set of rural settlements and reconstructed settlement densities for each sub-region, an analysis of potential land use for arable farming and animal husbandry was undertaken. Although scenarios were simulated using settlement sizes ranging from one to five households, archaeological evidence from the Lower Rhine delta indicates that large settlements were rare (see Sect. 7.3.5). The majority of settlements comprised just one or two households. Arable land use by small settlements in each sub-region was low enough for both surplus strategies that the availability of land was not a limiting factor (see Fig. 7.2). Only in those sub-regions with very little arable land, such as those in the peat areas of the central Lower Rhine delta, that were occupied homogenously by large settlements with five households did the availability of arable land restrict the settlements' ability to undertake arable extensification.

Comparisons were also made between the area of pasture and meadow land needed for different cattle herds managed by settlements in each sub-region. Settlements undertaking arable intensification need very few cattle resulting in only a relatively small proportion of the total area of pasture and meadow land being used in each sub-region each year. Conversely, settlements undertaking an extensive animal husbandry strategy by managing herds much larger than those simulated by ROMFARMS could potentially use almost all pasture and meadow land available. In landscapes with smaller settlements, the total number of animals that could be managed was limited most by the availability of labour. When landscapes were occupied by large settlements with three or five households, the availability of land did become more limiting in many sub-regions. Settlements in these scenarios had workforces that could manage more animals than could be supported by the natural landscape.

Only a few instances were recorded when the use of land for one agricultural task could limit the availability of land. In some sub-regions occupied by large settlements comprising three or five households, the use of arable land for pasturing animals can increase the total number of animals that can be managed. In these scenarios, the area of land available for animal husbandry is reduced because settlements undertake arable farming.

7.3.5 Mechanisms of Supply: Micro-regional and Macro-regional Supply Networks

Using a data-set of *castella*, *castra*, towns and *vici*, the demand for grain for human consumption, grain for animal fodder and animal products in each sub-region was estimated. In this paper, only grain for human consumption is considered. Two scales of supply network were envisaged. The micro-regional supply network is one where consumer-only settlements were supplied by rural agrarian settlements located in the same micro-region. The macro-regional supply network was denoted as a supply network where all settlements in the Lower Rhine delta were involved in the supply of all military settlements, towns and *vici* located in the Dutch *limes* zone.

The results from these comparisons showed that for grain supply for human consumption, a micro-regional supply network was infeasible in many scenarios. This is especially the case for scenarios with small settlements possessing one to two households whose surplus grain output was relatively low per settlement. The amount of grain that can be supplied is also lower when settlements undertake arable intensification (see Fig. 7.3). In scenarios where settlements comprised three or five households, a majority of the grain required for either human consumption or to be used as fodder could be supplied on a micro-regional scale when settlements undertake arable extensification. Changes in demand and supply were observed

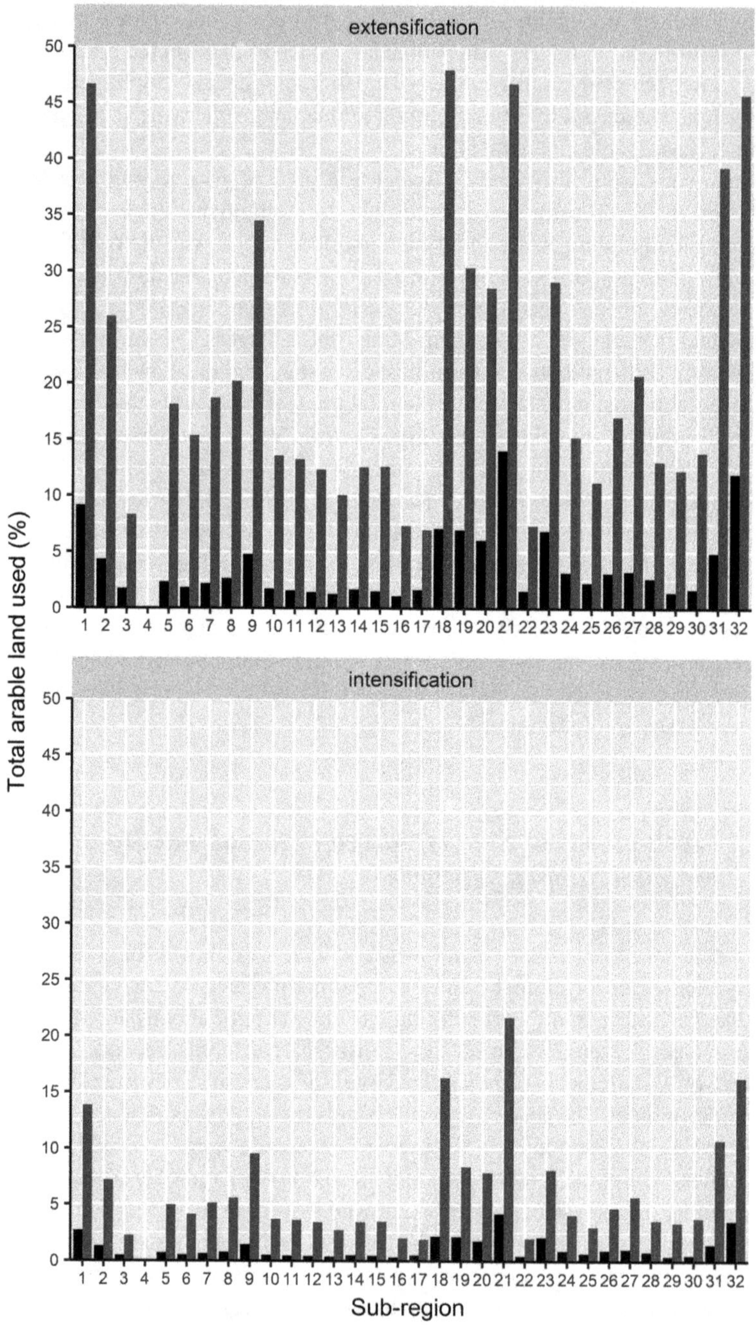

Fig. 7.2 Percentage of total arable land available used per sub-region in scenarios with homogenous occupation by settlements with one (black) or five (grey) households using settlement densities from the Middle Roman Period A

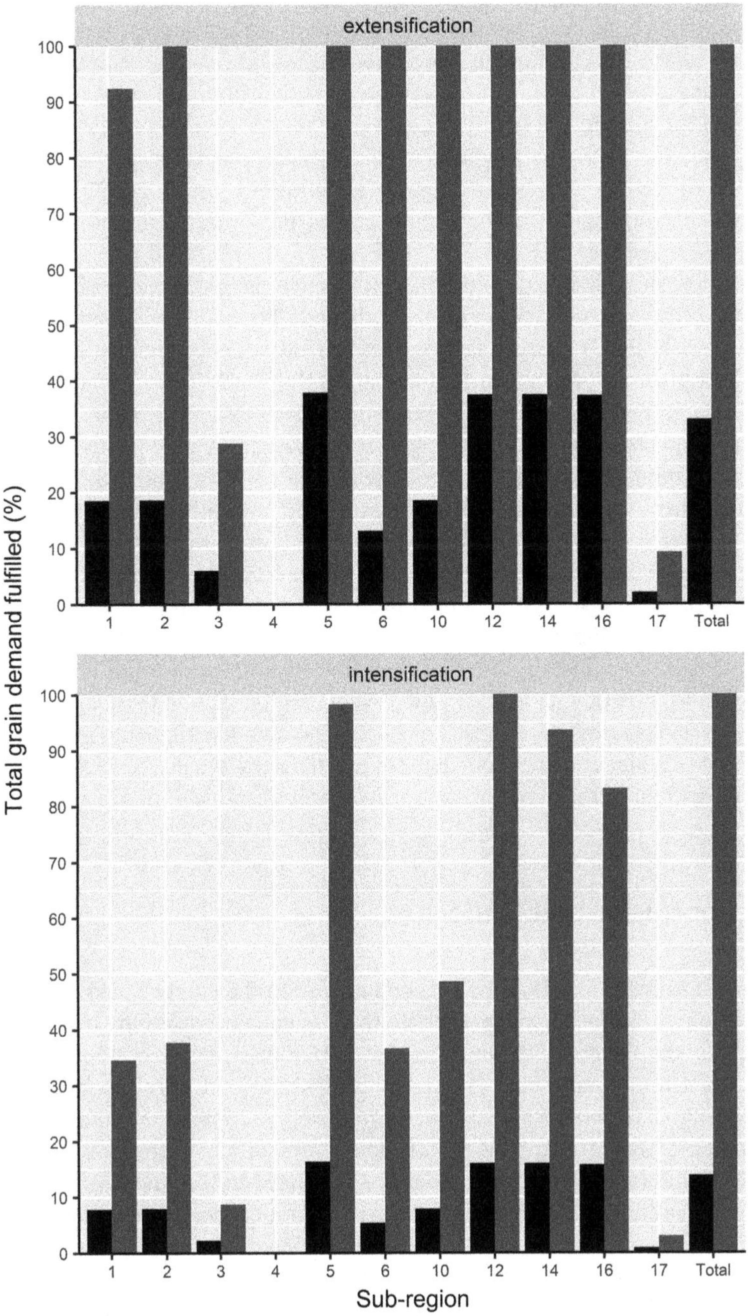

Fig. 7.3 Percentage of grain demand per micro-region and total macro-regional demand that can be fulfilled by supply in each micro-region from settlements with one (black) and five households (grey) during the Middle Roman Period A when demand was highest. Population estimates per *castella* and *vicus* are 350 per settlement (after Van Dinter et al. 2014) with a further 5500 civilians and soldiers in the larger settlements at Nijmegen and 1000 civilians in Forum Hadriani

over time with an increasing demand from military settlements, towns and *vici* from the Early to the Middle Roman period as well as increases in settlement density. These changes result in only slight variations in the pattern of surplus and deficits calculated for sub-regions however. Owing to the variation in settlement density in sub-regions, the surpluses produced in the sparsely populated peat regions (sub-regions 2–4, see Fig. 7.1) produce smaller quantities of surplus grain than the more densely occupied regions in the central part of the Lower Rhine delta (e.g. sub-regions 8–11, see Fig. 7.1).

With most sites identified from surface find-spots and few remains of actual buildings, only broad assumptions can be made about the typical size of a settlement in the region. Vossen (2003) argued that large settlements were exceptional in the region. Van Dinter et al. (2014) and De Kleijn et al. (2016, 2018) both assumed 1.5 households as the average size of a rural settlement. Landscapes occupied homogenously by settlements all comprising the same number of households are unrealistic. However, if the occupation of landscapes by small settlements was the norm, the results from scenarios where simulated settlements possess one or two households better reflect the situation in the past. A micro-regional supply network was unlikely to have been able to fulfil the demands of consumer-only settlements in all sub-region.

In contrast, the results show that a macro-regional supply network for grain is more feasible (see Figure 7.3). The sum total of grain produced, including where sub-regions are occupied by small settlements, is sufficient to fulfil a much higher proportion of the grain demanded in the whole region than in the majority of sub-regions. If landscapes were mostly occupied by small settlements in the Roman Dutch *limes* zone, a macro-regional supply network would be better suited to responding to the demands of *castra*, *castella*, towns and *vici* for grain.

7.4 Conclusion and Outlook

The development of ROMFARMS encountered several theoretical and methodological difficulties. Choosing an appropriate time scale to use in simulations as well as reconciling the different frequencies that agricultural activities took place was required. Each step represents 1 year in ROMFARMS and therefore processes that take place more than once per year were simulated multiple times within each step. This increased processing time significantly. In addition, there existed an upper limit to the number of agents that could be simulated in ROMFARMS. The use of sub-regions prevented simulation of the agricultural economy on a macro-regional scale. The economic activities of military settlements, towns and *vici* that could impact on the availability of land were not simulated. Furthermore, ROMFARMS includes only limited provision for agents to adapt. An inconsistent availability of data to generate different assumptions and estimates was noted. Assumptions were not available for many agricultural tasks. There were also significant uncertainties when estimating settlement densities for periods, the chronology of non-agrarian settlements and populations of *castella*, *vici* and towns. The calculations of supply and demand are based on currently available domain knowledge. As more domain knowledge becomes available, the accuracy of these estimates will improve.

ROMFARMS relies on the economic rationalism of agents. When farmers undertake surplus production in ROMFARMS, they are limited only by economic factors. Agents in ROMFARMS are not affected by exogenous socio-political or cultural factors. Concepts such as land ownership, land choice or Roman macro-economic policies are incorporated either superficially, or not at all. Although it was understood that these concepts would have impacted agricultural behaviour in the past, it was not possible to produce behavioural rules from them to implement in ROMFARMS. Instead, ROMFARMS has been used to simulate the baseline scenario: the first step in simulating agricultural behaviour in the study region in the past. Future approaches using ROMFARMS may wish to develop the model to incorporate social and cultural factors and observe how the results may differ from the null scenario.

As ROMFARMS is reliant on the sub-model of settlement population dynamics, the strength of this part of the simulation has a large impact on the results produced. The sub-model developed for this model uses simplifications of demographic processes. Marriage rules, for example, are simplified with few rules (c.f. Danielisová et al. 2015; Verhagen et al. 2016a). ROMFARMS assumes patrilocal marriage and the relocation of orphans and other dependents to the nearest settlement. Again, these assumptions are based on currently available domain knowledge which are subject to change and, hopefully, improvement. Further research could analyse the effect of recruitment of the local population into the Roman army which could have had a significant impact on the availability of labour and the marriage pool (see Van Dinter et al. 2014; Verhagen et al. 2016a). The use of life tables and fertility estimates provide usable approximations of mortality and birth rates in the past but should be treated with caution (Woods 2007).

Further development of ROMFARMS should focus on implementation of socio-political and cultural factors. In addition, development of the sub-models, particularly settlement population dynamics, will improve how representative the results are. ROMFARMS as a computational tool is a new contribution to the analysis of agriculture in the past, alongside other recent approaches (see, e.g. Cimler et al. 2012; Saqalli et al. 2014; Danielisová et al. 2015; Danielisová and Štekerová 2015; Baum 2016; Baum et al. 2016; Olševičová et al. 2014). The results from simulating multiple scenarios in both randomly generated and reconstructed landscapes have generated new hypotheses regarding the relative impact of land and labour availability on agricultural productivity and the possible ways in which rural agrarian settlements could have supplied military settlements, towns and *vici* that did not produce their own food. It has reduced the full spectrum of possibilities to a limited range of plausible scenarios which further research can be directed to. The results from ROMFARMS confirm that occupation of the Lower Rhine region by small settlements in relatively sparsely populated micro-regions reduced labour availability, thereby possibly limiting the production of surplus grain and animal products.

Appendix

Table 7.4 Parameter values for scenarios discussed in this chapter

Variable	Value	Increment	Notes
Experiment 1			
No-1-household-settlements	0/2	–	
No-2-household-settlements	0/2	–	
No-3-household-settlements	0/2	–	
No-5-households-settlements	0/2	–	
Runtime	100	–	
Region	"Hyp"	–	
Period	N/A	–	
Area-levee	0.5	–	
Area-floodbasin	0.5	–	
Forest-cover	0.1	–	
Fen-cover	0	–	
%-calories-from-crops	0.1–1.0	0.1	
Store-size	1.5	–	
Strategy-arable	"Extensification"/"intensi fication"	–	
Surplus-takeoff	0.1–1	0.1	For "extensification" (for "intensification" surplus takeoff = 1.0)
Daily-per-capita-fuel-use	6	–	
Coppicing?	Y	–	
Collection-frequency	1	–	
Reconstruction-frequency	20	–	
Cattle?	Y/N	–	
Sheep?	Y/N	–	
Horse?	Y/N	–	
Sheep-strategy	"Meat", "milk", "wool"	–	
Cattle-strategy	"Meat", "milk", "manure/traction"	–	
Experiment 2			
Region	1–32		
Period	"IJZ", "ROMVA", "ROMVB", "ROMMA", "ROMMB"		
	NB. Other values same as experiment 1		

References

Baum T (2016) Simulating land use of prehistoric wetland settlements: did excessive resource use necessitate a highly dynamic settlement system? In: Barceló JA, Del Castillo F (eds) Simulating prehistoric and ancient worlds. Springer, Cham, pp 255–279. https://doi.org/10.1007/978-3-319-31481-5_9

Baum T, Nendel C, Jacomet S, Colobran M, Ebersbach R (2016) "Slash and burn" or "weed and manure"? A modelling approach to explore hypotheses of late Neolithic crop cultivation in pre-alpine wetland sites. Veg Hist Archaeobotany 25(6):611–627. https://doi.org/10.1007/s00334-016-0583-x

Bieleman J (2010) Five centuries of farming. A short history of Dutch agriculture 1500–2000. Wageningen Academic Publishers, Wageningen. https://doi.org/10.3920/978-90-8686-693-9

Bloemers JHF (1983) Acculturation in the Rhine/Meuse basin in the Roman period: a preliminary survey. In: Brandt R, Slofstra J (eds) Roman and native in the Low Countries: spheres of interaction. BAR, Oxford, pp 159–209

Brouwer ID, Hoorweg JC, Van Liere MJ (1997) When households run out of fuel: responses of rural households to decreasing fuelwood availability, Ntcheu District, Malawi. World Dev 25(2):255–266

Cimler R, Olševičová K, Machálek T, Danielisová A (2012) Agent-base model of agricultural practices in Late Iron Age. In: Proceedings of the 15th Czech-Japan seminar on data analysis and decision making under uncertainty, September 24–27, 2012, Machikane facility. Osaka University, Osaka, pp 166–171

Coale AJ, Demeny P (1966) Regional model life tables and stable population. Princeton University Press, Princeton

Coale AJ, Trussell TJ (1978) Technical note: finding the two parameters that specify a model schedule of marital fertility. Popul Index 44:203–213. https://doi.org/10.2307/2733910

Danielisová A, Štekerová K (2015) Sociální simulace při zkoumání společnosti, ekonomiky a využívání krajiny v době železné: metoda a příklady/ Social simulations for exploring society, economy and land use in the Iron Age: method and examples. Památky archeologické 106:137–180

Danielisová A, Olševičová K, Cimler R, Machálek T (2015) Understanding the Iron Age economy: sustainability of agricultural practices under stable population growth. In: Wurzer G, Kowarik K, Reschreiter H (eds) Agent-based modelling and simulation in archaeology. Springer, Cham, pp 205–241. https://doi.org/10.1007/978-3-319-00008-4_9

De Hingh AE (2000) Food production and food procurement in the Bronze Age and Early Iron Age (2000-500 BC). University of Leiden, Leiden

De Kleijn M, Beijaard F, Van Manen N, Crumley C, Von Hackwitz K, Kolen J, Löwenborg D (2016) D2.3 Dynamic models for analyzing long-term landscape change (HERCULES deliverable). Available from www.hercules-landscape.eu/tartalom/HERCULES_WP2_D2_3_VU.pdf. Accessed on 30 April 2018

De Kleijn M, Beijaard F, Koomen E, Van Lanen RJ (2018) Simulating past land use patterns; the impact of Romans on the Lower Rhine delta in the first century AD. In: De Kleijn M (ed) Innovating landscape research through Geographic Information Science. Implications and opportunities of the digital revolution in science for the research of the archaeology, history and heritage of the landscape from a GIScience perspective. Vrije Universiteit Amsterdam, Amsterdam, pp 125–148. Available at http://dare.ubvu.vu.nl/handle/1871/55517. Accessed on 7 June 2018

Ellis F (1993) Peasant economics. Farm households and agrarian development, 2nd edn. Cambridge University Press, Cambridge

FAO (2004) Human energy requirements. Report of a Joint FAO/WHO/UNU Expert Consultation. FAO, Rome

Galic N (2014), Horse population dynamics (Version 1.3.0). CoMSES Computational Model Library. Available from https://www.comses.net/codebases/4031/releases/1.3.0. Accessed on 2 July 2018

Gregg SA (1988) Foragers and farmers. Population interaction and agricultural expansion in prehistoric Europe. University of Chicago Press, Chicago

Groot M (2008) Animals in ritual and economy in a Roman frontier community. Excavations in Tiel-Passewaaij. Vrije Universiteit Amsterdam, Amsterdam

Groot M, Kooistra LI (2009) Land use and agrarian economy in the Roman Dutch River Area. Internet Archaeol 27. https://doi.org/10.11141/ia.27.5

Joyce J (2019) Farming along the limes. Using agent-based modelling to investigate possibilities for subsistence and surplus-based agricultural production in the Lower Rhine delta between 12 BCE and 270 CE. Vrije Universiteit Amsterdam, Amsterdam

Joyce J, Verhagen P (2016) Simulating the farm: computational modelling of cattle and sheep herd dynamics for the analysis of past animal husbandry practices. In: Multi-, inter- and transdisciplinary research in landscape archaeology. Proceedings of LAC 2014 Conference, Rome, 19–20 September 2014. Vrije Universiteit Amsterdam, Amsterdam. https://doi.org/10.5463/lac.2014.59

Kooistra LI (1996) Borderland farming. Possibilities and limitations of farming in the Roman Period and Early Middle Ages between the Rhine and Meuse. Van Gorcum, Assen

Kooistra LI, Van Dinter M, Dütting MK, Van Rijn P, Cavallo C (2013) Could the local population of the Lower Rhine delta supply the Roman army? Part 1: the archaeological and historical framework. J Archaeol Low Ctries 4(2):5–23

Lauwerier RCGM, Robeerst JMM (2001) Horses in Roman times in the Netherlands. In: Buitenhuis H, Prummel W (eds) Animals and man in the past. Essays in honour of Dr. A. T. Clason emeritus professor of archaeozoology Rijksuniversiteit Groningen, the Netherlands. ARC Publicaties, Groningen, pp 275–290

Nicolay J (2008) Armed Batavians: use and significance of weaponry and horse gear from non-military contexts in the Rhine delta (50 BC to AD 450). Amsterdam University Press, Amsterdam

Olševičová K, Procházka J, Danielisová A (2014) Reconstruction of prehistoric settlement network using agent-based model in NetLogo. In: Bajo J, Hallenborg K, Pawlewski P, Botti V, Sánchez-Pi N, Darío Duque Méndez N, Lopes F, Julian V (eds) Highlights of practical applications of agents, multi-agent systems and sustainability. Springer, Cham, pp 165–178

Saqalli M, Salavert A, Bréhard S, Bendrey R, Vigne J-D, Tresset A (2014) Revisiting and modelling the woodland farming system of the early Neolithic Linear Pottery Culture (LBK) 5600–4900 B.C. Veg Hist Archaeobotany 23(1):37–50. https://doi.org/10.1007/s00334-014-0436-4

Shackleton, C, Prins FE (1992) Charcoal analysis and the "Principle of Least Effort"- a conceptual model. Journal of archaeological science, 19 (6): 631–637

Shaw, JD (2008) Driftwood as a resource: modeling fuelwood acquisition strategies in the mid- to late Holocene Gulf of Alaska. University of Washington, Seattle

Van Dijk J, Groot M (2013) The Late Iron Age-Roman transformation from subsistence to surplus production in animal husbandry in the Central and Western parts of the Netherlands. In: Groot M, Lentjes D, Zeiler J (eds) Barely surviving or more than enough. The environmental archaeology of subsistence, specialisation and surplus food production. Sidestone Press, Leiden, pp 175–200

Van Dinter M, Kooistra LI, Dütting MK, Van Rijn P, Cavallo C (2014) Could the local population of the Lower Rhine delta supply the Roman army? Part 2: modelling the carrying capacity using archaeological, palaeo-ecological and geomorphological data. J Archaeol Low Ctries 5(1):5–50

Van Driel-Murray C (2003) Ethnic soldiers: The experience of the Lower Rhine tribes. In: Grünewald T, Seibel S (eds) Kontinuität und diskontinuität. Germania inferior am Beginn und am Ende der römischen Herrschaft. Beiträge des deutsch-niederländischen Kolloquiums in der

Katholieke Universiteit Nijmegen (27. bis 30.06.2001). Walter de Gruyter, Berlin, pp 200–217. https://doi.org/10.1515/9783110900903.200
Van Driel-Murray C (2008) Those who wait at home: the effect of recruitment on women in the Lower Rhine area. In: Brandl U (ed) Frauen und römisches Militär: Beiträge eines Runden Tisches in Xanten vom 7. bis 9. Juli 2005. BAR, Oxford, pp 82–91
Van Es WA (1981) De Romeinen in Nederland. Fibula-Van Dishoeck, Bussum
Verhagen P, Joyce J, Groenhuijzen MR (2016a) Modelling the dynamics of demography in the Dutch limes zone. In: Multi-, inter- and transdisciplinary research in landscape archaeology. Proceedings of LAC 2014 Conference, Rome, 19–20 September 2014. Vrije Universiteit Amsterdam, Amsterdam. https://doi.org/10.5463/lac.2014.62
Verhagen P, Vossen I, Groenhuijzen MR, Joyce J (2016b) Now you see them now you don't: defining and using a flexible chronology of sites for spatial analysis of Roman settlement in the Dutch river area. J Archaeol Sci Rep 10:309–321. https://doi.org/10.1016/j.jasrep.2016.10.006
Vossen I (2003) The possibilities and limitations of demographic calculations in the Batavian area, In: Grünewald T, Seibel S (eds) Kontinuität und diskontinuität. Germania inferior am Beginn und am Ende der römischen Herrschaft. Beiträge des deutsch-niederländischen Kolloquiums in der Katholieke Universiteit Nijmegen (27. bis 30.06.2001) Walter de Gruyter, Berlin, pp 414–435. doi:https://doi.org/10.1515/9783110900903.414
Vossen I, Groot M (2009) Barley and horses: surplus and demand in the Civitas Batavorum. In: Driessen M, Heeren S, Hendriks J, Kemmers F, Visser RM (eds) TRAC 2008. Proceedings of the eighteenth annual theoretical Roman archaeology conference Amsterdam 2008. Oxbow Books, Oxford, pp 85–100. https://doi.org/10.16995/TRAC2008_85_100
Whittaker CR (2004) Rome and its frontiers. Routledge, London. https://doi.org/10.4324/9780203476314
Wilensky U (1999) NetLogo (and NetLogo user manual). Northwestern University, Evanston
Willems WJH (1986) Romans and Batavians. A Regional Study in the Dutch Eastern River Area. University of Amsterdam, Amsterdam
Woods R (2007) Ancient and early modern mortality: experience and understanding. Econ Hist Rev 60:373–399. https://doi.org/10.1111/j.1468-0289.2006.00367.x

Chapter 8
The Economy of Laetanian Wine: A Conceptual Framework to Analyse an Intensive/Specialized Winegrowing Production System and Trade (First Century BC to Third Century AD)

Antoni Martín i Oliveras and Víctor Revilla Calvo

Abstract The Roman economy has been defined as an agrarian regime, where wheat was mainly cultivated combined with livestock farming and intensive cash crops such as wine and olive oil. Possibilities for economic growth in a winegrowing area such as the Laetanian region in *Hispania Citerior* depended upon changes in agrarian productivity but were subject to agro-ecological and agroeconomic endowments that could affect the settlement patterns, the fluctuations in population, the forms of production related to the vineyard crop capacities, the spread of new techniques of cultivation and processing and the adoption of new technological advances. The combination of these factors explains how comparative advantages arose from other winegrowing territories, achieved through intensification and specialization processes that generated an increase of winemaking production surplus capable of being traded in different overseas markets.

Keywords Ancient viticulture · Laetanian Roman wine · Conceptual framework · Economic models · Intensive/specialised winegrowing production processes

8.1 Introduction

> Hispaniarum Laeetana copia nobilitantur, elegantia vero Tarraconensia atque Lauronensia et Baliarica ex insulis conferuntur Italiae primis.[1] – Gaius Plinius Secundus, Naturalis Historia XIV, 71

[1] "Among the Hispanian (wines), the Laietanian (wine) is famous for its large productivity; beside the Tarraconensian (wine), the Lauronensian (wine) and the Balearian (wine) from the islands, (these ones) gather a certain elegance comparable to the best Italian (wines)" (authors'

A. Martín i Oliveras (✉) · V. R. Calvo
Universitat de Barcelona/CEIPAC-Centre for the Study of Provincial Interdependence in Classical Antiquity, Barcelona, Spain
e-mail: amartinioliveras@ub.edu; vrevillac@ub.edu

P. Verhagen et al. (eds.), *Finding the Limits of the Limes*, Computational Social Sciences, https://doi.org/10.1007/978-3-030-04576-0_8

Ancient Roman viticulture has multiple fields of knowledge and expertise with enormous possibilities for research. Most studies dedicated to the development of viticulture in Hispania during Antiquity have in common the use of archaeological information and written sources as a complementary support to confirm the absolute chronology of a settlement, a socioeconomic phenomenon or an exact location of a winegrowing production or a pottery activity in a specific territory (Revilla 1995).

This research builds on previous work in which the theoretical and epistemological framework of study was established of the different variables, factors and endogenous and exogenous agents involved in every stage of the production, distribution, trade and consumption of wine in the ancient Laetanian region between the first century BC and third century AD (Martín i Oliveras 2015b). The intensive viticulture practised during the Roman period in this area situated in the centre of Catalan Coastal Depression was a widespread phenomenon with huge economic implications on the organization of this territory and the local communities.

The main aim of this study is to establish a specific conceptual framework where this phenomenon was developed, selecting the economic models susceptible to be applied and identifying the necessary variables, parameters and constraining factors to take into account to analyse its socioeconomic structure and evolution over the time. This first approach intends to evaluate the relations that could be generated between the development of viticulture and a set of complementary activities between the end of the Republic and the Early Roman Empire in this winegrowing area. In particular, it seeks to explore the impact of certain organizational forms, articulated by rational strategies, large investments in technology, resources and economic intensification processes, which involve labour needs and a precise organization of the global structure of settlement. This impact can be assessed from factors such as rural and urban habitat distribution and density, the calculation of labour needs also in agriculture and handicrafts, both fixed and variable, and its influence on living standards. These factors may be related to others more difficult to evaluate, such as the possible population growth, population mobility or the possibilities of enrichment and social promotion of certain groups related to the wine's economy such as the freedmen (Scheidel 2004).

Further specialized studies must be focused on specific geospatial and geoeconomic analysis, which supposes the identification of the settlement patterns, the organization of the rural habitat, the forms of production and management related to the crop capacities to obtain optimal yields for generating surpluses in a context of a growing population. The utilization of quantitative methods such as mathematics, statistics and linear programming models will allow us to interpret and make predictions, regressions and reconstructions of the evolution of the Laetanian wine economy, understood as a situation that includes all the aspects needed to produce wines of various qualities along with a group of complementary activities related to the production, elaboration, distribution, trade and consumption.

---

translation).

Thus, this chapter only attempts to make a first theoretical approach to this specific conceptual framework and its influence on the configuration of this ancient winegrowing socioeconomic system, analysing the possibilities of implementation with a scanty available dataset where estimations will play a decisive role.[2]

8.2 The Territorial Scope

The Laetanian region is an ill-defined area in historical terms, organized around some urban centres as, *Blanda* or *Blandae*, the *municipia* of *Iluro*, *Baetulo* and the colonia of *Barcino* on the coast and, among others, the Flavian *municipium* of *Egara*, the secondary settlement of *Arrago* and the thermal station and possible Augustan or Flavian *municipium* of *Aquae Calidae* (Caldes de Montbui) inland. The extension and limits of these cities' territories have not been precisely defined with the exception of the *ager Barcinonensis*, the constitution and legal status of which must have had an effect on the urban centres that were there before (Palet 1997; Palet et al. 2009, 2011, 2012). Otherwise, the process of urbanization and legal promotion of the interior territories seems to assume particular forms, with the constitution of *civitas sine urbe*, and culminates in the Flavian era. This evolution has been related to the development of new patterns of exploitation and agricultural occupation (Oller 2015).

The Laetanian territory also comprised the extensive plain situated between the *Baetulo* River (Besós) and the mouth of *Rubricatum* River (Llobregat), located on the southwest side of the Montjuïc promontory. The first foothills of the Garraf Massif would have risen from this point. Away from the coast, the colony's *ager* would have included the lower course of the Llobregat River as far as *Ad fines* (Martorell) and the lower course of the Besós River to where it joined the Ripoll River and the Congost-Mogent basin, spreading across the great Vallès plain as far as the Catalan Pre-Coastal Range. Attending the special features of the *Laeetana regio*, as regards its particular geospatial configuration, geoeconomic characteristics and historical evolution over time, we distinguish the following four specific research areas of study:

- Study Area 1: Barcelona Hinterland Plain – *Ager Barcinonensis* (Fig. 8.1)
- Study Area 2: Central Coast – *Territoria* of *Baetulo*, *Iluro* and *Blandae*
- Study Area 3: Lower Llobregat – *Rubricatum* estuary
- Study Area 4: Vallesian Plain – *Territoria* of *Arraona, Egara* and *Aquae Calidae.*

[2] Estimations are subject of debate among some scholars but have been accepted by most economic historians due to the scarcity of the archaeological data and the absence of more reliable information (De Sena 2005, 2, note 7).

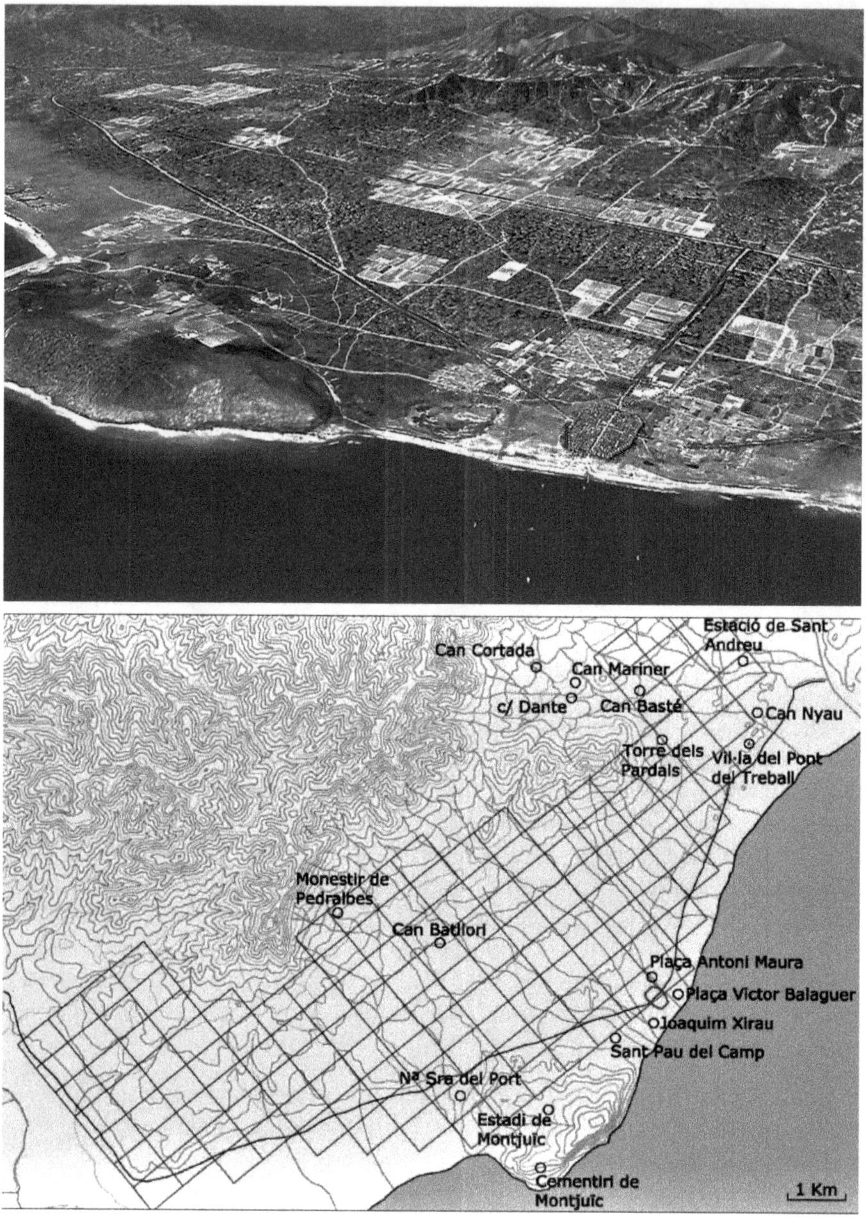

Fig. 8.1 (**a**) General view of Study Area 1: *Barcino* Roman colony hinterland plain in the third century CE – from *Barcino3D* (https://bit.ly/2Kpo4J8); (**b**) *Ager Barcinonensis centuriatio* proposal and main Roman *villae* attested from Palet et al. (2012)

8.3 Working Hypothesis

The amphoric studies carried out in recent decades and the suggestions put forward regarding how to interpret them make it possible to propose an evolutionary sequence of viticulture in this territory during the Roman period from both the perspective of production and trade.

We start with the premise that there are five main chronocultural phases of development, which we consider to correspond to the configuration of different agricultural and artisan production systems (Miró 1988; Martín i Oliveras 2015b; Martín i Oliveras et al. 2017):

- *Phase 1. Origins (1/3 2nd c. BC – ½ 1st c. BC):* First productions of *Citerior* amphoric containers imitating forms as Greco-Italic, Dressel 1A, 1B and 1C.
- *Phase 2. Expansion (½ 1st c. BC – middle decades of 1st c.* AD): The appearance of the first widely manufactured amphorae forms: *Tarraconense 1/Laietana 1* and *Pascual 1*, the latter being the first *Tarraconense amphora* intended for large scale trade. Appearance of first imitations of the Dressel 2–3 italic form.
- *Phase 3. Reorientation (middle decades of 1st c. AD – end of 1st c. AD):* Characterized by large-scale production of Dressel 2–3 *Tarraconense amphorae* form and maybe in *dolia* (big pottery jars) for the massive export of wine, both individually packaged and in bulk, mainly destined for the Italic Peninsula and the city of Rome itself.
- *Phase 4. Peak (early 2nd c. AD – mid 3rd c. AD):* Period when the production structures were transformed, probably connected to the transport of wine in bulk in other types of containers such as *cupae* (wooden barrels) for export and *culleii* (wineskins) for regional trade, possibly as a consequence of having to reduce costs when supplying heavily-used, strongly competitive markets.
- *Phase 5. Decline (½ 3rd c. AD-early 5th c. AD):* Crisis and the end of viticulture for export. The phenomenon could be due to the appearance of new producers with much lower costs, which would imply a change in market orientation. The viticultural centres were restructured for supplying only the internal demand for wine and carry out other agrarian activities or were gradually abandoned.

8.4 Operative Hypothesis

The intensive viticulture practised during the Roman period in the ancient Laetanian region was a widespread phenomenon with huge socioeconomic implications between the first century BCE and third century CE. Outstanding questions and key structural features suggest important conjunctural changes in the land use increase, the crop regimes, the landowner-tenancy relationships, the population fluctuations, the balance between production and consumption, the investment needs, the implantation of the "*villa* system" and its evolution as a cash-crop market-oriented surplus production and the prevalence of wine pressing and pottery facilities. This phenomenon can be only explained by an intensification process and the application of an *agency-oriented winegrowing specialization production* system related to a profit mentality that exploited a comparative advantage arose in productivity, a pulled force of product demand and the accessibility of larger distributed markets resulting from the reduction of production and transaction costs (Van Minnen 1998; Badía-Miró and Tello 2013).

8.5 Conceptual Framework

Every agrarian activity is determined by environmental conditions composed by multiple variables, factors, endogenous and exogenous agents involved in every stage of the production, distribution, trade and consumption of a good or product. The ancient viticulture production process and trade was not an exception. Our conceptual framework (Fig. 8.2) analyses the relationships among the agroecological and agroeconomic endowments such as paleoclimatic conditions, physical environment, landscape typology, settlement patterns, land use, optimal yields, tax control and other geographical, demographic, economic (price policies and markets), technological (new methods and mechanization), institutional (taxes and fiscality) and sociocultural (tradition and religion) driving forces that could influence and model the evolution of this complex system over time.

8.6 Agroecological and Agro-economic Endowments

Agroecological endowments are the combination of constraints that conditioned vineyard crops and the winegrowing production systems under which they are grown. It includes the resilience strategies harnessing ecosystem functions to the

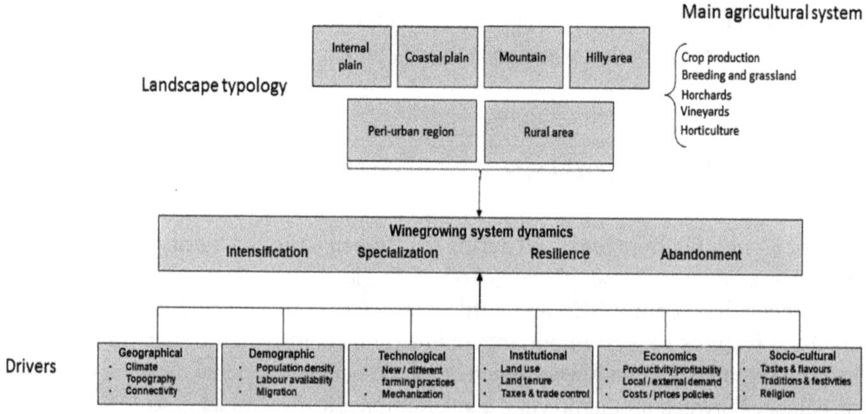

Fig. 8.2 Conceptual framework for land and farming system dynamics. Relationships among driving variables, processes and ecosystem properties. (Based on Debolini et al. 2016, Fig. 2)

maximum possible extent, to improve the existing land-use situation and winemaking facilities, either through increasing or diminishing the means of production in order to sustainably reconcile social, economic and environmental challenges.

Agro-economic endowments are the combination of constraints that conditioned productivity performance in a territorial or farming plot scale. It supposes the analysis of the economic factors which shaped the winemaking production function on a supply chain. It also means giving economic values to the initial investment for starting the activity and for all the factors of production needed (land, labour, capital, technology, processes etc.), to determine the profitability of winegrowing production and trade.

8.6.1 Palaeoclimatic Conditions

Specific macroclimate data as experienced by different regions of the Western Roman Empire and robustly documented by different independent palaeoclimatic proxy data sets testify a favourable and exceptionally stable climatic situation from 100 BC to 200 AD with a prolonged period of warming and wet conditions that favoured the rise of agrarian production yields. It is known as The Roman Warm Period or Roman Climate Optimum (McCormick et al. 2012). All agricultural activity is dependent upon and interconnected to climate and weather conditions; grapes are no exception. Wine composition and optimal productivity is largely dependent on mesoclimatic conditions of a territory and microclimatic environment conditions of a small restricted space such as a vineyard or a row of vines. As such, any shift in climate and weather patterns is bound to affect grapes and the subsequent production of wine. This is important because optimal wine production occurs only within very narrow climate ranges. While studies have indicated that initial climate changes even could have been beneficial for some Roman winegrowing regions in the short run, undoubtedly excessive climate changes were disastrous in the long run.

8.6.2 Physical Environment

The physical environment comprises the space where the winegrowing activity is embedded in and also the connectivity and transport infrastructure that are necessary for the efficient operational flow of the production and trade system, such as paths, roads, rivers, streams, ports, etc. Such a physical environment appears as a major external determinant of the movement of goods by terrestrial vehicles and vessels. It thus can become decisive for the success or the shortcoming of the production and distribution system. This follows the consideration of space as a barrier for the notion and the physics of flow. The physical environment plays a more sophisticated role, since it represents the entire pressure that is exerted by space on the supply chain, positively and critically. This happens particularly in those territories that are characterized by scarcity of access such as port hinterlands, or core urban areas that are problematic for distribution or delivery of goods. The agents of production and distribution have to arrange themselves with their physical environment conditions over the time.

8.6.3 *Viticulture Supply Chain*

A supply chain is a system of resources and processes involved in produce and trade of a good or service from a supplier to a customer. The viticulture supply chain involves both the production process and trade activities from its inception to its delivery to the end customer or consumer. The *production function* is the global system that characterizes a productive activity. The factors of production constitute the *inputs* of the economic system. A specific technology specifically combines these *inputs* – raw materials, labour, machinery, tools, facilities, etc. The *outputs* are the finished products, the goods or services resulting from the productive activity (Martín i Oliveras 2015a). In any type of socioeconomic organization, the production of goods and services may be in the hands of the state or in the hands of private producers. The Roman wine production process is not alien to all these factors, conditions and microeconomic variables and has also its particular production function with its own inputs intervening in the different stages of the productive chain.

8.6.4 *Yield Quantification*

Its calculation is fundamental for the study of agricultural production processes, so we will try to adapt it both to the vineyard crop and to the processes of transformation, production and exploitation, in the different stages of the viticulture supply chain (Amouretti and Brun 1993). The analysis of viticultural activities can be approached in several ways according to different parameters of study.

8.6.4.1 Vineyard Yields

Vineyard yields calculate both the yield of the crop itself and the yield from the harvest. To estimate the global vineyards yields we must take into account the following factors:

1. *Yield per strain*. This refers to the productive capacity of the plant, in order to obtain data on absolute yields and means of productivity of grapes from maximum to minimum. Factors related to both the configuration of the vineyard and the cultivated grape variety, the planting frame and the number of vines/hectare (*vitis/iugera*), the pruning and loading of buds, the number of hectares/*iugera*

cultivated, etc. Once the productive capacity of the plant and the variety of grapes chosen are fixed according to the geomorphological characteristics of the territory under study and the soil characteristics of the land to be cultivated, we will be able to analyse the different parameters and intervening factors, in order to obtain a whole series of values that we can compare with productivity data from the written sources themselves and statistical data of yields from modern and contemporary periods, basically from nineteenth and twentieth centuries.

2. *Harvesting yield*. Refers to grape collection prior to pressing. The data set and factors to be analysed are of different nature and origin. The most important are the spatial configuration of the vineyards, which can facilitate or hinder the manual grapes collecting of the clusters. This process is conditioned by the harvest time available, which can last from 15 to 30 days depending on the staff's picking expertise and the maturation time necessary for the cultivated grape variety.
3. *Winery yields*. This calculates the yields from the processes of treading and pressing the grapes, its transformation into must and then into wine, as the maximum productive capacity of the facilities with regard to the processing machinery and the capacity needs of the collecting, ageing, and storing structures.
4. *Productivity of the processing machinery*. Once we know the technical, mechanical and operational constraints of the Roman beam presses, we can analyse the different parameters and intervening factors that allow us to make an assessment of the productive performance of a winery installation in terms of productive capacity (Martín i Oliveras and Bayés 2009; Martín i Oliveras 2011–2012, 2012, 2015a, b). The productive capacity measures the ratio of the volume of grapes processed and the volume of must obtained, depending on the time used, counted in hours or days, taking into account the *vindemia* period related to the characteristics of the grape varieties to be processed. All these factors are connected to each other and influence in the final result, so we will have to calculate the yields in absolute values of maximum productivity in order to get an idea of the real and total capacity, both for the processing and pressing machinery as for the necessary collection and storage structures (*lacus*, *dolia*, *cupae*, etc.; Tchernia 2013). We can also compare the results with the absolute data of productivity and capacity of the installations coming from the written sources, especially from Cato (Cat. *Agri.11*) and Pliny the Elder (Plin. *N.H.XVIII, 317*), previously studied by modern scholars, with historical data from modern vintages and with data from experimental archaeology – currently we only have those from the *Mas de Tourelles* experience (Brun 2004; Tchernia & Brun 1999). Subsequently, we can extrapolate them to the extent of the vineyard fields to give us an idea of the amount of must and wine that a "typical" installation, with certain characteristics established according to the different typologies of Roman wineries documented in the area, can process, establishing models and systems of production. Their analysis can also inform us about the settlement patterns, the size of properties or *fundus* and the organization and tax control of the vine-growing and winemaking production in the former territory object of study.

Table 8.1 Behaviour of the total fixed cost (TFC), total variable cost (TVC) and total cost (TC) of each of the units produced in estimate economic calculation values

Quantities produced	Total fixed cost (TFC)	Total variable cost (TVC)	Total cost (TC)
0	2000	0	2000
1	2000	800	2800
2	2000	1360	3360
3	2000	1680	3680
4	2000	1910	3910
5	2000	2150	4150
6	2000	2550	4550
7	2000	3210	5210
…	…	…	…
22	2000	9610	11,610

8.6.4.2 Cost Quantification

The production of a particular good or service involves the use of a number of factors that have a quantifiable economic value, the *costs*. The cost structure of an economic activity is considered as a diagram of consecutive allocation of *direct costs* (raw materials, labour power and energy) and *indirect costs* (maintenance costs of tools, infrastructure and facilities and administrative, commercial and financial expenses) (Maza and González 1992). The calculation of production costs of a good or service is complex since it is necessary to take into account all the costs structure and the proportional part of the capital investment.

In order to calculate the productive and commercial costs of a wine *amphora*, the first thing we have to do is to try to obtain a scale of ancient real prices situated in the chronological context that we want to study. That allows us to make a calculation, as close as possible, to the real productive costs in a fixed-value Roman monetary unit, such as the *sestertius* (HS; Duncan-Jones 1974).[3] However, in order to understand the general theoretical framework of costs, we will randomly develop an example of production or service provision X, which can show us the behaviour of the variable costs and total costs of each one good or service produced in units, tens, hundreds or thousands values (Table 8.1; Jones 2014).[4]

The average cost per unit: The *average cost* (AC) is the total cost (TC) divided by the *quantity* (Q) of the units produced. Although the total costs are very important, the average costs per unit are even more important for the short-term analysis

[3] Quantitative studies have been developed related to the calculation of costs and yields of productive activities and price scales of goods and services in different places of the Roman Empire and chronological periods (Temin 2014, 2017). See also data sets from the written sources and other preserved documentation: *Mensa Ponderaria* and prices lists of Pompeii (first century AD), Edict of Maximum Prices of Diocletian (301 AD), etc.

[4] The units of value employed in this theoretical example are imaginary and only have a quantitative numeral value expressed in units, tens, hundreds or thousands of units to facilitate economic calculation.

of the production centre (exploitation), since by comparing them with the price of the product or with the average income, we will know when a profit is made. The average costs per unit are essential for the evaluation of inventories in matters related to the "design" of the product. These concepts also play an important role in the introduction of a new product in the market. In modern microeconomics, the decisions to buy or not to buy a product and the decision of reject or accept a new production line depend on the available information on the *average cost per unit*. Other short-term unit costs are usually calculated to complement the decisions, such as:

- *Average fixed cost* (AFC) = *fixed cost* (FC)/*quantity* (Q) of units produced
- *Average variable cost* (AVC) = variable cost (VC)/*quantity* (Q) of units prod
- *Marginal cost* (MC) = cost of each additional unit, defined as the change that affects the *total cost* (TC), when one more unit is produced:

$$\mathrm{MC} = \frac{\mathrm{Change\,in\,TC}}{\mathrm{Change\,in\,Q}}$$

where:

Change in TC = TC2 – TC1
Change in Q = Q2 – Q1

It is calculated by subtracting from the total cost (column 4 in Table 8.1) of row unit, n, the total cost of row unit, n – 1; it can also be obtained from the variable cost in column 3, because variable costs increase in exactly the same way.

The *average cost* (AC) and the *marginal cost* (MC) are known as short-term costs, because these act during the period of decision-making, in which some costs are fixed and others are variables. In this example, if the cost of producing 5 units is 20,750 units (where 48.2% are fixed costs and the remaining 51.8% are variable costs), and the *Average Cost* (AC) of production is 4150. If the centre produces one additional unit (6 units), the *average costs* (AC) are reduced to 3790, and by producing 7 units the *average cost* (AC) continues to decline but when there are 8 again begins to increase due to the *law of diminishing returns* and due to the increasing number of units for a fixed capital investment. These results are shown in the *marginal cost* (MC) column 5, in which it is observed as this one decreases to the fourth unit and from here again begins to increase (Table 8.2).

The marginal cost must always be lower than the average cost, but the more units are produced, this will be closer to the average cost, and to justify the production of more units when the marginal cost is above the medium cost, the selling price should be equal to the marginal cost of the last unit produced, so that the activity does not incur in losses when producing this last unit. Table 8.2 shows that the progression of unitary costs is not constant; this is initially decreasing, and then goes to constant progression, to then increases again, generating three moments.

The combination of available fixed resources with small amounts of variable resources will not achieve the full potential efficiency of the exploitation, which

Table 8.2 Behaviour of average fixed costs (AFC), average variable cost (AVC), average total cost (ACT) and marginal cost (MC) of each of the units produced in estimate economic calculation values (in thousands)

Quantities produced	Average fixed cost (TFC/Q)	Average variable cost (TVC/Q)	Average total cost (TC/Q)	Marginal cost (MC)
0	–	–	–	–
1	10.00	4.00	14.00	4.00
2	5.00	3.40	8.40	2.80
3	3.33	2.80	6.13	1.60
4	2.50	2.39	4.89	1.15
5	2.00	2.15	4.15	1.20
6	1.67	2.12	3.79	2.00
7	1.43	2.29	3.72	3.30
8	1.25	2.57	3.82	4.50
9	1.11	2.92	4.03	5.75
10	1.00	3.40	4.40	7.75

supposes high unitary costs for the first products. As the scale of units produced increases, the proportions of the combination of fixed resources with variable resources allows better overall returns, reducing these costs in proportion to the units produced. Production continues to rise until the fixed resources do no longer support the production of additional units under equal conditions so that they will be processed at higher proportions cost.

See the following graphs, which represent, on the one hand, the behaviour of the *total fixed cost* (TFC), the *total variable cost* (TVC) and the *total cost* (TC) (Fig. 8.3I) and, on the other hand, the behaviour of the *average variable cost* (AVC = TVC/Q) and the *marginal cost* (MC) (Fig. 8.3L).

The *total fixed costs* (TFC) are by definition equal and independent of the level of production, and the *average fixed cost* (AFC = TFC/Q) decreases as production increases and is represented by a continuously lowering curve. When the production increases by adding variable resources, because the *total variable cost* (TVC/Q) reflects the *law of diminishing returns*, we can first obtain increasing returns, but in the end it would yield diminishing returns; then the *average variable cost* (TVC /Q) decreases at the beginning, and it reaches a minimum and returns to increase, so the graph is U-shaped. The *marginal cost* curve (MC) reaches its level lower in four units, below cost mean variable (TVC/Q) or the *average total cost* (TC/Q) and cuts the mean the *total variable cost* curves (TVC/ Q) and the *average total cost* (TC/Q), respectively, low points, because while the cost (MC) is below the *average total cost* (TC/Q), the average presses down, and when it is above, the average presses upwards (Fig. 8.3K).

The long-term production costs: As a result of a successful operation, a winery can modify its installed production capacity to expand it, or in case of different results expected, in the long run it could also reduce their size. Either decision seeks to obtain the lowest *average total cost* (ATC) of possible production. The reduction

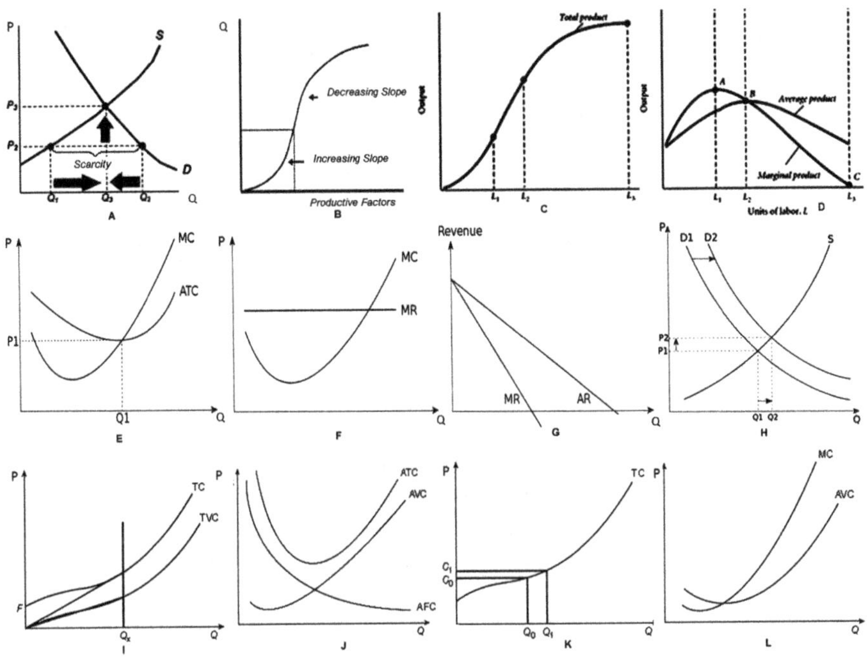

Fig. 8.3 (**A**) Principle of economic scarcity; (**B**) production function curve; (**C**) and (**D**) comparative charts of law of diminishing returns. (After Maza and González 1992); (**E**) economic efficiency graph; (**F**) curves of marginal cost (MC), in relation to marginal revenue (MR) in situation of perfect competition; (**G**) marginal revenue (MR) curve with respect to average revenue (AR) (**H**) supply (S) and demand (D) curves; (**I**) cost curves: total cost (TC) and total variable cost (TVC); (**J**) average total cost (ATC), average variable cost (AVC) and average fixed cost (AFC) curves; (**K**) the marginal cost concept; (**L**) marginal cost (MC) and average variable cost curves. (After Jones 2014)

in the price of resources and technological progress displace cost curves down. Similarly, the increase in the price of resources shifts it up (Fig. 8.3J; Vilcalpoma 1995; Jones 2014).

8.6.4.3 Economies of Scale

The decision to expand the winery seeks to achieve economies of scale or serial production. When the size of the centre increases, factors such as specialization of labour, better utilization of staff, efficient use of capital and technical resources, the allocation of indirect costs and other costs arising from the expansion of the producing centre in a number of units, contributes to reduce the unit costs for the producer, who can expand its scale of operation. It is, therefore, the set of circumstances that allow reducing the average cost of production as the total product increases. They are also defined as gains in production and the costs resulting from the increase in the size of the producing centre, which implies an improvement in the buying prices of the inputs or factors of production and a most efficient use of them. The improvements in economies of scale can be internal, due to the indivisibility of the factors of production, or external, due to the expansion of the producing centre as a whole. Economies of scale stimulate mass production and are achieved rapidly when the size of the producing centre increases, which means that the decreasing returns only appear when the scale of production is very high, the total average cost decreases over a wide interval of production. This can lead to the development of monopolies and oligopolies of producers and investors, due to the large initial investments required and the difficulty of obtaining minimum short-term yields and costs, in order to protect themselves against new competitors. For example, when an *amphora* of noble wine is produced, high fixed costs must be faced to buy the land, plant the vines, build the *torcularium*, the *cella vinaria* and other facilities, but when this entire infrastructure is already operating at full capacity, the cost of filling an *amphora* of wine is more or less the same. Thus, if these infrastructure costs hypothetically 20,000 units of investment and the production of each wine amphora costs hypothetically 500 units, the "real" unitary cost is 5 units producing 100 wine *amphorae*, 2.5 units for 200 wine *amphorae* and 1 unit for 500 wine *amphorae*.

8.7 Demographic Dynamics, Workforce Availability and Labour Division

Demographic studies of ancient societies have increased over the last years, trying to recognize the internal organization of the population's evolution and to identify possible settlement patterns related to resources management, urban development and agrarian exploitation of the territory. These studies allow us to revise basic concepts such as the relationship between the urban and rural world, as regards the urbanism development related to the implementation of an intensive agrarian production system and the different administrative status, sizes and ranges of ancient Roman cities (Morley 1996; for Hispania: Carreras 1996, 2014).

Quantitative and qualitative analyses of territories have been favoured by a better knowledge of the urban perimeters and the settlement patterns of rural distribution; either from the contribution of urban archaeology, field-surveys, and cadastral studies (Lo Cascio 1994, 1999; Scheidel 2002, 2007a, b; Fentress 2009; Launaro 2011). Therefore, the most important interrelations to take into account for the analysis of demographic inference and population dynamics is the total size of the population, its distribution – urban or rural – and its internal configuration trends, such as gender, age, social status, etc., for every chronological period in the study area. This serves to calculate, on one hand, the needs of foodstuffs in terms of maintenance and self-consumption and, on the other hand, the workforce availability necessary to make the different activities that allows the wine intensive system of production, distribution and trade works. In this same sense, some scholars attempted to convert

Table 8.3 Typology of rural Roman settlements and estimation of inhabitants according to Carreras (2014), after Perkins (1999)

Type	Size	Inhabitants
Large *vicus*	800 m^2	80 persons
Large *villa*	500 m^2	50 persons
Small *vicus*	400 m^2	40 persons
Small *villa*	300 m^2	30 persons
Large farm	100 m^2	10 persons
Small farm	60 m^2	5 persons

the results obtained from archaeological excavations and field-surveys into demographic data (Witcher 2005, 2008, 2011). Thus, some analyses achieve to develop ranges of estimated inhabitants by settlement typologies, despite important methodological problems, such as the nature of the samples and the partial data obtained, due to the fact that not the entire territory can be excavated or prospected properly and not all domestic or habitational spaces have been preserved (Table 8.3).

Others studies try to quantify the food supplies necessary to cover the basic diet of resident population in urban and rural settlements with regard to the main crops and other derivate products – wheat, vegetables, wine and olive oil – as well as animal husbandry, to transform them in estimates of units of land necessary to produce it (Garnsey 1979, 1983; Tchernia 1986; Amouretti 1986).

The Roman agronomists such as Cato (Agr.1-11), Varro (R.R 1.4-1.11), and Columella (R.R. 3.3.8-9) also inform us about some environmental aspects, labour requirements and facilities to consider for managing an agricultural holding. These can all help us to calculate the minimal unit of land necessary for self-sufficient maintenance[5]:

1 worker = 7 *iugera* (iug) vineyard
1 worker = 51 *modii* (m) wheat/1 year
1 iug × 4 m seed × 3 m wheat = 12 m/1 iug
51: 12 = 4.25 iug
6.138 iug for wheat and reposition of seed
6.138 × 3 (triennial rotation system) = 18.414 iug
18.414 + 7 = 25.414 iug/1 worker

The internal quote of wine consumption has been also an important parameter to take into account, so that the balance between intra-regional and extra-regional consumption can determine the performance of the intensive productive wine economy in our study area and the possibility to obtain surpluses for trade and benefits for increasing social position of intervenient agents such as *vilici, conductores, mercatores, negotiatores, argentari, naviculari, institores,* etc.

[5]Calculations made by Martín-Arroyo (2016), for modeling minimum needs of arable land for self-consumption labour maintenance in a standard fundus. According to Roman agronomists data, mainly Columella (R.R. 3.3.8-9).

Endogenous and exogenous factors such as economic success and wealth increment can stimulate population growth, otherwise poor harvests, wars, diseases, plagues, etc. can provoke social conflicts and economic crisis that makes the population decline. In this sense, where it concerns the Laetanian region, historical events such as the Antonine Plague (165–189 CE and the Plague of Cyprian (250–266 CE) could have caused widespread labour shortages in agriculture and important casualties in the Roman army that could make conditions change and affect the system.

Regarding workforce availability and labour division we don't dispose of datasets for the Laetanian region in these periods. It means that we should make estimations taking into account the information provided by the written sources and modern rental wage ratios from nineteenth and twentieth centuries. Another way is to develop a general scaling theoretical model to study the relationship between the population and functional diversity of settlements as an indicator of the division of labour (Hanson et al. 2017).

8.7.1 Settlement Patterns: The Archaeological Dataset

The progress in archaeological field research has shown itself to be an essential resource for defining the geography of vineyards, since the technological evidence relating to the production and storage of wine or the manufacture of *amphorae* containers can, in many cases, be located and dated with reasonable accuracy. Archaeology's contribution has also been essential for increasing our knowledge about the rural habitat, settlement patterns and how the territory was occupied and exploited (Revilla et al. 2008–2011).[6]

The establishment of viticulture in the Laetanian region is already confirmed in the final third of the second century BC supposing a progressive transformation of the settlement patterns and the forms of production (Revilla 2004b, 2010b). This development brought with it a need to manufacture specific containers for transport, in the form of imitations of the Dressel 1 and Lamboglia 2 Italic *amphorae* ("El vi a l'antiguitat" 1987, 1999; Prevosti and Martín i Oliveras 2007; López Mullor and Martín i Menéndez 2008). However, the spread of vineyards geared towards commercialization for overseas markets did not come about until the second half of the first century BC, specifically in the final third of that century. This incipient vine-growing and winemaking intensification process is confirmed by the foundation chronologies of many pottery workshops and numerous villa-type settlements and other rural centres, equipped with facilities for pressing and storing wine production (Revilla 1995, 2008). All this suggests that these were places given over to specialized, intensive work processes forming part of a production structure organized elsewhere, possibly a nearby villa. Indeed, some buildings were occupied only sea-

[6]The bibliography on rural settlement patterns in the Laetanian region is difficult to summarise.

sonally, during certain phases of the agricultural cycle (some examples in Burch et al. 2005 and Revilla 2010a).

Almost ninety agrarian establishments have been identified in Laetanian Region having traces of pressing facilities or spaces for storing liquids, mainly wine. These facilities vary greatly in importance, from modestly-built settlements with a single press to large buildings with four or more presses (Sánchez 1997; Prevosti 2005; Revilla 1998, 2010a; Martín i Oliveras 2009, 2012, 2015b; Palahí and Nolla 2010[7]; Alcubierre et al. 2015, in press[8]; Peña 2010, 2011–2012.

So, we can distinguish three different sizes:

1. *Small establishments* 400/500 m^2 with a simple spatial organization formed by one or two spaces compartmented also dedicated to winemaking production with a single press without *cella vinaria* or with limited storage capacity (5–10 *dolia*). These facilities often are integrated into small or medium size villa or urban *domus* and are different from other small buildings or huts dedicated to diverse functions (sheds, tool warehouse, etc.), equally related to the main building unit. The production seems aimed at self-consumption or for local and regional trade.
2. *Medium establishments* 1000/1200 m^2 with a wide range of buildings for agrarian activities. Most were used for producing wine and had one or two presses, a collecting *lacus* and a *cella vinaria* of between 30 and 50 *dolia*. These are the most common winegrowing facilities documented in the Laetanian region during the intensification process. The production seems aimed at interregional and interprovincial trade.
3. *Large establishments* 1500/2000 m^2 with a complex spatial organization and a basically productive function geared towards winegrowing specialization and long-distance trade. These places would contain all infrastructure needed for making and storing wine on a certain scale. There are several *calcatoria* for crushing the grapes, some pressing rooms or *torcularia* with from 4 to 6 presses, various tanks or *lacus* for collecting the must and different storing spaces set aside of between 100 and 200 *dolia* called *cellae vinariae*. Viticulture seems to remain in some of these facilities during the second to fourth centuries AD.

Artisan activities such as pottery workshops, forges and so on; have also been identified in most of these settlements. This type of viticulture geared towards exporting to overseas markets would continue, depending on the area, until the mid or late second or even the early third century AD, when agricultural establishments would see the abandonment or gradually reduction of pressing facilities between the second half of the second and the beginning of the third century AD. In the case of pottery workshops, almost fifty of them have been documented at Laetanian Region and some would disappear between the middle of the first century (Flavian period)

---

[7] Facilities with 4 bean presses were attested in Vallmora (Teià, Maresme, Barcelona), Can Pedrerol de Baix (Castellbisbal, Baix Llobregat, Barcelona) or Els Ametllers (Tossa de Mar, la Selva, Girona) Roman Villa.

[8] Facilities with 5–6 presses were attested in Pont del Treball Digne -La Sagrera- (Barcelona, Barcelonès) Roman Villa.

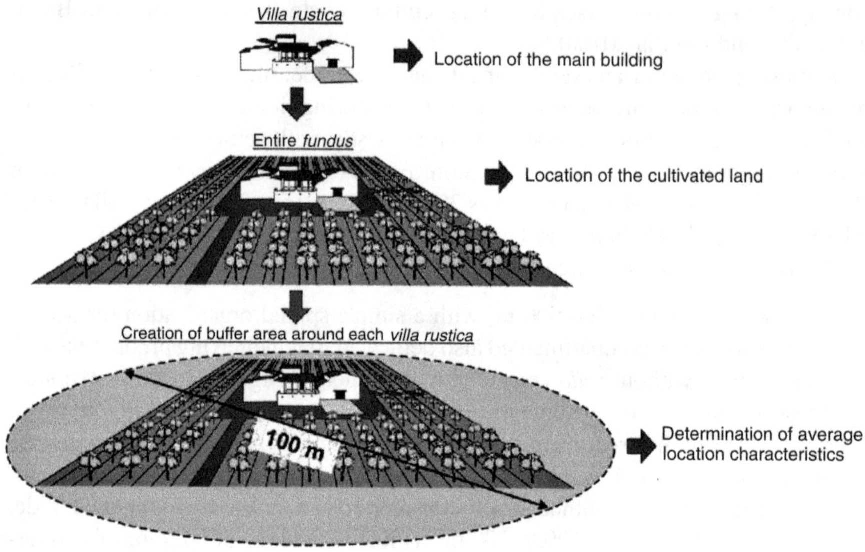

Fig. 8.4 Determination of average location characteristics of the *villae rusticae* and their surrounding cultivated land using buffer areas. (After Vogel et al. 2016, Fig. 4)

and the start of the second century AD (Antonine period), while others would convert and diversify their production. This ensured their continuity during the second and third centuries AD (Revilla 1995, 1998, 2004a, 2015; Martín i Oliveras et al. 2017; Tremoleda 2008[9]) (Fig. 8.4).

8.7.2 Land Use, Tenure and Ownership Management

Land use is the management and modification of natural environment into an anthropised landscape with the development of rural and urban settlements and other open areas such as arable fields, vineyards, pastures, grasslands and managed woods. It necessarily implies the distribution of land resources among the population developing different land ownership and tenure systems.

Land tenure is the legal regime in which land is owned by one or various individuals who hold the property. Land tenure and ownership management can be studied as ancient social traditions according to territoriality and kinship relationships.[10]

[9] Where it concerns the management of *torcularia* and *figlinae*.

[10] *Territoriality* refers to the ways in which people create and utilize landscape boundaries (both natural and constructed) to define the extent of their properties. *Kinship* refers to the web of social relationships that increases the land tenure whether by affinity (marriage) or consanguine links (inheritance).

This makes it possible to study the long-term consequences of change and development in land tenure systems and agricultural productivity.

During the Roman period the distribution of lands in conquered territories such as the Laetanian region was unequal. Some ancient properties and tenure traditions were respected among the inhabitants and ancient Iberian elites not opposed to the Romans. Notwithstanding, the Roman state's need of land for paying veteran soldiers by *deductio* implies that land tenure changed especially during the first quarter and the end of the second half of the first century BC. It coincides with the end of some war episodes such as Sertorian War (80–72 BC), Triunviral Civil Wars (49–31 BC), Cantabrian and Asturian Wars (29–19 BC) and with the foundations dates of some main cities like *Baetulo* (ca. 100 BC), *Iluro* (ca. 80–75 BC) and the *colonia* of *Barcino* (ca. 15–13 BC). The new Roman landlords were to keep the yearly income from land exploitation as stable as possible, and solving this economic constraint supposes that in the first stage they took toward managing their own farming states. However, tenancy practices were also a good way to assure a certain economic security.

The term "tenancy" refers to a type of sharecropping arrangement in which a landowner can make full use of the property he may not otherwise be able to develop properly. A "tenant" or nonlandowner will take residency on the *fundus* and work on the land in exchange for giving a percentage of the profits from the eventual vineyard crop or winegrowing yield. In this case the landowner would extend to the farmer's house-holding food and necessary items on credit to be repaid out of the tenant's share. The landowner could, if he desired, charge the tenant extremely high interest on the advanced pay since there were no lending laws applicable to migrant or tenant workers at the time. This could ultimately result in the tenant owing the landowner more money than his share of the crop at harvest and forcing the farmer to be further indentured to the landowner. This practice was used frequently by landowners after slaves were manumitted (Kehoe 1997[11]; Kloppenborg 2010[12]; Olesti 2006, 2009; Olesti and Carreras 2012, 2013[13]) (Fig. 8.5).

8.7.3 Connectivity, Transport Infrastructures and Taxation

Regional, inter-regional and extra-regional trade was a common feature of the Roman world. A mixture within state control and a free market approach ensured that consumer goods produced in one territory could be exported far and wide. Foodstuffs such as cereals and agrarian processed goods such as wine and olive oil were exported in huge quantities. The Roman Empire included regions which were completely different from one another. Notwithstanding, all of these agrarian

[11] Approaches to profit and management in Roman agriculture.

[12] Some examples of vineyard tenancy in Roman times.

[13] Concerns some cases of freedmen's social promotion and landownership's evolution in Laetanian region during the Roman period.

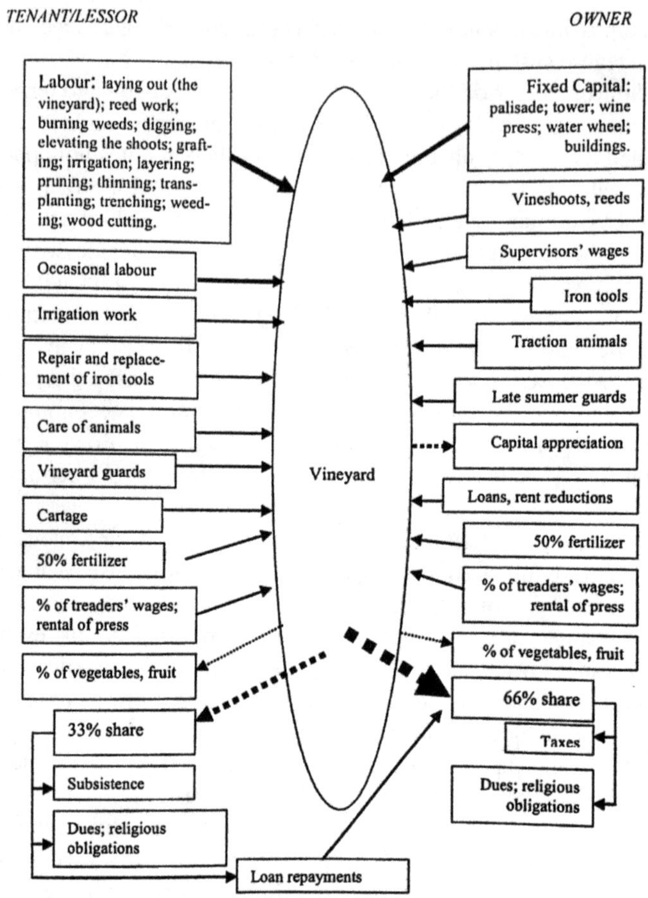

Fig. 8.5 Inputs and outputs of crop-share leased vineyard. (After Kloppenborg 2010, Fig. 6)

regions were linked through a network of trade routes (nautical and terrestrial) that supposes an important mobility of goods and people but integrated in a larger common tax structure. All the inhabitants of these regions pay taxes directly or indirectly to the Roman state. Taxes could be raised in money, earned through regional, inter-regional or extra-regional trade, or in kind, through agrarian production surpluses obtained by the exploitation of land. Public or private investments of capital were also an important factor to take into account. When the state did not spend much money on connectivity infrastructure between the internal production centres, cities and ports, the region had to finance this deficit through the revenues obtained by the internal and the external trade of goods produced and sold.

In the case of Laetanian region, winegrowing intensification/specialisation combined with other related crafts and trade activities could develop recurrent patterns and rhythms in the forms and scale of places, spaces, connectivity and mobility of goods and people over time. We will consider the structure and organisation of the physical environment, the settlement patterns, the regional structure and the transport corridors, the relationships between city and countryside and the changes in the labour market within the wider context of demographic, social, and institutional infrastructure, considering issues such as the impact of migration and slavery on the economic opportunities available to the freeborn access to training, apprenticeships, and capital. We also have to consider the potential roles of work's organisation and social relationships related such as chattel slavery, wage labour, patronage and clientelism that could have created important floating population dynamics mainly during the *vindemia* seasonal periods (Martín i Oliveras et al. forthcoming[14]).

8.8 Economic Models Applied: Agrarian Systems, Population Dynamics, Taxes and Trade Policies

Most of the recent attempts on quantification of Roman economic activities were made on the wide-scale of the Roman Empire and have adopted a *top-down* rather than a *bottom-up* approach (Scheidel and Friesen 2009; Bowman and Wilson 2013). They often pay too little attention to territorial or chronological variation in terms of change in the forms of production, to its diachronic evolution over the time and make no attempt to identify and aggregate individual, local or regional production, as well as consumption and income distribution. On the one hand, they do not take into account the minimum level of subsistence and, on the other hand, they do not calculate the maximum surplus capacity in an intensive and specialized winegrowing production situation such as the case study we have. Here we try to show, from a necessary joint perspective, different economic formal models and demographic analyses systems that could be adopted for explaining this evolution in our different study areas and scenarios of the Laetanian region.

8.8.1 The "Roman Villa" System

The "Catonian" *villa* was originally defined as an autarchic agrarian production system where its main aim was to be self-sufficient in a context of a closed economy, meaning from a theoretical point of view, that no imports are brought in and no exports are sent out. Varro and Columella both dutifully observe that agricultural production and not residential building is the main theme of an agronomical treatise, placing the agricultural activity as the productive system's reason of being, (Wallace-Hadrill 1998). Andrea Carandini went further and presented the "Roman

[14] Concerns winegrowing production and demographic dynamics in Laetanian region. Floating population dynamics are still present between some winegrowing regions of Europe and all over the world.

Villa" as a "bisectorial" model where the agrarian productivity and technological autarchy responds to a competitive strategy in a context of a global economy mainly regulated by market constrains (Carandini 1980, 1983, 1989a, b).[15] Therefore, the main goals are first to cover the own needs in terms of suitability and second to generate surpluses from their agroecosystem borders for sale and trade, in terms of profitability (Gliessman et al. 2006).[16] It supposes that every agrarian economic unit should produce the required supplies for maintenance of its own inhabitants and the population of a determined territorial scope. Most *villae* were food-production centres made up from cultivated fields, meadows and forests. Watermills, cowsheds, grain dryers, wine cellars and kilns were other typical farm facilities. Artisan activities such as pottery production and blacksmith workshops related to farming processes have been also documented. *Villae* produced wool, leather and tallow in addition to food. Hunting, fowling and fishing were also common activities and sources of food protein as well.

Slave-based *villae* existed in large numbers in Italy, but we can suppose that free peasants and tenant farmers working for v*illae* were the common workforce in other provinces. The Roman institution of slavery in the empire also provided other options and incentives. Many slaves were rewarded for their good services and there were also opportunities to earn money and buy their own freedom. A promising young slave might attend lessons of specialized studies. Thus, the *domini* could bring up secretaries, accountants, administrators, and tutors for their own use or for renting them out. By the end of the second century AD, up to 80% of the Roman population were composed by old citizens, freedmen (emancipated slaves) or by their descendants and at the end of the empire most slaves worked in domestic service rather than as labourers on the agrarian properties (Dyson 2003; Johnston 2004; Bowman and Wilson 2013).

The landscape of north-west *Hispania Citerior* shows a diversity of situations. More fields were used for pasture than for crops because of the need for cattle, sheep and forage. Local people also managed the forest intensely for wood and wild products. Villages and hamlets were denser in the countryside during the Iberian period (fifth–third centuries BC) and tribal areas probably were divided into borough parcels. Each one usually had a settlement at its centre, and sometimes they were located closer to a road, stream or waterway. The Romans enhanced this agrarian system without dramatically altering it. An appropriate water source was the primary site-location factor for a villa. Cisterns for collecting rainwater and deep wells were often build and dug to ensure enough drinking and clean water for the family, labour and livestock. Clean water was also essential for watermills and eventually baths, the Roman indicator of a fully civilized life. The *villae* were also

[15] It supposes the production of fixed assets as a precondition for to the production of exchange goods but also for trading; ultimately both situations involve a regular link with market structures.

[16] An agroecosystem is the basic unit of study in agro-ecology, and is somewhat arbitrarily defined as a spatially and functionally coherent unit of agricultural activity, and includes the living and non-living components involved in that unit as well as their interactions.

related to a broader Roman economy through a system of primary, secondary and tertiary roads. These were sometimes built or maintained by *villa* owners or tenants, especially if crossed their lands.

The establishment of intensive viticulture in the Laetanian region is related to the thorough transformations brought about by the Roman conquest. Especially interesting in this sense is the existence of early wine production in the territory close to the indigenous *oppida* of the central Catalan coast, which survived until the mid-first century BC. This situation is already confirmed in the final third of the second century BC, in connection with a global transformation of the settlement patterns and the production structures probably associated with the displacement of some Italic immigrants (Miret et al. 1991; Revilla 2004b, 2010b).

Roman viticulture spread rapidly close to the change of era and throughout the first half of the first century AD, covering new territories or exploiting more intensively those spaces that were already occupied. The first evidence are placing in the north coastal area situated between the *Baetulo flumen* (Besós River) and the *Arnum flumen* (Tordera River), where the *villa* system had been strongly established since the Augustan period, organized around two *municipia*, *Baetulo* and *Iluro*, and the small *oppidum* of *Blanda* or *Blandae*. These rivers and other minor streams connected the coastal settlements with the inland territory, ensuring access to other agricultural spaces and their resources. It also affected the plain area situated between the *Rubricatum* (Llobregat River) and *Baetulo* (Besós River), where the *deductio* of the colony of *Barcino* supposes an important territorial reorganization. During the first century AD, increasing economic interests of important *gentes* from the colony would consolidate their presence in this whole area. This explains the socioeconomic development of *Barcino* over the first and second centuries AD (Rodà et al. 2005). This specific distribution responds to different ways of exploiting the territory, characterized by a particular architecture defined by a differentiated spatial planning. In general, the technology for winemaking, including several presses along with one or more tanks for collecting the must, is found in buildings close to the residential sector. But they could also be a little further away. Some *villae* had the agricultural and artisan sectors set apart from the residential area. In some places, however, there is evidence of the simultaneous storage of a cereal production, either for personal use or for trading (Revilla 2011–2012). Some of these establishments had also a pottery workshop where *amphorae* and other ceramic products were made. So far over 90 *figlinae* have been identified in the NE of *Citerior*'s province and almost 50 of them are located in the Laetanian region (for *figlinae* see Tremoleda 2008, 116, Fig. 2 and Martín i Oliveras et al. 2017, 221, map 1; for *torcularia* see Revilla et al. 2008–2011, 88, Fig. 2 and Martín i Oliveras et al. 2017, 222, map 2). These features suggests that these were places given over to intensive and specialized work processes forming part of a production structure organized from elsewhere, possibly a nearby *villa*. Indeed, some buildings were occupied only seasonally during certain phases of the agricultural cycle (Burch et al. 2005; Revilla 2010a).[17]

[17] With some examples of secondary winemaking productive settlements.

The Roman *villae* documented in Laetanian region were often settlements with a former occupation in an already intensely farmed landscape. These settlements took the form of large investments and technological improvements enhancing the economic structure which included the transport of raw materials and the transformed goods to distant and large markets. The primary early-Roman modifications were technical and technological improvements, which often meant an intensification of agrarian production and its orientation towards a proto-market economy. One of the major technological innovations was a bigger plough, which could break up the heavier soil. This new plough cut deeper into the soil, and the peasant could regulate its depth. It was usually pulled by two to eight oxen. Other techno-functional innovations on cultivation, tools and machinery for transforming processes were applied in different intensive cash-crops as winegrowing production activities (Martín i Oliveras 2012, 2015a, b). The results of these innovations were the spread of vineyards, the emergence of large estates with great winemaking facilities, population growth and wealth increase with the large-scale surplus of food produced and trade.

8.8.2 Boserup's Model of Population Growth and Agricultural Intensification

Archaeological conceptions of agricultural productive intensification during the Roman period related to the abandonment of subsistence model, the rise of an intensive agrarian production, the spread of large-scale trade, the population's growth and the development of social complexity in an open economy context are still an unresolved debate, and there are different explanations for it.

Boserup's model claims that intensification of production refers to an increase in the productive output per unit of land or labour (Boserup 1965). This increase may be achieved in a number of different ways. The variables that held constants are: land, in reference to capacity of food production on a given area by agriculture, hunting, fishing or gathering; labour, in reference to workforce needed for increasing efficiency in yields, craft production and so on; and the capital, necessary for investments and maintenance of transforming facilities and technology (tools and machinery). Alternate temporal parameters as compulsory fallow for grain crops or growing and mature periods for viticulture, are also important factors to take into account in the economic strategies adopted for obtain an optimal amount of productive diversity or specialized intensive production. Boserup's model also defines population pressure as a pushing force driving intensification of agricultural production and, at the same time, as a resilience factor for balancing the change in land, in order to guarantee its sustainability.

On the contrary, the Malthusian proposal defends an agroecosystem collapse (Malthus 1798). Thus, while Malthus saw land and particularly the availability of arable soils as limiting factors in terms of frequency of cropping for the increase in production that eventually would be outstripped by a decontrolled growing population, Boserup turned the double production-population pair around the land and labour use along an adaptable extensive-intensive continuum (Rubin 1972). Other variables such as the technical or technological advantage in cultivation systems, the diversity of crops such as productive strategies, the importance of mobility and the access to resources can contribute to sustain a growing density of population by the intensification of production (Morrison 1994).

The notion of population pressure is also associated with agroecosystem carrying capacity. The calculation of carrying capacity requires the specification of two main concepts related to environmental potential and agro-economic pattern (Dewar 1984). Then, agricultural productive intensity is not only a simple consequence of human-land ratios. Decisions taken by producers to intensify or extensify crops to face contingent conditions or negative factors such as bad harvests by adverse climatology; non-availability of labour due to wars, plagues or diseases; increase of land rents by increase in taxes and prices; fluctuations of internal or external demand, increase or decrease in costs or sales prices; and so on respond rather economic strategies than changes in population size. It does not mean that demographic factors are not important, but they may be affected by other proximate factors and constitute only one aspect of human productive organization. Human populations possess not only size but also structure, so that population size and growth rates will be determined by age-specific fertility and mortality rates. In age-structured populations the distributions of various age groups and the nature of the domestic cycle impinge directly on the organization of labour. Other factors as the social condition either as free citizen, freedman or slave, the administrative situation and relationships between owner and tenant, master and servant, patron and client, will be determinant for an overall analysis of the population dynamics and the social relationships. Thus, from a socioeconomic point of view, these dynamics and relationships must be considered an aspect of the organization of labour and consumption. Often intensification or specialization practices were applied to only a part of the total productive system, specifically to the part obtaining high revenue, having an ideological or ritual significance (e.g. wine as a sacred, prestige or consumption good), or were used in large-scale social or political loans as the *annona* system for supply grain, meat, wine and olive oil to the Roman army and the inhabitants of Rome (Pavis d'Escurac 1976; Remesal 1990; Sirks 1991), although wine apparently seems was not included in the *annona* until the reign of Aurelian (270–275 CE; Conison 2012).

8.8.3 The Agency-Oriented Winegrowing Specialization Production Model

The agency-oriented model adopted for explaining the spread of vineyard cultivation and vine-growing specialization system in the Laetanian region during the Roman period (first century BC to third century AD), is an applied version of the

Heckscher-Ohlin-Samuelson economic model (Heckscher 1919; Ohlin 1967; Samuelson 1948, 1953–1954). This model combines the theoretical insights of the Adam Smith's principle of absolute advantage (Smith 1776), that refers to the ability of a party or territory to produce a greater or most efficient quantity of a good, product, or service than competitors, using the same amount of resources; with the 'Ricardian' principle of comparative advantage (Ricardo 1817), that considered what goods and services a party or territory should produce, and suggested what they should specialise by allocating their scarce resources to produce goods and services for which they have a comparative cost advantage.[18] Thus, there are two types of cost advantage, absolute and comparative. Absolute advantage means being more productive or cost-efficient than another territory whereas comparative advantage relates to how much productive or cost efficient one is than another. All of these are in a context of a "Boserupian" pushing force of increasing population densities that triggered more intensive land use and a "Smithian" market pulling force exerted by an overseas demand for wine which induced the reallocation of land and labour towards vine-growing specialization and more capital investment in larger wine-making production centres. According to it, vine-growing specialization would have developed in the territories with more favourable factor endowments to meet the increasing demand for wine. Thus, vines tended to spread where land and labour endowments were more suitable. However, there are a set of driving forces to be considered. Some of them can be regarded as naturally given, such as agro-climatic conditions. Others depended on human agency, like migrations that changed population densities or the readiness of many landless peasants to invest their labour force in own tenancy. This could be an important factor to explain the evolution in the productive forms and in the land use changes.

This agency-oriented model of land-use change combines what environmental historians and geographers call first-nature and second-nature variables. While agro-climatic endowments are first-nature factors, the dynamic interaction between the other variables becomes a set of second-nature drivers including time-distances to the nearest seaport (network analysis), that is taken as a proxy for the market-pulling force (Badía-Miró and Tello 2014; De Soto 2010).

What eventually really matters is the combination between them. Except for the demand, all variables had to move along a specific range of values, higher than a minimum but not exceeding an upper level, so as to fit with the rest in a suitable

[18]The Heckscher-Ohlin-Samuelson economic model features that the best effective combination of relative factor endowments such as a favourable agroecological conditions, suitable factors of production (land, labour and capital), high technical expertise in the production processes, availability for applying technological advances and a good transportation network can determine that a comparative advantage arises. Territories have comparatives advantages in those goods for which the required factors of production are relatively abundant or suitable. This is because the profitability of goods is determined by input costs. Goods that require conditions and inputs that are locally abundant will be cheaper to produce than those goods that require inputs that are locally scarce. Technical expertise and technological advances can contribute also that these comparative advantage improves being even determinant.

economic factor endowment. Local suitability to vine-growing was the outcome of a myriad of decisions taken by a lot of people interacting in a given set of challenges and opportunities which in turn they transformed. This agency-driven impulse set in motion self-reinforcing processes of vineyard planting works, and some technical advantages could be established within them. Planting vines in bush/head training system using the *alveus/goblet* technique without trellis infrastructure combined with the spur pruning system supposes an important technical advantage which favours both grape's productivity and harvesting efficiency (Martín i Oliveras 2015b, Figs. 16 and 17).[19] In this sense, Columella (*De Arboribus* IV, 1–2) indicates that these efficient planting and pruning systems were already used by Carthaginians and were adopted in *Hispania* by native peasants and Italic colonists. André Tchernia hypothetically proposes that during the Roman period the Laetanian vineyards planted and pruned with these techniques were maintained at a height of between one Roman foot and a half (44.4 cm) and three Roman feet (88.8 cm). This fact facilitates the recollection and increased the labour productivity during the harvesting, improving its performance and reducing the production costs greatly. According to the same author, this fact, combined with strong investments in processing and storage facilities and in applying technology (tools and machinery), would explain in large part the great production capacity and the strong competitiveness of the Laetanian wines (Tchernia 1986; Martín i Oliveras 2015b).

This winegrowing specialization stops when one or several key variables exceed or diminish certain threshold values, for example, reaching population densities higher than the ones capable to be sustained by a still mainly agrarian economy, exhausting the marginal lands available for planting vineyards or dropping the external demand of wine and derivatives due the irruption of more competitive producers. The result is a dilemma. Or local economies have to start a structural change for returning to an autarchic self-sufficient system in resilience, in which demographic surpluses have to emigrate towards other places; or either they have to expand towards new economic activities. It should be noted that this agency-oriented model was previously applied by economic historians in a cross-sectional analysis in the same territory in a similar context of wine-growing specialization in the mid-nineteenth century, basing on the theoretical comparative advantages, factor endowment and the impact of trade openness to international markets (Tello et al. 2008; Tello and Badía-Miró 2011; Badía-Miró and Tello 2013, 2014) (Fig. 8.6).

[19] The head-trained and spur-pruned training system was one the most ancient vines driving techniques employed. Traditionally it was used in the coastal vineyards as well as in the foothills and interior valleys because it was inexpensive and very easy to manage because it did not need trellis infrastructure. An additional advantage to this system was that it could be cross-cultivated for weed control, a very important water conservation tool in non-irrigated vineyards (Tchernia 1986; Togores 2003; Martín i Oliveras 2015b).

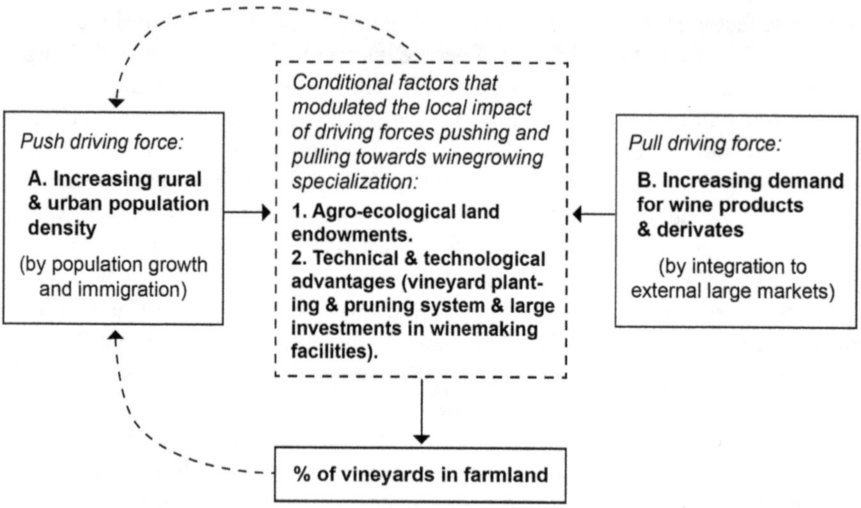

Fig. 8.6 Pushing or pulling drivers and conditioning factors of the Laetanian region's winegrowing specialization. (After Badía-Miró and Tello 2013, 22, Fig. 1)

8.8.4 The Taxes-and-Trade Model

Hopkins' *taxes-and-trade model* is a good point of departure for a further research on production and distribution economic dynamics. Insofar as it takes into account the fact that the ancient economy was in constant flux, it could be useful to analyse long-term changes and be versatile enough to accommodate local circumstances. Substantial growth in the scale of an economy is impossible without quantitative and qualitative changes in the means of production. Economic success often is matched by a growth in population. Hopkins thinks that regional trade was mainly in raw materials and foodstuffs in bulk and interregional, interprovincial and international trade were processed food products, consumer and luxury goods. He also calculates, from a macroeconomic point of view, that the Roman state needed an amount of capital about 825 million sesterces every year in the first century AD. This money was raised mainly in the form of direct and indirect taxes, and these represented 10% of the value of all economic activities in the Early Roman Empire, and they do not seem to have increased over time (Hopkins 1978; Duncan-Jones 1990; Kehoe 2013).

The "Roman *villa*" system, considered as an agricultural economic phenomenon with a tendency to intensification and specialization in the production and commercialization of larger cash-crop surpluses, reflects a profit mentality that exploited the accessibility to a larger distributive markets resulting in the lowering of production and transportation costs combined with the development of empire-wide political and economic institutions in which taxation plays a central role. This taxation affects the vine-growing and winemaking production and trade and all the stages of the productive function such as land tenure, yields, sales, revenues and so on. The internal relationships and the tensions generated by the competition for the control of the wealth and the resources by the state, civic communities and private individuals will be the key issue to understand its evolution and the changes over the time. The fact is that there was extensive Roman commerce and trade accompanied by a highly sophisticated law body to regulate it. The provinces were to carry on the heavy weight of administering the Empire. Roman state imposed a considerable number of indirect taxes, in particular customs and some taxes on trade – *portoria*. There were also crop taxes of 1/10 – *decima vectigalis* – for grain (Cic. *Verr.* IV-103: "*agros populo Romano ex parte decima... vectigalis fuisse*"); 1/5 – *quinta vectigalis* – for wine and olive oil; sales taxes of 1/100 – *centesima rerum venalium*; property tax; emergency tax; and so on, but the burden of taxation was distributed unevenly across the economy. Other issues related to land tenancy levied the crop yields and the incomes as leases and the share-cropping practices where the yield was proportionally split between landowner and tenant. These rents could oscillate around 50% of the yields, depending on the region and the product produced (Van Minnen 1998).

8.9 Discussion and Conclusion

There is a relationship between the processes of agrarian intensification and specialization, which are evident in the field of viticulture, and the structure and dynamics of settlement and population. These processes seem to promote the occupation of new spaces in specific territories on a regional scale. Ancient Laetania's viticulture seems to provide a good case study research.

The application of economic theory concepts could be an important tool to calculate production costs on the study of different systems of production, packing, shipment and distribution of wine. The evolution of supply and demand is determined by changes in consumption and in markets. Thus, a change of commercial orientation necessarily implies changes in the production system as well as in the system of transport and distribution of the product.

Demographic studies can also help us to calculate the amount of population, its distribution and its fluctuations over the time, trying to identify the causes of increases or decreases as regards the quantification of self-consumption needs, available workforce and hand labour division.

The extension of new productive forms requires a minimal amount of labour, necessary for the functioning of the agricultural and artisanal productive function with a complex technology and the extension of the crops. In turn, this economy can boost population growth and generate processes of increasing socio-economic inequality and the promotion of some social groups as a result of an uneven distribution of incomes and wealth generated. Part of this population growth can be evidenced by the intensification and unequal density of rural habitat and urban population growth, though it is hardly perceptible through the data provided by archaeological record.

The unequal extent of new economic forms of production along with other factors, not only the administrative ones, can help us to understand the different evolution of some cities and secondary settlements, in particular their function with respect to a territory and its demography, and to deepen into the global analysis of the urbanization process of the region.

Therefore, regional variability is one of the key points in understanding the changing patterns of rural settlement of any ancient historical period. Intra-regional and extra-regional economic networks seem to have been an important catalyst of specific interaction between agroecosystem and population in the ancient Laetanian region as regards the evolution of settlement patterns (urban and rural), land use, tenure, ownership management and labour division as well.

The level of dependence of the rural population of a given area in the regional market, respect the local urban centres and their subsequent screening in foreign markets, in our case study Western Europe and the Italian peninsula and Rome itself, are matters that respond to a series of socio-economic patterns and behaviours which are likely to be studied and modelled economical & econometrically.

The wide utilization of mathematics, statistics and linear programming models allows us to analyse, interpret and make predictions, regressions and reconstructions about the evolution of an ancient economic system, in relation with potential calculation of crop yields, the consumption level, the productive surplus susceptible of being traded in external markets and the study of several variables as the sales prices, the market reactions, the production trade and transportation costs, the business tendency and the consequences of economic policies in the socio-political affairs.

Acknowledgement Special thanks to Dr. Philip Verhagen for accepting our contribution in the "Finding the Limits of the *Limes* Project. Final Conference" held at Vrije Universiteit Amsterdam in January 2017, and also for his confidence in commissioning us one of the chapters of this book. Many thanks also to the two peer-reviewers whose invaluable suggestions have contributed to improving the quality of this chapter. All errors of course remain on our own.

This research was funded through the projects "EPNet Project-Economic and Political Networks" (ERC-2013-ADG 340828), "Relaciones interprovinciales en el Imperio Romano. Producción y comercio de alimentos hispanos (provincias *Baeticae* y *Tarraconensis*)"(MINECO, HAR2017-85635-P) and AGAUR (2017SGR512).

References

Alcubierre D, Hinojo E, Rigo A (2015) Primers resultats de la intervenció a la vil·la romana del Pont del Treball a Barcelona. In: Tribuna d'Arqueologia 2012–2013. Departament de Cultura, Generalitat de Catalunya, Barcelona, pp 372–398

Alcubierre D, Ardiaca J, Artigues PL, Llobet S (in press) Resultats preliminars de la nova intervenció arqueològica a la vil·la romana del Pont del Treball a Barcelona. In: Tribuna d'Arqueologia 2013–2014. Departament de Cultura, Generalitat de Catalunya, Barcelona

Amouretti M-C (1986) Le pain et l'huile dans la Grèce antique: de l'araire au moulin. Les Belles Lettres, Paris

Amouretti M-C, Brun J-P (1993) Les Rendements. In: Amouretti M-C, Brun J-P (eds) La production du vin et de l'huile en MéditerranéeÉcole Française d'Athènes, Athens/Paris, pp 551–562

Badía-Miró M, Tello E (2013) An agency-oriented model to explain vine-growing specialization in the province of Barcelona (Catalonia, Spain) in the mid-nineteenth century. In: Documents de Treball de la Facultat d'Economia i Empresa. Col·lecció d'Economia E13/290. Universitat de Barcelona, Barcelona, pp 1–31

Badía-Miró M, Tello E (2014) Vine-growing in Catalonia: the main agricultural change underlying the earliest industrialization in Mediterranean Europe (1720–1939). Eur Rev Econ Hist 18(2):203–226

Boserup E (1965) The conditions of agricultural growth. George Allen and Urwin, London

Bowman A, Wilson A (eds) (2013) The Roman agricultural economy: organization, investment and production. Oxford University Press, Oxford

Brun J-P (2004) Archéologie du vin et de l'huile. De la préhistoire à l'époque hellénistique, Errance, Paris

Burch J, Jiménez F, Nolla JM, Palahí L (2005) El fundus de Turissa entre el segle I aC i l'I dC. Arqueología de dos establiments rurals. Mas Carbotí i Ses Alzines, Girona

Carandini A (1980) Il vigneto e la Villa del fondo di Settefinestre nel Cosano: un caso di produzione agricola per il mercato transmarino. In: D'Arms JH, Kopff EC (eds) The Seaborne commerce of Ancient Rome. American Academy in Rome, Rome, pp 1–10

Carandini A (1983) Columella's vineyard and the rationality of the Roman economy. Opus 2:177–204

Carandini A (1989a) L'economia italica fra tarda Repubblica e medio impero considerata dal punto de vista di una merce: il vino. In: Amphores romaines et histoire économique. Dix ans de recherches. Actes du colloque de Sienne (22–24 mai 1986). École Française de Rome, Rome, pp 505–521

Carandini A (1989b) La villa romana e la piantagione schiavistica, In: Gabba A, Schiavone E (eds) Storia di Roma, vol 4, Caratteri e morfologie. Einaudi, Turín, pp 101–200

Carreras C (1996) A new perspective for the demographic study of Roman Spain. Revista da Historia da Arte e Arqueologia 2:59–82

Carreras C (2014) Nuevas tendencias y datos sobre la demografía romana en la Península Ibérica. Boletín del Seminario de Estudios de Arqueología LXXX:53–82

Conison A (2012) The organization of Rome's wine trade. University of Michigan, Ann Arbor

De Sena EC (2005) An assessment of wine and oil production in Rome's hinterland: ceramic, literary, art historical and modern evidence. In: Santillo Fritzell B, Klynne A (eds) Roman villas around the Urbs : interaction with landscape and environment : proceedings of a conference at the Swedish Institute in Rome, September 17–18, 2004. The Swedish Institute in Rome, Rome, pp 1–15

De Soto P (2010) Anàlisi de la xarxa de comunicacions i del transport a la Catalunya romana: estudis de distribució i mobilitat. Universitat Autònoma de Barcelona, Barcelona

Debolini M, Marraccini E, Dubeuf J-P, Geijzendorffer I, Simon-Rojo M, Targetti S, Napoleone C (2016) A Meta-analysis of land and farming system dynamics in Mediterranean basin. Paper presented at Agromed International Conference. December 1–2, 2016, Avignon

Dewar RE (1984) Environmental productivity, population regulation and carrying capacity. Am Anthropol 86:601–614. https://doi.org/10.1525/aa.1984.86.3.02a00040

Duncan-Jones R (1974) The economy of the Roman empire. Cambridge University Press, Cambridge

Duncan-Jones R (1990) Structure & scale in the Roman economy. Cambridge University Press, Cambridge

Dyson SL (2003) The Roman countryside. Duckworth, London

El Vi a l'Antiguitat: Economia, Producció i Comerç al Mediterrani Occidental (1987) Actes I Colloqui d'arqueologia romana. Museu de Badalona, Badalona

El Vi a l'Antiguitat: Economia, Producció i Comerç al Mediterrani Occidental (1999) II Col·loqui Internacional d'Arqueologia Romana, actes (Barcelona 6–9 de maig de 1998). Museu de Badalona, Badalona

Fentress E (2009) Peopling the countryside: Roman demography in the Albegna Valley and Jerba. In: Bowman A, Wilson AI (eds) Quantifying the Roman economy: methods and problems. Oxford UniversityPress, Oxford, pp 127–162

Garnsey P (1979) Where did Italian peasants live? Proc Camb Philol Soc 25:1–25

Garnsey P (1983) Grain for Rome. In: Garnsey P, Hopkins K, Whittaker CR (eds) Trade in the ancient economy, Chatto & Windus, London, pp 118–130

Gliessman SR, Engles E, Krieger R (2006) Agroecology: ecological processes in sustainable agriculture, 2nd edn. CRC Press, Boca Ratón

Hanson JW, Ormant SG, Lobo J (2017) Urbanism and the division of labour in the Roman Empire. J R Soc Interface 14:20170367. https://doi.org/10.1098/rsif.2017.0367

Heckscher E (1919) The effect of foreign trade on the distribution of income. Ekonomisk Tidskrift 21:497–512

Hopkins K (1978) Economic growth and towns in classical antiquity. In: Abrams P, Wrigley EA (eds) Towns in societies. Cambridge University Press, Cambridge, pp 35–79

Jones DW (2014) Economic theory and the ancient Mediterranean. Wiley Blackwell, Malden (MA)

Johnston DE (2004) Roman villas, 5th edn. Shire Publications, Buckinghamshire

Kehoe DP (1997) Investment, profit, and tenancy: the jurists and the Roman agrarian economy. The University of Michigan Press, Ann Arbor

Kehoe DP (2013) The state and production in the Roman agrarian economy. In: Bowman A, Wilson A (eds) The Roman agricultural economy: organization, investment and production. Oxford University Press, Oxford, pp 33–53

Kloppenborg JS (2010) Reading ancient viticulture. In: The tenants in the vineyard. Ideology, economics and agrarian conflict. Mohr-Siebeck, Tübingen

Launaro A (2011) Peasants and slaves: the rural population of Roman Italy (200 BC to AD 100). Cambridge University Press, Cambridge

Lo Cascio E (1994) The size of the Roman population: Beloch and the meaning of the Augustan census figures. J Roman Stud 83:24–40

Lo Cascio E (1999) The population of Roman Italy in town and country. In: Bintliff J, Sbonias K (eds) Reconstructing past population trends in Mediterranean Europe (3000 BC–AD 1800). Oxbow Books, Oxford, pp 161–172

López Mullor A, Martín i Menéndez A (2008) Las ánforas de la Tarraconense. In: Bernal D, Ribera A (eds) Cerámicas hipanorromanas. Un estado de la cuestión. Universidad de Cádiz, Cádiz, pp 689–724

Malthus TR (1798) An essay on the principle of population, as it affects the future improvement of society with remarks on the speculations of Mr. Godwin, M. Condorcet, and Other Writers. J. Johnston, London. Available at http://oll.libertyfund.org/titles/malthus-an-essay-on-the-principle-of-population-1798-1st-ed. Accessed on 30 July 2018

Martín i Oliveras A (2009) Parc Arqueològic Cella Vinaria (Teià-Maresme-Barcelona) Descobrint el celler romà de Vallmora. In: Prevosti M, Martín i Oliveras A (eds) El Vi Tarraconense i Laietà. Ahir i Avui. Actes del Simposi. Institut Català d'Arqueologia Clàssica, Tarragona, pp 193–213

Martín i Oliveras A (2011–2012) Arqueología del vino en época romana: El Proyecto Cella Vinaria y el complejo vitivinícola de Vallmora (Teià – Maresme – Barcelona). Nuevas aportaciones a la investigación. Anales de Prehistória y Arqueologia 27–28:101–127. Available at https://digitum.um.es/xmlui/handle/10201/46034. Accessed on 30 July 2018

Martín i Oliveras A (2012) Anàlisi tecnofuncional d'estructures productives i vitivinícoles d'època romana. Identificació i localització a Catalunya de fosses de maniobra de premses de biga amb contrapès tipus arca lapidum. Pyrenae 43(2):59–98

Martín i Oliveras A (2015a) Arqueología del Vino en Época Romana: Teoría económica, lógica productiva y comercial aplicada al envasado, la expedición, el transporte y la distribución de ánforas vinarias del nordeste peninsular (s. I a.C.-I d.C.). In: Martínez Ferreras V (ed) La difusión Comercial de las Ánforas Vinarias de Hispania Citerior Tarraconensis (s.I aC-I dC). Archaeopress, Oxford, pp 19–38

Martín i Oliveras A (2015b) Arqueologia del vi a l'època romana. Del cultiu al consum. Marc teòric i epistemològic, Premi d'Arqueologia Memorial Josep Barberà i Farràs (12a edició). Societat Catalana d'Arqueologia, Barcelona

Martín i Oliveras A, Bayés F (2009) Cella Vinaria de Vallmora (Teià-Maresme-Barcelona). Estudi per la reconstrucció de dues premses romanes. In: Prevosti M, Martín i Oliveras A (eds) El Vi Tarraconense i Laietà. Ahir i Avui. Actes del Simposi. Institut Català d'Arqueologia Clàssica, Tarragona, pp 215–248

Martín i Oliveras A, Martín-Arroyo DJ, Revilla V (2017) The wine economy in Roman Hispania. Archaeological data and modellization. In: Remesal J (ed) Economía Romana Nuevas perspectivas/the Roman economy new perspectives. Universitat de Barcelona, Barcelona, pp 189–236

Martín i Oliveras A, Revilla V, Carreras C, Remesal J, Van Limbergen D (forthcoming) Viticulture and demography in Laetanian Region (Hispania Citerior Tarraconensis) from 1sy century BC to 3rd century AD. Oxbow books, Oxford

Martín-Arroyo DJ (2016) Modelización de la ratio riparia/vinea: El emparrado romano entre Hasta Regia y Gades. In: Lagóstena LG (ed) Lacus autem idem et stagnus, ubi inmensa aqua convenit. Universidad de Cádiz, Cádiz, pp 105–124

Maza DF, González AJ (1992) Tratado de Economía Moderna, Ed. Panapo, Carácas

McCormick M, Büntgen U, Cane MA, Cook ER, Harper K, Huybers P, Litt T, Manning SW, Mayewski PA, More AFM, Nicolussi K, Tegel W (2012) Climate change during and after the Roman empire: reconstructing the past from scientific and historical evidence. J Interdiscip Hist 43(2):169–220. https://doi.org/10.1162/JINH_a_00379

Miret M, Sanmartí J, Santacana J (1991) From indigenous structures to the Roman world: models for the occupation of central coastal Catalonia. In: Barker G, Lloyd J (eds) Roman landscapes. Archaeological survey in the Mediterranean region. British School at Rome, London, pp 47–53

Miró J (1988) La producción de ánforas romanas en Catalunya. Un estudio sobre el comercio del vino de la Tarraconense (siglos I a.C.-I d.C.). BAR, Oxford

Morley N (1996) Metropolis and hinterland: the city of Rome and the Italian economy 200 B.C. – A.D.200. Cambridge University Press, Cambridge

Morrison KD (1994) The intensification of production: archaeological approaches. J Archaeol Method Theory 1(2):111–159

Ohlin B (1967) Interregional and international trade. Harvard University Press, Cambridge (MA)

Olesti O (2006) Propiedad de la tierra y élites locales. El ejemplo del ager Barcinonensis. In: Garrido-Hory M, Gonzales A (eds) Histoire, Espaces et Marges de l'Antiquité: Hommages à Monique Clavel-Lévêque. Université de Franche-Comté, Besançon, pp 175–200

Olesti O (2009) Propietat i riquesa a l'ager Barcinonensis. In: Carreras C, Guitart J (eds) Barcino I. Marques i terrisseries d'àmfores al Pla de Barcelona. Institut d'Estudis Catalan, Barcelona, pp 141–158

Olesti O, Carreras C (2012) Esclavos y libertos en la producción vinícola y alfarera en el Ager Barcinonensis: De la marginalidad al éxito económico. In: Reduzzi Merola F (ed) Dependenza ed emarginazione nel mondo antico e moderno. Atti del 33 Convegno G.I.R.E.A. Aracne, Rome, pp 309–333

Olesti O, Carreras C (2013) Le paysage social de la production vitivinicole dans l'ager Barcinonensis. Dialogues d'Histoire Ancienne 39(2):147–189

Oller J (2015) El territorio y poblamiento de la Layetania interior en época antigua (ss. IV a.C-I d.C). Universitat de Barcelona, Barcelona

Palahí L, Nolla JM (2010) Felix Turissa. La vil·la romana dels Ametllers i el seu fundus (Tossa de Mar, la Selva). Institut Català d'Arqueologia Clàssica, Tarragona

Palet JM (1997) Estudi territorial del Pla de Barcelona. Estructuració i evolució del territori entre l'època ibero-romana i l'altmedieval. Segles II/I aC-IX/X dC. Universitat de Barcelona, Barcelona

Palet JM, Fiz JL, Orengo HA (2009) Centuriació i estructuració de l'ager de la Colònia de Barcino: Anàlisi arqueomorfològica i modelació del paisatge. Quaderns d'Història i Arqueologia de la Ciutat de Barcelona 5:106–123

Palet JM, Julià R, Riera S, Orengo HA, Picornell L, Llergo Y (2012) The role of the Montjuïc promontory (Barcelona). In: Bertoncello F, Braemer F (eds) Variabilités environnementales, mutations sociales: Nature, intensités, échelles et Temporalités des changements. Éditions APDCA, Antibes, pp 341–352

Palet JM, Orengo HA, Riera S (2011) Centuriación del territorio y modelación del paisaje en los llanos litorales de Barcino y Tarraco. Una investigación interdisciplinar a través de la integración de datos arqueomorfológicos y paleoambientales. In: Dall'aglio PL, Rosada G (eds) Sistemi Centuriali e Opere di Assetto Agrario tra Età Romana e primo Medioevo. Atti del convegno borgoricco (Padova)-Lugo (Ravenna) 10–12 Settembre 2009. Fabrizio Serra, Pisa, pp 113–129

Pavis d'Escurac H (1976) La préfecture de l'annone, service administratif impérial d'Auguste à Constantin. École française de Rome, Rome

Peña Y (2010) Torcularia. La producción de vino y aceite en Hispania. Institut Català d'Arqueologia Clàssica, Tarragona

Peña Y (2011–2012) Variantes tecnológicas hispanas en los procesos de elaboración de vino y aceite en época romana. Anales de Prehistoria y Arqueologia 27–28:37–57

Perkins P (1999) Etruscan settlement, society and material cultura in central coastal Etruria. BAR, Oxford

Prevosti M (2005) L'època romana. In: Giralt E (ed) Història agrària dels Països Catalans, vol I, L'antiguitat. Universitat de Barcelona, Barcelona, pp 345–445

Prevosti M, Martín i Oliveras A (2007) El vi tarraconense i laietà. Ahir i avui. Actes del Simposi, Tarragona-Teià. Institut Català d'Arqueologia Clàssica, Tarragona

Remesal J (1990) El sistema annonario como base de la evolución económica del Imperio romano. In: Hackens T, Miró M (eds) Le commerce maritime romain en Méditerranée occidentale. Conseil d'Europe, Rixensart, pp 355–367

Revilla V (1995) Producción cerámica, viticultura y propiedad rural en Hispania Tarraconensis (siglos I a.C.-III d.C.). L'Estaquirot, Barcelona

Revilla V (1998) Modelos económicos y modelos culturales en una sociedad provincial romana: El vino en Hispania. Boletim do CPA 5/6:181–202

Revilla V (2004a) Ánforas y epigrafía anfórica en Hispania Tarraconensis. In: Remesal J (ed) Epigrafía anfórica. Universitat de Barcelona, Barcelona, pp 159–196

Revilla V (2004b) El poblamiento rural en el noreste de Hispania entre los siglos II a.C. y I d.C.: organización y dinámicas culturales y socioeconómicas. In: Moret P, Chapa T (eds) Torres, atalayas y casas fortificadas. Explotación y control del Territorio en Hispania (S. III a. de C. – S. I d. de C.). Universidad de Jaén, Jaén, pp 175–202

Revilla V (2008) La producción anfórica en el sector meridional de Cataluña: prácticas artesanales, viticultura y representaciones culturales. In: Aquilue J, López A, Pascual i Guasch R (eds) La producció i el comerç de les àmfores de la provincia Hispania Tarraconensis. Homenatge a Ricard Pascual i Guasch (Barcelona, 17 i 18 de novembre de 2005). Museu d'Arqueologia de Catalunya, Barcelona, pp 189–226

Revilla V (2010a) Hábitat rural y territorio en el litoral oriental de Hispania Citerior: perspectivas de análisis. In: Noguera JM (ed) El poblamiento rural romano en el sureste de Hispania 15 años después. Universidad de Murcia, Murcia, pp 20–75

Revilla V (2010b) Rural settlement in the central littoral area and the interior regions of Catalonia in the 1st and 2nd centuries BC Studies on the Rural World in the Roman Period 5:139–159. Available at https://www.documentauniversitaria.media/labarqueologia/index.php/srw/article/view/126. Accessed on 30 July 2018

Revilla V (2011–2012) Viticultura, territorio y hábitat en el litoral nororiental de Hispania Citerior durante el Alto Imperio. Anales de Prehistoria y Arqueologia 27–28:67–83

Revilla V (2015) Agricultura, artesanado rural y territorio en el noreste de Hispania Citerior: estructuras y dinámicas. In: Martínez V (ed) La difusión comercial de las ánforas vinarias de Hispania Citerior-Tarraconensis (siglos I a.C. -I d.C.). Archaeopress, Oxford, pp 1–17

Revilla V, González JR, Prevosti M (eds) (2008–2011) Actes del Simposi Les vil·les romanes a la Tarraconense. Implantació, evolució i transformació. Estat actual de la investigació del món rural en època romana (Lleida, 28–30 novembre 2007), 2 vols. Museu d'Arqueologia de Catalunya, Barcelona

Ricardo D (1817) On the principles of political economy and taxation. John Murray, London

Rodà I, Martín i Oliveras A, Velasco C, Pou R (2005) Personatges de Barcino i el vi Laietà. Localització d'un fundus dels Pedanii Clementes a Teià (El Maresme) a partir de la troballa d'un signaculum de plom amb inscripció (segle II dC). Quaderns d'Arqueologia i Història de la ciutat de Barcelona 1:47–57

Rubin J (1972) Expulsion from the garden (Boserup and Malthus). Peasant Studies Newsletter 135–38

Samuelson PA (1948) International trade and the equalisation of factor prices. Econ J 58(230):163–184

Samuelson PA (1953–1954) Prices of goods and factors in general equilibrium. Rev Econ Stud 21(1):1–209

Sánchez E (ed) (1997) El jaciment romà del Morè. Sant Pol de Mar, Maresme. Departament de Cultura, Generalitat de Catalunya, Barcelona

Scheidel W (2002) A model of demographic and economic change in Roman Egypt after the Antonine plague. J Roman Archaeol 15:97–114

Scheidel W (2004) Human mobility in Roman Italy I: the free population. J Roman Stud 94:1–26

Scheidel W (2007a) Roman population size: the logic of the debate. Stanford University, Stanford

Scheidel W (2007b) Demography. In: Scheidel W, Morris I, Saller R (eds) The Cambridge economic history of the Greco-Roman world. Cambridge University Press, Cambridge, pp 38–86. https://doi.org/10.1017/CHOL9780521780537

Scheidel W, Friesen J (2009) The size of the economy and the distribution of income in the Roman Empire. J Roman Stud 99:61–91

Sirks B (1991) Food for Rome. The legal structure of the transportation and processing of supplies for the imperial distributions in Rome and Constantinople. J.C. Gieben, Amsterdam, pp vi, 44

Smith A (1776) An inquiry into the nature and causes of the wealth of nations. Thomas Dobson, Philadelphia

Tchernia A (1986) Le vin de l'Italie romaine. École Française de Rome, Rome

Tchernia A (2013) Les dimensions de quelques vignobles Romains. In: Salviat F, Tchernia A (eds) Vins, Vignerons et Buveurs de l'Antiquité. L'Erma di Bretschneider, Rome, pp 153–166

Tchernia A, Brun JP (1999) Le Vin Romain Antique, Grenoble.

Tello E, Badía-Miró M, Cussó X, Garrabou R, Valls F (2008) Explaining vineyard specialization in the province of Barcelona (Spain) in the mid-19 century. In: Documents de Treball de la Facultat de Ciències Econòmiques i Empresarials. Col·lecció d'Economia E08/201. Universitat de Barcelona, Barcelona, pp 1–42

Tello E, Badía-Miró M (2011) Land-use profiles of agrarian income and land ownership inequality in the province of Barcelona in mid-nineteenth century. In: Documentos de Trabajo, 11-01. Sociedad Española de Historia Agraria, Girona, pp 1–30

Temin P (2014) Price behaviour in the Roman Empire. In: De Callataÿ F (ed) Quantifying the Greco-Roman economy and beyond. Edipuglia, Bari, pp 189–207

Temin P (2017) The Roman market economy. Princeton University Press, Princeton

Togores JH (2003) Tratado de Enología. 2 vols. S.A Mundi, Barcelona

Tremoleda J (2008) Les instal·lacions productives d'àmfores tarraconenses. In: Aquilue J, López A, Pascual i Guasch R (eds) La producció i el comerç de les àmfores de la provincia Hispania Tarraconensis. Homenatge a Ricard Pascual i Guasch (Barcelona, 17 i 18 de novembre de 2005). Museu Arqueològic de Catalunya, Barcelona, pp 113–150

Van Minnen P (1998) Agriculture and the 'Taxes-and-Trade' model in Roman Egypt. Z Papyrol Epigr 133:205–220

Vilcalpoma L (1995) Teoría de la producción y costos. Una exposición didáctica. Universidad Católica del Perú, Lima

Vogel S, Märker M, Esposito D, Seiler F (2016) The ancient rural settlement structure un the Hinterland of Pompeii inferred from spatial analysis and predictive modeling of Villae Rusticae. Geoarchaeol Int J 31:121–139

Wallace-Hadrill A (1998) The Villa as cultural symbol. In: Frazer A (ed) Roman Villa. Villa Urbana. The University Museum, University of Pennsylvania, Philadelphia, pp 43–54

Witcher RE (2005) The extended metropolis – city, suburbium and population. J Roman Archaeol 18:120–138

Witcher RE (2008) Regional field survey and the demography of Roman Italy. In: De Ligt L, Northwood S (eds) People, land and politics. Demographic developments and the transformation of Roman Italy, 300BC–AD14. Brill, Leiden, pp 273–303

Witcher RE (2011) Missing persons? Models of Mediterranean regional survey and ancient populations. In: Bowman A, Wilson A (eds) Settlement, urbanization, and population, Oxford studies on the Roman economy. Oxford University Press, Oxford, pp 36–75

Chapter 9
The Role of Forts in the Local Market System in the Lower Rhine: Towards a Method of Multiple Hypothesis Testing Through Comparative Modelling

Eli J. S. Weaverdyck

Abstract This paper analyses rural settlement patterns in the Lower Rhine frontier zone to elucidate the role of forts in the rural economy. Von Thünen's model of rural marketing suggests that market centres attract intensive cultivation, making them identifiable through spatial analysis of rural settlements. Environmental factors that influenced production capacity, however, can also be expected to exert a strong influence on settlement location, so a multivariate method of spatial analysis is necessary. Using a process of comparative modelling with logistic regression analysis, I test the hypotheses that rural settlements responded to the location of market centres, both civilian and military. I use univariate analysis of settlement territories to identify influential local environmental factors and combine these into a logistic regression model. Then I add a market potential (MP) variable that quantifies the accessibility of marketing opportunities from any location within a market system to see if this factor also shaped settlement patterns. Finally, I vary the centres included in the MP variable to determine whether rural settlements responded to the locations of forts in addition to civilian centres. I find that forts did not generally attract settlements and conclude that smallholders sold their produce primarily in civilian market places.

Keywords Rural marketing · Lower Rhine frontier · Location analysis · Logistic regression analysis · Landscape archaeology

---

E. J. S. Weaverdyck (✉)
Seminar für Alte Geschichte, University of Freiburg, Freiburg im Breisgau, Germany
e-mail: eli.weaverdyck@geschichte.uni-freiburg.de

P. Verhagen et al. (eds.), *Finding the Limits of the Limes*, Computational Social Sciences, https://doi.org/10.1007/978-3-030-04576-0_9

9.1 Introduction

In the first and second centuries CE, the Roman Empire established a network of military bases stretching from the mouth of the Rhine to the mouth of the Danube. In addition to the soldiers, their families as well as merchants and craftspeople who depended on the soldiers' salaries for their livelihood lived around these bases. While imperial officials arranged for the provision of rations to soldiers, their demand for supplementary goods and the needs of the civilians would have been filled through other mechanisms. If this included market exchange between soldiers and local peasants, military bases would have provided important opportunities for locals to engage in commerce and tap into empire-wide networks of exchange (for a more detailed account of the roles of peasants in Roman frontier economies, see Weaverdyck 2016, 1–22).

Recent scholarship in the lower Rhine *limes* zone has contributed significantly to our understanding of the economic relationship between the soldiers who manned the forts and the people living in the countryside (Groenhuijzen and Verhagen 2015; Groot 2008; Groot et al. 2009; Groot 2016; Joyce and Verhagen 2016; Kooistra 1996, 2009; Kooistra et al. 2013; Van Dinter 2017; Van Dinter et al. 2014; Verhagen et al. 2016b; Vos 2009). The question of rural marketing in particular has been studied using zooarchaeological remains (Groot 2016; Groot et al. 2009). In particular, Wouter Vos has argued that the military bases and their attendant settlements acted as local market centres (Vos 2009, 226–229). These studies have not only thrown the impact of the military in the area into sharp relief; they have also highlighted the agency of the local inhabitants in seizing the market opportunities afforded by the presence of soldiers. At the same time, there are some indications that the rural inhabitants might not have been in particularly close contact with the soldiers on a day-to-day basis. Network analysis has revealed that most local travel occurred well south of the major military highway (Groenhuijzen and Verhagen 2015). This contribution seeks to shed new light on the problem using location analysis.

Locations of settlements can provide evidence for marketing practices because distance constrains marketing opportunities. Transportation costs in time, money, and other resources can make it impossible for producers to sell their products in certain places. Similarly, if the sale of products is important, production will occur in locations close to markets. The spatial relationship between production and markets was first rigorously studied by Von Thünen in the nineteenth century. His famous model of an isolated market place surrounded by concentric rings of land use of declining intensity remains influential in archaeology today (Bintliff 2002; Casarotto et al. 2016; De Neeve 1984; Goodchild 2007, 31–35; Morley 1996; Patterson 2004. For critiques, see Horden and Purcell 2000, 115–122 and Witcher 2008). Von Thünen's basic insight was that the combination of the price of a crop, its production cost, and its transportation cost would encourage the intensive cultivation of land nearest to the market (Von Thünen 1966 [1842–1850]; Haggett 1965, 161–167). Because the actual crops produced and the precise agricultural strategies of ancient agriculturalists are difficult to determine, settlement density is sometimes used as a proxy indicator for intensity of cultivation (e.g. Casarotto et al. 2016; Patterson 2004).

Of course, transportation cost varies depending on the product being moved, and this has important consequences both for the spatial distribution of production and for the economic strategies of producers. For instance, many animals can transport themselves and require only a herder. While grain is bulky and must be carried, it also preserves well, so the transport of grain need not be frequent if one can invest in storage facilities. Fresh fruits, vegetables, and flowers, on the other hand, are lighter, but spoil quickly and so must be moved as soon as they are harvested (Morley 1996, 86–90 collects literary evidence for the production of perishable goods near Rome). In addition, these products require greater inputs of labour than grain. This makes the production and sale of perishable goods more advantageous for small-scale producers who lack the capital to invest in storage but often have surplus labour (see Weaverdyck 2016, 4–7 with literature for peasant production and marketing strategies). Thus, a high density of settlement near market centres implies not only the existence of market production but a type of market production that is highly sensitive to transportation costs, which in turn suggests that smallholders may have been directly involved in the sale of their own produce.

However, these smallholders relied on their own production for a large portion of their sustenance. The ability to sell a surplus would have been less important than the ability to produce enough to survive, so it would be unrealistic to expect the density of settlements in the Lower Rhine to simply decline with distance to markets without taking into account the productive capacity of the landscape.

This paper employs a method of location analysis and comparative modelling that is designed to detect the influence of rural marketing under the assumption that it would have been subordinate in importance to production. The method was first developed to analyse rural settlements in central Moesia Inferior, but it is applicable to any context where a large number of rural settlements can be distinguished from potential locations of exchange (Weaverdyck 2016). It relies on statistical models that attempt to distinguish between locations that contained an ancient settlement and those that did not on the basis of environmental factors. First, the factors influencing production are identified through univariate analysis of settlement territories – discs centred on settlement locations with a fixed radius. Then, these factors are used to create a multivariate logistic regression model, and the fit of the model to the data is measured. Finally, a market potential variable is added to the model to see if it significantly improves the model's performance.

This method also allows for different, specific hypotheses about the marketing system to be tested. The hypothesis under examination is that military bases on the Roman frontier acted as markets for the local producers living in the nearby countryside, making proximity to forts desirable. For each chronological period, I construct two market potential variables: one that includes forts and one that includes only civil settlements. The one that has the greatest positive impact on model performance can be understood to be the closest approximation of ancient reality. If neither improves on the performance of the baseline model, it can be concluded that marketing did not significantly influence settlement locations, either because marketing itself was not important or because the market relations were not meaningfully constrained by transportation costs at the current scale of analysis.

This type of narrowly focussed analysis has been referred to as a "scaffolding model" (Llobera 2012, 503–505). The goal is not to create an overarching model of the rural economy in Lower Rhine region, but to investigate one particular aspect of the economy – marketing – and specifically the role of forts within it. To accomplish this, I take advantage of one of the inherent strengths of quantitative modelling: the ability to rigorously compare the empirical support for competing hypotheses (this advantage has long been recognized. See, e.g. Gaffney and Van Leusen 1995, 370; Kvamme 1988, 386; Verhagen and Whitley 2012, 83). All modelling requires that potentially important factors be transformed into measurable variables, and modellers will often experiment with a variety of transformations to choose the one that produces the most statistically meaningful results. This makes it more likely that the resulting model will be useful in distinguishing areas that were preferred for settlement (e.g. Kay and Witcher 2009; Tourneux 2003; Verhagen et al. 2013). In the present case, the influence of marketing is transformed into market potential variables in accordance with specific hypotheses. If the resulting models fail to effectively identify preferred settlement locations, this too is a meaningful result in that it shows the underlying hypotheses lack empirical support in the currently available data (Weaverdyck 2016, 30–34).

9.2 Data

Data suitable for spatial analysis have recently been compiled by Philip Verhagen, Mark Groenhuijzen and Jamie Joyce as part of the project "Finding the Limits of the Limes". They consist of a palaeogeographic reconstruction of the lower Rhine and a geographic database of archaeological sites dating from the Late Iron Age to the Late Roman period. The palaeogeography of the region was reconstructed by Mark Groenhuijzen using the methods published by Van Dinter (2013). Ancient landform units are represented by polygons in a shapefile. The archaeological data are based primarily on the records of the Netherlands' national archaeological database, ARCHIS. When individual find spots were located within 250 m of each other, they were aggregated into a single site represented by a point at its centroid (Verhagen et al. 2016a). Settlements and potential market centres were identified on the basis of finds and features. These were categorized as *castra* (legionary camp), *castellum* (auxiliary fort), *vicus* (civil settlement), cult site, or rural settlement. In addition, two civil settlements were classified as cities in specific periods. The *canabae*, the civil settlement that surrounded the *castra* in the Middle Roman A period, is treated as a unique type due to its great size. The functional categorization of sites was not exclusive; a site could simultaneously be a *castellum* and a civil settlement, for example. Crucially, this allows both forts and their attendant military *vici* to be included as distinct entities within the analysis even when they occupy the same location.

Verhagen et al. (2016) calculated the chronology of the sites using a combination of aoristic analysis and Monte Carlo simulation. This resulted in a dataset that allows for the selection of precisely dated sites, ideal for statistical analysis aiming

Table 9.1 Periodization and archaeological sites

Period	Date range	Sites	Rural settlements
Late Iron Age	250–12 BCE	C: 141 E: 126	C: 137 E: 123
Early Roman A	12 BCE–25 CE	C: 138 E: 111	C: 131 E: 97
Early Roman B	25–70 CE	C: 163 E: 130	C: 153 E: 116
Middle Roman A	70–150 CE	C: 233 E: 197	C: 222 E: 177
Middle Roman B	150–270 CE	C: 248 E: 224	C: 237 E: 208
Late Roman A	270–350 CE	C: 158 E: 128	C: 153 E: 118
Late Roman B	350–450 CE	C: 176 E: 144	C: 170 E: 133

Periodization from Verhagen et al. (2016a, Table 1)
C: Central River Area, E: Eastern River Area

to understand diachronic change. As in Verhagen et al. (2016a), sites where the probability of 10 or more finds coming from a specific period is greater than 50% were selected for this analysis. The date ranges of the chronological periods, the total number of sites, and the number of rural settlements in each period, divided by zone, are presented in Table 9.1.

9.3 Methods

If the locational tendencies of rural settlements are to be used to elucidate marketing behaviour, it is necessary to understand and distinguish the other factors that influence settlement location. Assuming that most rural settlements relied on their own production for the majority of their sustenance, the productive capacity of the landscape must have exercised a powerful influence on settlement location decisions. Other factors, such as security from human and natural threats, might also have influenced settlement location choices, but they are excluded from this analysis for the sake of simplicity. Productive capacity depends on the physical characteristics of the environment as well as the social characteristics of the cultivators, which include the available technology, labour, and the particular goals and strategies of each household. Rather than try to anticipate the relevant combinations of these factors to model productive capacity, I take an inductive approach that identifies influential environmental factors by analysing their prevalence in settlement territories, building on a method developed in the 1990s during the Archaeomedes project (Van der Leeuw 1998, 2003) and extended by Verhagen et al. (2013).

9.3.1 Settlement Territories

Two different sizes of territories were used in this analysis consisting of simple circles with radii of 0.5 and 1.5 km. The former distance is based on the results of earlier cluster analysis which identified particularly tight groupings at this distance

(Verhagen et al. 2016a). These territories would contain an area of just under 80 ha, which is a reasonable estimate of the maximum size of a smallholding (Nuninger et al. 2016). The latter distance is based on Chisholm's cross-cultural investigations showing that the amount of labour invested in fields tends to drop sharply beyond 1–2 km from the settlement. A territory with a radius of 1.5 km represents the area that is likely to contain the fields worked by the inhabitants of a settlement, rather than the extent of a contiguous estate. No attempt was made to avoid overlapping settlement territories. Since it is impossible to prove exact contemporaneity of nearby settlements, and because land can change hands, an exclusive assignation of territory to a single settlement is unrealistic.

9.3.2 Study Areas

The study area was divided into three zones to homogenize the environmental constraints experienced by the settlements within each zone as much as possible. These were identified based on a cluster analysis of the palaeogeographic units within 20 km of sites (Verhagen et al. 2016a, Fig. 2).[1] The western zone contains large areas of uninhabited peat and few archaeological sites, possibly as a result of fluvial activity in the area. The central zone is characterized by broad floodplains interspersed with levees, and the eastern zone is characterized by large areas of sandy soil interspersed with levees. Because of the scarcity of archaeological sites in the western zone, and because of the large areas of uninhabited peat, only the central and eastern zones are included in this analysis (Fig. 9.1).

In order to learn about settlement preferences, settled locations are compared to the total area that was available for settlement. Large swathes of the study area were uninhabitable, and these must be eliminated before the other factors influencing settlement location can be identified. To identify the habitable area, all landforms that contained no archaeological sites were eliminated.[2] Thus, tendencies observed in settlement locations cannot be explained by the impossibility of living on certain landforms.

9.3.3 Univariate Analysis

In this first stage of analysis, the locations of settlements are compared to all the areas available for settlement. The landform classification system was simplified to combine landforms with similar agricultural capacities as described by Verhagen

[1] Some of the sites included in the western zone by the cluster analysis were included in the central zone here because they were geographically contiguous with the rest of the sites in the central zone.

[2] Eliminated landforms include oligotrophic sphagnum peat dome, mesotrophic peatland, eutrophic peatland, salt marsh, estuary, open sweet water, and Roman river.

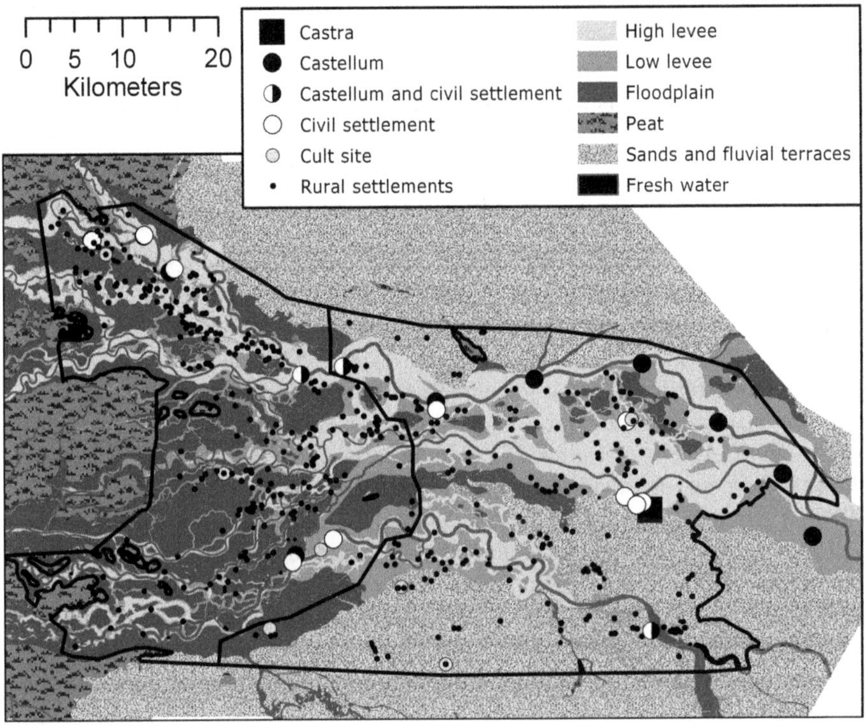

Fig. 9.1 The study area in the Middle Roman A period. (Courtesy of Mark Groenhuijzen)

Table 9.2 Simplification of palaeogeographic landforms and walking coefficients

Specific landform	Simplified landform	Walking coefficient
High floodplain	Floodplain	1.5
Low floodplain	Floodplain	1.8
Rivers and streams	Fresh water	20
Medium high levee	High levee	1.2
High levee	High levee	1.2
Low levee	Low levee	1.2
Residual gully	Low levee	1.5
Eutrophic peatland	Peat	1.8
Mesotrophic peatland	Peat	1.8
Oligotrophic peatland	Peat	1.8
Cover sands	Sands and fluvial terraces	1.2
Fluvial terraces	Sands and fluvial terraces	1.2
High Pleistocene sands	Sands and fluvial terraces	1.5
River dune	Sands and fluvial terraces	1.2

et al. (2016a). This simplified classification is shown in Fig. 9.1 and in Table 9.2. Each simplified landform was converted from the polygon shapefile to a raster with 10 m resolution. Cells containing that landform were coded 1, and the others were coded 0. The Focal Statistics tool in ArcGIS Pro 10.2.1 was used to calculate the number of cells within 500 m and 1500 m of each cell that contained the landform. This was then converted to a percentage of the entire territory around that cell.

The Kolmogorov-Smirnov (K-S) test was used to compare the portion of settlement territories covered by each landform to the landscape as a whole.[3] The K-S test is a non-parametric test that is able to compare continuous variables from two samples with radically different sizes (Wheatley and Gillings 2002, 136–142). This makes it an excellent tool for comparing the environmental context of archaeological sites to the entire study area (Kvamme 1990). While the K-S test identifies significant differences between settlements and the territory as a whole, it does not show the magnitude or the direction of difference. Effect size was measured using Vargha and Delaney's A estimate (Vargha and Delaney 2000).[4] This test has been shown to be more robust than other measures of effect size with non-normal data (Li 2016). It estimates the likelihood that a randomly selected case from one population will have a higher score on a certain variable than a case randomly selected from another population. If the two populations are identical, the statistic will be 0.5. If all of the members of the first population have higher scores than every member of the second population, the statistic will be 1, and if the opposite is true, it will be 0. Variables with a p value less than 0.05 on the K-S test were selected for inclusion in the multivariate analysis.

9.3.4 Multivariate Analysis

In the second stage of analysis, the variables identified as significant through univariate analysis were combined into a "postdictive", baseline model using logistic regression analysis.[5] This baseline model attempts to distinguish locations with settlements from those without by using only the quantities of landforms found in the surroundings of those locations. Next, a second model was created using the same landform variables as in the baseline model with the addition of a variable quantifying the location's access to marketing opportunities, a market potential (MP) variable. Improvement in the performance of the model suggests that those marketing opportunities affected the desirability of a location for settlement.

The use of logistic regression analysis to study archaeological settlement patterns is well established (Kohler and Parker 1986; Kvamme 1988; Warren 1990;

[3] This was done in R using the ks.test tool in the stats package (R Core Team 2017).

[4] Also performed in R using the VD.A tool in the package effsize (Torchiano 2017)

[5] The term "postdictive" applies to mathematical models that are designed to elucidate why known sites are located where they are rather than predict the locations of unknown sites (Citter and Arnoldus-Huyzendveld 2014).

Warren and Asch 2000; Woodman 2000; Woodman and Woodward 2002). The method is able to quantify the relationships between a number of independent variables of different types and a single, binary, dependent variable. In short, it calculates the probability between 0 and 1 that a location with certain characteristics contains a settlement. It also assigns a coefficient to each independent variable expressing whether an increase in that variable makes a settlement more or less likely, as well as a p value quantifying the statistical significance of each coefficient.

The root mean square error (RMSE) was used to measure model fit and has the advantage of being relatively simple and intuitive. Locations with a settlement are given a value of 1, and those without a settlement are given a value of 0. The probability of that location being a settlement as calculated by the model is subtracted from this value, and the difference is squared. The RMSE is the square root of the average of these squared errors. RMSEs are calculated for the baseline models and for models containing each of the four MPs in addition to landform data. Improvement is measured as a percentage of the baseline RMSE. The MP variable that improves model performance the most is the most important result.

9.3.4.1 The Dependent Variable

Logistic regression analysis uses a binary response variable, in this case either settlement or non-site. It would be inappropriate to compare settlement locations to the entire habitable zone used in the univariate analysis described above, as this includes places that were settlements. Logistic regression analysis also works best when the numbers of observations in each category are roughly similar. Therefore, for each time period, 250 non-sites were created. Because sites represent an aggregation of find spots within 250 m of each other, non-sites were restricted to areas that are more than 250 m from a settlement. This made it necessary to create separate sets of non-sites for each chronological period.[6]

With only 250 non-sites, the results could potentially reflect the characteristics of a particular set of these points rather than settlements. Therefore, for each time period and zone, five different sets of non-sites were constructed. By combining each set of non-sites with the settlements, five unique datasets were constructed for each period and zone, and the entire modelling process was performed on all five. If the same MP variable improves model performance the most in all five datasets, the result is likely to reflect the locations of settlements rather than non-sites.

[6]There is a chance that non-sites fall in areas where settlements existed but have not yet been discovered. The problem can be mitigated by analysing research and taphonomic biasing factors and subjecting non-sites to the same biases, but this was outside the scope of this project (Weaverdyck 2016, 125–130).

9.3.4.2 The Independent Variables

Landforms

The landform variables analysed in the first stage of analysis pose challenges for logistic regression because some are likely to be correlated. This is both because they are measured in terms of percentage of territory – and therefore must all sum to 100 – and because the processes by which they were formed cause the spatial relationships between them to follow certain patterns. This was confirmed by calculating correlation matrices using the Collect Band Statistics tool in ArcGIS Pro.[7] In order to arrive at truly independent variables that capture the character of settlement territories, principal component analysis (PCA) was performed on each dataset of settlements and non-sites. The principal components (PCs) that account for over 90% of the variance were used to construct the baseline models.

Market Potential

Unlike landforms, the accessibility of marketing opportunities was measured at the location of the settlement rather than in a territory around it. MP variables were constructed using the archaeological dataset and least cost surfaces calculated from the palaeogeographic reconstruction. Market potential is a measure of the relative accessibility of marketing opportunities from any given location.[8] It varies directly with the population or purchasing power of market places and inversely with the distance to those locations. The advantage of using market potential over simple distance measures is that it accounts for the accessibility of all markets in a system, not just the closest one. Two versions of the MP variable were calculated for each chronological period: one that included only cities, civil settlements, and cult sites and a second that included forts as well. In the Early Roman A and Middle Roman A period, further variations on these MP variables were also calculated (see below).

Without reliable data on population or purchasing power, it is necessary to assign weights that capture their relative importance to different types of market centres in the system (Table 9.3). Cult sites, which might have hosted periodic markets but had no large, permanent population, are given a weight of 1. Civil settlements – places of permanent habitation with some evidence for permanent population larger than rural settlements – and *castella* are given a weight of 5. This is based on the average size of auxiliary forts (1.4–3.2 ha for infantry cohorts and up to 6.1 ha for cavalry *alae*; Hanel 2007) and on the size of the *vicus* at Kesteren (4.5–5 ha; Groot 2016, 53).

---

[7] The correlation coefficient varies by zone and territory size, but high and low levees are negatively correlated with floodplains in the central zone and with sands and fluvial terraces in the eastern zone.

[8] This use of market potential is inspired by Jan De Vries' use of urban potential in the study of early modern European urbanization (De Vries 1984, 154–67).

Table 9.3 Market types and weights

Type	Weight
Cult site	1
Civil settlement	5
Castellum	5
City	25
Castra	25
Canabae	75

Note that variations on the weighting of the *castra* and *canabae* are also tested

There are two places that, at different times, might be termed cities: Oppidum Batavorum on the Valkhof in Nijmegen was the capital of the Batavi in Early Roman periods and occupied an area of around 20 ha. Ulpia Noviomagus in the Waterkwartier in Nijmegen was built after the Batavian revolt and remained an important city throughout the Middle Roman period. Its built-up area was between 35 and 40 ha, but more of this space was occupied by monumental buildings than was the case at Oppidum Batavorum (Willems and Van Enckevort 2009, 69–79). Since precise sizes fluctuated through time, it seems best to give these two cities the same weight of 25, five times the weight of the civil settlements.

A *castra* (legionary fortress) was present at two different periods: the Early Roman A period and the Middle Roman A period. The Augustan period castra covered 42 ha, but was only in use for a few years – possibly less than a decade – and seems not to have been accompanied by a civilian settlement (*canabae*) (Kemmers 2007; Willems and Van Enckevort 2009). The brief period of its occupancy makes analysis complicated, so two alternative reconstructions were tested. In the first, the fortress is given a weight of 25 because its size is of the same order of magnitude as Ulpia Noviomagus. In the second, it is excluded altogether because of its brief occupation.

The second, a Flavian period legionary camp, was only 16 ha, but it was surrounded by a *canabae* that brought the total built-up area to around 100 ha, far larger than either city in the region. The *castra* and *canabae* were occupied from just after the Batavian revolt to 104 CE, when Trajan shifted the legion to the Danube (Willems and Van Enckevort 2009, 56–57), which roughly corresponds to the first half of the Middle Roman A period. This makes weighting difficult. Two alternatives were implemented. In the first, the market is given its full weight for the entire period: the legionary fortress is given a weight of 25 because its size is of the same order of magnitude as the city Oppidum Batavorum. The civil settlement accompanying it was assigned a weight of 75, bringing the total weight to 100. In the second alternative, these weights are halved to correspond to the period of occupation.

Distance is calculated in terms of the time it would take to walk to each market centre. The travel-time model employed here is the same as the one used by

Groenhuijzen and Verhagen (2015, 2017). In contrast to most other distance models, it relies on assigning coefficients to land cover classes rather than slope, which is appropriate since the study area is mostly flat (see Table 9.1 for coefficients).

Cost distance surfaces for every possible market were computed using the Cost Distance tool in Esri's ArcGIS Pro 10.2.1. For each time period, the MP variables were calculated by taking the inverse of each cost surface, multiplying it by the appropriate weight, and summing the results.

9.4 Results

9.4.1 Univariate Analysis

The univariate analysis showed fairly consistent results across time periods. In both zones, at both territorial radii, and in every time period, the K-S test showed that settlement territories had significantly different amounts of high and low levees from the habitable zone ($p < 0.05$). In the central zone, floodplains also differed significantly at both territorial radii and in every time period. In the 1500 m territories, peat differed significantly in every time period, as did fresh water, with the exception of the Early Roman B. The p values for sands and fluvial terraces in the 1500 m territories were consistently low, but only dipped below the 0.05 threshold in the Mid-Roman periods and in the Late Roman B period. In the eastern zone, the results of the K-S test were more consistent between the two settlement territories. In addition to high and low levees, sands and fluvial terraces always differed significantly from the habitable zone. There were also differences in the area of the 1500 m territories covered by fresh water in the Late Iron Age and the Early Roman periods, but in the Early Roman B period, the p value was above the 0.05 threshold.

The estimation of Vargha and Delaney's A statistic showed that, while the differences between settlement territories and the entire habitable zone were statistically significant, they were often small (Fig. 9.2). The largest effect sizes are found in the central zone settlements' preference for high levees, but even here the A statistic never rises above 0.75. Figure 9.2 displays the A statistics for landforms in each zone and territory size. To ease interpretation, 0.5 has been subtracted from each value, so that landforms that are more prevalent in settlement territories have positive values and those that are less prevalent have negative values. These results demonstrate that levees were consistently favoured and other landforms either ignored or avoided. In the central zone, high levees were most preferred and floodplains avoided, while in the eastern zone, low levees were the most preferred and sandy soil was avoided. The high A statistics for low levees is a result of their relative prevalence in the eastern zone as a whole, where high levees are more common. The average percentage of settlement territories covered by high levees is actually greater than low levees, but many locations in the eastern zone have very high percentages of high levee in their territory, so the settlement locations are less unusual in this regard.

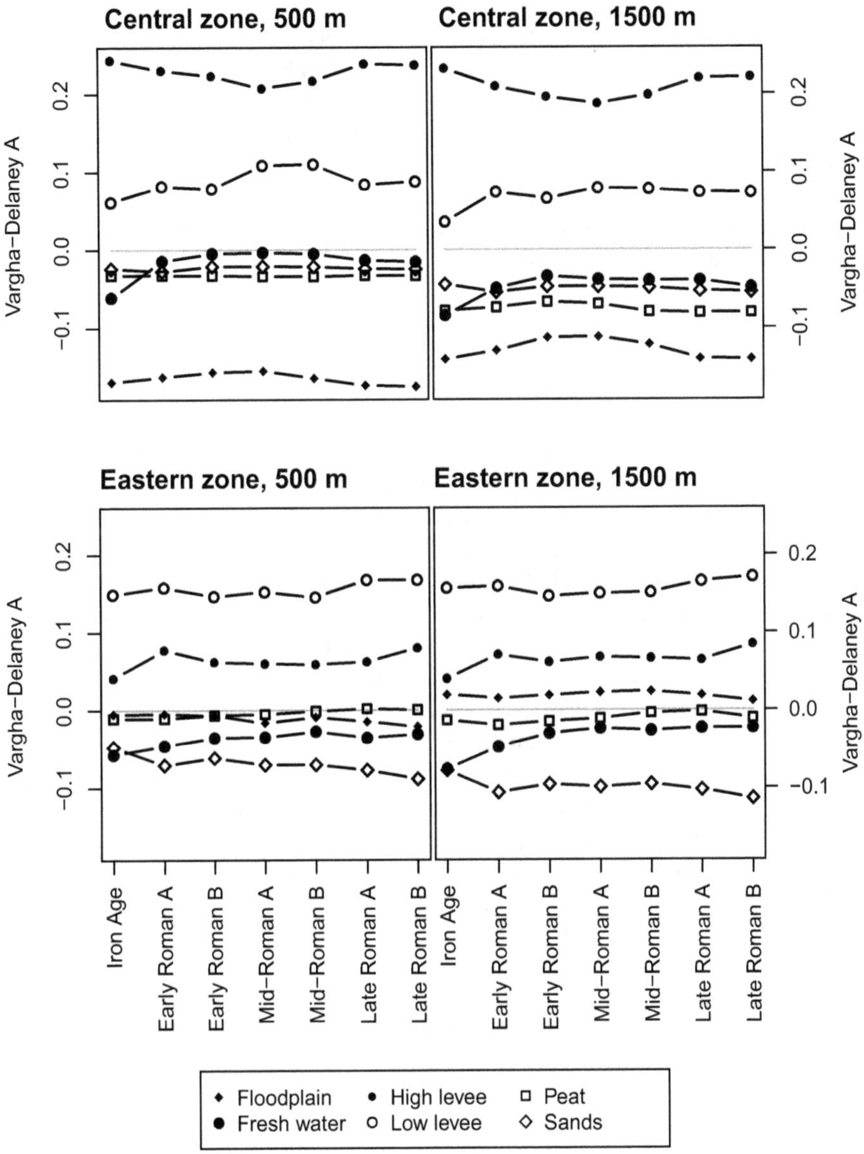

Fig. 9.2 Graphs showing the Vargha and Delaney A statistics. Note that 0.5 has been subtracted from the A statistic to make the results more easily interpretable

Within this pattern, some diachronic trends can be observed. In the central zone, in 500 m territories, the A statistic decreases for high levees and increases for low levees until the Middle Roman A period, after which they separate again. At the same time, the A statistic for floodplains in 1500 m territories rises until the Middle Roman A period before falling again. This mirrors the results of the cluster analysis performed by Verhagen et al. (2016) on all rural settlements in the Lower Rhine. They identified clusters of sites whose 500 m territory was dominated by one landform and found that the proportion of sites in the "floodplain" cluster peaked in the Middle Roman A period at the expense of the "high levee" cluster.

In the eastern zone, there is a distinct jump in the A statistic for high levees in both 500 m and 1500 m territories, which is accompanied by a drop in the A statistic for sands and fluvial terraces, in the Early Roman A period. The gap narrows slightly in the Early Roman B period and then remains stable until the Late Roman B period when the A statistics diverge further.

9.4.2 Multivariate Analysis

The baseline logistic regression models were only moderately successful at distinguishing settlements from non-sites on the basis of the landforms in their territories. Nevertheless, some diachronic trends emerge. RMSEs fall in the eastern zone between the Late Iron Age and the Early Roman A period. In both zones, they rise until the Mid-Roman periods before falling in in the Late Roman A and beginning to rise again in the Late Roman B (Fig. 9.3). This is the same trend as observed in settlement numbers suggesting that as population increased, settlement extended into more marginal areas that resemble non-sites in their territory profiles. Alternatively, factors other than the landforms present in settlement territories could have been influencing settlement location.

The addition of MP variables improved model performance little – never more than 3% – but their contribution was often statistically significant. The results are presented in tabular form in the appendix. Beyond the percentage of improvement, three pieces of information are encoded in these tables: which MP variable improved model performance the most within each settlement/non-site dataset, the statistical significance of the MP variable ($p < 0.1$ or $p < 0.05$), and the sign of the coefficient.

The Late Iron Age, with no forts, had only one MP variable. In the eastern zone, it was significant for 4/5 datasets with 500 m territories and 3/5 datasets with 1500 m territories ($p < 0.05$). Proximity to larger centres, then, seems to have been attractive in the late Iron Age, at least in the eastern zone.

In the Early Roman A period in the central zone, no MP variable consistently improves model performance more than the other nor were any of the variables significant. In the eastern zone, the MP variable without forts consistently improves model performance most with both 500 m and 1500 m settlement territories, but it was significant ($p < 0.1$) in only two of the datasets with 500 m territories. Maximizing access to markets might have mattered somewhat to some people at this early period, but the impact was small. If marketing did matter, however, the market system was centred on the civilian settlements, not the forts.

In the Early Roman B period, in the central zone, the civilian MP variable always outperformed the variable that included forts when examining 1500 m territories.

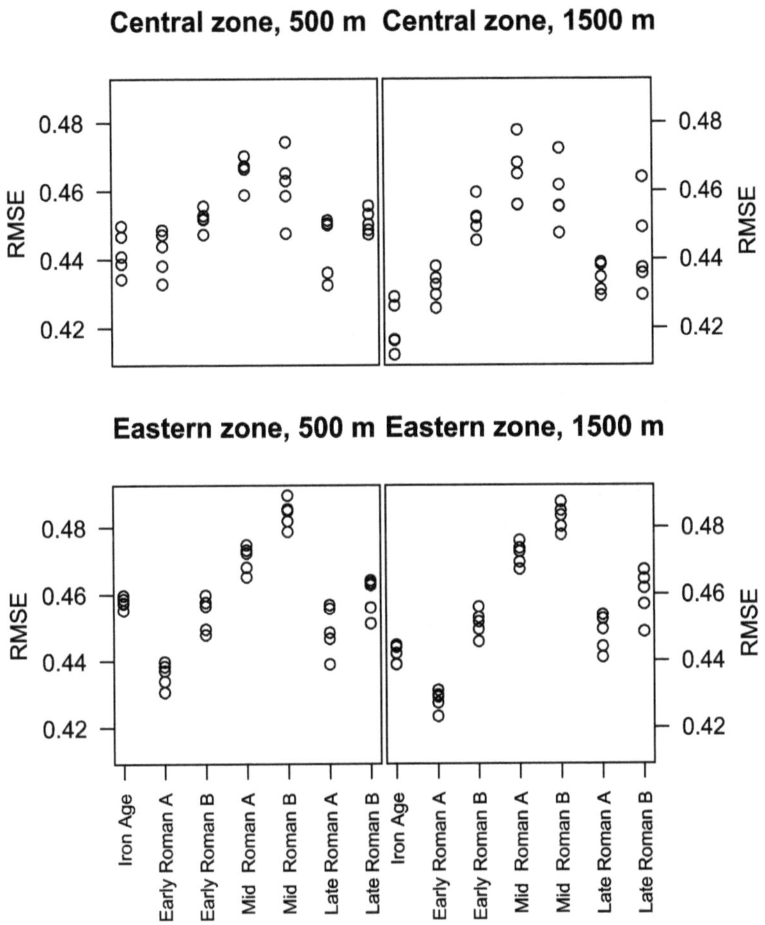

Fig. 9.3 Root mean square errors. Each point represents one dataset combining settlements and non-sites

This variable was significant in 3/5 datasets, and the coefficient was consistently negative. This makes the role of forts difficult to understand. Rural settlements seem to favour areas far from markets, but the effect is less pronounced when forts are included. The eastern zone settlements show a slight tendency to favour civilian centres over forts, but significant MP variables are almost entirely confined to a single dataset. As in the previous period, evidence that proximity to markets shaped settlement location trends is weak, but there is no evidence at all that forts attracted settlements.

The Middle Roman A period shows more consistent results. In the eastern zone, civilian MP variables consistently outperform civilian and military MP variables at both sizes of territory. The variable that assigns a weight of 37.5 to the *canabae* around the legionary *castra* performs better than the variable in which the *canabae* has a weight of 75. The former variable is significant in three out of five datasets, while the latter is significant only once. Therefore, despite the great size of this settlement, it did not completely dominate the rural market.

The Middle Roman B period shows inconsistent results in terms of improvement. Significant variables are confined to the eastern zone where three datasets produced at least one. These improvements were also the largest of any in the analysis: 2.69% in the eastern zone using 1500 m territories and the civilian MP variable. However, both variables performed well: the civilian MP variable performed best three times with 500 m territories and four times with 1500 m territories. It seems that proximity to market centres was more attractive at this time than any other, but the evidence that forts acted as market centres is ambiguous.

The Late Roman A period was also highly inconsistent and produced very few significant variables.

The Late Roman B period produced more significant MP variables than any other. In the central zone, using 1500 m territories, both MP variables are significant ($p < 0.01$) in every dataset except one, where the p value is less than 0.101. The civilian and military MP variable improves model performance the most four out of five times with 1500 m territories and every time using 500 m territories. As in previous periods, the coefficient is always negative.

In the eastern zone, the civilian MP variable is significant in every dataset with both territory sizes, and the civilian and military MP variable is significant in four out of five datasets at both sizes of territory. Which variable improves model performance the most is ambiguous, though. As in the Middle Roman period, proximity to market centres was clearly attractive, but the role of forts remains murky.

9.5 Discussion

9.5.1 Modelling Results

While much remains obscure, one conclusion is certain: the MP variable that includes forts consistently improves model performance more than the variable that excludes them in only one time and place, the central zone in the Late Roman B period, and in that case it has a negative coefficient. When the results are consistent in other contexts, the MP variable that includes only civil settlements improves model performance more. At the same time, the fact that MP variables had negative coefficients in the central zone complicates the matter.

To understand why MP variables so often had negative coefficients in the central zone and the relative improvements of the MP variables, it is helpful to visually compare the distribution of settlements and non-sites relative to each MP variable (Fig. 9.4). Using the civilian MP variable, there are five high MP areas, and the heart of each is devoid of rural settlements but contains several non-sites. Their unusually high MP score allowed the model to successfully identify these locations as belonging to the category of non-sites rather than sites, which explains why the MP vari-

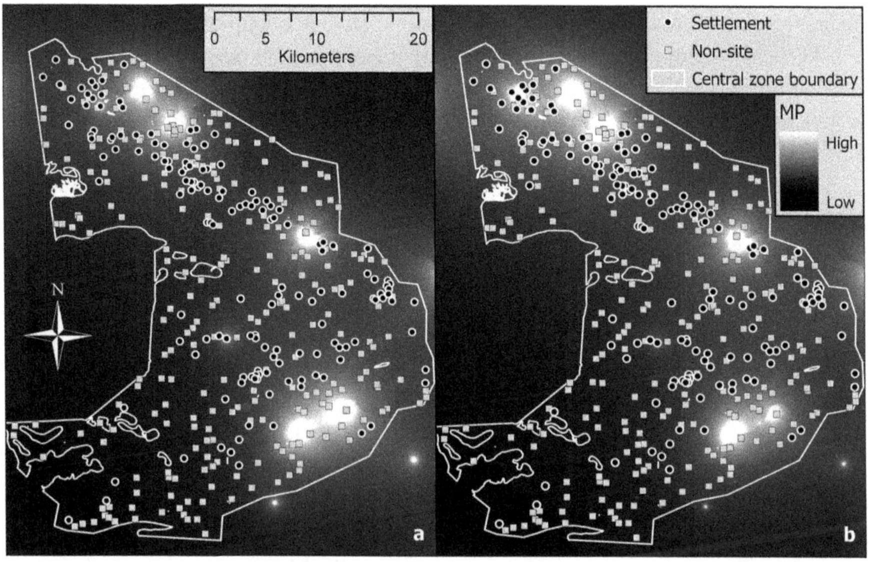

Fig. 9.4 Early Roman B settlements and the second set of non-sites overlaid on the civilian (**a**) and civilian and military (**b**) MP variables. MP variables were most significant and produced the largest improvements over the baseline model with this combination of settlements and non-sites

able has a negative coefficient. Using the civilian and military MP variable, a sixth high MP area emerges in the extreme northwest of the central zone. Unlike the others, this area contains a cluster of settlements. Using this variable, high MP values were found among both settlements and non-sites, confusing the model. This cluster suggests that the fort at De Meern might have attracted rural settlement, but in this it was unusual.

9.5.2 *Historical Implications*

The shift in location preferences identified in the eastern zone in the early Roman A period supports the idea that there was a shift in agricultural practice already in the earliest phase of Roman occupation to supply the new population. Maaike Groot has recently shown that livestock production changed in the early Roman period with an increased emphasis on sheep and a focus on meat production in cattle (Groot 2016, 211–215). Laura Kooistra has emphasized the presence of cereals in Nijmegen and Vechten from this period that could have been locally grown and pointed out the possibility that grain was grown around Meinerswijk and that spelt might have been grown at the behest of the army (Kooistra 2009, 223–226). Groot further argues that, with the exception of the initial conquest, rural producers had a fair degree of freedom in how they responded to the increase in demand (Groot 2016, 213). If the rural settlements did indeed favour proximity to civilian centres, this would support the notion of a mutually beneficial relationship between occupiers and rural producers. At the same time, the fact that the civilian MP variable outperformed the civilian and military MP variable suggests that the new forts themselves did not attract many settlers. Farmers are more likely to have sold their products in civilian markets.

Changes in land use in the central zone are identifiable in the Middle Roman A period, when more settlements have territories that contain larger areas of floodplain and low levees rather than high levees. This coincides with the peak in the RMSEs of the baseline models. With no significant MP variables and negative MP coefficients, there is no indication that the inhabitants of the area were compromising the quality of their land in order to maximize marketing opportunities. Either population pressure was forcing people to inhabit less desirable locales or a large portion of the rural population preferred floodplains. The first option seems unlikely as the number of sites increased in the Middle Roman B period, but the RMSEs of the baseline models fell. Areas with high water tables would have been unsuitable for arable agriculture but well suited to animal husbandry. On the basis of zoological remains and an increase in the sizes of granaries, Groot has argued that both arable farming and animal husbandry intensified in the Middle Roman period (Groot et al. 2009; Groot 2016, 125–128, 215–218). Horse breeding, in particular, became very important in the Middle Roman B period, but increases in the proportion of horse remains are already visible in the Middle Roman A period (Groot 2016, 87–90). Furthermore, variations in species proportions between sites have led her to suggest that settlements were specializing to some extent in the production of different animals for market. If some settlements were focusing on raising animals while others were focusing on agriculture, this would explain the greater variety in environmental preferences observed in this period. This would also help to explain why, even as production for market increased, proximity to markets was not particularly appealing. Livestock has very low transportation costs. The increase in granary size in this period is also consistent with the settlement preferences identified here. Wouter Vos has argued that these large granaries collected produce from other rural settlements (2009, 256–257). By bulking cargo in the countryside, fewer trips to the places of consumption are necessary. Again, this reduces transportation costs. While surplus production for market occurred in the central zone, it seems unlikely that most smallholders were selling their produce directly to consumers. If the forts and *vici* were acting as local market centres, as Vos has argued (2009, 226–229), this function did not influence settlement locations in the central zone.

In the eastern zone, the situation is different. The significant improvements achieved by adding MP variables show that settlers favoured proximity to market centres, which could also help to explain the increasingly poor performance of the baseline model. The peak in model improvement occurs during the Middle Roman B period, which fits well with Groot's conclusions drawn from archaeozoological analysis (Groot 2016). In contrast to the central zone, it seems that access to market centres influenced settlement location tendencies, which in turn suggests that transportation costs were intentionally minimized. This would be consistent with the sale of perishable fruits and vegetables, an undertaking in which the advantages of large landowners are less pronounced than in the sale of grain (Weaverdyck 2016, 4–5), but other scenarios cannot be ruled out.

The forts might have played a role in this process, but it was not particularly large. The civilian MP variable outperformed the civilian and military MP variable consistently in the Middle Roman A period and in the majority of datasets in the Middle Roman B period. What is more, assigning massive weights to the legionary fortress and *canabae* in the Middle Roman A period did not improve model performance as much as assigning them a more moderate weight. Overemphasizing the role of the military only confused the model. The city of Ulpia Noviomagus and the civilian settlements seem to have been the most important market places.

These results should not be taken to deny the importance of the army in the economy of the region as a whole. Many of the civilian settlements were closely tied to the army, military demand surely played a major role in stimulating production, and the salaries paid to soldiers brought significant quantities of coined money to the region. What this does show is that the forts themselves, with the possible exception of De Meern in the Early Roman B period, were not particularly important market centres. The economic relationship between the army and rural producers was usually mediated through civilian institutions. The role of the city of Ulpia Noviomagus would have been crucial. This conclusion mirrors the result of my previous study in the central Lower Danube (Weaverdyck 2016). There too I found that forts failed to influence rural settlement locations despite the undeniable importance of the military in the regional economy. This means that cities and civilian settlements should be seen as an integrated part of the military supply network. It also means, however, that forts played a distinct role as centres of consumption but not necessarily of exchange.

9.6 Conclusion

Comparative logistic regression analysis of rural settlement landscapes has proven to be a useful tool in detecting the subtle influence of marketing behaviour among a population that was likely more focused on production than on transporting their goods to market centres. As with any statistical tool, however, its results require careful interpretation. Improvements in model fit, significance of MP variables, and coefficients of MP variables all proved crucial in drawing conclusions from the results of the modelling process. Furthermore, the comparison data, the non-sites, have as much of an impact on the model as the settlements, so it is crucial to construct multiple sets of non-sites to avoid drawing spurious conclusions. One significant improvement would be to analyse biases in the archaeological record to minimize the risk of placing non-sites in locations that contain undiscovered settlements.

As with any approach, the results of comparative modelling are most meaningful when interpreted in light of other evidence. The Lower Rhine region has the advantage of a long history of excellent research on military, urban, and rural sites.

Location analysis has reinforced and added nuance to the conclusions drawn by other scholars. The presence of the army spurred agricultural intensification and surplus production for market, but this surplus was exchanged in civilian market centres. If the rural population interacted frequently with military personnel, there is little reason to think these interactions occurred in forts. If the military created a landscape of opportunity on the frontier, peasants seized those opportunities primarily in cities and towns.

Acknowledgements I gratefully acknowledge the assistance of the "Finding the Limits of the Limes" project in providing me with the data on which this analysis is based. In particular, I would like to thank Philip Verhagen and Mark Groenhuijzen for their help in understanding the structure and genesis of the data. Verhagen and Groenhuijzen also provided insightful comments on an earlier draft of this paper, as did an anonymous reviewer. Their advice greatly improved my methodology, my interpretations, and my presentation of both. Any errors remain my own.

Appendix 9.1

The improvement in RMSE achieved by the addition of MP variables is presented in the tables below. N-S stands for non-site and indicates which set of non-sites was used in each model. Each column corresponds to a different MP variable. When multiple MP variables were tested, the maximum improvement for each set of non-sites is written in bold. When the coefficient of the MP variable was negative, the improvement figure is printed in italics. A single set of parentheses indicates that the *p* value of the MP variable is less than 0.1, and a double set of parentheses indicates the *p* values is less than 0.05.

"Civ" indicates MP variables that include only cities, civil settlements, and cult sites. "Civ & Mil" indicates MP variables that also include *castella* and *castra*. "Civ & Mil*" is an MP variable used in the Early Roman A, which contains *castella* but not the *castra*. "Civ**" and "Civ & Mil**" are MP variables used in the Middle Roman A period which assign half weights to the *castra* and legionary *canabae*. The weighting scheme is described above (see Table 9.2).

Late Iron Age				
	Central zone		Eastern zone	
	500 m	1500 m	500 m	1500 m
N-S	Civ	Civ	Civ	Civ
1	*0.64%*	*0.15%*	((0.87%))	((0.77%))
2	*0.30%*	*0.14%*	0.31%	0.16%

(continued)

Late Iron Age				
	Central zone		**Eastern zone**	
	500 m	1500 m	500 m	1500 m
N-S	Civ	Civ	Civ	Civ
3	*0.18%*	*0.00%*	((0.66%))	0.47%
4	*0.15%*	*0.03%*	((1.38%))	((1.27%))
5	*0.12%*	*0.16%*	((0.72%))	(0.54%)

Early Roman A						
	500 m			1500 m		
N-S	Civ	Civ & Mil	Civ & Mil*	Civ	Civ & Mil	Civ & Mil*
Central zone						
1	0.02%	0.09%	**0.10%**	*−0.01%*	*−0.01%*	***0.00%***
2	0.01%	0.01%	**0.02%**	*0.00%*	***0.02%***	*0.00%*
3	***0.45%***	*0.30%*	*0.31%*	***0.27%***	*0.24%*	*0.23%*
4	***0.13%***	*0.02%*	*0.02%*	***0.14%***	*0.10%*	*0.09%*
5	***0.05%***	*0.00%*	*0.00%*	*−0.02%*	*−0.02%*	***−0.02%***
Eastern zone						
1	**0.28%**	*0.00%*	0.00%	**0.14%**	*0.00%*	0.00%
2	**(0.58%)**	0.21%	0.20%	**(0.58%)**	0.16%	0.22%
3	**0.36%**	0.02%	0.12%	**0.23%**	*0.00%*	0.03%
4	**(0.51%)**	0.45%	0.43%	**0.31%**	0.16%	0.15%
5	**0.06%**	*0.01%*	*0.00%*	**0.05%**	*0.03%*	*0.00%*

Early Roman B				
	500 m		1500 m	
N-S	Civ	Civ & Mil	Civ	Civ & Mil
Central zone				
1	***0.06%***	0.02%	***0.30%***	*0.04%*
2	***((0.85%))***	*(0.45%)*	***((1.43%))***	*((0.76%))*
3	*0.01%*	**0.04%**	***(0.32%)***	*0.02%*
4	*0.02%*	**0.06%**	***(0.42%)***	*0.04%*
5	*0.01%*	**0.14%**	***0.18%***	*0.01%*
Eastern zone				
	500 m		1500 m	
1	**0.00%**	*0.00%*	**0.02%**	0.00%
2	*0.00%*	***0.00%***	*0.00%*	***0.00%***
3	**((0.65%))**	(0.35%)	**((0.81%))**	(0.44%)
4	**0.07%**	0.02%	**0.12%**	0.05%
5	**0.24%**	*0.01%*	**(0.36%)**	*0.00%*

Middle Roman A				
N-S	Civ	Civ & Mil	Civ**	Civ & Mil**
Central zone				
	500 m			
1	***0.04%***	*0.02%*	*0.04%*	*0.02%*
2	0.05%	0.11%	0.08%	**0.13%**
3	0.00%	0.09%	0.01%	**0.10%**
4	*0.06%*	*0.00%*	***0.06%***	*0.00%*
5	***0.05%***	*0.01%*	*0.04%*	*0.01%*
	1500 m			
1	***0.25%***	*0.21%*	*0.23%*	*0.19%*
2	***0.10%***	*0.05%*	*0.07%*	*0.04%*
3	***0.24%***	*0.01%*	*0.14%*	*0.00%*
4	***0.11%***	*−0.01%*	*0.08%*	0.00%
5	***0.20%***	*0.13%*	*0.18%*	*0.11%*
Eastern zone				
	500 m			
1	0.09%	0.07%	**0.15%**	0.12%
2	0.27%	0.18%	**(0.38%)**	0.24%
3	0.00%	0.00%	**0.01%**	0.01%
4	(0.33%)	0.17%	**((0.52%))**	0.25%
5	((0.67%))	((0.60%))	**((0.89%))**	((0.79%))
	1500 m			
1	0.17%	0.14%	**0.26%**	0.23%
2	(0.38%)	0.28%	**((0.52%))**	0.35%
3	0.01%	0.00%	**0.04%**	0.03%
4	((0.54%))	(0.35%)	**((0.80%))**	(0.48%)
5	((0.89%))	((0.82%))	**((1.14%))**	((1.06%))

Middle Roman B				
	500 m		1500 m	
N-S	Civ	Civ & Mil	Civ	Civ & Mil
Central zone				
1	**0.02%**	*0.01%*	*0.01%*	***0.04%***
2	***0.01%***	*0.00%*	***0.15%***	*0.05%*
3	0.05%	**0.10%**	*−0.01%*	***0.00%***
4	0.15%	**0.26%**	0.04%	**0.15%**
5	0.29%	**0.41%**	0.00%	**0.01%**
Eastern zone				
1	0.33%	**0.34%**	**0.45%**	0.43%
2	**((0.58%))**	0.20%	**((0.76%))**	0.31%
3	0.24%	**0.24%**	0.33%	**0.34%**
4	**((2.25%))**	((2.04%))	**((2.69%))**	((2.47%))
5	**((0.82%))**	((0.56%))	**((1.00%))**	((0.68%))

(continued)

Late Roman A				
	500 m		1500 m	
N-S	Civ	Civ & Mil	Civ	Civ & Mil
Central zone				
1	0.00%	***0.02%***	*−0.01%*	***−0.01%***
2	*0.05%*	***0.11%***	*0.03%*	***0.05%***
3	*0.33%*	***0.34%***	***0.23%***	*0.18%*
4	***0.10%***	*0.09%*	*−0.01%*	***−0.01%***
5	**0.03%**	0.00%	**0.04%**	0.02%
Eastern zone				
1	**((0.83%))**	((0.69%))	**((0.98%))**	((0.87%))
2	(0.51%)	**((0.66%))**	((0.68%))	**((0.93%))**
3	0.02%	**0.03%**	0.02%	**0.03%**
4	0.03%	**0.03%**	0.04%	**0.06%**
5	0.00%	**0.10%**	0.01%	**0.15%**

Late Roman B				
	500 m		1500 m	
N-S	Civ	Civ & Mil	Civ	Civ & Mil
Central zone				
1	*0.34%*	***(0.59%)***	*((0.28%))*	***((0.42%))***
2	*0.05%*	***0.20%***	*(0.24%)*	***0.25%***
3	*0.03%*	***0.05%***	***(0.20%)***	*(0.15%)*
4	*0.14%*	***0.19%***	*(0.57%)*	***((0.90%))***
5	*(0.46%)*	***(0.62%)***	*((0.68%))*	***((0.89%))***
Eastern zone				
1	((1.05%))	**((1.16%))**	((1.32%))	**((1.45%))**
2	**(0.44%)**	0.28%	**(0.52%)**	0.35%
3	**((0.88%))**	((0.81%))	**((0.92%))**	((0.88%))
4	(0.42%)	**(0.54%)**	(0.50%)	**((0.64%))**
5	((0.81%))	**((0.93%))**	((0.88%))	**((1.00%))**

References

Bintliff J (2002) Going to market in antiquity. In: Olshausen E, Sonnabend H (eds) Stuttgarter Kolloquium zur historischen Geographie in Altertums 7, 1999: Zu Wasser und zu Land. Verkehrswege in der Antiken Welt. Franz Steiner, Stuttgart, pp 209–250

Casarotto A, Pelgrom J, Stek TD (2016) Testing settlement models in the early Roman colonial landscapes of Venusia (291 B.C.), Cosa (273 B.C.) and Aesernia (263 B.C.). J Field Archaeol 41:568–586. https://doi.org/10.1080/00934690.2016.1211474

Citter C, Arnoldus-Huyzendveld A (2014) Site location and resources exploitation: predictive models for the plain of Grosseto. Archeologia Medievale 41:65–78

De Neeve PW (1984) Peasants in peril: location and economy in Italy in the second century B.C. J.C. Gieben, Amsterdam

De Vries J (1984) European urbanization 1500–1800. Harvard University Press, Cambridge, MA

Gaffney V, Van Leusen M (1995) Postscript – GIS, environmental determinism and archaeology: a parallel text. In: Lock GR, Stančič Z (eds) Archaeology and geographical information systems: a European perspective. Taylor & Francis, London

Goodchild H (2007) Modelling Roman agricultural production in the middle Tiber valley, central Italy. University of Birmingham, Birmingham. Available at http://etheses.bham.ac.uk/175/. Accessed on 14 May 2018

Groenhuijzen MR, Verhagen P (2015) Exploring the dynamics of transport in the Dutch limes. eTopoi J Anc Stud 4:25–47. Available at http://journal.topoi.org/index.php/etopoi/article/view/203. Accessed on 14 May 2018

Groenhuijzen MR, Verhagen P (2017) Comparing network construction techniques in the context of local transport networks in the Dutch part of the Roman *limes*. J Archaeol Sci Rep 15:235–251. https://doi.org/10.1016/j.jasrep.2017.07.024

Groot M (2008) Surplus production of animal products for the Roman army in a rural settlement in the Dutch River Area. In: Stallibrass S, Thomas R (eds) Feeding the Roman army: the archaeology of production and supply in NW Europe. Oxbow Books, Oxford, pp 83–98

Groot M (2016) Livestock for sale: animal husbandry in a Roman frontier zone: the case study of the Civitas Batavorum. Amsterdam University Press, Amsterdam

Groot M, Heeren S, Kooistra LI, Vos WK (2009) Surplus production for the market? The agrarian economy in the non-villa landscapes of Germania Inferior. J Roman Archaeol 22:231–252. https://doi.org/10.1017/S1047759400020687

Haggett P (1965) Locational analysis in human geography. Edward Arnold (Publishers) Ltd, London

Hanel N (2007) Military camps, canabae, and vici: the archaeological evidence. In: Erdkamp P (ed) A companion to the Roman army. Blackwell, Malden, pp 395–416. https://doi.org/10.1002/9780470996577.ch23

Horden P, Purcell N (2000) The corrupting sea: a study of Mediterranean history. Blackwell, Oxford

Joyce J, Verhagen P (2016) Simulating the farm: computational modelling of cattle and sheep herd dynamics for the analysis of past animal husbandry practices. In: Multi-, inter- and transdisciplinary research in landscape archaeology. Proceedings of LAC 2014 Conference, Rome, 19–20 September 2014. Vrije Universiteit Amsterdam, Amsterdam. https://doi.org/10.5463/lac.2014.59

Kay SJ, Witcher RE (2009) Predictive modelling of Roman settlement in the middle Tiber valley. Archeologia e calcolatori 20:277–290. Available at http://www.archcalc.cnr.it/indice/PDF20/21_Kay.pdf. Accessed on 14 May 2018

Kemmers F (2007) Coins for a legion. An analysis of the coin finds from the Augustan legionary fortress and Flavian canabae legionis at Nijmegen. Philipp von Zabern, Mainz am Rhein

Kohler TA, Parker SC (1986) Predictive models for archaeological resource location. In: Schiffer MB (ed) Advances in archaeological method and theory 9. Academic Press, New York, pp 397–452. https://doi.org/10.1016/B978-0-12-003109-2.50011-8

Kooistra LI (1996) Borderland farming: possibilities and limitation of farming in the Roman period and early middle ages between the Rhine and Meuse. Van Gorcum, Assen

Kooistra L (2009) The provisioning of the Roman Army in the Rhine Delta between c. AD 40 and 140. In: Morillo A, Hanel N, Martín E (eds) Limes XX: XX Congreso Internacional de Estudios sobre la Frontera Romana/XXth International Congress of Roman Frontier Studies, Léon (España), Septiembre, 2006. Consejo Superior de Investigaciones Científicas/Polifemo, Madrid, pp 1309–1315

Kooistra LI, van Dinter M, Dütting MK, Van Rijn P, Cavallo C (2013) Could the local population of the Lower Rhine delta supply the Roman army? Part 1: The archaeological and historical framework. J Archaeol Low Countr 4:5–23

Kvamme KL (1988) Development and testing of quantitative models. In: Judge WJ, Sebastian L (eds) Quantifying the present and predicting the past: theory, method, and application of archeological predictive modeling. U.S. Department of the Interior, Bureau of Land Management, Denver, pp 325–428

Kvamme KL (1990) One-sample tests in regional archaeological analysis: new possibilities through computer technology. Am Antiq 55:367–381. https://doi.org/10.2307/281655

Li JC-H (2016) Effect size measures in a two-independent-samples case with nonnormal and nonhomogeneous data. Behav Res Methods 48:1560–1574. https://doi.org/10.3758/s13428-015-0667-z

Llobera M (2012) Life on a pixel: challenges in the development of digital methods within an "interpretive" landscape archaeology framework. J Archaeol Method Theory 19:495–509. https://doi.org/10.1007/s10816-012-9139-2

Morley N (1996) Metropolis and hinterland: the city of Rome and the Italian economy, 200 B.C.-A.D. 200. Cambridge University Press, Cambridge. https://doi.org/10.1017/CBO9780511518584

Nuninger L, Verhagen P, Bertoncello F, Castrorao Barba A (2016) Estimating "land use heritage" to model changes in archaeological settlement patterns. In: Multi-, inter- and transdisciplinary research in landscape archaeology. Proceedings of LAC 2014 Conference, Rome, 19–20 September 2014. Vrije Universiteit Amsterdam, Amsterdam. https://doi.org/10.5463/lac.2014.60

Patterson JR (2004) City, territory and metropolis: the case of the Tiber valley. In: Patterson H (ed) Bridging the Tiber: approaches to regional archaeology in the Middle Tiber Valley. British School at Rome, London, pp 61–73

R Core Team (2017) R: A language environment for statistical computing. R Foundation for Statistical Computing, Vienna. Online resource available at http://www.R-project.org/

Torchiano M (2017) effsize: Efficient effect size computation. Online resource available at https://CRAN.R-project.org/package=effsize

Tourneux F-P (2003) Analyse de l'environnement des établissements. In: Van der Leeuw SE (ed) Archéologie et systèmes socio-environnementaux: études multiscalaires sur la vallée du Rhône dans le programme Archaeomedes. CNRS Éditions, Paris, pp 255–275

Van der Leeuw SE (1998) The Archaeomedes project: understanding the natural and anthropogenic causes of land degradation and desertification in the Mediterranean basin; research results. Office for Official Publications of the European Communities, Luxembourg

Van der Leeuw SE (ed) (2003) Archéologie et systèmes socio-environnementaux: études multiscalaires sur la vallée du Rhône dans le programme Archaeomedes. CNRS Éditions, Paris

Van Dinter M (2013) The Roman Limes in the Netherlands: how a delta landscape determined the location of the military structures. Neth J Geosci 92:11–32. https://doi.org/10.1017/S0016774600000251

Van Dinter M (2017) Living along the Limes: landscape and settlement in the Lower Rhine Delta during Roman and early Medieval times. University of Utrecht, Utrecht

Van Dinter M, Kooistra LI, Dütting MK, Van Rijn P, Cavallo C (2014) Could the local population of the Lower Rhine delta supply the Roman army? Part 2: Modelling the carrying capacity using archaeological, palaeo-ecological and geomorphological data. J Archaeol Low Countr 5:5–50

Vargha A, Delaney HD (2000) A critique and improvement of the CL common language effect size statistics of McGraw and Wong. J Educ Behav Stat 25:101–132. https://doi.org/10.3102/10769986025002101

Verhagen P, Whitley TG (2012) Integrating archaeological theory and predictive modeling: a live report from the scene. J Archaeol Method Theory 19:49–100. https://doi.org/10.1007/s10816-011-9102-7

Verhagen P, Nuninger L, Bertoncello F, Tourneux F-P, Jeneson K (2013) Introducing the human factor in predictive modelling: a work in progress. In: Earl G, Sly T, Chrysanthi A, Murrieta-Flores P, Papadopoulos C, Romanowska I, Wheatley D (eds) Archaeology in the Digital Era: Papers from the 40th Annual conference of Computer Applications and Quantitative

Methods in Archaeology (CAA), Southampton, 26–29 March 2012. Amsterdam University Press, Amsterdam, pp 379–388. Available at http://arno.uva.nl/cgi/arno/show.cgi?fid=516092. Accessed on 14 May 2018

Verhagen P, Vossen I, Groenhuijzen MR, Joyce J (2016a) Now you see them, now you don't: defining and using a flexible chronology of sites for spatial analysis of Roman settlement in the Dutch river area. J Archaeol Sci Rep 10:309–332. https://doi.org/10.1016/j.jasrep.2016.10.006

Verhagen P, Joyce J, Groenhuizen M (2016b) Modelling the dynamics of demography in the Dutch Roman Limes zone. In: In: Multi-, inter- and transdisciplinary research in landscape archaeology. Proceedings of LAC 2014 Conference, Rome, 19–20 September 2014. Vrije Universiteit Amsterdam, Amsterdam. https://doi.org/10.5463/lac.2014.62

Von Thünen, JH (1966) Der isolierte Staat in Beziehung auf Landwirtschaft und Nationalökonomie, Neudr. von 1842 bzw. 1850, 4., unveränd. Aufl. Fischer, Stuttgart

Vos WK (2009) Bataafs platteland: Het Romeinse nederzettingslandschap in het Nederlandse Kromme-Rijngebied. Rijksdienst Voor Het Cultureel Erfgoed, Amersfoort

Warren RE (1990) Predictive modelling of archaeological site location: a primer. In: Allen K, Green S, Zubrow E (eds) Interpreting space: GIS and archaeology. Taylor & Francis, London, pp 90–111

Warren RE, Asch DL (2000) A predictive model of archaeological site location in the Eastern Prairie Peninsula. In: Wescott K, Brandon J (eds) Practical applications of GIS for archaeologists: a predictive modeling toolkit. Taylor and Francis, London/New York, pp 5–32

Weaverdyck E (2016) Isolation or integration? A spatial analytical approach to the local impact of the roman army on the northern frontier. University of California, Berkeley. Available at https://escholarship.org/uc/item/5h65s74k. Accessed on 14 May 2018

Wheatley D, Gillings M (2002) Spatial technology and archaeology: the archaeological applications of GIS. CRC Press, London

Willems WJH, Van Enckevort H (2009) Ulpia Noviomagus, Roman Nijmegen: the Batavian capital at the imperial frontier. J Roman Archaeol, Portsmouth, RI

Witcher R (2008) The middle Tiber valley in the imperial period. In: Coarelli F, Patterson H (eds) Mercator Placidissimus: the Tiber valley in antiquity. Edizioni Quasar, Rome, pp 467–487

Woodman PE (2000) A predictive model for Mesolithic site location on Islay using logistic regression and GIS. In: Mithen SJ (ed) Hunter-gatherer landscape archaeology: the Southern Hebrides Mesolithic project, 1988–98. McDonald Institute for Archaeological Research, Cambridge, pp 445–464

Woodman PE, Woodward M (2002) The use and abuse of statistical methods in archaeological site location modelling. In: Wheatley D, Earl G, Poppy S (eds) Contemporary themes in archaeological computing. Oxbow Books, Oxford, pp 22–27

Chapter 10
A Multi-scalar Approach to Long-Term Dynamics, Spatial Relations and Economic Networks of Roman Secondary Settlements in Italy and the Ombrone Valley System (Southern Tuscany): Towards a Model?

Stefano Bertoldi, Gabriele Castiglia, and Angelo Castrorao Barba

Abstract In Roman landscapes, the particular sites defined as secondary settlements (also known as *vici*/villages, minor centres, *agglomérations secondaires* and/or *stationes/mansiones*) have played an 'intermediary' role between the cities and other rural structures (*villae*/farms), linked to medium- and long-distance economic and commercial trajectories. The aim of this paper is to apply a multi-scalar approach to model their long-term spatial relationships and connectivity with the Mediterranean exchange network. On the macro-scale, we have analysed a sample of 219 reviewed sites to understand the diachronic trends and spatial dynamics of attraction/proximity to significant elements of the landscape such as towns, roads, rivers and coastline. The Ombrone Valley (Tuscany, Italy) represents a micro-scale case study of a complex system, in which the imported pottery (*amphorae*, African Red Slip ware, *ingobbiata di rosso*) found in the *vicus/mansio* of Santa Cristina in Caio, the Roman *villa* of La Befa and the town of Siena (*Saena Iulia*) provided diagnostic 'macroeconomic' perspectives. The results show how the secondary settlements occupied a nodal position in the Roman landscape in terms of resilience (long period of occupation until the Early Middle Ages) and spatial organization with a close relationship to natural and anthropic infrastructures and trade functions linked to Mediterranean routes.

Keywords Settlement patterns · Diachrony · Roman pottery · Network analysis · Statistics · GIS

S. Bertoldi
University of Siena, Siena, Italy

G. Castiglia
Pontifical Institute of Christian Archaeology, Rome, Italy

A. Castrorao Barba (✉)
University of Palermo, Palermo, Italy
e-mail: angelo.castroraobarba@unipa.it

P. Verhagen et al. (eds.), *Finding the Limits of the Limes*, Computational Social Sciences, https://doi.org/10.1007/978-3-030-04576-0_10

10.1 Introduction to the Study of Secondary Settlements: Theory and Method

Archaeological research into indicators for defining Roman settlements as 'secondary' (*agglomération secondaire*) (Leveau 2012; Garmy 2012), a theoretical intermediate between towns and *villae*, is still emerging (see Crogiez 1990, 391; Chevallier 1997, 284; Mezzolani 1992 113; Corsi 2000, 186; Maggi and Zaccaria 1994, 163–168; Cantino Wataghin et al. 2007, 88; Goffredo et al. 2013) (Fig. 10.1). This interpretation related to settlement hierarchy is also expressed in the definition of these sites as 'minor centres' (Tol et al. 2014). In the archaeological record, however, only a certain number of excavated sites were identified as secondary settlements: they are characterized as places with a specific role in the roads of the *cursus publicus* and/or rural agglomerations of the *vicanico* type (communities living in nucleated villages; Tarpin 2006).

Studying the topic of 'secondary settlements' requires the inclusion of a wide variety of themes, including the role of these sites, their abandonment and reuse, the organization of rural areas, trade, production, Christianization and land and river traffics.

The hypothesis that some of these sites seem to respect certain rules of spatial order oriented our research aimed to determine whether a trend or pattern in the spatial order of secondary settlements can be detected.

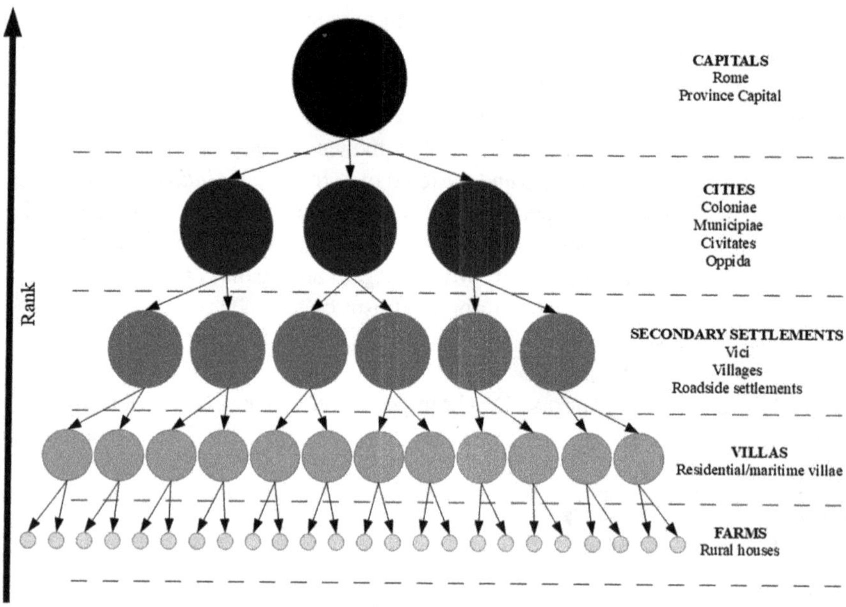

Fig. 10.1 Theoretical dendrogram of rank-size classification of Roman settlements, reworked from Garmy (2002, 31). About the classification of settlement types have been re-elaborated the macro generic groups proposed in Witcher (2012), and the typology of Roman cities has been taken from Nevett and Perkins (2000)

This kind of settlement is closely associated with economic functions: secondary settlements appear to fulfil the role of centres promoting and providing trades and services. The 'amount of services offered by a settlement' is a concept introduced in geography by Christaller (1980), who argues that it could be used as an indicator for defining the importance of an inhabited site with greater accuracy than the population of the site. The approach of the German geographer is crucial for addressing the problem of secondary settlements, the materiality and magnificence of which are insignificant in comparison to the monumental *villae*, but which held strategic importance in the 'State system'.

In this regard, the definition given by M. Corbier concerning the Gallo-Roman *vicus* is extraordinarily effective: 'A village that lives by exploiting a territory but not necessarily only through agriculture' (Corbier 1986, 691). A settlement of this kind often is involved in various productive crafts, such as the procurement of raw materials, leading to the construction of a system in which there are patterns ruling the space (Bischi et al. 2004); however, the outcomes are still influenced by many variables. In this system, even small changes can lead to very different results. Therefore, as in climatology and economics, it is very difficult to predict what may occur in the future. Following this line of reasoning, we can compare archaeology to burning matchsticks. Even with similar initial conditions, the smoke of each matchstick will follow very different trajectories, its path difficult to predict (De Guio 1992). This 'chaos theory' has also been studied in Physics, to explain how an attractor regulates a system governed by deterministic and causal dynamics (Lorenz 1963).

By looking at the settlements' network and its analytical composition, and the transformations and degradation thereof, one can observe a few spatial rules: whatever these rules are, we wonder what the driving forces behind them are.

In our work, the concept of 'cause' that Bloch had identified as 'the misstep of a man walking in the mountains' (Bloch 1998, 138–143) and that Flannery (1968, 67–87) and Plog (1975, 213–216) called the differential or 'kicking' element lost importance. What matters more here is to identify the forces generating these causations in their entirety. We will not aim to predict the past, nor will we deal with overly complex phenomena, thus leaving room for physicists, philosophers and theologians (Citter 2012, 13). We will use geographical and statistical methods only for descriptive analysis.

The theme of 'attractors' and the ability of some elements of the natural and human landscape to attract and/or repel goods, settlements, etc. is certainly not a novelty in archaeology (Wheatley and Gillings 2002, 134–135). The study of the diffusion of finds (in this case imported pottery) in certain types of settlements transforms us into a kind of Hop-o'My-Thumb (Perrault 2012, 42–46), in search of the traces left in the woods, with the goal of returning home. Unlike Hop-o'My-Thumb, however, we cannot tell if we are in front of a white stone or a crumb of bread. The truth of the past is difficult to grasp: not all of the material culture has survived, not all of the material culture can be found, not all the material culture has been excavated, not all the material culture indicates trade. However, studying the relationships and trade flows through pottery imports, and the products they carried, requires investigating 'traces', without aiming for the completeness of the record, but nevertheless using the same methodology as the other branches of archaeology. Ultimately, rules exist in archaeology; however they are very complex.

10.2 Quantitative Approaches to the Analysis of Secondary Settlements in Italy in the Long Term

With a full knowledge of certain physiological problems of interpretation, we have tried to establish a program of cataloguing all of the published contexts in Italy, from both excavations and surface surveys, and interpreted in various ways (*stationes*, *mansiones*, *mutationes*, villages/*vici*, etc.), which may all be categorized as part of the group of 'secondary settlements' (Castrorao Barba 2016).

The compilation of a significant sample of sites formed the basis from which to undertake a quantitative approach to comparing the description of long-term historical trends with the spatial relationships to significant elements, both natural (natural coastlines and rivers) and anthropogenic (towns and roads).

The bibliographic inventory was stored in a database with information on the initial and final phases of the various settlements. The sites included in this study are those with a chronology dating between the first and sixth centuries CE and which have been identified by the excavators/publishers as those that may be defined as secondary settlements.[1] A sample of 219 sites (Fig. 10.2a) was collected (Table 10.1): 68.9% of them have been subject to excavation, while 31.1% are known only through field surveys.

For the purpose of 'data mining', descriptive statistics and spatial analysis were undertaken on this sample, in order to answer the following questions:

- When was the first phase of occupation of these secondary settlements?
- What percentage of the sites was active in the long term (third century BCE to thirteenth century CE)?
- How often did the sites remain active for a number of centuries?
- What is the relationship between abandoned sites and those permanently reoccupied after the end of the stage referred to as 'secondary settlement'?
- When did the phenomenon of reuse begin?
- What percentage of the sites being reused was characterized by the construction of a church?
- Was the location of the secondary settlements determined by the proximity (attractiveness) to certain important elements of the landscape (coastlines, rivers, towns, roads)?
- Which of the four 'attractors' appears to be the closest to a single site?

[1] This database is part of a PhD research project granted by the University of Siena (Castrorao Barba 2013), using the DBMS 'Carta Archeologica' (Fronza 2005) managed by the LIAAM laboratory at the University of Siena, under the direction of Marco Valenti.

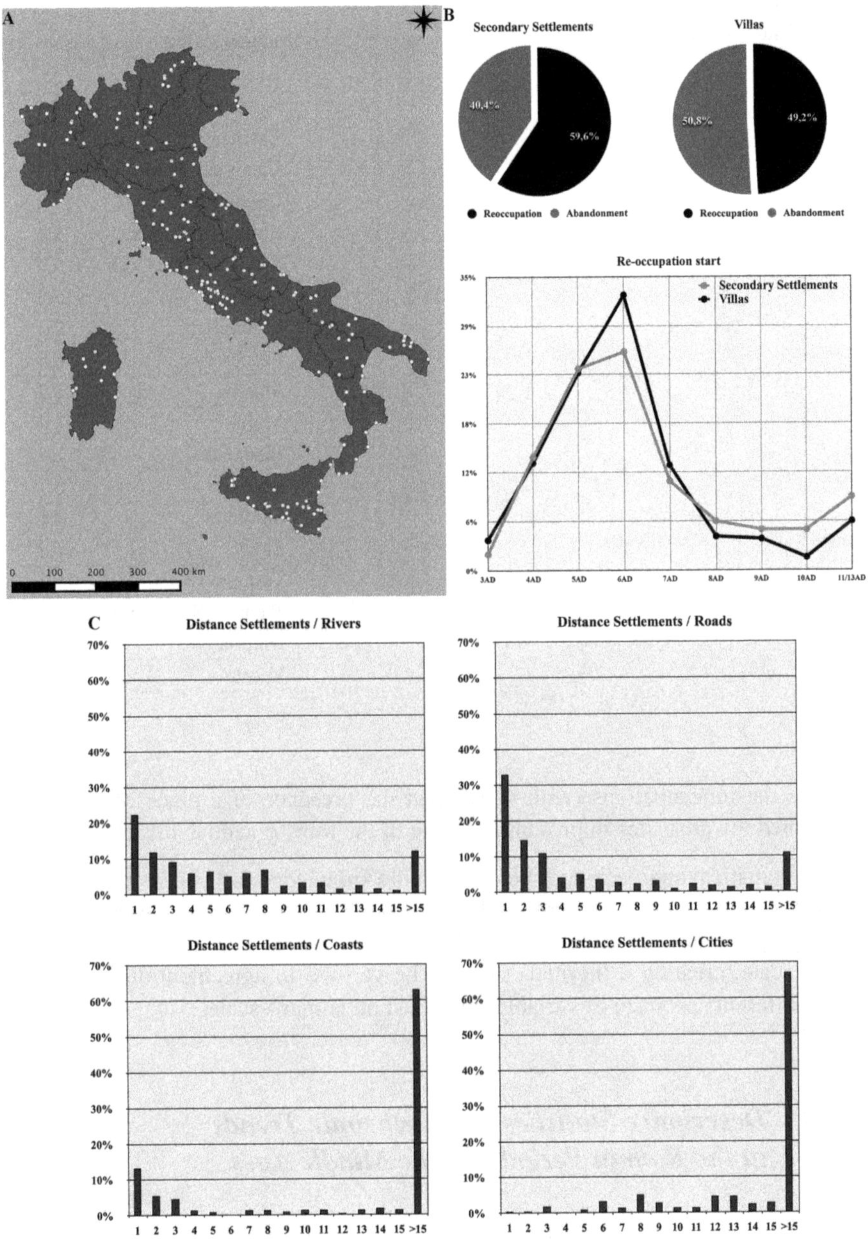

Fig. 10.2 (**a**) Distribution map with the sample of 219 sites used for the spatial and statistical analyses. (**b**) Comparison between *villae* and secondary settlements: percentages of deserted sites, of reoccupied sites and chronology of the reoccupation. (**c**) Frequency histograms of percentages related to distances (one class of 1 km from 0 to 15 km and then a unique class superior to 15 km) between secondary settlements and landscape elements (rivers, roads, coastlines, towns)

Table 10.1 Proportions of collected sites per region

Italian regions	% of sites
Abruzzo	4.6
Aosta Valley	1.4
Basilicata	3.2
Calabria	5
Campania	3.2
Emilia-Romagna	4.6
Friuli-Venezia Giulia	0.9
Latium	15.5
Liguria	2.3
Lombardy	5.5
Marche	3.2
Molise	1.4
Piemonte	2.7
Apulia	8.7
Sardinia	4.1
Sicily	14.2
Tuscany	11.4
Trentino-South Tyrol	4.6
Umbria	0.5
Veneto	3.2

- Were the reoccupations (with or without the presence of a place of worship) oriented towards sites in proximity to one of the four 'potential attractors'?

This statistical approach does not exhaust the knowledge that can be gained from this data source, nor is it its purpose. However, it is a robust tool for describing and quantifying a material reality (spatial relationships between sites and landscape) on a large scale, creating a 'normal' trend to be verified in agreement/disagreement with a different spectrum of variables observed on a micro-scale.

10.2.1 Descriptive Statistics on Diachronic Trends in the Roman Period and the Middle Ages

The quantification of the initial chronologies of secondary settlements shows that traces of human occupation dating from before the third century BCE can be detected in a fairly high percentage of sites (14.2%), while just over half of the sample (51.1%) shows an early stage dating to the first century BCE/first century CE. Following this, we see an accelerating decline in the number of new sites being settled, except for a brief period in the fourth century CE (8.2%).

By looking at the distribution of the frequency of sites in the individual centuries (Fig. 10.3a) between the third century BCE and the thirteenth century CE, a peak is observed in the fourth century CE (83.6%) and in the first century CE (81.7%) with

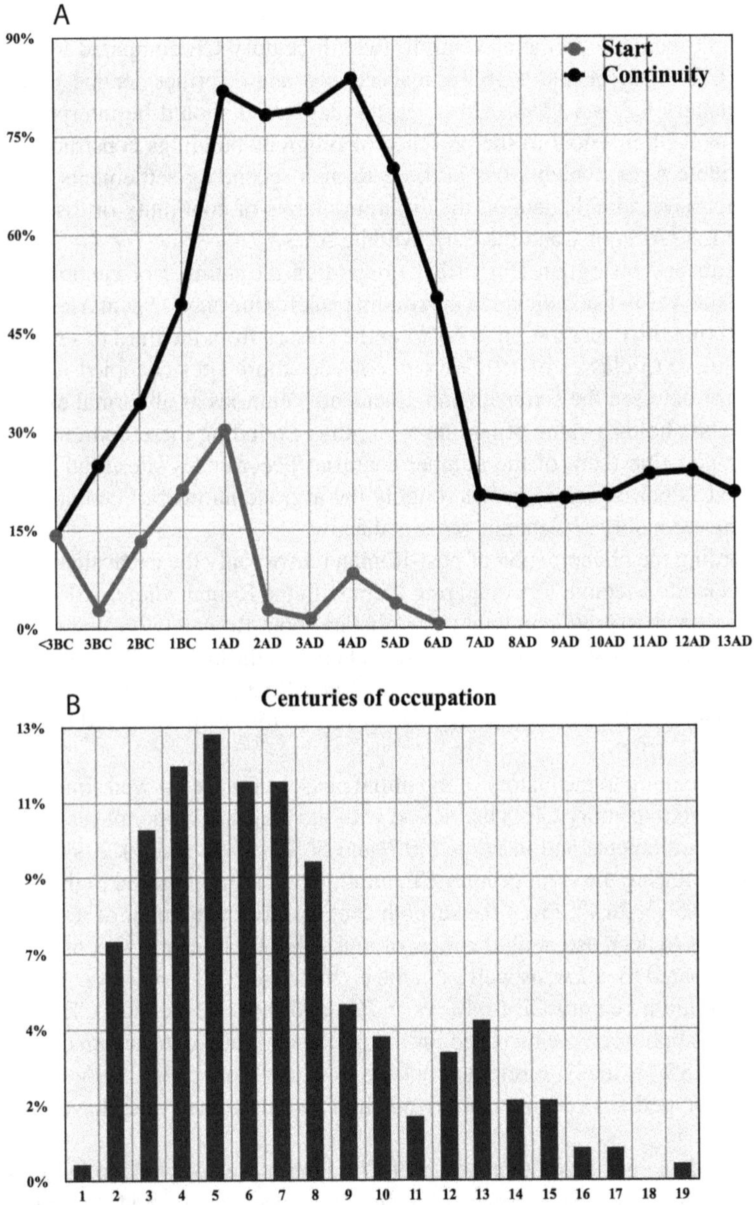

Fig. 10.3 (**a**) Diachronic trend of secondary settlements in Italy: start and continuity of occupation. (**b**) Frequency histogram with the secondary settlements' centuries of life

the period between the first and the fourth centuries CE containing an average 80.6% of the sample. In the following period, between the fifth and the seventh centuries CE, we see a progressive reduction of occupied sites with a growing decline: −16.4% between the fourth and the fifth centuries CE, −28.1% between the fifth and sixth centuries, and – 60% between the sixth and seventh centuries. After a stabilization between the seventh and ninth centuries CE (average – 3.4%), there were slight increases in the eleventh to twelfth century CE compared to the tenth century CE, + 18.1% and + 15.9% respectively, and a further decline in the thirteenth century CE (−13.5%). However, this last trend should be interpreted with caution as it often refers to the presence of religious buildings constructed in the High Middle Ages, which arose in those Roman secondary settlements for which we do not have reliable data on the different phases of continuity or discontinuity between Late Antiquity and the Early Middle Ages.

A frequency histogram (Fig. 10.3b) regarding the number of centuries during which a site was in use indicates a maximum peak for the class '5 centuries' (18.8%) and a maximum concentration (57.5%) in the classes from the third to seventh century inclusive (5 classes of 19). We can consider those sites occupied for the first century, or between the sixteenth and nineteenth centuries as abnormal exceptions, as each class holds a value of less than 1%, thus excluding these 'extreme' values. An average value (sum of the number centuries/occurrences sites/total sites) was calculated as 6.5, which indicates roughly the average number of centuries during which the secondary settlements remained active.

Regarding the phenomenon of post-Roman reuses, only the excavated sites have been taken into account, by comparing them with the Roman *villae*, 151 secondary settlements and 768 *villae* in total (for statistics about Roman *villae* and reuses, see Castrorao Barba 2014a, b). The comparison between the cases with traces of reuses and the definitively deserted sites reveals a clear difference between the two groups, with secondary settlements most likely to be reused (59.6%), compared to the villae (49.2%) (Fig. 10.2b).

Curves relating to the history of the initial phases of reuse showed similar trends: the fifth to sixth century CE is the period with the highest number of reuses both in secondary settlements and in *villae* (50% and 56.2% respectively). A similar peak can be seen during the sixth century CE, although more pronounced in the group of *villae* (32.8% vs. 26%). From the seventh century CE, the number of new cases of reuse begins to decrease, with the rates of reuse slightly higher in secondary settlements compared to *villae*, as well as in the eighth century CE (5.8% vs. 4% respectively), the ninth century CE (4.8% vs. 3.7%) and the tenth century CE (4.8% vs. 1.5%). The slight increase recorded for the period eleventh to thirteenth century CE (8.7% vs. 5.8%) is likely to refer to contexts in which reuse phases prior to the construction (or perhaps reconstruction) of churches in Roman sites have not been recognized.

Further data concerns the presence of Christian places of worship built on pre-existing Roman sites: the presence of a church is documented in 44.2% of cases of reuse of secondary settlements, with a lower proportion of reuses of *villae* (34.6%). In absolute terms, the number of *villae* in which a church has been identified is higher, but this figure is highly biased by the higher total number of Roman *villae* and the greater spread of their territory. The high percentage for the secondary settlements indicates that this type of site was more attractive for the construction of churches, while *villae* had proportionally higher rates of other types of reuses (housing units or groups of tombs).

10.2.2 Spatial Statistics for the 'Attractive Force' of the Landscape's Significant Elements on Secondary Settlements

Assessing the relationship between settlement choices and landscape elements on a large scale, whether natural (rivers and coast lines) or anthropogenic (roads and towns), required an extensive amount of data processing.

To quantify the concept of 'attraction', it was necessary to connect it to the idea of 'distance': the closer site *x* is to place *y*, the greatest the attractiveness of *y* on *x*. Through a further effort of abstraction, the Earth's surface was considered flat and smooth, eliminating all geomorphological roughness, as if it were a two-dimensional Cartesian plane (Euclidean space). GIS-based spatial analysis made it possible to calculate all distances in meters between the individual sites and the four potential attractors: rivers, coastlines, roads and towns. The goal was to understand the distribution of the sample in various intervals of linear distances in relation to the attractors, in order to numerically verify the different levels of proximity.

A statistical indicator was used to summarize the relative percentage frequency of the values of the site/attractor distances within 15 size classes. This operation expresses the number of times (as a percentage of the total) in which a distance value is included in a class (Coccarda 2011, 64). The definition of the number and amplitude of the classes included only the sites' attractors within a 15 km limit, beyond which the relationship between the entities is practically irrelevant.

The reading of the frequency histograms allows us to make some observations. In general, the majority of sites are located within 1 km of a river (22.4%) or a road (32.9%), with the terrestrial communication routes representing the main attractor. A much lower proportion of sites are located within 1 km of the coastline (13.2%), while those in close proximity to urban settlements (0–1 km) represent only 0.5% of sites. The low combined force exerted by coasts and cities can be also observed in the high number of inhabited centres located over 15 km away: 63% and 67.1% for coastal and urban areas, respectively, while only 11 0.9% and 11% are positioned that far from rivers and roads (Fig. 10.2c).

The data on the first quartile for the four attractors, i.e. the value falling in the first 25% of the distances sorted in ascending order, mirror the patterns seen in the frequencies. The roads show the lowest values, an indicator of the higher proximity of sites to roads, followed by rivers and then by coasts and cities, where 75% of sites are at a distance that exceeds at least 4 km from the attractor.

A different spatial analysis allowed us to identify the 'unique element' closest to rivers, roads, coasts and cities for each settlement: also in this case, the proximity to roads constitutes the most attractive element with 46.6%, followed by rivers (41.1%), coastlines (11.4%) and towns (0.9%).

In order to evaluate the impact of the different surface occupied by the buffer zones of 1 km around rivers, cities, coastlines and roads, the statistics are weighed. The percentage of the sites inside this proximity area was subtracted from the total area covered by the single buffer zones in the entire surface of Italy. The results show – also in comparison with the villas – the stronger relationship between the secondary settlements and the roads, the coastlines and the rivers.

These percentages are a numerical representation of the close spatial link between secondary settlements and communication systems (major roads and rivers), a characteristic that demonstrates the importance of the inclusion of these populations within a complex system of interactions and flows of people, ideas and goods. In contrast, towns appear to exercise a centrifugal and bumping force, creating an area of 'respect' related to the authority of the town, which is not seen around 'secondary rank' settlement types. This 'hegemonic' role of the cities characterized by its surroundings empty of large sites, such as secondary settlements, is well explained in the classic geographical theories of central places (Christaller 1980) and rank-size law (Zipf 1949). Secondary settlements appear to have an alternative role and perhaps competition compared to cities.

The same pattern (proximity to rivers and roads and distance from towns) is also found in sites that were reoccupied for an extended period, with new functions between the Late Antiquity and the Middle Ages (fourth to thirteenth century CE), 47.5% of the total sample. Fifty per cent of the reused settlements were located at a short distance from a road compared to the other landscape elements (39.4% from a river, 9.6% from the coast, 1% from towns). Furthermore, the relative frequency percentages indicate the same trend outlined for secondary settlements: a maximum peak in the sites located 0–1 km from roads (34%) and rivers (27.9%) and a minimum for coasts (12.5%) and cities (0%). If we compare the histograms of the total with those of the reused sites, we notice an increase in the incidence of proximity to rivers in the reused sites (+5.5%) and a sharp decline in reused complexes in the vicinity of a city (& gt;15 km 73.1%, +6% compared to all sites).

Within the reused contexts, there were 46 cases (44.2%) in which the presence of a Christian place of worship can be identified. The places chosen for reuse for the construction of a church were those in proximity to a road (50%) or river (37%) and further from the coast line (13%); 39.1% of the sites were located within 2 km of a road, 30.4% within 2 km of a river and 13% within 2 km of the coastline.

10.3 From Global to Local: The 'Ombrone System'

The objective of the data presented thus far is the definition of an economic landscape that we have defined as the 'Ombrone System' (Fig. 10.4). The strength of our analysis comes from the fact that this system was not conceived a priori but was

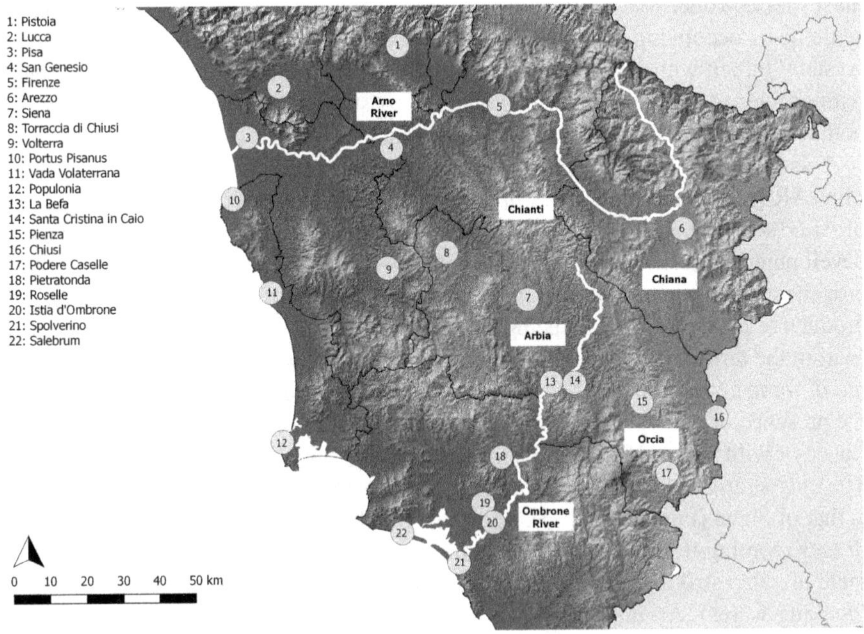

Fig. 10.4 Map of central and southern Tuscany (Arno and Ombrone valleys) with the sites mentioned in the text

based on analysis made in previous research (Bertoldi and Castiglia 2015; Bertoldi et al. 2015) which embraced landscape studies, spatial analysis and the study of material culture and settlements, which have gradually come to define the economic landscape. Research based primarily on the analysis of the secondary settlement of Santa Cristina in Caio (Bertoldi and Valenti 2016) gradually led to the framing of a much wider network, made up of roads, towns, commodities, rivers and people. From a positivist point of view, a base of quantitative data allows us to understand how countryside, urbanization and commercial trade (in different hierarchies) can interact with each other, despite some significant differences. The rigorous analysis of the origin of *amphorae* was undoubtedly one of the indicators with the greatest impact in this respect. This is not the place to dwell into the details of individual *amphora* types observed in the different contexts we have considered, as it would serve only to repeat a precise assessment already made in another study (Bertoldi and Castiglia 2015), but rather we want to dwell on a range of selected indicators, fundamental to the definition of the 'Ombrone system'. One of the most striking points in the comparison between the town and countryside is dictated by the presence/absence of the so-called '*amphora* of Forlimpopoli'. These were produced in the Adriatic side of Italy (in different types: see Aldini 1978; Aldini 1999; Panella 1989; Panella 2001) predominantly between the first century BCE and the third century CE. It is common in Santa Cristina in Caio, present in smaller quantities at La Befa, but is completely absent in Siena. In order to discuss this phenomenon, we must first consider this important fact: Santa Cristina and La Befa, despite being settlements occupying different hierarchic levels, form part of the same economic 'system' (albeit with different roles). They were in dialogue with each other but also with entities at both the hinterland and the coast (via Ombrone), a 'block' that is both different and complementary to towns such as Siena.

This dichotomy is well readable also in the proportional values of African Red Slip (ARS) ware and *ingobbiata di rosso* (local red slipware produced as imitation of ARS, see Fontana 1998), which allows us to develop a hypothesis regarding the development of relationships within a network of settlements which, even on a heterogeneous hierarchical scale, seems to consist of a solid network of commercial/productive exchanges. Introducing the Roman *villa* of Aiano-Torraccia di Chiusi (within the territory of Siena) into these comparisons, we can see that the *ingobbiata di rosso* coming from this site (quite plausibly produced in situ, as indicated by the presence of a kiln; see Cavalieri 2008) is not comparable either with the area of Lucca or with that of Florence, Pisa or Empoli and only minimally so with Fiesole. The only stratigraphic basin with which there are actual and demonstrable affinities is that of Siena (Fumo 2010, 33). The same trend can be detected in the *ingobbiata di rosso* coming from Santa Cristina in Caio and the Chianti region, sites with which there are also striking comparisons for coarse ware, especially regarding the *ollae* (cooking wares). An important aspect of these three contexts is also the fact that they are, respectively, to the north, south and east of the city of Siena, with a practically equidistant mileage from the city centre. It is therefore plausible to think about this complex of settlements as a deeply interconnected economic system, in which each vector acts as both an origin and a destination for certain types of pottery.

Based on the fact that a kiln has been identified in Torraccia di Chiusi and on production waste from the Chianti region, the presence of *ingobbiata di rosso* manufacturing workshops has been hypothesized (Valenti 1995). This leads us to believe that the town of Siena was the primary destination of a production chain originating in rural areas. Furthermore, the interdependence of Siena with rural settlements seems well demonstrated by its relationship with the third region, namely, Santa Cristina in Caio. In fact, remarkable similarities between the artefacts can be recognized here too, so on the one hand, Siena could be the starting point of what was produced in the other two settlements/distribution areas but at the same time also the destination of the goods passing by Santa Cristina. In this regard, in fact, in a recent and already quoted article (Bertoldi and Castiglia 2015), we have shown (or at least have proposed an interpretive key worthy of further consideration) that the Ombrone river, on the banks of which Santa Cristina was located, represented a constant artery in the period between the first and seventh centuries CE, ensuring supplies to the hinterland of Siena to a greater degree than the roads. This, therefore, explains the arrival of *amphorae* to the city from overseas during the seventh century CE (Cantini 2005, 197), right through the *vicus/mansio* of Santa Cristina in Caio.

The River Ombrone was navigable for at least part of its course; Plinius describes it as *navigiorum capax* (Naturalis Historia, III, 51) and Rutilius Namatianus as *non ignobile flumen* (De Reditu Suo, I, 337). The Ombrone's navigability is controversial. Some argue that the river, at most, was passable until Istia d'Ombrone (a few kilometres north-east of Rusellae) (Cardarelli 1971, 15), while others more recently have denied its navigability (Arnoldus-Huyzendveld 2011, 41).

However, addressing the problem from a wider standpoint, its navigability becomes a 'non-issue': the importance of a river is not determined only in terms of its use for aquatic transport. It is no coincidence that in Italy the systems of the Po and Arno rivers have been thoroughly studied. In order to understand the role of a river network, it is sufficient to look at the permeability (north-south) and convenience (east-west) of the Danube in Roman times, apparently used only as a natural border.

Returning to our subject, we know that there must have been a road that connected Siena with Populonia; at first, it was assumed that this road accessed not only the area of Siena but also the whole countryside south of the city.

Noting, however, the distribution of the extra Italic pottery findings, there is a clear 'penetration line' stretching from the coastlines to the hinterland, independent of the previously mentioned line of access, which connected Populonia and Siena. In this system, Roselle becomes a point of departure/sorting of products coming from ports along the coastline (as previously supposed for the town of Siena and the *ingobbiata di rosso*). From here, the goods traced the course of the Ombrone until the current town of Civitella Paganico, home to a site identified as a Roman *villa*, called Pietratonda (Barbieri 2004: the author thinks actually of a *vicus* or of a *mansio*, due to the thermal baths for public use). This site would act as a junction, with the goods that had been travelling north-east and then crossing the Ombrone at the confluence of the river Orcia and bypassing the hill of Montalcino in the south. This route guaranteed faster communication between the coastal area and the valleys of the Orcia and Arbia and the site of Santa Cristina in Caio. This settlement was the terminal of the trade network and a market place for a large area, south of the city of Siena. A similar settlement is likely to have existed in Val d'Orcia (likely in the south-east), although the current state of knowledge is insufficient for estimating its location.

10.3.1 Pottery Imports in the Sites of Siena, Santa Cristina in Caio and La Befa

As already noted in other papers (e.g. Bertoldi and Castiglia 2015), the definition of relational systems between settlements and other forms of secondary agglomerates, at different hierarchical levels, must be accompanied by a systematic analysis of the pottery finds, in order to identify commercial relations at various distances. *Amphorae* should be considered a key part of the economic system and, therefore, an indication of contact between human settlements. This approach should be complemented with the fundamental study of ARS ware and its imitations. This brief introduction is essential, as this methodological approach is useful not only for purely 'descriptive' goals but also for an understanding of what will be defined as the ‘Ombrone system’. In this context, it was decided to enrich previous research (Bertoldi and Castiglia 2015) with the analysis of a little-known and previously overlooked site, the Roman villa of La Befa. Located only a few kilometres away from Santa Cristina in Caio, it was partially investigated archaeologically during the 1970s. It is not necessary here to describe the entire stratigraphy and structural evolution of the complex (for that, see the integral edition of the excavation in Dobbins 1980). It is sufficient to point out how the structures, at least in the investigated area, were abandoned at the end of the fourth century CE and that traces of later settling are not recorded. What aim to outline here is the assemblage of the identified pottery types, which will be integrated with the assessment of the Santa Cristina in Caio archaeological record, in order to later compare them with the data related to the urban context of Siena.

It must be stressed from the start that *amphorae*, and in particular the ARS ware, are not found in large quantities in La Befa, although qualitative analysis can be used to draw significant conclusions. The chronological frame of interest was divided into two main macro-blocks, one from the first century CE to the first half of the third century and the other from the second half of the third century CE to the end of the sixth century. It can be noted that in the earlier centuries, imports coming from the coastlines formed greater than 78% of the total, while the goods coming from inland areas make up the remaining to 22%. In the second chronological period, the disparity increases further, with a coastline/hinterland relationship of 98%/2%. With regard to the ARS ware, only five fragments of this typology were identified throughout the stratigraphic sequence, with only two having a reliable chronology, dating back to the half of the third century CE (Dobbins 1980, 143). In the period between the first century CE and the first half of the third century, 63% of the amphorae originated from the coastline, while 37% was from inland areas; between the second half of the third century CE and the end of the sixth century, these values diverge further, with 74% of the goods travelling from the coast and 26% originating inland. Using the same kind of analysis on Siena shows that in the first period there is a prevalence of coastline-sourced (and therefore maritime) items comprising 91% compared to 9%. In the second period, this trend remains almost unchanged, with a ratio of 89–11% (for Siena, see Cantini 2005; Castiglia 2014, 2015).

These analyses reflect very clear trends: La Befa and Santa Cristina, while playing different roles in the landscape and having heterogeneous ‘settlement hierarchies’ (being in the first place a *villa* and secondly a *vicus/mansio*, probably acting in the role of ‘central place’), reflect the same tendency towards trade related to coastal environments (and, therefore, in close relationship with the Ombrone river, as we shall see in the following paragraphs). The town of Siena itself displays the same trend, reflecting the inclusion of the urban centre in the same system. It does not seem to be accidental that the fraction reflected in the two chronological macro-groups corresponds to a very specific economic phenomenon that swept much of the Mediterranean from the third century CE. In all three analysed settlements, we witness, in the Early Imperial Age, a majority of goods coming mainly from the Iberian Peninsula (primarily from Baetica but partly also from Tarraconensis, especially *garum* and oil), as well as high-quality *amphorae* coming from Italy, associated with the transport of wine. From the third century CE, a sharp decline in both Hispanic and Italian products is documented, corresponding to the explosion of goods from North African markets, which become a characteristic feature in the archaeological record.

This evidence is derived exclusively from *amphorae*, as the ARS ware is present in very low quantities, in some cases close to zero, although higher quantities are seen in towns. In this sense, it is very important to consider the role of local products imitating the ARS such as the *ingobbiata di rosso*. These are characterized by almost slavish reproductions of the original North African pottery, although are of lower quality, especially in the coatings (consisting of reddish or brownish engobe), and peak chronologically in Tuscia between the late fourth and the sixth to early seventh centuries CE (Valenti 1991, 1995, 1996; Cantini 2015; Vaccaro 2015). This class is widely seen in both Siena and Santa Cristina, revealing a desire to imitate forms that no longer reached inland markets and, a need to fill the gaps to which the available supply could not respond. This indicates that a demand for ARS ware still existed, so the lack of certain types of ARS ware reflects a decline in trade routes. At the same time, the need to imitate, and therefore produce, these morphologically similar types ties to Roman tradition, mirror of the presence of still configured (although resized) needs and requirements that cannot yet plausibly be read as a reflection of a real crisis, which instead will accrue and be completed only in later centuries (Valenti 1999, 85). The absence of this pottery class in La Befa, however, could simply be due to the fact that, following the disintegration and subsequent abandonment of the facilities of the villa at the end of the fourth century CE, it has not been possible to record anthropogenic activities for those centuries in which the *ingobbiata di rosso* was a 'guide fossil'.

Since we have completed all the 'descriptive' and quantitative assessment, in the following section dedicated to the definition of the so-called Ombrone system, we will trace the implications of the material culture on the 'settlement hierarchies' and how we believe that these implications can be read.

10.4 Approaching Network Analysis: The Case of the Ombrone Valley

Trade relations in archaeology, especially for products for which we know the origin, contribute to the understanding of the complex interchange systems, especially within the Roman globalized world (Pitts and Versluys 2015).

In archaeology, the concept of networks is not a novelty: commercial exchanges, ideas, artisans and road networks are studied, but generally the term is used in a very generic way, or as a synonym of connectivity (Leidwanger et al. 2014). Like many other disciplines, such as statistics and geography, the network analysis had already been intuited by the New Archaeologists (see Clarke 1998), long before the development of software able to help us in the application of such methodologies. With the development of post-processual theories, during the 1980s and 1990s, an anti-network thought was affirmed, which criticized the excessive rigidity of the system, technique and analysis (Knappett 2013; Collar et al. 2015).

We used the software Cytoscape (version 3.4), which is created for the visualization of molecular interaction in bioinformatics.[2]

We have selected the sites where a specific ARS form has been identified (e.g. Hayes 61), to create series of relationships and then linking the sites with the GIS least-cost path algorithm, for example, from the Salebrum harbour to the city of Roselle, from Roselle to Santa Cristina in Caio, and from Santa Cristina in Caio to the La Befa *villa*.

Fundamental statistics in network analysis are those linked to the concept of centrality: the calculation of the degree of centrality for each vertex and the degree of centralization of the network in general (Freeman 1978).

Besides the graphic representation, it is interesting to analyse some values that the network analysis generates: in particular, the betweenness centrality, which corresponds to the sum of the length of the shortest paths between each node and all the others to which it is directly connected and the edge betweenness, that is defined as the number of the shortest paths that go through an edge in a graph or network (Girvan and Newman 2002; Fig. 10.5).

Between the second and the third centuries, the chronological period chosen for network analysis, we identify three major commercial flows: the Mediterranean imports (arriving in the Tuscan hinterland from the Tyrrhenian ports), the Empoli *amphorae* and the Adriatic productions.

Santa Cristina is a central place in the commercial network of Roman Tuscany and in particular in the subnetwork of the southern part of the region. In particular, the settlement was a node of the three commercial routes described. The Mediterranean imports arrived in Santa Cristina from the Ombrone valley and were sold in the valleys of the Arbia and Orcia (and perhaps up to Chiusi). The Adriatic productions came from the valleys of Chiana and Orcia and are sold in nearby areas (such as the La Befa villa). The amphora of Empoli came to Santa Cristina from Siena and then in Roselle via the Ombrone river.

During the second century, Santa Cristina in Caio was the third site for betweenness centrality: the settlement had a role of distribution of Mediterranean products coming from the coast, towards Pienza, La Befa and Podere Caselle, and the Adriatic products coming from the Chiana valley towards Roselle, La Befa, Siena and then Volterra. The other nine sites on the top ten list are Pisa, Vada Volaterrana, Portus Scabris, Lucca, Roselle, Pistoia, San Genesio, Firenze and Portus Pisanus.

During the third century, among the top ten settlements with higher betweenness centrality, there are four cities (Pisa, Firenze, Arezzo and Lucca), four ports (Vada Volaterrana, Portus Pisanus, Portus Scabris and Spolverino) and two inland secondary settlements (San Genesio and Santa Cristina), connected to Roman roads and

[2] This software was developed in Seattle by the Institute for Systems Biology in 2002, then released under an Open license and currently maintained by a group of developers.

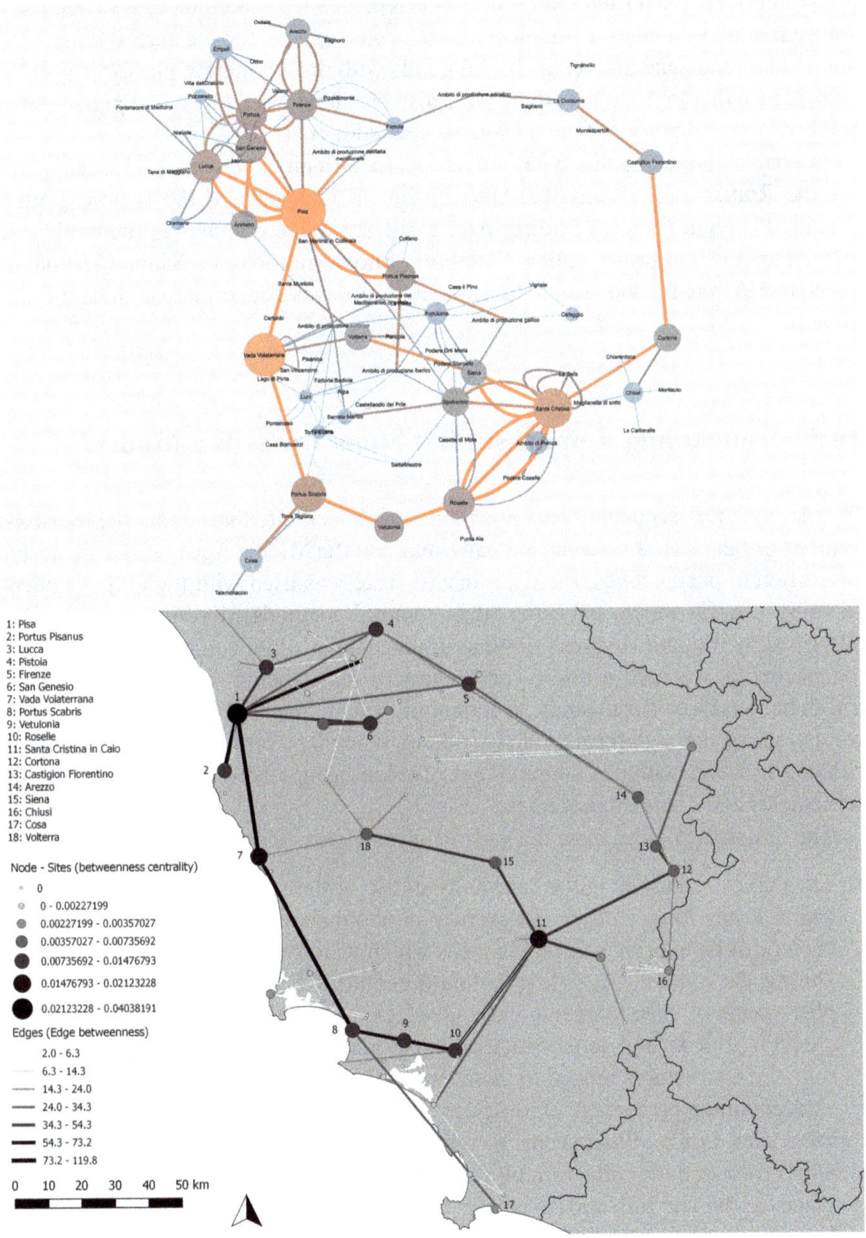

Fig. 10.5 (**a**) Network analysis of Tuscan settlements with ARS ware. The size of the sites is based on the factor named betweenness centrality, and the size of the edge is based on the edge betweenness. (**b**) GIS spatial representation of network analysis

important rivers (Arno and Ombrone). This type of sites was connected to commercial function. Secondary settlements were central places for the surrounding economic landscape and also to exchange goods with distant market places. It is not a coincidence that in these sites there were also productive activities, like pottery, iron and bricks (for Santa Cristina in Caio, see Bertoldi et al. 2017).

In conclusion, using this type of analysis, the principal network of Tuscany during the Roman period was the Arno system in the north of the region (Portus Pisanus-Pisa-San Genesio-Firenze-Arezzo). The second commercial network was located in the Ombrone valley (Salebrum-Spolverino-Roselle-Santa Cristina in Caio-Siena/Chiusi), and Santa Cristina in Caio was the principal node of the system.

10.5 Concluding Remarks: First Steps Towards a Model?

In order to define secondary settlements in their specificity throughout the transformations of landscapes between Roman times and the Middle Ages, we have chosen two different perspectives. Firstly, a macro-scale was used with the aim of understanding general trends by using 'data mining' methods (descriptive statistics), described by Richard Hodges (1989) as a 'parachutist's job' equipped with calculator. Secondly, we used a micro- or semimicro-scale (being 'cyclists' rather than truffle hunters) in order to study an economic system, the Ombrone valley, in which we can grasp the significance of the role of secondary settlements such as Santa Cristina in Caio, within a complex net of relationships between the hierarchy of settlements and commercial routes.

The first data coming from the sample of reviewed sites show some trends:

- The curves representing the continuity of use of the secondary settlements indicate a strong *longue durée* (an average of about six centuries), with a high percentage of Roman sites settled in areas which were previously already occupied.
- During the Imperial Age (first to fourth century CE), we do not record drastic phenomena of abandonment, and, indeed, in the fourth century CE, there is the creation of new rural settlements, contemporary to the maintenance of the vital role of the structures related to the *cursus publicus*.
- The remaining percentage of reuses, even more significant when compared to the trend seen in the *villae*, seems to reflect a greater attractiveness to new settlements formed during the difficult centuries of the deconstruction of Roman landscapes in the late fifth and especially the sixth century CE.
- In the secondary settlements (higher than in villae), the high percentage of reuses characterized by the construction of a church is a quantitative indicator connected to the organizational strategies of the Christianization of rural areas, probably planned by the Church itself from the fifth century CE onwards (this phenomenon finds a similar comparison in the Tiber Valley and is highlighted by the excavations at the Mola di Monte Gelato; see Potter and King 1997; more in

general, for Lazio, see also the fundamental Fiocchi Nicolai 1994). The position of secondary settlements in the landscape, favourable both for the interaction of man and environment and for its proximity to the crucial areas of the economic framework (roads, rivers and the sea), may have played an important role in the choice of secondary settlements as ideal places for the construction of rural churches, in a view of 'a precise plan of territorial occupation by the diocesan authority' (Cantino Wataghin et al. 2007, 105; Castiglia 2018).

- From a simplified and bi-dimensional point of view, the infrastructures of communication (roads and rivers) where goods and people travelled are phenomena of great importance in relation to the secondary settlements, which tend to be located in proximity to these infrastructures. In contrast, towns had their own area of influence 'rejecting' secondary settlements with a centripetal force, as in Coulomb's law, the coexistence of two poles with a strong 'charge' is impossible, especially in the paradigm of economic production, consumption and distribution of goods.
- The link of settlements with trade and the tendency of these to occupy nodes within economic trajectories in medium and large geographical areas is very important for understanding the continuity of employment of a site throughout the deconstruction of the Roman 'world system' and the complex emergence of the new Early Medieval world.

Under this general framework, however, lies a greater complexity in which certain factors and variables play a key role in our understanding of the historical processes.

The analysis of the 'Ombrone system' allowed us to compare the data of different kinds of sites (town-secondary settlement-villa) in the context of relations between sea and land along communication routes. In this framework, using the pottery analysis (*amphorae*, ARS and *ingobbiata di rosso*) as an indicator of economic flows has enabled us to better delineate connections between sites and between sites and the wider economic system.

Moreover, the detailed analysis of pottery held diagnostic 'macro-economic' perspectives, revealing how towns, secondary settlements and *villae* within this system, although playing different roles, managed to silently communicate. The city seems to be both the point of arrival and departure of certain types of goods, especially the *ingobbiata di rosso* produced in rural areas. The urban context, therefore, seems to remain an important point of reference in the hierarchy of commercial exchanges, despite the context of deep structural and topographic reconfigurations, such as the transition between Late Antiquity and Middle Ages. Nevertheless, the actual production needs to take place in rural areas and in the infrastructure connected to them, with workshops now constructed *extra urbem*, aiming to satisfy needs no longer tied to a large economic system such as that of the Empire but still anchored in the requirements of a market still influenced by it. The real turning point will take place only in the fully Early Medieval period, from the seventh century onwards. If we look at the nearby regional case of Lazio, the Tiber Valley Project, carried by the British School at Rome (Patterson 2010), represents a significant and interesting comparison. In this case, from the third century onwards, there is a marked drop of settlements, with just an ephemeral reprise in the fourth and fifth centuries, with the secondary settlements going through a deep crisis: in the Tiber valley, only some *villae* and those sites that were reused for the building of churches ensured some tendencies of continuity (see Fiocchi Nicolai 1994; Patterson 2010, 145). But if we look at the material culture, mainly pottery, the trends are similar to those we identified in the Ombrone valley: from the fifth century onwards, in fact – quite analogously to what happens in our research area – the markets' needs were satisfied mainly thanks to local production that somehow guaranteed 'standardized good quality products' (Patterson 2010, 146).

Another interesting comparison is the Arno river: there were some secondary settlements that alternated with the cities in the valley. These minor settlements had a strong commercial vocation, as evidenced by the findings of imported ceramics (Cantini et al. 2009).

The Ombrone river is then a complex socio-economic system that favours long-term trade from the coastlines to the hinterland, through a 'winning' settlement type, the *vicus*. Santa Cristina in Caio and perhaps Pietratonda are the nodes of the system, living mainly on trade and crafts.

In conclusion, to define the economic and commercial role of secondary settlements in greater detail in the long term, two main things are needed: an increase in stratigraphic investigations of these contexts and an intensification of comparative analysis between the different provinces of the Empire and the individual systems, where rivers, roads and secondary settlements formed a segment of the economic history of the countryside between Roman times and the Early Middle Ages.

Authorship per Section

- Section 1 by Stefano Bertoldi & Angelo Castrorao Barba
- Section 2 by Angelo Castrorao Barba
- Section 3 by Gabriele Castiglia
- Section 4 by Stefano Bertoldi
- Section 5 by Stefano Bertoldi, Gabriele Castiglia & Angelo Castrorao Barba

References

Aldini T (1978) Anfore foropopilensi. Archeologia Classica 30:230–245

Aldini T (1999) Anfore foropopiliensi in Italia, Forlimpopoli. Documenti e studi 10:23–56

Arnoldus-Huyzendveld A (2011) Fiumi e sorgenti. In: Citter C, Arnoldus-Huyzendveld A (eds) Uso del suolo e sfruttamento delle risorse nella pianura grossetana nel medioevo: verso una storia del parcellario e del paesaggio agrario. Artemide, Rome, pp 39–41

Barbieri G (2004) Le terme di Pietratonda presso Civitella Paganico (GR). Fasti On Line Documents Res 67:1–4

Bertoldi S, Castiglia A (2015) Santa Cristina in Caio: paesaggi economici in trasformazione tra tarda antichità e alto medioevo. In: Cambi F, De Venuto G, Goffredo R (eds) I pascoli, i campi, il mare. Paesaggi d'altura e di pianura in Italia dall'Età del Bronzo al Medioevo. Edipuglia, Bari, pp 129–145

Bertoldi S, Castiglia G, Castrorao Barba A (2015) Processualismo critico: un approcio allo studio delle relazioni spaziali ed economiche (paesaggi, insediamenti, merci). In: Arthur P, Leo Imperiale M (eds) VII Congresso nazionale di archeologia medievale. All'Insegna del Giglio, Florence, pp 18–22

Bertoldi S, Castiglia G, Menghini C (2017) La produzione di ceramica a pareti sottili di Poggio alle Fonti a Santa Cristina in Caio. Tipologie, cronologie e quantificazioni. Fasti Online Documents Res 389. Available at http://www.fastionline.org/docs/FOLDER-it-2017-389.pdf. Last accessed on 17 May 2018

Bertoldi S, Valenti M (2016) Santa Cristina in Caio a Buonconvento (SI): diacronia di un central place. In: Basso P, Zanini E (eds) Statio Amoena. Sostare e vivere lungo le strade romane. Archaeopress, Oxford, pp 185–196

Bischi GI, Carini R, Gardini L, Tenti P (2004) Sulle orme del caos. Comportamenti complessi in modelli matematici semplici. B. Mondadori, Milan

Bloch M (1998) Apologia della storia o mestiere dello storico. Einaudi, Turin

Cantini F (2005) Archeologia urbana a Siena. All'Insegna del Giglio, Florence

Cantini F (2015) Produzioni ceramiche e dinamiche commerciali nel territorio toscano (III-metà VIII secolo): l'area interna. In: Cirelli E, Diosono F, Patterson H (eds) Le forme della crisi. Produzioni ceramiche e commerci nell'Italia centrale tra Romani e Longobardi (III-VIII sec. d.C.). Ante quem, Bologna, pp 183–190

Cantini F, Buonincontri S, Serugeri S (2009) Al centro della rete: archeologia e storia di un "centraipiace" della Toscana settentrionale tra V e XIII secolo. Il caso di "Vicus Wallari"-borgo San Genesio. In: Volpe G, Favia P (eds) Atti del V congresso di Archeologia Medievale. All'Insegna del Giglio, Florence, pp 255–261

Cantino Wataghin G, Fiocchi Nicolai V, Volpe G (2007) Aspetti della cristianizzazione degli agglomerati secondari. In: Bonacasa Carra RM, Vitale E (eds) La cristianizzazione in Italia fra tardoantico ed altomedioevo: aspetti e problemi. Atti del IX Congresso nazionale di archeologia cristiana. C. Saladino, Palermo, pp 85–134

Cardarelli R (1971) La costa del territorio rosellano vetuloniese nell'antichità. Archivio Piombinese di Studi Storici 1:11–23

Castiglia G (2014) Il Duomo di Siena. Excavations and pottery below Siena cathedral. Archaeopress, Oxford

Castiglia G (2015) Siena e i ritmi della crisi. Lo scavo del Duomo e i reperti ceramici come lente sull'età della transizione. In: Cirelli E, Diosono F, Patterson H (eds) Le forme della crisi. Produzioni ceramiche e commerci nell'Italia centrale tra Romani e Longobardi (III-VIII sec. d.C.). Ante quem, Bologna, pp 201–210

Castiglia G (2018) Si legitur in villa: il rapporto tra chiese e ville nella Toscana centro-settentrionale in età tardo antica e altomedievale. Amoenitas. Rivista Internazionale di Studi Miscellanei sulla Villa Romana Antica 6:43–60

Castrorao Barba A (2013) La fine delle ville romane in Italia tra Tarda Antichità e Alto Medioevo (III-VIII secolo). University of Siena, Siena

Castrorao Barba A (2014a) Continuità topografica in discontinuità funzionale: trasformazioni e riusi delle ville romane in italia tra III e VIII secolo. Post-Classical Archaeologies 4:259–296

Castrorao Barba A (2014b) Le ville romane in Italia tra III e VI sec. d C.: approccio statistico e considerazioni generali. Amoenitas. Rivista internazionale di studi miscellanei sulla Villa Romana antica 3:9–24

Castrorao Barba A (2016) Alcune statistiche sulle dinamiche cronologiche degli insediamenti secondari. In: Basso P, Zanini E (eds) Statio Amoena. Sostare e vivere lungo le strade romane. Archaeopress, Oxford, pp 121–128

Cavalieri M (2008) La villa romana di Aiano-Torraccia di Chiusi, III campagna di scavi 2007. Il progetto internazionale "VII Regio. Il caso della Val d'Elsa in età romana e tardoantica. Fasti Online Documents Res. 110. Available at http://www.fastionline.org/docs/FOLDER-it-2008-110.pdf. Last accessed on 17 May 2018.

Chevallier R (1997) Les voies Romaines. Picard, Paris

Christaller W (1980) Le località centrali della Germani Meridionale. Una indagine geografica sulla regolarità della distribuzione dello sviluppo degli insediamenti con funzioni urbane. F. Angeli, Milan

Citter C (2012) Modelli predittivi e archeologia postclassica: vecchi strumenti e nuove prospettive. In: Redi F, Forgione A (eds) Atti del VI congresso di Archeologia Medievale. All'Insegna del Giglio, Florence, pp 12–15

Clarke DL (1998) Archeologia Analitica. Electa, Milan

Coccarda R (2011) Manuale di statistica: statistica descrittiva, inferenziale e calcolo delle probabilità. Maggioli, Santarcangelo di Romagna

Collar A, Coward F, Brughmans T, Mills BJ (2015) Networks in archaeology: phenomena, abstraction, representation. J Archaeol Method Theory 22(1):1–32. https://doi.org/10.1007/s10816-014-9235-6

Corbier M (1986) Grande proprietà fondiaria e piccole aziende: la Gallia settentrionale in epoca romana. In: Giardina A (ed) Società romana e impero tardoantico III – Le merci, gli insediamenti. Laterza, Rome/Bari, pp 687–702

Corsi C (2000) Le Strutture di Servizio del Cursus Publicus in Italia. BAR, Oxford

Crogiez S (1990) Les stations du cursus publicus en Calabre. Un état de la recherche. Mélanges de l'École française de Rome Antiquité 102(1):389–431. https://doi.org/10.3406/mefr.1990.1673

De Guio A (1992) Archeologia della complessità e calcolatori: un percorso di sopravvivenza tra teorie del caos, attrattori strani, frattali e... frattaglie del postmoderno. In: Bernardi M (ed) Archeologia del Paesaggio. IV ciclo di lezioni sulla Ricerca applicata in Archeologia. All'Insegna del Giglio, Florence, pp 305–389

Dobbins JJ (1980) The excavation of the Roman Villa at La Befa, Italy. BAR, Oxford

Fiocchi Nicolai V (1994) Considerazioni sull'archeologia del territorio lazialenell'altomedioevo. In: Francovich R, Noyé G (eds) La storia dell'altomedioevo italiano alla luce dell'archeologia. All'Insegna del Giglio, Florence, pp 403–406

Flannery KV (1968) Archaeological systems theory and early Mesopotamia. In: Meggars BJ (ed) Anthropological archeology in the Americas. Anthropological Society of Washington, Washington, pp 67–87

Fontana S (1998) Le "imitazioni" della sigillata africana e le ceramiche da mensa italiche tardoantiche. In: Saguì L (ed) Ceramica in Italia VI-VII secolo. All'Insegna del Giglio, Florence, pp 83–100

Freeman LC (1978) Centrality in social networks. I Conceptual clarification. Soc Netw 1(3):215–239. https://doi.org/10.1016/0378-8733(78)90021-7

Fronza V (2005) Database Management applicato all'Archeologia nell'ambito del Progetto "Paesaggi Medievali". In: Francovich R, Valenti M (eds) Archeologia dei Paesaggi Medievali. Relazione progetto (2000–2005). Fondazione Monte dei Paschi di Siena, Siena, pp 399–451

Fumo A (2010) Le ceramiche rivestite di rosso della villa di Aiano-Torraccia di Chiusi (San Gimignano, Siena): uno studio archeologico e archeometrico. Fasti Online Documents Res 178 Available at http://www.fastionline.org/docs/FOLDER-it-2010-178.pdf. Last accessed on 17 May 2018.

Garmy P (2002) Villa-vicus. Une question d'espace. Revue archéologique de Narbonnaise 35:27–37

Garmy P (2012) Les mots et la chose: à propos des agglomérations secondaires antiques. Revue Archeologique du Centre de la France 42:183–187

Girvan M, Newman MEJ (2002) Community Structure in Social and Biological Networks. Proc Natl Acad Sci 99:7821–7826. https://doi.org/10.1073/pnas.122653799

Goffredo R, Ficco V, Costantino C (2013) Ville e vici della valle del Carapelle (Puglia settentrionale). Mélanges de l'École française de Rome Antiquité 125(1). https://doi.org/10.4000/mefra.1310

Hodges R (1989) Parachutists and truffle-hunters: at the frontiers of archaeology and history. In: Aston M, Austin DA, Dyer C (eds) Rural settlements of medieval England. Studies dedicated to Maurice Beredsford and John Hurst. Basil Blackwell, Oxford, pp 287–306

Knappett C (2013) Introduction: why networks? In: Knappett C (ed) Network analysis in archaeology, new approaches to regional interaction. Oxford University Press, Oxford, pp 3–16. https://doi.org/10.1093/acprof:oso/9780199697090.003.0001

Leidwanger J, Knappett C, Arnaud P, Arthur P, Blake E, Broodbank C, Brughmans T, Evans T, Graham S, Greene ES, Kowalzig B, Mills B, Rivers R, Tartaron TF, Van de Noort R (2014) A Manifesto for the Study of Ancient Mediterranean Maritime Networks. Antiquity Project Gallery 88(342). Available at https://www.antiquity.ac.uk/projgall/leidwanger342. Last accessed on 17 May 2018.

Leveau P (2012) Vicus, "agglomération secondaire", des mots différents pour une même entité. In: Cribelier C, Ferdière A (eds) Actes de la Table ronde d'Orléans Agglomérations secondaires romaines en Région Centre. FERACF, Tours, pp 165–175

Lorenz EN (1963) Deterministic nonperiodic flow. J Atmos Sci 20:130–141. https://doi.org/10.1175/1520-0469(1963)020<0130:DNF>2.0.CO;2

Maggi P, Zaccaria C (1994) Considerazioni sugli insediamenti minori di età romana nell'Italia settentrionale. In: Petit JP, Mangin M (eds) Les Agglomérations secondaires. La Gaule Belgique, les Germanies et l'Occident romain. Actes du colloque de Bliesbruck-Reinheim/Bitche. Errance, pp 163-80

Mezzolani A (1992) Appunti sulle mansiones in base ai dati archeologici. In: Quilici L, Quilici Gigli S (eds) Tecnica Stradale Romana. L'Erma di Bretschneider, Rome, pp 105–113

Nevett L, Perkins P (2000) Essay Eight: Urbanism and urbanization in the Roman world. In: Huskinson J (ed) Experiencing Rome: culture, identity and power in the Roman Empire. Routledge, London, pp 213–244

Panella C (1989) Le anfore italiche di II secolo d.C. In: di Panella C (ed) Amphores romaines et histoire économique. Dix ans de recherche. École Française de Rome, Rome, pp 139–178

Panella C (2001) Le anfore di età imperiale nel Mediterraneo occidentale. In: Geny E (ed) Céramiques héllenistiques et romaines 3. Les Belles Lettres, Paris, pp 177–275

Patterson H (2010) Rural Settlement and Economy in the Middle Tiber Valley: AD 300-1000. Archeologia Medievale 27:143–161

Perrault C (2012) I racconti di Mamma Oca – Racconti e storie del passato con una morale. Aonia edizioni, Pisa (translated by F. Verdinois from the original book Histoires ou contes du temps passé, avec des moralités. Contes de ma mère l'Oye, 1697, Paris)

Pitts M, Versluys MJ (2015) Globalisation and the Roman world: perspectives and opportunities. Cambridge University Press, Cambridge

Plog FT (1975) Systems Theory in Archaeology Research. Annu Rev Anthropol 4:207–224. https://doi.org/10.1146/annurev.an.04.100175.001231

Potter TW, King AC (1997) Excavations at the Mola di Monte Gelato: a Roman and medieval settlement in south Etruria. The British School at Rome, London

Tarpin M (2006) Les formes d'agrégation dans le monde romain: diversité et spontanéité. In: Lo Cascio E, Merola GD (eds) Forme di aggregazione nel mondo romano. Edipuglia, Bari, pp 379–391

Tol G, De Haas T, Armstrong K, Attema P (2014) Minor centres in the Pontine plain: the cases of Forum Appii and Ad Medias. Papers of the British School at Rome 82:109–134. https://doi.org/10.1017/S0068246214000063

Vaccaro E (2015) Ceramic Production and trade in Tuscany (3rd – mid 9th c. AD): New Evidence from the South-West. In: Cirelli E, Diosono F, Patterson H (eds). Le forme della crisi. Produzioni ceramiche e commerci nell'Italia centrale tra Romani e Longobardi (III-VIII sec. d.C.). Ante quem, Bologna, pp 211–228

Valenti M (1991) Materiali ceramici tardoantichi dal territorio senese. Contributo alla tipologizzazione della ceramica comune di produzione locale. Archeologia Medievale 18:737–754

Valenti M (1995) Carta archeologica della provincia di Siena, Il Chianti senese, vol 3. Nuova immagine, Siena

Valenti M (1996) La ceramica comune nel territorio settentrionale senese tra V-inizi X secolo. In: Brogiolo GP, Gelichi S (eds) Le ceramiche altomedievali (fine VI-X secolo) in Italia settentrionale: produzione e commerci. SAP, Mantova, pp 143–169

Valenti M (1999) Carta archeologica della provincia di Siena, La Val d'Elsa, vol 3. Nuova immagine, Siena

Wheatley D, Gillings M (2002) Spatial technology and archaeology: the archaeological applications of GIS. CRC Press, New York

Witcher RE (2012) That from a long way off look like farms: the classification of roman rural sites. In: PAJ A, Schörner G (eds) Comparative issues in the archaeology of the roman rural landscape. Site classification between survey, excavation and historical Journal of Roman Archaeology. Journal of Roman Archaeology, Portsmouth, pp 11–30

Zipf GK (1949) Human Behavior and the Principle of Least Effort: An Introduction to Human Ecology. Addison Wesley, Cambridge, MA

Part III
Transport and Movement

Chapter 11
Modelling of Pathways and Movement Networks in Archaeology: An Overview of Current Approaches

Philip Verhagen, Laure Nuninger, and Mark R. Groenhuijzen

Abstract This chapter presents and discusses current approaches and trends in computer-based modelling of pathways and movement networks in archaeology. After an introduction to the theoretical concepts involved, we present a state of the art of methodologies applied for reconstructing pathways and movement in ancient landscapes and discuss the various difficulties in using these methods as well as the most important technical hurdles involved. The problems of integrating optimal pathfinding algorithms with 'softer' socio-cultural variables are highlighted, as well as the limitations of modelling connections between places using least-cost path techniques. Network analysis reconstruction and analysis approaches are then reviewed as tools to better understand the overall structure of movement and communication in ancient landscapes. It is concluded that, while the potential of current approaches for understanding ancient movement is considerable, improvement is still needed in three main areas: the integration of approaches, sensitivity analysis and validation, and the theoretical underpinning of models of ancient movement.

Keywords Movement · Pathways · Landscape archaeology · Least-cost paths · Network analysis

11.1 Introduction

In this chapter, we provide an overview of the current approaches to computer modelling of pathways and movement networks in archaeology. The subject has been of interest to archaeologists since the early 1990s, when the first studies were published that tried to reconstruct ancient pathways using GIS (e.g. Van Leusen 1993; Verhagen et al. 1995). Since then, a considerable amount of research has focused on

P. Verhagen (✉) · M. R. Groenhuijzen
Faculty of Humanities, Vrije Universiteit Amsterdam, Amsterdam, The Netherlands
e-mail: j.w.h.p.verhagen@vu.nl; m.r.groenhuijzen@vu.nl

L. Nuninger
Chrono-Environnement UMR 6249/MSHE C.N. Ledoux USR 3124, Besançon, France
e-mail: laure.nuninger@univ-fcomte.fr

P. Verhagen et al. (eds.), *Finding the Limits of the Limes*, Computational Social Sciences, https://doi.org/10.1007/978-3-030-04576-0_11

the modelling process itself, by trying to find ways to incorporate the factors that influence movement into the models as realistically as possible in order to arrive at good reconstructions of ancient routes and movement patterns. While clear successes can be observed in this respect, some major questions remain. These are centred around the possibilities of accurately modelling human movement and navigation practices on the basis of archaeological and experimental data, the validation of the models, and the relationship between the modelled routes, communication and transport networks and settlement patterns.

The purpose of this chapter is to summarize the main issues in the debate and put them into a larger theoretical and methodological perspective, since such a comprehensive overview is currently lacking. However, we refrain from discussing the results of individual modelling projects in terms of their archaeological interpretation. The chapters that follow (Chaps. 12, Groenhuijzen; 13, De Soto; 14, Parcero-Oubiña et al.; and 15, Crawford) provide a number of case studies in which this aspect is addressed.

11.2 What is Movement, and How Do People Move?

11.2.1 Affordances and Movement Potential

When discussing modelling of movement and pathways, it is useful to think in terms of *affordances* (Gibson 1977, 1979; Ingold 1992; Llobera 1996; Murrieta-Flores 2010). The concept of affordances was formulated by the psychologist James Gibson in 1977, and the term is a neologism based on the verb 'to afford'. Thus, the affordance of an environment corresponds to what it can offer to an individual (in the broad sense of the term including humans and non-humans), for better or for worse. It implies an interdependency between the individual and the environment. It is not only the set of abstract physical properties of the environment that can be measured in standard units, scales, etc. but a set of properties that are relative to the individual considered. Affordance could thus be defined as the potential offered by the environment in relation to an individual's properties and abilities to act in that environment (to move, obtain food, etc.): it is a set of environmental properties related to individual behaviour. According to Gibson (1979), the affordance of an environment is not the sum of its qualities but is more related to what the individual will normally pay attention to when doing something, like moving for example. Gaver (1991) supplemented the definition of affordance as the properties of the environment that make certain actions possible for an individual who is equipped for this purpose. In addition, he distinguished three types of affordances:

- The *perceptible* affordance which both affords and suggests an action
- The *hidden* affordance which affords an action but does not suggest it
- The *false* affordance that suggests an action but does not afford it (e.g., quicksand when moving on the ground)

When moving, the affordance thus is the potential offered to an individual within a specific environment to move from one place to another, even when the individual is unaware of this or is not able to take advantage. It is only by considering the reciprocal influence of the environment (geographical, cultural) and the *movement capability* (technical, social) of individuals that we will arrive at identifying a set of movement affordances.

The basic premise of modelling of pathways and movement in archaeology is that we can use the affordance properties of the environment for movement in order to compute the *past movement potential* for a set of locations, using a GIS, for example (Llobera 2000).

Closely related to movement potential is the concept of *accessibility*. While movement potential is origin-oriented, accessibility considers movement from the perspective of the destination. In a completely isotropic environment, accessibility is the reciprocal of movement potential. In reality, the affordances can vary according to the direction of movement. For example, a site located on a hilltop can have a large movement potential, but not be very accessible.

Movement potential and accessibility are, however, only a set of possible, as-yet unfulfilled movement patterns. Modelling the actual movement of people and the pathways they have taken requires us to understand not only the affordances associated with movement but also the goals of movement and the cognitive and social processes that guide movement and structure the development of pathways that may eventually take on a permanent nature, and thereby change the affordances.

How to model movement, accessibility, and pathways has therefore been the subject of a substantial and lively debate characterized by a large number of experimental studies that heavily rely on GIS-based data and techniques. Underlying these are a number of assumptions about (ancient) movement that we will shortly discuss in the following sections. The main elements to consider are the movement capability of individuals, the definition of movement potential and accessibility by means of cost surfaces, and the use of least-cost paths as a technique based on optimal path-finding routines.

11.2.2 Movement Capability

11.2.2.1 Energy or Speed?

It is common practice in path modelling studies to measure movement capability in either *energy expenditure* or *movement speed*. Both are innate to the individual considered: humans walk slower than horses and spend less calories per time unit of movement. However, we have to take into account that modelling of movement capability is usually determined on the basis of averages for healthy individuals. Furthermore, individuals will not always maintain an average speed but can decide to go slower or faster.

The calculation of energy expenditure is often preferred because it is a direct measure of the effort that humans or animals will have to make in order to go somewhere while maintaining a certain speed. Ultimately, energy will run out and will need to be replenished with food and/or fuel and rest. It therefore poses a limit to the amount of time that can be spent on movement and thus on the distance covered.

Movement speed is more relevant for dealing with types of movement that prioritize speed, such as the deployment of troops, the trade in perishable goods, or the transfer of messages. It is also easier to understand when interpreting and comparing modelled pathways. Movement speed and energy expenditure are of course related, and there are even conversion formulae available (e.g. Groenhuijzen and Verhagen 2015).

11.2.2.2 Transport Modes

The human capability for movement differs depending on the mode of transport used, which is in turn dependent on the transport medium (land or water). Almost all studies on modelling land-based movement up to date have focused on walking as the primary mode of transport. This has been studied in sufficient detail to allow for realistic modelling of movement capability, including the effects of carrying a load (see Sect. 11.3.1.1).

For other modes of transport, there is much less reliable data available. Riding animals, in particular horses, can obtain much higher speeds than humans and will have been used when longer distances needed to be covered quickly. While average speeds and maximum distances per day covered on horseback or by riding other animals are known from historical sources, good data on the energy expenditure of riding animals are scarce. Some comparisons were made between human and donkey by Yousef et al. (1972), and the effect of loads on the movement speed of horses were studied by Wickler et al. (2001).

For carrying heavy loads, pack animals and wheeled transport will have been preferred, although these were not available to all ancient societies. In all probability, the use of pack animals (mostly mules, donkeys, and horses, but also camels, llamas, and elephants) will not have greatly influenced the speed of movement and the distance covered, since there would always be humans accompanying the transport animals. However, in the case of llamas, it seems that they could not travel for more than two days consecutively and would only cover distances of up to 20 km per day (D'Altroy 2015).

In the case of wheeled transport, there is only very general information available on the types of carts used, the number and type of traction animals employed to draw them, the maximum loads carried, and the accompanying movement speeds and distances (Bachrach 1993; Roth 1998; Kolb 2000; Yeo 1946; Laurence 1999; Raepsaet 2002; Adams 2007).

Water-based transport is another often overlooked transport mode in the modelling of movement, even though rivers in many areas form natural corridors of movement from the hinterland to the sea (Laurence 1999; see also Chap. 10, Bertoldi,

Castiglia and Castrorao Barba). Water transport is also capable of transporting much heavier loads than land transport. Relatively little research has been done on the quantification of ancient movement over water. The speed or energy expenditure is dependent on various factors, including the ship type, manner of propulsion (floating, paddling, rowing, sailing, towing, and/or using a push pole), the direction of travel, and the flow of the river. Some information is available on long-distance movement, for example using prams on the Rhine in the Roman period (Jansma and Morel 2007). However, most local transport over water probably made use of dugouts (also known as dugout canoes or logboats), a type of watercraft that has been used at least since the Mesolithic. McGrail (1978) and Gregory (1997) provide an overview of dugouts from the UK and Ireland, including some quantification on speed and load capacity. Ancient sea transport, while having been studied in considerable detail (e.g. Casson 1994; Pomey 1997; Arnaud 2005), is even more challenging to model given the lack of (historical) data on how ships responded to weather and water conditions.

11.2.3 External Factors Influencing Movement Capability

11.2.3.1 The Natural Environment

The human capability for movement is influenced by external factors that are out of control of the individual, in particular terrain conditions – although atmospheric conditions can play a role as well. Topography, and in particular slope, is the most frequently used environmental factor considered. Steep slopes hinder movement for all modes of land-based transport, up to the point where zones may become impassable. The effect of slope on energy expenditure for walkers has been studied in detail (see Sect. 11.3.1.1). For other modes of land transport, however, the effects of slope are less well defined.

A number of other environmental constraints can influence movement capability. One of the most important is the presence of muddy and boggy terrain that can considerably slow down movement or even impede it. Unlike topography, hydrological conditions can change relatively quickly and may have a distinct seasonal component. In tidal zones, conditions will even change within hours. In colder regions, the presence of snow and ice in winter is a factor to consider as well. Movement potential in winter may be quite different from summer, when wet areas will be frozen over that are difficult to negotiate in summer. Vegetation, especially high brush, can also reduce movement capability.

There is some experimental evidence available that relates different terrain conditions to the energy expenditure of walkers (Soule and Goldman 1972; Pandolf et al. 1976, 1977; De Gruchy et al. 2017). This evidence is rather limited, and similar data for other modes of transport are not available. Pack animals, however, seem to have no difficulties in keeping up with humans in any form of terrain, although for steep slopes mules and donkeys were usually preferred over horses, since they are better at negotiating this type of terrain. For wheeled transport, critical slopes are clearly lower than for walking (Herzog 2013a), and in difficult terrain, wagons and carts will experience more difficulties than humans and pack animals (Haisman and Goldman 1974).

The effects of river crossings on movement capability across land have also been considered in a number of path modelling studies (see e.g. Van Leusen 2002; Fiz and Orengo 2008; Whitley et al. 2010). The procedure followed is usually to consider rivers (and other water bodies) as if they are zones that hinder movement in the same way as very steep slopes. Whitley et al. (2010) instead took the energy expenditure of wading and swimming as input for their models and this would seem to be the most realistic approach to estimate movement capability of walkers in wet terrain. Again, no similar data is available for other forms of land-based transport. We also have to keep in mind that getting one's feet or body wet comes with additional disadvantages, so the use of water-based transport will quickly become attractive even when the total distance to be covered over water is not very large.

For water-based transport, however, much less data is available on the effects of the natural environment on movement, even when some research has been done into modelling the effects of winds and currents on sea transport (see for example the ORBIS project http://orbis.stanford.edu).

11.2.3.2 Infrastructure

Human intervention in the landscape can improve movement conditions considerably. Whether humans tried to overcome or reduce the effects of terrain conditions on movement will have depended on the importance attached to moving with little effort from one place to the next and on the technical abilities of ancient societies. Relatively simple measures include clearing the ground to make the going easier in the case of dense vegetation or boulders, the use of stepping stones to negotiate small rivers, and using switchbacks, steps, and stairs to climb steep slopes. More complex solutions are the construction of bridges to cross wider rivers and ravines, paving of roads in the case of wet terrain, and even cutting tunnels to pass steep rock faces.

In order to travel larger distances, people and animals also need places to stock up on food and water and find shelter to safely spend the night (Murrieta-Flores 2010). Locations where these facilities are found can be both natural and anthropogenic. Also, places where people could shift between modes of transport, like harbours and horse stables, will have been important logistical facilities. In the Roman period, for example, an empire-wide infrastructure of *mansiones*, *mutationes*, and *stationes* was maintained to provide food, rest, and, if needed, fresh horses. The stageposts along the Inka road system known as *tampus* also provide a very good example of such an infrastructure. Hyslop (1984) estimates there were around 2000 of them along the ca. 40,000 km of the road network.

An important effect of infrastructural improvement is that it will concentrate movement in specific locations, and thereby also increase the possibilities for control of travel and transport (see Sect. 11.2.3.4). Modelling the effects of infrastructural improvement on movement patterns has however not been explored in depth.

11.2.3.3 Safety

The factors considered so far are primarily concerned with energy efficiency and maximizing the speed of movement, i.e., they have direct effects on the movement capability of individuals. Many factors that influence movement, however, do not just have an effect on movement capability but also or even predominantly on the perceived affordances of the environment.

Unsafe areas in particular will have been avoided by travellers unless they were sufficiently prepared to deal with any dangers on the road. Knowing where enemy groups or wild animals lived – not to mention the residential areas of evil spirits or grumpy ancestors – will thus have been a very important consideration when choosing a route. Many ancient routes will therefore have been determined by the ability to avoid potential dangers, or if this could not be done, to equip them with protective infrastructure, such as forts and watchtowers.

Other aspects of safety have to do with weather conditions: a route could become unsafe or even inaccessible because of rainfall, snow or drought, and may have had specific infrastructure to deal with the effects of excessive water, cold or aridity.

Modelling safety of movement is highly complex since we usually don't have much evidence on where hostile groups of humans or animals, or even malicious spirits could be found (see Whitley 2000 for an exception). Visibility must have been an important aspect for this, and in some contexts it is therefore possible to analyse if routes are safer or more unsafe than others on the basis of being hidden from sight (Lock et al. 2014). However, we should not underestimate the role of sound and smell either. Estimating the effects of extreme weather conditions would seem more feasible, but as far as we know there are no studies around that have specifically addressed these questions from a route modelling perspective.

11.2.3.4 Control

Control of routes was important for guaranteeing the safety of travellers, but many societies also used roads and other infrastructure to impose political and economic control on their own or hostile populations. Roads and waterways facilitate the movement of troops and can be used to regulate the access of travellers and goods by means of tolls. Travellers could also be forced to pay for the use of infrastructure and logistic facilities. Obviously, this kind of control system may also have led people to take different, non-controlled routes to escape paying the taxes.

A different type of control is supposed to have played a role in the positioning of the Inka imperial road system (Lynch and Parcero-Oubiña 2017). The Inka placed great importance on the symbolic appropriation of spiritual landmarks, in particular the snow-capped mountaintops of the Andes. It is suggested that the positioning of the imperial roads can at least partly be explained by the wish to keep the mountain tops within view over a long stretch of road, and in this way assert the empire's power over places of spiritual importance.

11.2.3.5 Navigation

Various authors have pointed out that navigation is inherent to movement (e.g. Lock and Pouncett 2010; Murrieta-Flores 2010), and thus the ease of navigation constitutes one of the major factors determining the affordances for movement on both land and water. Humans rely on sequential and mostly visual cues to find their way in the landscape. Cognition plays a vital role in the human ability to navigate, and the more local knowledge the traveller has, the easier it will become to find one's way. When travelling in unfamiliar terrain, however, navigational markers are necessary to help travellers arrive at their destination as they allow to provide oral or written instructions for wayfinding, like the famous indigenous Australian songlines. This latter aspect of creating a 'mental map' rather than using distance calculations was also relevant for maritime navigation in the Pacific (Turnbull 2000, 136). Permanent roads and water courses will even better guide movement, but even then markers will help the traveller to decide where to go, for example when arriving at a junction.

Navigational markers can be both natural and anthropogenic. The most important natural ones are terrain morphology (e.g. peaks, valleys, slope breaks, caves, horizon profiles), hydrology, vegetation, and geology (rock outcrops, boulders). They can be related to both short-distance and long-distance travel. A mountain top or river, or in the absence of such a landmark, the position of the sun or the stars, may provide the general orientation of travel. For navigation over short distances, and especially in circumstances of reduced visibility, local markers are more important. We should also be aware that markers can change their appearance over the seasons: ground can be covered in snow, trees will lose their leaves and water courses may flood or disappear in the dry season.

In the absence of suitable natural markers, humans have for a long time created their own ones, for example by erecting standing stones, cairns and milestones or by planting trees. Lighthouses were already in use in Antiquity to aid maritime navigation. Markers can also be used to emphasize the visibility of natural features, for example by placing cairns on hilltops, or by creating rock art (Fairén-Jiménez 2007). However, there will have been myriads of other anthropogenic markers available to travellers, since paths and routes express their character in a number of ways, for example because of their mode of construction, their trajectory including curves and crossings, and the presence of related infrastructure and other human activity in the vicinity of the path.

Understanding the role of navigation and markers in movement is a complex exercise, as is demonstrated in the studies by Murrieta-Flores (2014) and Llobera (2015). Researchers have therefore also focused on more general indicators to model the influence of navigation on path location, such as the general direction of movement (Zakšek et al. 2008; Lock and Pouncett 2010) and overall visibility (Lock and Pouncett 2010). Visibility, while being the sense that still provides 'most information on the structure of space to the brain compared to the rest' (Llobera 2007, 52), is however only one aspect of how people navigate; smell, sound, and even the touch of the feet on the ground also provide clues on the position of the traveller and will change according to the season.

11.3 Modelling Approaches to Ancient Movement

The interest in modelling ancient movement was initially triggered by site catchment analysis studies in the 1970s (Vita-Finzi and Higgs 1970; Higgs and Vita-Finzi 1972). This approach can be characterized as establishing the affordances of a settlement's environment for agriculture or hunting-gathering, for which movement potential was considered to be the major factor. The area that could be reached within a certain amount of time from the settlement was considered to be the extent of its territory (see e.g. Ericson and Goldstein 1980). Since this analysis involved actually walking the areas around archaeological sites to map the extent of the territories, the utility of creating cost surfaces to quickly calculate and analyse the movement potential around settlements was therefore already clear when GIS arrived on the scene (see e.g. Gaffney and Stančič 1991; Verhagen et al. 1995).

However, the possibility to calculate least-cost paths (LCPs) in order to reconstruct ancient movement patterns and pathways was a new addition to the quantitative archaeological toolbox (Van Leusen 1993) and attracted much interest from the mid-1990s onwards. Least-cost path modelling is a method to find the optimal path between two or more locations. First, a cost surface is defined that determines the costs of crossing one grid cell, usually specified in time or energy units spent. A cumulative cost surface is then created from a starting point which will provide the cost distance from the starting point to every grid cell in the study area. Finally, we can then determine the least-cost path between the starting location and any other location, giving us some idea on where transport and movement may have taken place. The cumulative cost surface can also be used to find the area that can be reached within a certain amount of time (or by spending a maximum amount of energy).

Applications of path modelling are not just found in archaeology but also in economic and human geography (see Rodrigue et al. 2017) and to a lesser extent in ecology (see Cushman et al. 2013). In these disciplines path modelling is used to understand and predict movement patterns of traffic, goods and people (in geography) and animals (in ecology) within a constrained environment. These constraints are either natural, or created by human intervention. In contrast to archaeology, however, the movement processes modelled in geography and ecology can still be observed today.

Archaeologists and historians, on the other hand, are confronted with the fact that factors influencing movement patterns and transport networks have changed considerably in the recent past. Both the capacity of humans to intervene in the landscape and create new possibilities for movement, as well as the modes of transportation are completely different from those in prehistory, or even from a period as recent as the nineteenth century (see e.g. Lawton 2004). Analogies from modern day transportation are therefore not very suitable for archaeological applications. However, reliable information on how people dealt with these issues in the past is limited. Researchers therefore have to rely on modern-day data, such as physiological research into the speed of movement of humans in different environments, and use the scant historical evidence, for example by applying data from historical military sources to situations that did not involve the movement of troops.

Furthermore, the underlying premise of GIS-based modelling of movement and pathways is the calculation of optimal, least-cost or least-effort paths. This is an assumption that is very restrictive when investigating past movement (see e.g. Ingold 2011), and many studies in archaeological path modelling over the past decade have tried to come to grip with this. The main issues to be considered have been summarized in various papers (e.g. Murrieta-Flores 2010; Herzog 2014), but it is useful to provide a condensed overview here.

11.3.1 Cost Surfaces and Cost Definitions

11.3.1.1 Defining Movement Capability

Most modelling studies in archaeology have been explicitly interested in movement on foot and assume that slope was the main constraint to movement. While slope clearly is a major factor influencing movement capability, we already listed a number of other factors that can be considered. The popularity of slope as the primary cost factor is therefore not just related to its (perceived) archaeological importance, but also to the fact that elevation data is relatively easy to obtain, and can usually be considered a reasonable approximation of the topography in the past, since it is the most stable and enduring geographical factor. Also, walking on slope is the only type of movement for which there is reasonably detailed experimental evidence (Margaria 1938; Imhof 1950; Givoni and Goldman 1971; Pandolf et al. 1977; Ericson and Goldstein 1980; Minetti et al. 2002; Langmuir 2004; Kondo and Seino 2010).

Herzog (2013a) provides an overview of the different cost (or 'hiking') functions that have been used to estimate the effect of slope on walking speed and energy expenditure. She compares these functions to the data collected by Minetti et al. (2002) when walking on a slope and presents a 6th order polynomial function that best approximates the experimental data. The alternative equation developed by Llobera and Sluckin (2007), however, seems to better match the empirical data. Since these equations only provide values for energy expenditure, they cannot be directly converted to time units, which are easier to understand and compare. By far the most popular hiking function in archaeology has therefore been the one attributed to Tobler (1993).

Similar functions for riding or pack animals and wheeled transport are not available because of a lack of experimental data. It has been noted (Llobera and Sluckin 2007; Herzog 2013a) that there is a critical upward slope for vehicles beyond which movement is not possible. As far as we can tell, however, the only equation that directly connects slope, and to some extent terrain friction, to movement of carts is given by Raepsaet (2002).

When calculating LCPs using slope-based hiking functions, it is important to keep in mind that upslope movement will lead to different paths than downslope movement, and therefore 'isotropic' cost distance calculations are unsuitable to estimate the optimal paths. A further problem with slope-based cost surfaces is that slope in GIS is always calculated as the average of slope from a grid cell to its 8 neighbouring cells. However, in order to find the optimal path, we need to know the slope in the direction of movement, or effective slope. Solutions to this problem have been implemented in various GIS packages (IDRISI, SAGA, ArcGIS), but Herzog (2013d) showed that the existing tools are either not implemented correctly or lack sufficient documentation to judge their performance. Alternative approaches, taking into account the general direction of movement, have been presented by Zakšek et al. (2008) and Lock and Pouncett (2010), but in practice there does not seem to be agreement on the best way to proceed.

11.3.1.2 The Role of DEMs

Herzog (2014) also discusses the problems associated with creating LCPs from digital elevation model (DEMs). Most available DEMs are not well suited to create cost surfaces and least-cost paths for archaeological research questions. LiDAR-based elevation models are very popular with archaeologists nowadays because of the level of detail they provide. However, their high resolution is also a drawback for path modelling since many modern-day, anthropogenic landscape features are present in the models as well, and filtering techniques to easily suppress these are not sufficiently developed yet. The vertical and horizontal accuracy and/or precision of the popular and free Aster and SRTM products on the other hand is often not sufficient for a realistic calculation of the accumulated cost surfaces. Also, interpolation techniques used to create DEMs from digitized contour lines and irregularly spaced point elevations can greatly influence the results. A well-known effect is the creation of artificial elevation 'steps' in relatively flat terrain because of very widely spaced contour lines. Ideally, DEMs used for LCP modelling should be based on corrected and sufficiently detailed height information that ignores recent anthropogenic features, and takes into account recent natural changes in topography as well. This often still implies correcting the DEMs manually, for example by consulting and (partly) digitizing historical elevation maps.

Lock and Pouncett (2010) and Lock et al. (2014) point out that scale is also an important factor influencing the results of slope-based path modelling. The horizontal resolution of a DEM will have a marked effect on the end results, as is for example shown by Verhagen et al. (2014). A DEM at a resolution that is too coarse may obscure difficult passages, especially the occurrence of cliffs, since these have a very limited horizontal extent (width). A cliff with only a few meters height difference is in practice impassable, but an elevation difference of 5 m will not seem very important when the cell size is large enough. The slope at 5 × 5 m resolution will be 100%, but at 50 × 50 m only 10%. DEM resolution also influences the results of path modelling when introducing linear features like rivers and cliffs as barriers or zones of difficult access, because of the effect of diagonal crossing (Van Leusen 2002).

11.3.1.3 Modelling Other Terrain Costs

Other terrain factors directly influencing movement capability, in particular vegetation and soil type, would seem easier to model since their effects are isotropic, but in practice they are more difficult to estimate. Experimental data on energy expenditure when walking through various types of terrain were published by Soule and Goldman (1972) and Pandolf et al. (1976) and converted to terrain coefficients reflecting the difficulty of movement (summarized by Herzog 2014). A recent study by De Gruchy et al. (2017), however, indicates that these coefficients cannot be translated directly to movement speeds. For movement of vehicles, it is even more difficult to obtain reliable estimates. Groenhuijzen and Verhagen (2015) therefore combined the terrain coefficients obtained for handcarts by Haisman and Goldman (1974) with data on average movement speeds of vehicles reported from historical sources (Roth 1998).

Water-based transport has to take into account the direction of movement (upstream of downstream, which can be included through artificial slope; Groenhuijzen 2018), the flow of the river and the costs of moving between land and water. Wheatley and Gillings (2002, 156–157) suggest to model waterways as part of multimodal pathways as low-cost corridors which can be accessed through a barrier of high costs. Whitley et al. (2010) included portage of canoes as a cost factor as well. As mentioned in Sect. 11.2.2.2, some experimental and historical information is available on sailing speeds for different types of vessels, but in practice it is very challenging to model all aspects influencing movement capability on water.

11.3.1.4 Visibility as a Movement Cost

Possibly the most frequently considered non-terrain-based cost factor in pathway modelling is visibility, because of its close relationship to navigation, safety, and road construction practices but also because it can be relatively easily modelled on the basis of DEMs. The interest in visibility as an aspect of strategic placement of settlements, military infrastructure and monuments has a long history, and has been extensively explored in archaeological GIS studies (e.g. Gaffney and Stančič 1991;

Wheatley 1995; Ruggles and Medyckyj-Scott 1997; Loots et al. 1999; Lake and Woodman 2003; Llobera 2003; Trifković 2006; Gillings 2009).

The inclusion of visibility as a cost factor for movement is usually approached through the calculation of *total viewsheds* (Llobera 2003) within the region of interest, and then adding the relative visibility of each grid cell as an additional cost. The drawback of this approach is the heavy computational load associated with total viewshed calculations. For this reason, Verhagen and Jeneson (2012) used openness (Yokoyama et al. 2002) as a proxy for visibility.

Recent studies (Bourgeois 2013, 105–158; Čučković 2015) have drawn attention to the fact that networks of intervisibility of archaeological sites and prominent landscape features can be successfully modelled and analysed, and may be of interest for understanding navigation and movement as well.

11.3.1.5 Modelling Socio-cultural Costs

Herzog (2013a) discusses how to use parameters not related to movement speed in path modelling, like visibility or the presence of particular features attracting or repelling travel. 'Socio-cultural' costs are not based on expenditure of energy, and the resulting models will therefore not necessarily result in 'optimal' paths. Since the costs cannot be expressed in units of time and energy they need to be translated into a different 'currency', using some form of subjective weighting. This can produce confusing end results, since the costs then calculated are no longer real costs but 'pseudo-costs'.

The basic procedures for combining factors that are not intrinsically comparable are covered by the literature on multi-criteria analysis (MCA; Saaty 1980; Nijkamp et al. 1990; Malczewski 1999), a technique that is quite commonly applied in archaeological predictive modelling (Dalla Bona 1994; Verhagen 2006) and which has also been used for path modelling (Howey 2007). Importantly, the weighting of factors can take place at two levels: the attribute level (e.g. where it concerns the importance of visibility with increasing distance) and the criterion level (e.g. whether visibility is a more or less important factor to consider than slope). Normally, the weightings in MCA are based on expert judgement, preferably obtained by consulting a number of experts who then express their weight preferences using a procedure known as pair-wise comparison (Saaty 1980; Verhagen 2006). However, there is no objection to using different weighting methods or to include 'fuzzy' weights.

11.3.2 Calculating Routes and Movement Potential

11.3.2.1 LCPs and Corridors

Many published case studies in archaeology concerned with the reconstruction or prediction of ancient movement are modelling linear connections between two or more locations. This is mostly because the LCP toolboxes in GIS packages only calculate a single optimal route between start- and endpoints. The shortest path algorithms used in GIS are based on the work of Dijkstra (1959) and other computer scientists (Hart et al. 1968) who wanted to find efficient solutions to the problem of finding the shortest path in a graph consisting of multiple, unevenly spaced nodes. Movement in a grid is a special case of this, since all the nodes (grid cells) are evenly spaced. It is only by attaching differential costs to moving from one grid cell to the next that we can apply shortest path algorithms in a raster-GIS environment.

The assumption of a linear route is true for single travels, but the paths taken for multiple travels may shift in location, especially if these are continued over long periods of time, and when the routes are not consolidated by means of infrastructural amenities. Therefore, archaeologists have also explored the possibility of defining corridors of movement on the basis of cost surfaces, as a more fuzzy and possibly more realistic approach to reconstructing and predicting ancient movement patterns (e.g. Howey 2011; Murrieta-Flores 2012; Van Lanen et al. 2015a; Howey and Brouwer Burg 2017).

Some attempts have also been made to model potential movement patterns via agent-based modelling (ABM; Herzog 2016). The advantage of this approach is that the modelled paths are not deterministic: the agents can react to stimuli of the environment, and they can interact with other agents moving in the landscape. These models can also be used to simulate the spatio-temporal development of movement patterns. Simulation models are very well suited to investigate all kinds of sociocultural processes, but they are often based on highly abstracted representations of environmental and archaeological settings involved, whereas GIS-based studies often aim for more realistic representations. Furthermore, the few ABM studies around (e.g. Lake 2001; Wren et al. 2014) have mostly focused on dispersal, for example in the context of foragers looking for food or hominids moving out of Africa, rather than on the goal-oriented movement that is more commonly modelled in GIS. An exception to this is the study into army movement by Murgatroyd et al. (2012), who used computer-intensive ABM to model the logistics and most probable marching route of Byzantine troops on their way to the lost battle of Manzikert.

11.3.2.2 Movement Potential

LCPs and corridors assume travel between fixed start- and endpoints, an assumption that is not necessarily valid when studying movement in the past. Non-agricultural societies, for example, can be highly mobile, so routes and pathways will be highly variable as well, depending on the availability of mobile or seasonal resources. Furthermore, the archaeological data sets we use are incomplete and do not provide us with all the clues we need to model ancient routes. Methods to predict *potential* routes can therefore be very useful.

A first step in this direction can be to model the movement potential for a set of locations (see Herzog 2013c for an in-depth overview). As indicated earlier, movement potential is closely related to accessibility but not its exact reciprocal. Llobera (2000) introduced the concept of 'total path costs' as a proxy for movement potential. By calculating for each grid cell the average costs of moving to every other grid cell within a predefined radius it can be analysed at various scales (local, middle range, global). Mlekuž (2013, 2014) developed a similar method of calculating 'potential path fields', which proceeds by summing accumulated cost surfaces ('site catchments') for every single grid cell. This method can also be used to analyse movement potential at multiple scales. Herzog and Yépez (2013), lastly, introduced 'least-cost kernel density estimation' to obtain movement potential maps, giving a higher weight to the areas closer to the point of departure. All these methods are computationally intensive on larger grids. It has to be emphasized that all published examples are based on the calculation of terrain costs influencing walking speed, in particular slope.

A map of movement potential based on least effort is not yet an indicator of probable movement patterns. Whitley and Hicks (2003) therefore experimented with creating multiple LCPs crossing a region from edge to edge, maintaining a regular distance between the start- and endpoints, and then cumulated the results. This idea was also applied by Zakšek et al. (2008) and Fovet and Zakšek (2014), using multiple LCPs connecting known settlements, and was further explored by Murrieta-Flores (2012). Using this approach, the LCPs will concentrate in specific locations, and their density can then be used as a proxy for the probability of movement.

This concept was taken further by creating LCPs from regularly placed departure points in a region, running either to the edges of the study region or to a number of terminus points within a predefined radius of movement. This approach was independently developed by White and Barber (2012), who named it 'From Everywhere To Everywhere' or FETE modelling and by Verhagen (2013) who referred to it as 'cumulative cost path' or CCP modelling. Llobera (2015) created similar patterns by calculating LCPs between random locations at varying distances. Herzog (2013c) notes that this approach has drawbacks in application: the concentration of paths is not dependent on the absolute costs involved, so even in areas where movement costs are generally high there still will be many paths.

A different approach to the problem of modelling potential routes is presented by Llobera et al. (2011), who used hydrological flow accumulation algorithms on accumulated cost surfaces, first experimented with by Fábrega Álvarez (2006), to create a 'focal mobility network'. A similar procedure was published in the same year by Frachetti (2006). It results in the creation of multiple, converging paths from the edge of the accumulated cost surface to the point of departure (see also Chap. 14, Parcero-Oubiña et al.). The locations where the paths converge can be considered as nodes in a network, and a 'mobility basin' is then defined as the number of cells 'draining' into a node.

11.3.3 Sensitivity Analysis and Validation

While substantial debate has thus been directed towards the definition of cost parameters and the best ways to calculate movement potential and pathways, sensitivity analysis and validation of the models has been of less concern (see also Kantner 2012). Sensitivity analysis will reveal the effects of changing the parameters that are entered into the model, and it has a solid tradition in computational modelling outside archaeology (Brouwer Burg et al. 2016).

Since path modelling is based on three different steps (cost definition, creation of accumulated cost surfaces, and least-cost path calculation), we can make comparisons and perform sensitivity analyses in all three stages. Of these, the comparison of cost definitions is the easiest, since we know the equations and/or weighted costs involved, and GIS offers good tools to compare these by making overlays and obtaining spatial statistics. It therefore may come as a surprise that such simple analyses are never presented (the authors of this paper plead guilty as well). Comparing accumulated cost surfaces is more complicated, since we will have to compare them for each and every starting point (and maximum distance, if applicable). This is an exercise that has never been published either, as far as we are aware.

Comparison of individual LCPs or movement corridors is a more common procedure (e.g. Howey 2007; Gietl et al. 2008; Verhagen and Jeneson 2012; Kantner 2012; Herzog 2013a, d; Verhagen et al. 2014). In most cases this is only done visually. Aspects like path length, deviation, sinuosity (Mueller 1968) and path travel time, however, are relatively easy to calculate, and can be used to assess the relative efficiency of the routes. Also, the characteristics of the paths can be quickly analysed by overlaying them on one or more of the cost factors used or on other environmental characteristics, for example to see where the paths are crossing difficult terrain. However, this becomes computationally expensive when doing this for a large number of paths.

Validation of path models is very comparable to sensitivity analysis, the only difference being that it compares the model outcomes to empirical data such as field observations, indigenous knowledge or ethnographic accounts and/or historical documents (e.g. Howey 2007; Becker and Altschul 2008; Fiz and Orengo 2008; Polla 2009; Fovet 2010; Murrieta-Flores 2014; Verhagen et al. 2014; Güimil-Fariña and Parcero-Oubiña 2015; van Lanen et al. 2015b; Supernant 2017; Fonte et al. 2017). Most work so far has been concerned with establishing the accuracy of the reconstructed routes in comparison to the available evidence. This is because a correct prediction is desirable from a heritage management perspective, but also because the interpretation of the functioning of the path or road system can only give meaningful results if it departs from a correct reconstruction. The chances of successfully predicting a stretch of road will obviously increase with the number of available independent sources for testing the model.

There currently seem to be no standard methods for judging the reliability of the predictions of pathways, even when methods for assessing predictive model performance are well established (Kvamme 1988; Verhagen 2008; Verhagen and Whitley 2012). The most commonly applied approach is to analyse the distance of the modelled paths to the archaeological and historical evidence (e.g. Bell and Lock 2000; Ejstrud 2005; Fovet 2010; Güimil-Fariña and Parcero-Oubiña 2015; Van Lanen et al. 2015b; Fonte et al. 2017): the more traces of roads and other evidence that are found close to or aligned with the modelled pathways, the better the model is thought to perform. However, some of these studies do not provide a statistical assessment of the reliability of the modelling results.

In terms of computational efficiency, the comparison of large numbers of path models can only be profitably approached through statistical simulation modelling techniques. These have not been applied extensively to questions of path modelling yet (in contrast to visibility analysis; see Lake and Ortega 2013), and this is almost certainly due to the use of GIS as the exclusive toolbox for path modelling. While GIS has many virtues, efficient statistical computing is not one of them, whereas standard statistical simulation techniques such as Monte Carlo-analysis and bootstrapping are not primarily intended for use with spatial data. A middle ground between the two is not available at the moment, so performing sensitivity analysis and validation of path models still requires combining different software solutions and programming.

11.4 Movement, Pathways, and Networks

Pathways are always part of a network. They are connected to other paths that can be combined into routes that can be travelled in any order, not just the shortest or most efficient one. The network perspective changes the way in which we analyse movement: whereas cost surfaces consider the totality of the space that can be travelled, a network of paths represents a linear set of affordances for movement that limits travel to the network's structure. While this has some disadvantages from a theoretical point of view because it neglects the possibility of movement outside the path network, it also has strong analytical advantages since the properties of the network can be used to better understand the structure and development of (reconstructed) networks (see e.g. Gorenflo and Bell 1991; Brughmans 2010; Collar et al. 2015).

Social network analysis was developed in sociology in the 1970s and was initially only concerned with non-spatial relationships. Over the past decade, network analysis has become a major field of archaeological and historical investigation as well (see Knappett 2013a; Brughmans et al. 2016) with studies focusing on (supra-) regional trade and communication networks (e.g. Earl and Keay 2007; Sindbæk 2007, 2015; Knappett et al. 2008; Knappett et al. 2011; Carreras and De Soto 2013) and the possible development of social networks on the basis of observed finds (e.g. Mills et al. 2013; Coward 2013; Golitko and Feinman 2015). Archaeologists, however, have been keen to include geographical aspects in their studies as well (e.g. Carreras 1994; Isaksen 2007; Brughmans 2010; Coward 2013).

From a network analysis perspective, LCPs are graphs connecting two or more nodes via (weighted) edges. The only real difference with 'standard' network models is that the 'edges' have an irregularly shaped spatial extent. The shape of the pathways is not essential for performing network analysis, but the cost-distance between nodes is. Using relative distances instead of Euclidean ones can potentially lead to different configurations and thus interpretations of the networks. Several authors (Kaddouri 2004; Llobera et al. 2011; Herzog 2013b; Verhagen et al. 2013; Verhagen et al. 2014; Groenhuijzen and Verhagen 2015, 2016; Orengo and Livarda

2016) have explored the potential of using network analysis techniques with path modelling. Moving from LCPs to network analysis however implies that we first need to reconstruct the full network of possible connections.

11.4.1 *What to Connect?*

Network analysis can only be undertaken when we know which places to connect. In the majority of case studies, the places where movement starts and ends are taken from settlement data, and to a lesser extent from places of symbolic or strategic interest, or where resources could be obtained. The existence of these connections is mostly inferred from theoretical considerations and from material evidence of exchange of goods and people. The nature of movement, its frequency and the distances covered, however, are more difficult to establish, which is where LCP modelling comes in.

Connections can be modelled most easily when we only consider direct links between the two nearest points (see e.g. Van Lanen et al. 2015b). This conceptually simple model is however problematic for two reasons. First of all, direct connections to places further away may have existed as well. And secondly, the archaeological record will not always tell us where the nearest connected place was. Both chronological inaccuracy and incompleteness of survey data sets will complicate the reconstruction of all existing connections.

Apart from the supposed start- and endpoints of movement, waypoints should be considered as well. Waypoints can be defined as locations that provide navigational aid and/or logistical support during travel. Certain waypoints will strongly concentrate movement because they provide easy access through difficult terrain, like fords, bridges and stairs. Many waypoints, however, are of a more ephemeral nature than settlements, and are therefore difficult to include in path models. There is also a reciprocal relationship between the two: paths may be chosen because of the presence of natural features that support travel, but since humans adapt the landscape, human-made waypoints may become an integral part of the path system as well. From a technical point of view we can either treat them as additional nodes to be connected, or add them as attractors to the cost surfaces using a distance decay function, so that the modelled paths will have a higher probability of passing through the waypoints.

11.4.2 *Network (Re)construction Techniques*

Path modelling routines in GIS are not very efficient for network (re)construction since they do not allow for simultaneously connecting multiple nodes on the basis of standardized criteria. Commonly used and effective network construction techniques limit the number of allowed connections on the basis of distance and/or the number of closest neighbours (see Gorenflo and Bell 1991; Jiménez Badillo 2004;

Rivers et al. 2013; Groenhuijzen and Verhagen 2017; Fulminante et al. 2017). This limitation is necessary in order to prevent the creation of spurious connections, since direct links from everywhere to everywhere are not realistic. Note that this approach does not exclude the existence of long-distance connections, it only constrains the number and length of *direct* connections.

A common approach to define the thresholds for direct connections between places is to use gravity models derived from economic theory and urban geography (see Hodder and Orton 1976, 187–195 for an introduction). These are based on the assumption of a decrease in interaction potential with increasing (cost) distance. Gravity models can be created by simply calculating accumulated cost surfaces around sites. Instead of assuming a linear decrease in interaction potential with increasing travel time or energy expenditure, an exponential decrease is then specified in a *deterrence* (Evans and Rivers 2017) or distance decay function (Nuninger et al. 2006). This assumption is based on the consideration that interactions are much more probable over short distances.

The functions can further be weighted according to the (hypothesized) importance of nodes in the network. Archaeologists who explored the utility of gravity models in the 1970s (e.g. Plog 1976; Crumley 1979) often used settlement size as a weighting factor, but other factors were included as well (e.g. Hodder 1974; Jochim 1976). Nuninger et al. (2006), for example, considered distance, hierarchical categorization of settlements and visual control to estimate the strength of interaction between nodes.

A network can then be set up by creating direct connections between places that fall within a predefined maximum weighted (cost) distance threshold. A further refinement can be introduced by limiting the number of allowed connections, using some form of nearest neighbour analysis (e.g. Broodbank 2000).

However, depending on the approach chosen, these techniques can result in the creation of unconnected network clusters, and the various methods will inevitably result in different configurations. Furthermore, creating optimal connections between pairs of points is not necessarily optimal for the network as a whole. So-called Steiner points (extra nodes to be used as junctions) can be inserted in order to optimize the connectivity of the whole network, but applying this principle to cost surfaces is very challenging (Frommer and Golden 2007; Verhagen et al. 2014). Sensitivity analysis and validation of the resulting networks would therefore seem an important issue, but best practices for assessing the realism of (re)constructed networks are still largely lacking (Knappett 2013b; Groenhuijzen and Verhagen 2017).

The realism of the (re)constructed networks is also influenced by the completeness of the dataset of places to connect. Lack of information on presence and dating of sites is a common feature in archaeology and may influence not just the network configuration, but also all resulting analyses. Bevan and Wilson (2013) and Paliou and Bevan (2016) approached this by adding simulated settlements in the modelled network, based on a prediction of suitable site locations. By repeating this procedure a large number of times, it could be assessed whether the resulting networks' characteristics were stable or not. Davies et al. (2014) and Groenhuijzen and Verhagen (2016) used a similar approach. In their case the site dataset was assumed to be relatively complete but lacking in chronological precision, making it difficult to interpret the evolution of the network through time. By repeatedly taking subsamples of the dataset and creating networks from them, the robustness of the observed patterns could be established.

11.4.3 Network Analysis Techniques

Network analysis metrics come in two flavours, global and local (Wasserman and Faust 1994; Collar et al. 2015). Global descriptors, such as average shortest path length and clustering coefficient, give insight into the level of integration of the network: are all places well connected to each other, or is the network fragmented? Local descriptors are primarily used to understand the position of individual nodes in the network through the concept of centrality: which nodes are most advantageously positioned in the network? These local metrics, such as degree and betweenness centrality, are well suited to study the hierarchical structure of the network.

Analysis of the network links (edges) is less common (Knappett 2013b). Weighted edges are however a common feature in studies analysing the exchange of material culture (e.g. Golitko and Feinman 2015) in order to understand the relative importance of the connections. The studies by Kaddouri (2004) and Nuninger et al. (2006) similarly attached weights to links on the basis of the size of the settlements involved. In most published studies the edges are undirected, i.e. there is no difference between going to and from a place. However, some places will act as 'hubs', attracting goods, wealth, and workforce, whereas others are only net suppliers of, for example, mineral resources, food, or people. The edges between the network nodes will then be directed and have different weights depending on the direction of flow (see e.g. Rivers, Knappett & Evans 2013).

Alternatively, network analysis can be approached through *space syntax* (Hillier and Hanson 1984; Bafna 2003), which analyses the movement through the network (the routes), rather than the flow to and from the nodes. Unlike the approaches discussed earlier, space syntax assumes an existing fabric of connections and is not concerned with the (re)construction of networks. Nodes are only recognized as junctions of routes and carry no weight. Archaeological examples are mainly restricted to the analysis of architectural complexes (e.g. Chapman 1990; Blanton 1994; Banning 1997; Van Dyke 1999; Clark 2007) and urban street networks (Stöger 2008, 2015), although it has been extended to non-urban contexts as well (Hudson 2012; Craane 2013), and it can be combined with other network analysis approaches (Verhagen et al. 2013).

Networks created using least-cost path modelling are relatively easily integrated with space syntax (Verhagen 2013; Verhagen et al. 2013). Combining path models with node-based network analysis is also feasible and gradually becoming more common (Coward 2013; Bevan and Wilson 2013; Groenhuijzen and Verhagen 2015, 2017; Paliou and Bevan 2016), but we are still a long way from a full integration of both approaches. A significant obstacle is still found in the fact that common network analysis tools are not capable of directly using cost surfaces to (re)construct networks, or to calculate network metrics using non-Euclidean distances.

Also, the question of model validation looms large and was mostly ignored in earlier studies. Validation attempts have tried to establish the validity of either the (re)constructed connections or the assumed importance of the nodes in the network. Nuninger et al. (2006), for example, compared the results of their network reconstructions to archaeological expert judgement. Rivers et al. (2013) similarly ranked a set of sites for importance based on archaeological considerations and compared this to the ranking obtained from the constructed networks. Davies et al. (2014) reported that the modelled distribution of site sizes in their case study was in good agreement with the archaeological evidence. Even then, it was not possible to make precise predictions, and this was attributed to the influence of other, non-geographical factors. As far as we can tell, similar studies attempting to establish the relative importance of routes are lacking. Fulminante et al. (2017), however, present a straightforward method to compare modelled networks to observed ones by taking into account the differences in network descriptors.

An advantage of using formal network analysis is that it can be applied independently of assumptions about political, social, and economic structure and interaction. At the same time, this can be a drawback if we want to understand how real-world networks of movement and transport originate, function, and develop. The centrality metrics are only measures of potential interaction in a spatial or non-spatial network. In the context of transport and communication networks, this means that a node in an advantageous position does not necessarily attract movement. The actual movement patterns also depend on many other factors such as the importance of sites for trade, administration, and/or ritual purposes and the availability of logistical facilities.

11.5 Discussion and Conclusions

The overview of approaches presented in this paper shows that the scope for understanding movement on the basis of computer modelling is as substantial as it is complex. Improvements are still needed on a number of topics, especially where it concerns a better integration of tools and methods with theoretical insights.

11.5.1 Technical Issues

11.5.1.1 Software

There still is a lack of comprehensive and user-friendly tools for both path modelling and spatial network analysis. The available modules are highly inflexible when it comes to experimenting with different parameters. Also, many tools lack good documentation of the algorithms employed, essentially providing nothing more than a 'black box'. At the same time, adapting and reprogramming existing software is a task that is beyond the capabilities of individual researchers. Open source software development, which is needed for this, has clear advantages in terms of low costs to end users and the options it offers for collaborative work with scientists from different disciplines, but its weakness is its dependence on volunteer and project-based work, leading to the uneven development of toolboxes and the release of software packages that are not fully tested. The current interest in R as a spatial analysis tool, however (see, e.g. http://www.rspatial.org/ and https://elementr.hypotheses.org/), shows that open-source toolbox development can rapidly gain momentum, given sufficient interest.

11.5.1.2 Algorithms

Unfortunately, most archaeologists, including those working with GIS on a regular basis, do not have the required mathematical background to fully understand the algorithms used for LCP modelling and network reconstructions. Herzog (2013a) cites a number of papers where equations are represented wrongly, or interpreted in the wrong way. Improvement of the existing algorithms, coupled to tools that can create models using multiple algorithms, is therefore urgently needed. These tools would also need sophisticated options for sensitivity analysis of the model outcomes.

11.5.2 Methodological Issues

11.5.2.1 Validation of Pathway Models

A fundamental issue for pathway modelling is validation of the modelling results. This is only partly a matter of having sufficiently detailed archaeological data to judge the realism of model outcomes. A side-by-side comparison of different modelling outcomes is currently often a very demanding exercise, even when the goals and approaches are fairly similar – see e.g. Verhagen et al. (2013) on comparing space syntax and SNA, or Gietl et al. (2008) on comparing different LCP algorithms. In practice, therefore, the outcomes of single models are often presented as the only possible representation of the research results.

Even while chronological uncertainty and incompleteness of datasets will always be part archaeological research practice, sensitivity analysis therefore needs to become part of the standard methodology for pathway and network modelling in order to assess the quality of the presented models (see Bevan and Wilson 2013; Groenhuijzen and Verhagen 2017).

11.5.2.2 Dealing with Model Complexity

There are good reasons for advocating parsimony in modelling: sensitivity analysis of models will be less challenging, and most of the variation in model outcomes is often due to a limited number of variables anyway.

The middle-range theoretical approach advocated by Verhagen and Whitley (2012) can be applied to reduce the complexity of modelling by exploring cause-and-effect relationships in clearly circumscribed spaces, especially since much archaeological data is providing anecdotal rather than quantitative information (see also Lovis 2016). 'Scaffolding' of models is then a good approach to sequentially introduce extra complications into the models without making them unmanageable, as is for example demonstrated by Güimil-Fariña and Parcero-Oubiña (2015).

Nevertheless, we should remain aware that all models are inherently flawed. Using GIS is best seen as a dynamic and eclectic practice of research (cf. Hacıgüzeller 2012) or even a form of experimental archaeology (Whitley 2017). However, this does not imply an attitude of 'anything goes'. Providing a clear argumentation for the choice of parameters, equations, and/or algorithms used will avoid the danger of applying 'push-button' approaches without understanding their implications (Brouwer Burg 2017).

11.5.3 Theoretical Issues

11.5.3.1 The Value of Experimental Data

Much of the debate on LCP modelling has centred around the question of the realism of hiking functions and the estimation of energy expenditure and movement speed for other forms of transport. The experimental data available are mainly dating from the 1970s, and little work has been done to repeat and evaluate the experimental results. Some of this is going to be highly challenging, for example, if we want to understand the movement capabilities of ancient wheeled and water transport. A more thorough study of historical accounts, however, might be valuable to obtain more quantitative data on speeds of movement and energy expenditure.

11.5.3.2 Understanding Movement Practices

One of the enduring criticisms of LCP modelling is its emphasis on establishing optimal connections between places, whether these are based on consideration of energy expenditure or other aspects, such as optimal visibility. The relationship between theoretical principles of movement and navigation, observed and hypothesized movement practices, material traces of pathways, and modelling therefore needs to be further explored. This is a very complex field of study that should be addressed at various scale levels and for different movement practices. For example, the practice of *wayfaring* (Ingold 2011) implies a completely different movement strategy than when transporting trade goods or when moving in a ritual procession. Yet, these types of movement can occur over the same pathways and will be very difficult to disentangle on the basis of the material traces of pathways alone.

11.5.3.3 Understanding Networks

Finally, in order to fully understand patterns of movement and their long-term development, ancient pathways cannot be studied in isolation from settlement patterns. The nodes in the network are where the decisions on movement are taken, where people and goods flow to and from. Questions of structuring of networks of communication and transport have however only recently begun to be approached by considering both the routes and the settlements, and standard methods to do so still need to be developed.

11.5.4 Final Remarks

The presented overview of current approaches to computer modelling of pathways and movement networks in archaeology shows its considerable potential for understanding ancient movement.

Nevertheless, the technological integration of approaches needs to be much improved, or simply still to be done, in order to aid and clarify the analytical process. Within this integration, specific efforts must be dedicated to documenting the algorithms used and to offer a better understanding of their use by archaeologists.

From a methodological point of view, this technological effort should be coupled to a systematic description of the data, analytical process, sensitivity analysis, and validation. These last two require new software tools, but can be done using straightforward and existing techniques. The major challenge is defining the best practices that we need adopt.

Lastly, many debates remain open regarding the social interpretation of the materiality of past movement. The strong assumption of optimality behind most of LCP models deserves a deeper investigation and a more relativistic attitude, where optimality is seen as a hypothesis rather than a basic assumption. In a broad sense, the theoretical underpinning of models of ancient movement needs to be clarified and related to various conceptual frameworks of past movement. The use of ontologies could be a way to pursue this challenge.

References

Adams CEP (2007) Land transport in Roman Egypt: economics and administration in a Roman province. Oxford University Press, Oxford

Arnaud P (2005) Les routes de la navigation antique: Itinéraires en Méditerranée. Éditions Errance, Paris

Bachrach BS (1993) Animals and warfare in Early Medieval Europe. In: Bachrach BS (ed) Armies and politics in the Early Medieval West. Hampshire, Aldershot, pp 708–751

Bafna S (2003) Space Syntax. A brief introduction to its logic and analytical techniques. Environ Behav 35:1–29. https://doi.org/10.1177/0013916502238863

Banning EB (1997) Spatial perspectives on early urban development in Mesopotamia. In: Aufrecht WE, Mirau NA, Gauley SW (eds) Urbanism in antiquity, from Mesopotamia to Crete. Sheffield University Press, Sheffield, pp 17–34

Becker KM, Altschul JH (2008) Path finding: the archaeology of trails and trail systems. In: Altschul JH, Rankin AG (eds) Fragile patterns: the archaeology of the Western Papaguería. SRI Press, Tucson, pp 420–446

Bell T, Lock G (2000) Topographic and cultural influences on walking the Ridgeway in later prehistoric times. In: Lock G (ed) Beyond the map. Archaeology and spatial technologies. IOS Press/Ohmsha, Amsterdam, pp 85–100

Bevan A, Wilson A (2013) Models of settlement hierarchy based on partial evidence. J Archaeol Sci 40:2415–2427. https://doi.org/10.1016/j.jas.2012.12.025

Blanton RE (1994) Houses and households. A comparative study. Plenum Press, New York

Bourgeois Q (2013) Monuments on the Horizon. The formation of the barrow landscape throughout the 3rd and 2nd millennium BC. Sidestone Press, Leiden

Broodbank C (2000) An island archaeology of the Early Cyclades. Cambridge University Press, Cambridge

Brouwer Burg M (2017) It must be right, GIS told me so! Questioning the infallibility of GIS as a methodological tool. J Archaeol Sci 84:115–120. https://doi.org/10.1016/j.jas.2017.05.010

Brouwer Burg M, Peeters H, Lovis WA (eds) (2016) Uncertainty and sensitivity analysis in archaeological computational modeling. Springer, Berlin

Brughmans T (2010) Connecting the dots: towards archaeological network analysis. Oxf J Archaeol 29:277–303. https://doi.org/10.1111/j.1468-0092.2010.00349.x

Brughmans T, Collar A, Coward F (eds) (2016) The connected past. Challenges to network studies in archaeology and history. Oxford University Press, Oxford

Carreras C (1994) Una reconstrucción del comercio en cerámicas: la red de transportes en Britannia. Ed. Estaquirot, Barcelona

Carreras C, De Soto P (2013) The Roman transport network: a precedent for the integration of the European mobility. Hist Methods: J Quant Interdisciplinary Hist 46(3):117–133. https://doi.org/10.1080/01615440.2013.803403

Casson L (1994) Ships and seafaring in ancient times. University of Texas Press, Austin

Chapman J (1990) Social inequality on Bulgarian tells and the Varna problem. In: Samson R (ed) The social archaeology of houses. Edinburgh University Press, Edinburgh

Clark DLC (2007) Viewing the liturgy: a space syntax study of changing visibility and accessibility in the development of the Byzantine Church in Jordan. World Archaeol 39:84–104

Collar A, Coward F, Brughmans T, Mills BJ (2015) Networks in archaeology: phenomena, abstraction, representation. J Archaeol Method Theory 22:1–32. https://doi.org/10.1007/s10816-014-9235-6

Coward F (2013) Grounding the net: social networks, material culture, and geography in the Epipalaeolithic and early Neolithic of the Near East (~21-6,000 cal bce). In: Knappett C (ed) Network analysis in archaeology: new approaches to regional interaction. Oxford University Press, Oxford, pp 247–280

Craane ML (2013) Spatial patterns: the Late Medieval and Early-Modern movement economy of the Bailiwick of 's Hertogenbosch from an interregional, regional and local spatial perspective. University of Tilburg, Tilburg

Crumley CL (1979) Three locational models: an epistemological assessment for anthropology and archaeology. In: Schiffer MB (ed) Advances in archaeological method and theory, vol 2. Academic Press, New York, pp 141–173

Čučković Z (2015) Exploring intervisibility networks: a case study from Bronze and Iron age Istria (Croatia and Slovenia). In: Giligny F, Djindjian F, Costa L, Moscati P, Robert S (eds) CAA2014. 21st century archaeology. Concepts, methods and tools. Proceedings of the 42nd annual conference on computer applications and quantitative methods in archaeology. Archaeopress, Oxford, pp 469–478

Cushman SA, McRae B, Adriaensen F, Beier P, Shirley M, Zeller K (2013) Biological corridors and connectivity. In: MacDonald DW, Willis KJ (eds) Key topics in conservation biology 2. John Wiley & Sons, New York, pp 385–404

D'Altroy T (2015) The Incas, 2nd edn. Wiley-Blackwell, Oxford

Dalla Bona L (1994) Ontario Ministry of Natural Resources archaeological predictive modeling project. Lakehead University, Thunder Bay

Davies T, Fry H, Wilson A, Palmisano A, Altaweel M, Radner K (2014) Application of an entropy maximizing and dynamics model for understanding settlement structure: the Khabur Triangle in the Middle Bronze and Iron Ages. J Archaeol Sci 43:141–154. https://doi.org/10.1016/j.jas.2013.12.014

De Gruchy M, Caswell E, Edwards J (2017) Velocity-based terrain coefficients for time-based models of human movement. Internet Archaeol 45. https://doi.org/10.11141/ia.45.4

Dijkstra EW (1959) A note on two problems in connexion with graphs. Numer Math 1:269–271. https://doi.org/10.1007/BF01386390

Earl G, Keay S (2007) Urban connectivity of Iberian and Roman towns in Southern Spain: a network analysis approach. In: Clark JT, Hagemeister EM (eds) Digital discovery. Exploring new frontiers in human heritage. CAA2006. Computer applications and quantitative methods in archaeology. Proceedings of the 34th conference, Fargo, United States, April 2006. Archeaeolingua, Budapest, CD-ROM, pp 77–86

Ejstrud B (2005) Cost surface analysis and ancient roads: a comparison. In: Berger J-F, Bertoncello F, Braemer F, Davtian G, Gazenbeek M (eds) Temps et espaces de l'homme en société, analyses et modèles sociaux en archéologie. XXVe rencontres internationales d'archéologie et d'histoire d'Antibes. Éditions APDCA, Antibes, pp 135–139

Ericson JE, Goldstein R (1980) Work space: a new approach to the analysis of energy expenditure within site catchments. In: Findlow FJ, Ericson JE (eds) Catchment analysis: essays on prehistoric resource space. Department of Anthropology, University of California, Los Angeles, pp 21–30

Evans TS, Rivers RJ (2017) Was Thebes necessary? Contingency in spatial modeling. Front Digit Humanities 4(8). https://doi.org/10.3389/fdigh.2017.00008

Fábrega Álvarez P (2006) Moving without destination. A theoretical GIS-based determination of movement from a given origin. Archeologia e Calcolatori 64:7–11. Available at http://www.archcalc.cnr.it//acn/per_ACN64/ACN64_testo.pdf. Accessed on 18 July 2018

Fairén-Jiménez S (2007) British Neolithic rock art in its landscape. J Field Archaeol 32:283–295. https://doi.org/10.1179/009346907791071584

Fiz I, Orengo H (2008) Simulating communication routes in Mediterranean alluvial plains. In: Posluschny A, Lambers K, Herzog I (eds) Layers of perception. Proceedings of the 35th international conference on computer applications and quantitative methods in archaeology (CAA), Berlin, Germany, April 2-6, 2007. Dr. Rudolf Habelt GmbH, Bonn, pp 316–321

Fonte J, Parcero Oubiña C, Costa-García J-M (2017) A GIS-based analysis of the rationale of Roman roads. The Iter XVII (NW Iberian Peninsula). MAA 17:163–189. https://doi.org/10.5281/zenodo.1005562

Fovet É (2010) Dynamiques socio-environnementales durant l'Antiquité: approche micro-régionale du peuplement en Languedoc oriental. University of Franche-Comté, Besançon

Fovet É, Zakšek K (2014) Path network modelling and network of aggregated settlements: a case study in Languedoc (Southeastern France). In: Polla S, Verhagen P (eds) Computational approaches to the study of movement in archaeology. Theory, practice and interpretation of factors and effects of long term landscape formation and transformation. De Gruyter, Berlin, pp 43–72

Frachetti MD (2006) Digital archaeology and the scalar structure of pastoral landscapes. In: Evans TL, Daly P (eds) Digital archaeology: bridging method and theory. Routledge, London, pp 114–131

Frommer I, Golden B (2007) A genetic algorithm for solving the Euclidean Non-Uniform Steiner Tree problem. In: Baker EK, Joseph A, Mehrotra A, Trick MA (eds) Extending the horizons: advances in computing, optimization, and decision technologies. Springer, New York, pp 31–48

Fulminante F, Prignano L, Morer I, Lozano S (2017) Coordinated decisions and unbalanced power. How Latin cities shaped their terrestrial transportation network. Front Digit Humanities 4(4). https://doi.org/10.3389/fdigh.2017.00004

Gaffney V, Stančič Z (1991) GIS approaches to regional analysis: a case study of the island of Hvar. Znanstveni inštitut Filozofske fakultete Ljubljana, Ljubljana
Gaver WW (1991) Technology affordances. In: CHI '91. Proceedings of the SIGCHI Conference on Human Factors in Computing Systems. New Orleans, Louisiana, USA - April 27-May 02, 1991. https://doi.org/10.1145/108844.108856
Gibson JJ (1977) The theory of affordances. In: Shaw R, Bransford J (eds) Perceiving, acting, and knowing: toward an ecological psychology. Lawrence Erlbaum, Hillsdale, pp 67–82
Gibson JJ (1979) The ecological approach to visual perception. Houghton Mifflin Harcourt, Boston
Gietl R, Doneus M, Fera M (2008) Cost distance analysis in an alpine environment. Comparison of different cost-surface modules. In: Posluschny A, Lambers K, Herzog I (eds) Layers of perception. Proceedings of the 35th international conference on computer applications and quantitative methods in archaeology (CAA), Berlin, Germany, April 2-6, 2007. Dr. Rudolf Habelt GmbH, Bonn, pp 336–341
Gillings M (2009) Visual affordance, landscape and the megaliths of Alderney. Oxf J Archaeol 28:335–356. https://doi.org/10.1111/j.1468-0092.2009.00332.x
Givoni B, Goldman RF (1971) Predicting metabolic energy cost. J Appl Physiol 30:429–433
Golitko M, Feinman GM (2015) Procurement and distribution of Pre-Hispanic Mesoamerican Obsidian 900 BC-AD 1520: a social network analysis. J Archaeol Method Theory 22:206–247. https://doi.org/10.1007/s10816-014-9211-1
Gorenflo LJ, Bell TL (1991) Network analysis and the study of past regional organisation. In: Trombold CD (ed) Ancient road networks and settlement hierarchies in the New World. Cambridge University Press, Cambridge, pp 80–98
Gregory NTN (1997) A comparative study of Irish and Scottish Logboats. University of Edinburgh, Edinburgh
Groenhuijzen MR (2018) Palaeogeographic analysis of the Dutch part of the Roman limes. Vrije Universiteit Amsterdam, Amsterdam
Groenhuijzen MR, Verhagen P (2015) Exploring the dynamics of transport in the Dutch Limes. eTopoi Journal for Ancient Studies Special Volume 4:25–47. Available at http://journal.topoi.org/index.php/etopoi/article/view/203/227. Accessed on 10 May 2018
Groenhuijzen MR, Verhagen P (2016) Testing the robustness of local network metrics in research on archeological local transport networks. Front Digit Humanities 3(6). https://doi.org/10.3389/fdigh.2016.00006
Groenhuijzen MR, Verhagen P (2017) Comparing network construction techniques in the context of local transport networks in the Dutch part of the Roman limes. J Archaeol Sci Rep 15:235–251. https://doi.org/10.1016/j.jasrep.2017.07.024
Güimil-Fariña A, Parcero-Oubiña C (2015) “Dotting the joins”: a non-reconstructive use of Least Cost Paths to approach ancient roads. The case of the Roman roads in the NW Iberian Peninsula. J Archaeol Sci 54:31–44. https://doi.org/10.1016/j.jas.2014.11.030
Hacıgüzeller P (2012) GIS, critique, representation and beyond. J Soc Archaeol 12:245–263. https://doi.org/10.1177/1469605312439139
Haisman MF, Goldman RF (1974) Effect of terrain on the energy cost of walking with back loads and handcart loads. J Appl Physiol 36:545–548
Hart PE, Nilsson NJ, Raphael B (1968) A formal basis for the heuristic determination of minimum cost paths. IEEE Trans Syst Sci Cybern 4:100–107. https://doi.org/10.1109/TSSC.1968.300136
Herzog I (2013a) Theory and practice of cost functions. In: Contreras F, Farjas M, Melero FJ (eds) Fusion of cultures. Proceedings of the 38th Annual Conference on Computer Applications and Quantitative Methods in Archaeology, Granada, Spain, April 2010. Archaeopress, Oxford, pp 375–382
Herzog I (2013b) Least cost networks. In: Earl G, Sly T, Chrysanthi A, Murrieta-Flores P, Papadopoulos C, Romanowska I, Wheatley D (eds) Archaeology in the digital era. Papers from the 40th Annual Conference of Computer Applications and Quantitative Methods in Archaeology (CAA), Southampton, 26-29 March 2012. Amsterdam University Press, Amsterdam, pp 240–251

Herzog I (2013c) Calculating accessibility. In: Earl G, Sly T, Chrysanthi A, Murrieta-Flores P, Papadopoulos C, Romanowska I, Wheatley D (eds) Archaeology in the digital era. Papers from the 40th Annual Conference of Computer Applications and Quantitative Methods in Archaeology (CAA), Southampton, 26–29 March 2012, vol II. Amsterdam University Press, Amsterdam, pp 720–734

Herzog I (2013d) The potential and limits of optimal path analysis. In: Bevan A, Lake M (eds) Computational approaches to archaeological spaces. Left Coast Press, Walnut Creek, pp 179–211

Herzog I (2014) Least cost paths – some methodological issues. Internet Archaeol 36. https://doi.org/10.11141/ia.36.5

Herzog I (2016) Dispersal versus optimal path calculation. In: Campana S, Scopigno R, Carpentiero G, Cirillo M (eds) Keep the revolution going. Proceedings of the 43rd Annual Conference on Computer Applications and Quantitative Methods in Archaeology. Archaeopress, Oxford, pp 567-578

Herzog I, Yépez A (2013) Least-cost Kernel density estimation and interpolation-based density analysis applied to survey data. In: Contreras F, Farjas M, Melero FJ (eds) Fusion of cultures. Proceedings of the 38th Annual Conference on Computer Applications and Quantitative Methods in Archaeology, Granada, Spain, April 2010. Archaeopress, Oxford, pp 367–374

Higgs ES, Vita-Finzi C (1972) Prehistoric economies: a territorial approach. In: Higgs ES (ed) Papers in economic prehistory. Cambridge University Press, Cambridge, pp 27–36

Hillier B, Hanson J (1984) The social logic of space. Cambridge University Press, Cambridge

Hodder I (1974) Some marketing models for Romano-British coarse pottery. Britannia 5:340–359. https://doi.org/10.2307/525737

Hodder I, Orton C (1976) Spatial analysis in archaeology. Cambridge University Press, Cambridge

Howey MCL (2007) Using multi-criteria cost surface analysis to explore past regional landscapes: a case study of ritual activity and social interaction in Michigan, AD 1200-1600. J Archaeol Sci 34:1830–1846. https://doi.org/10.1016/j.jas.2007.01.002

Howey MCL (2011) Multiple pathways across past landscapes: circuit theory as a complementary geospatial method to least cost path for modeling past movement. J Archaeol Sci 38:2523–2535. https://doi.org/10.1016/j.jas.2011.03.024

Howey MCL, Brouwer Burg M (2017) Assessing the state of archaeological GIS research: unbinding analyses of past landscapes. J Archaeol Sci 84:1–9. https://doi.org/10.1016/j.jas.2017.05.002

Hudson EJ (2012) Walking and watching: new approaches to reconstructing cultural landscapes through space syntax analysis. In: White DA, Surface-Evans SL (eds) Least cost analysis of social landscapes: archaeological case studies. University of Utah Press, Salt Lake City, pp 97–108

Hyslop J (1984) The Inka road system. Academic Press, Orlando

Imhof E (1950) Gelände und Karte. Rentsch, Erlenbach bei Zürich

Ingold T (1992) Culture and the perception of the environment. In: Croll E, Parkin D (eds) Bush base: forest farm. Culture, environment and development. Routledge, London, pp 39–56

Ingold T (2011) Being alive. Essays on movement, knowledge and description. Routledge, London

Isaksen L (2007) Network analysis of transport vectors in Roman Baetica. In: Clark JT, Hagemeister EM (eds) Digital discovery. Exploring new frontiers in human heritage. CAA2006. Computer Applications and Quantitative Methods in Archaeology. Proceedings of the 34th conference, Fargo, United States, April 2006. Archeaeolingua, Budapest, CD-ROM, pp 64–76

Jansma E, Morel JMAW (2007) Een Romeinse Rijnaak, gevonden in Utrecht-De Meern. Resultaten van het onderzoek naar de platbodem 'De Meern 1'. Rijksdienst voor Archeologie, Cultuurlandschap en Monumenten, Amersfoort

Jiménez Badillo D (2004) A method for interactive recognition of three-dimensional adjacency patterns in point sets, based on relative neighbourhood graphs. An archaeological application. University College London, London

Jochim MA (1976) Hunter-gatherer subsistence and settlement: a predictive model. Academic Press, New York

Kaddouri L (2004) Structures spatiales et mises en réseaux de villes pour la régionalisation des territoires. Université Paul Valéry - Montpellier III, Montpellier

Kantner J (2012) Realism, reality, and routes: evaluating cost-surface and cost-path algorithms. In: White DA, Surface-Evans SL (eds) Least cost analysis of social landscapes: archaeological case studies. University of Utah Press, Salt Lake City, pp 225–238

Knappett C (ed) (2013a) Network analysis in archaeology: new approaches to regional interaction. Oxford University Press, Oxford

Knappett C (2013b) Introduction: why networks? In: Knappett C (ed) Network analysis in archaeology: new approaches to regional interaction. Oxford University Press, Oxford, pp 3–16

Knappett C, Evans T, Rivers R (2008) Modelling maritime interaction in the Aegean Bronze Age. Antiquity 82:1009–1024. https://doi.org/10.1017/S0003598X0009774X

Knappett C, Rivers R, Evans T (2011) The Theran eruption and Minoan palatial collapse: new interpretations gained from modelling the maritime network. Antiquity 85:1008–1023

Kolb A (2000) Transport und Nachrichtentransfer im Römischen Reich. De Gruyter, Berlin

Kondo Y, Seino Y (2010) GPS-aided walking experiments and data-driven travel cost modeling on the historical road of Nakasendō-Kisoji (Central Highland Japan). In: Frischer B, Webb Crawford J, Koller D (eds) Making history interactive. Computer Applications and Quantitative Methods in Archaeology (CAA). Proceedings of the 37th international conference, Williamsburg, Virginia, United States of America, March 22–26. Archaeopress, Oxford, pp 158–165

Kvamme KL (1988) Development and testing of quantitative models. In: Judge WJ, Sebastian L (eds) Quantifying the present and predicting the past: theory, method, and application of archaeological predictive modelling. U.S. Department of the Interior, Bureau of Land Management Service Center, Denver, pp 325–348

Lake M (2001) The use of pedestrian modelling in archaeology, with an example from the study of cultural learning. Environ Plann B Plann Des 28:385–403. https://doi.org/10.1068/b2726

Lake M, Ortega D (2013) Compute-intensive GIS visibility analysis of the settings of prehistoric stone circles. In: Bevan A, Lake M (eds) Computational approaches to archaeological spaces. Left Coast Press, Walnut Creek, pp 213–243

Lake MW, Woodman PE (2003) Visibility studies in archaeology: a review and case study. Environ Plann B Plann Des 30:689–707. https://doi.org/10.1068/b29122

Langmuir E (2004) Mountaincraft and Leadership. Revised Third Edition. Cordee, Leicester

Laurence R (1999) The Roads of Roman Italy. Mobility and cultural change. Routledge, London

Lawton B (2004) Various and ingenious machines, vol 1: Power generation and transport. Brill, Leiden

Llobera M (1996) Exploring the topography of mind: GIS, social space and archaeology. Antiquity 70:612–622. https://doi.org/10.1017/S0003598X00083745

Llobera M (2000) Understanding movement: a pilot model towards the sociology of movement. In: Lock G (ed) Beyond the map. Archaeology and spatial technologies. IOS Press/Ohmsha, Amsterdam, pp 66–84

Llobera M (2003) Extending GIS-based visual analysis: the concept of visualscapes. Int J Geogr Inf Sci 17:25–48. https://doi.org/10.1080/713811741

Llobera M (2007) Reconstructing visual landscapes. World Archaeol 39(1):51–69. https://doi.org/10.1080/00438240601136496

Llobera M (2015) Working the digital: some thoughts from landscape archaeology. In: Chapman R, Wylie A (eds) Material evidence: learning from archaeological practice. Routledge, Abingdon, pp 173–188

Llobera M, Sluckin TJ (2007) Zigzagging: theoretical insights on climbing strategies. J Theor Biol 249:206–217. https://doi.org/10.1016/j.jtbi.2007.07.020

Llobera M, Fábrega-Álvarez P, Parcero-Oubiña C (2011) Order in movement: a GIS approach to accessibility. J Archaeol Sci 38:843–851. https://doi.org/10.1016/j.jas.2010.11.006

Lock G, Pouncett J (2010) Walking the Ridgeway revisited: the methodological and theoretical implications of scale dependency for the derivation of slope and the calculation of least-cost pathways. In: Frischer B, Webb Crawford J, Koller D (eds) Making history interactive. Computer Applications and Quantitative Methods in Archaeology (CAA). Proceedings of the 37th international conference, Williamsburg, Virginia, United States of America, March 22–26. Archaeopress, Oxford, pp 192–203

Lock G, Kormann M, Pouncett J (2014) Visibility and movement: towards a GIS-based integrated approach. In: Polla S, Verhagen P (eds) Computational approaches to the study of movement in archaeology. Theory, practice and interpretation of factors and effects of long term landscape formation and transformation. De Gruyter, Berlin, pp 23–42

Loots L, Nackaerts K, Waelkens M (1999) Fuzzy Viewshed Analysis of the Hellenistic City Defence System at Sagalassos, Turkey. In: Dingwall L, Exon S, Gaffney V et al (eds) Archaeology in the age of the internet. CAA97. Computer Applications and Quantitative Methods in Archaeology. Proceedings of the 25th anniversary conference, University of Birmingham, April 1997. BAR, Oxford, p 82 + CD-ROM

Lovis WA (2016) Is there a research design role for sensitivity analysis (SA) in archaeological modeling? In: Brouwer Burg M, Peeters H, Lovis WA (eds) Uncertainty and sensitivity analysis in archaeological computational modeling. Springer, Berlin, pp 21–36

Lynch J, Parcero-Oubiña C (2017) Under the eye of the Apu. Paths and mountains in the Inka settlement of the Hualfín and Quimivil valleys, NW Argentina. J Archaeol Sci Rep 16:44–56. https://doi.org/10.1016/j.jasrep.2017.09.019

Malczewski J (1999) GIS and multicriteria decision analysis. John Wiley and Sons, New York

Margaria R (1938) Sulla fisiologia e specialmente sul consumo energetico della marcia e della corsa a varia velocità ed inclinazione del terreno. Atti Accademia Nazionale dei Lincei 7:299–368

McGrail S (1978) The Logboats of England and Wales. University of London, London

Mills BJ, Clark JJ, Peeples MA et al (2013) Transformation of social networks in the late pre-Hispanic US Southwest. PNAS 110:5785–5790. https://doi.org/10.1073/pnas.1219966110

Minetti AE, Moia C, Roi GS, Susta D, Ferretti G (2002) Energy cost of walking and running at extreme uphill and downhill slopes. J Appl Physiol 93:1039–1046

Mlekuž D (2013) Time geography, GIS and archaeology. In: Contreras F, Farjas M, Melero FJ (eds) Fusion of cultures. Proceedings of the 38th Annual Conference on Computer Applications and Quantitative Methods in Archaeology, Granada, Spain, April 2010. Archaeopress, Oxford, pp 359–369

Mlekuž D (2014) Exploring the topography of movement. In: Polla S, Verhagen P (eds) Computational approaches to the study of movement in archaeology. Theory, practice and interpretation of factors and effects of long term landscape formation and transformation. De Gruyter, Berlin, pp 5–22

Mueller JE (1968) An introduction to the hydraulic and topographic sinuosity indexes. Ann Assoc Am Geogr 58:371–385

Murgatroyd P, Craenen B, Theodoropoulos G, Gaffney V, Haldon J (2012) Modelling medieval military logistics: an agent-based simulation of a Byzantine army on the march. Comput Math Organ Theory 18:488–506. https://doi.org/10.1007/s10588-011-9103-9

Murrieta-Flores PA (2010) Traveling in a prehistoric landscape: exploring the influences that shaped human movement. In: Frischer B, Webb Crawford J, Koller D (eds) Making history interactive. Computer applications and quantitative methods in archaeology (CAA). Proceedings of the 37th International Conference, Williamsburg, Virginia, United States of America, March 22–26. Archaeopress, Oxford, pp 249–267

Murrieta-Flores P (2012) Understanding human movement through spatial technologies. The role of natural areas of transit in the Late Prehistory of South-western Iberia. Trab Prehist 69:103–122. https://doi.org/10.3989/tp.2012.12082

Murrieta-Flores P (2014) Developing computational approaches for the study of movement: assessing the role of visibility and landscape markers in terrestrial navigation during Iberian Late Prehistory. In: Polla S, Verhagen P (eds) Computational approaches to the study of movement in archaeology. Theory, practice and interpretation of factors and effects of long term landscape formation and transformation. De Gruyter, Berlin, pp 99–132

Nijkamp P, Rietveld P, Voogd H (1990) Multicriteria evaluation in physical planning. North-Holland, Amsterdam

Nuninger L, Sanders L, Favory F, Garmy P, Raynaud C, Rozenblat C, Kaddouri L, Mathian H, Schneider L (2006) La modélisation des réseaux d'habitat: trois expériences. Mappemonde 3:1–28

Orengo HA, Livarda A (2016) The seeds of commerce: A network analysis-based approach to the Romano-British transport system. J Archaeol Sci 66:21–35. https://doi.org/10.1016/j.jas.2015.12.003

Paliou E, Bevan A (2016) Evolving settlement patterns, spatial interaction and the socio-political organisation of late Prepalatial south-central Crete. J Anthropol Archaeol 42:184–197. https://doi.org/10.1016/j.jaa.2016.04.006

Pandolf KB, Givoni B, Goldman RF (1976) Metabolic energy expenditure and terrain coefficients for walking on snow. Ergonomics 19:683–690. https://doi.org/10.1080/00140137608931583

Pandolf KB, Givoni B, Goldman RF (1977) Predicting energy expenditure with loads while standing or walking very slowly. J Appl Physiol 43:577–581

Plog S (1976) Measurement of prehistoric interaction between communities. In: Flannery KV (ed) The early Mesoamerican Village. Academic Press, New York, pp 255–272

Polla S (2009) GIS-basierte Modellierung der Strecken des Stadiasmos. In: Graßhoff G, Mittenhuber F (eds) Untersuchungen zum Stadiasmos von Patara: Modellierung und Analyse eines antiken geographischen Streckennetzes. University of Bern, Bern, pp 121–145

Pomey P (ed) (1997) La navigation dans l'Antiquité. Édisud, Aix-en-Provence

Raepsaet G (2002) Attelages et Techniques de Transport Dans Le Monde Gréco-Romaine. Le Livre Timperman, Brussels

Rivers R, Knappett C, Evans T (2013) What makes a site important? Centrality, gateways and gravity. In: Knappett C (ed) Network analysis in archaeology: new approaches to regional interaction. Oxford University Press, Oxford, pp 125–150

Rodrigue J-P, Comtois C, Slack B (2017) The geography of transport systems, 4th edn. Routledge, New York

Roth JP (1998) The logistics of the Roman Army at War (264 B.C. – A.D. 235). Brill, Leiden

Ruggles C, Medyckyj-Scott D (1997) Site location, landscape visibility, and symbolic astronomy: a Scottish case study. In: Maschner HDG (ed) New methods, old problems: geographic information systems in modern archaeological research. Southern Illinois University, Carbondale, pp 127–146

Saaty TL (1980) The analytic hierarchy process: planning, priority setting, resource allocation. McGraw-Hill, New York

Sindbæk SM (2007) The small world of the Vikings: networks in early medieval communication and exchange. Nor Archaeol Rev 40:59–74. https://doi.org/10.1080/00293650701327619

Sindbæk SM (2015) Northern emporia and maritime networks. Modelling past communication using archaeological network analysis. In: Preiser-Kapeller J, Daim F (eds) Harbours and maritime networks as complex adaptive systems. Verlag des Römisch-Germanischen Zentralmuseums, Mainz, pp 105–118

Soule RG, Goldman RF (1972) Terrain coefficients for energy cost prediction. J Appl Physiol 32:706–708. https://doi.org/10.1152/jappl.1972.32.5.706

Stöger JJ (2008) Roman Ostia: Space syntax and the domestication of space. In: Posluschny A, Lambers K, Herzog I (eds) Layers of Perception. Proceedings of the 35th international conference on Computer Applications and Quantitative Methods in Archaeology (CAA), Berlin, Germany, April 2–6, 2007. Dr. Rudolf Habelt GmbH, Bonn, pp 322–327

Stöger JJ (2015) Roman neighbourhoods by the numbers: a space syntax view on ancient city quarters and their social life. J Space Syntax 6:61–80

Supernant K (2017) Modeling Métis mobility? Evaluating least cost paths and indigenous landscapes in the Canadian west. J Archaeol Sci 84:63–73. https://doi.org/10.1016/j.jas.2017.05.006

Tobler W (1993) Three presentations on geographical analysis and modelling. National Center for Geographic Information and Analysis, Santa Barbara

Trifković V (2006) Persons and landscapes: shifting scales of landscape archaeology. In: Lock G, Molyneaux BL (eds) Confronting scale in archaeology. Issues of theory and practice. Springer, New York, pp 217–324

Turnbull D (2000) Masons, tricksters and cartographers: comparative studies in the sociology of scientific and indigenous knowledge. Taylor and Francis, London

Van Dyke RM (1999) Space syntax analysis at the Chacoan outlier of Guadalupe. Am Antiq 64:461–473. https://doi.org/10.2307/2694146

Van Lanen RJ, Kosian MC, Groenewoudt BJ, Jansma E (2015a) Finding a way: modeling landscape prerequisites for Roman and early-medieval routes in the Netherlands. Geoarchaeol Int J 30:200–222. https://doi.org/10.1002/gea.21510

Van Lanen RJ, Kosian MC, Groenewoudt BJ, Spek T, Jansma E (2015b) Best travel options: modelling Roman and early-medieval routes in the Netherlands using a multi-proxy approach. J Archaeol Sci Rep 3:144–159. https://doi.org/10.1016/j.jasrep.2015.05.024

Van Leusen M (1993) Cartographic modelling in a cell-based GIS. In: Andresen J, Madsen T, Scollar I (eds) Computing the past. Computer applications and quantitative methods in archaeology. CAA92. Aarhus University Press, Aarhus, pp 105–124

Van Leusen PM (2002) Pattern to process: methodological investigations into the formation and interpretation of spatial patterns in archaeological landscapes. Rijksuniversiteit Groningen, Groningen. Available at http://www.rug.nl/research/portal/files/7002343/thesis.pdf. Accessed on 11 May 2018

Verhagen P (2006) Quantifying the qualified: the use of multicriteria methods and Bayesian statistics for the development of archaeological predictive models. In: Mehrer M, Wescott K (eds) GIS and archaeological site location modeling. CRC Press, Boca Raton, pp 191–216

Verhagen P (2008) Testing archaeological predictive models: a rough guide. In: Posluschny A, Lambers K, Herzog I (eds) Layers of perception. Proceedings of the 35th international conference on Computer Applications and Quantitative Methods in Archaeology (CAA), Berlin, Germany, April 2–6, 2007. Dr Rudolf Habelt GmbH, Bonn, pp 285–291

Verhagen P (2013) On the road to nowhere? Least cost paths, accessibility and the predictive modelling perspective. In: Contreras F, Farjas M, Melero FJ (eds) Fusion of cultures. Proceedings of the 38th annual conference on computer applications and quantitative methods in archaeology, Granada, Spain, April 2010. Archaeopress, Oxford, pp 383–389

Verhagen P, Jeneson K (2012) A Roman puzzle. Trying to find the via Belgica with GIS. In: Chrysanthi A, Murrieta Flores P, Papadopoulos C (eds) Thinking beyond the tool: archaeological computing & the interpretive process. Archaeopress, Oxford, pp 123–130

Verhagen P, Whitley TG (2012) Integrating archaeological theory and predictive modeling: a live report from the scene. J Archaeol Method Theory 19:49–100. https://doi.org/10.1007/s10816-011-9102-7

Verhagen P, McGlade J, Gili S, Risch R (1995) Some criteria for modelling socio-economic activities in the Bronze Age of south-east Spain. In: Lock G, Stančič Z (eds) GIS and archaeology: a European perspective. Taylor and Francis, London, pp 187–209

Verhagen P, Brughmans T, Nuninger L, Bertoncello F (2013) The long and winding road: combining least cost paths and network analysis techniques for settlement location analysis and predictive modelling. In: Earl G, Sly T, Chrysanthi A, Murrieta-Flores P, Papadopoulos C, Romanowska I, Wheatley D (eds) Archaeology in the digital era. Papers from the 40th Annual Conference of Computer Applications and Quantitative Methods in Archaeology (CAA), Southampton, 26–29 March 2012. Amsterdam University Press, Amsterdam, pp 357–366

Verhagen P, Polla S, Frommer I (2014) Finding Byzantine junctions with Steiner trees. In: Polla S, Verhagen P (eds) Computational approaches to the study of movement in archaeology. Theory, practice and interpretation of factors and effects of long term landscape formation and transformation. De Gruyter, Berlin, pp 73–98

Vita-Finzi C, Higgs ES (1970) Prehistoric economy in the Mount Carmel area of Palestine: site catchment analysis. Proc Prehist Soc 36:1–36. https://doi.org/10.1017/S0079497X00013074

Wasserman S, Faust K (1994) Social network analysis. Methods and applications. Cambridge University Press, Cambridge

Wheatley D (1995) Cumulative viewshed analysis: a GIS-based method for investigating intervisibility, and its archaeological application. In: Lock G, Stančič Z (eds) Archaeology and geographical information systems: a European perspective. Taylor and Francis, London

Wheatley D, Gillings M (2002) Spatial technology and archaeology. CRC Press, London

White DA, Barber SB (2012) Geospatial modeling of pedestrian transportation networks: a case study from precolumbian Oaxaca, Mexico. J Archaeol Sci 39:2684–2696. https://doi.org/10.1016/j.jas.2012.04.017

Whitley TG (2000) Dynamical systems modelling in archaeology: a GIS approach to site selection processes in the Greater Yellowstone Region. University of Pittsburgh, Pittsburgh

Whitley TG (2017) Geospatial analysis as experimental archaeology. J Archaeol Sci 84:103–114. https://doi.org/10.1016/j.jas.2017.05.008

Whitley TG, Hicks LM (2003) A geographic information systems approach to understanding potential prehistoric and historic travel corridors. Southeast Archaeol 22:77–91

Whitley TG, Moore G, Goel G, Jackson D (2010) Beyond the Marsh: settlement choice, perception and spatial decision-making on the Georgia Coastal Plain. In: Frischer B, Webb Crawford J, Koller D (eds) Making history interactive. Computer Applications and Quantitative Methods in Archaeology (CAA). Proceedings of the 37th international conference, Williamsburg, Virginia, United States of America, March 22–26, 2009. Archaeopress, Oxford, pp 380–390

Wickler SJ, Hoyt DF, Cogger EA, Hall KM (2001) Effect of load on preferred speed and cost of transport. J Appl Physiol 90:1548–1551

Wren CD, Xue JZ, Costopoulos A, Burke A (2014) The role of spatial foresight in models of hominin dispersal. J Hum Evol 69:70–78. https://doi.org/10.1016/j.jhevol.2014.02.004

Yeo CA (1946) Land and sea transport in imperial Italy. Trans Proc Am Philol Assoc 77:221–244

Yokoyama R, Shirasawa M, Pike RJ (2002) Visualizing topography by openness: a new application of image processing to digital elevation models. Photogramm Eng Remote Sens 68:257–265

Yousef MK, Dill DB, Freeland DV (1972) Energetic cost of grade walking in man and burro, Equus asinus: desert and mountain. J Appl Physiol 33:337–340

Zakšek K, Fovet É, Nuninger L, Pobodnikar T (2008) Path modelling and settlement pattern. In: Posluschny A, Lambers K, Herzog I (eds) Layers of perception. Proceedings of the 35th international conference on Computer Applications and Quantitative Methods in Archaeology (CAA), Berlin, Germany, April 2–6, 2007. Dr. Rudolf Habelt GmbH, Bonn, pp 309–315

Chapter 12
Palaeogeographic-Analysis Approaches to Transport and Settlement in the Dutch Part of the Roman *Limes*

Mark R. Groenhuijzen

Abstract The aim of the PhD research on which this chapter is based is to reconstruct and analyse the cultural landscape of the Dutch *limes* area using computational approaches, specifically to model and analyse transport networks, settlement patterns and their relationship with the natural environment, to better understand the interactions between the Roman military population and the local population that lived in this frontier region. The goal of this chapter is to present the general results of this study and showcase the technical, methodological and interpretative aspects that it has contributed to the research field of computational archaeology and to the archaeological understanding of the Dutch part of the Roman *limes*.

Keywords LCP analysis · Network science · Network analysis · Palaeogeography · Transport networks

12.1 Introduction

12.1.1 General Introduction

The main aim of the 'Finding the limits of the *limes*' project is to reconstruct and understand the cultural landscape of the Dutch part of the Roman *limes*, specifically looking at the spatial and economic interactions between the Roman military population and the local population. The spatial component is evidently an important part of the research project, and the palaeogeographic analysis of the Dutch *limes* area thus became the main focus of the PhD thesis on which this chapter is based (Groenhuijzen 2018). The general aim of this PhD study was to reconstruct and analyse the cultural landscape of the Dutch *limes* area using computational approaches; more specifically, it models and analyses transport networks and settlement patterns and includes their relationship with the natural environment.

M. R. Groenhuijzen (✉)
Faculty of Humanities, Vrije Universiteit Amsterdam, Amsterdam, The Netherlands
e-mail: m.r.groenhuijzen@vu.nl

P. Verhagen et al. (eds.), *Finding the Limits of the Limes*, Computational Social Sciences, https://doi.org/10.1007/978-3-030-04576-0_12

This chapter will present the general results of the aforementioned PhD study and place it in the wider research context. It aims to showcase some of the innovative aspects of the study, either from technical, methodological or interpretative viewpoints. To do this, case studies from this PhD study in the realm of transport networks and settlement location in the Dutch part of the Roman *limes* are utilised. The questions that form the basis of these case studies are: how were goods transported from the local population to the military population, and what is the role of stone-built rural settlements in these transport networks; can location preferences shed light on the interaction between the local population and the military population?

Formulated in a more general question, the goal of this chapter is as follows: what has this spatial analytical study of the cultural landscape of the Dutch *limes* area contributed to the research field of computational archaeology and related fields, and what has it contributed to the archaeological understanding of the Dutch part of the Roman *limes*? Furthermore, what are the prospects for future research?

12.1.2 Palaeogeographic Analysis of the Dutch Limes Area

The palaeogeographic analysis of the Dutch part of the Roman *limes* that is performed as a PhD study within the 'Finding the limits of the *limes*' project can be subdivided into three parts: firstly, a reconstruction of the natural palaeogeography of the Rhine-Meuse delta in the Roman period; secondly, a reconstruction and analysis of local transport networks; and thirdly, an analysis of settlement location in the landscape. This section provides a summary of these three branches of the study, with more elaboration on the analyses and results and their place in the wider research context presented in the following sections.

In order to understand spatial developments and patterns in the cultural landscape in relation to the natural landscape, the natural landscape must be accurately known first. There is a strong tradition of reconstructing the natural environment in the Netherlands (e.g. Cohen et al. 2012; Vos 2015), and for the Roman period a great advance was made following the study of Van Dinter (2013) on the Old Rhine area between Utrecht and Katwijk. Using a similar methodology, this study has extended the 1:50,000 reconstruction of Van Dinter to cover the entire Rhine-Meuse delta, the geographic area roughly equal to what is considered the Dutch part of the Roman *limes*.

Transport as part of the cultural landscape is often understudied in archaeology, both due to the focus on settlements in archaeology and due to the immaterial nature of transport, particularly that of transport on the local scale. However, when we are interested in the interaction between the local and the Roman military population, most transport occurs on the local scale. In this research, computational modelling approaches are used to study local transport networks. A least-cost path (LCP) approach is applied to reconstruct local transport connections (e.g. Groenhuijzen and Verhagen 2015), and concepts of network science and formal network analysis are applied to reconstruct and analyse local transport networks (e.g. Groenhuijzen and Verhagen 2016, 2017). The resulting networks are used to study archaeological questions such as the provisioning of the Roman military population from the local population and the potential role of intermediary sites in such provisioning networks. A significant part of the PhD study was focussed on local transport networks, and this aspect thus serves as the largest contribution to this chapter.

The study on the location of settlements in the landscape has had a traditional following in processual archaeology and predictive modelling (e.g. Brandt et al. 1992; Verhagen 2007). Most focus has traditionally been on site location in the natural landscape, but other aspects may also have played a role, among them (distance to) forts, transport networks and the influence of the historical landscape (e.g. Nuninger et al. 2016). This study has used a multivariate approach (e.g. Stančič and Veljanovski 2000; Fernandes et al. 2011; Chap. 9, Weaverdyck) to find how these various factors determined the location of rural settlements.

12.2 Natural Palaeogeography

The Rhine-Meuse delta in the Netherlands is a highly dynamic region, and the modern landscape is hardly a representative of the Roman landscape. To reconstruct the natural palaeogeography of the Dutch part of the Roman *limes*, a methodology was adopted from Van Dinter (2013). For the central part of the Dutch *limes* area this involves the manual combination of various source datasets in a GIS, ranging from geomorphological maps, soil maps, elevation maps, earlier palaeogeographic reconstructions and data from archaeological research. For the eastern part of the study area, this methodology is less applicable because the corridor through which the Rhine and Meuse move is narrower here, resulting in more erosion and burial of older channel belts. Therefore, a simple overlay of the existing geomorphological and palaeogeographic maps was used. The reconstructed natural palaeogeography represents the landscape roughly around CE 100 (Fig. 12.1a).

From a technical and methodological point of view, the reconstruction of the natural landscape for archaeological analysis is not innovative. A number of palaeogeographic datasets were already developed in the Netherlands, but they are often either on a coarse (1:500,000) national scale (e.g. Vos and De Vries 2013) or on a local scale (e.g. Vos and Gerrets 2005; Cohen et al. 2009), sometimes focussed on particular geomorphological elements rather than the landscape as a whole. Van Dinter (2013) provided a reconstruction that is suitable for the required level of analysis at the local and regional level, which is why this methodology was also used for extending the reconstruction to encompass the entire Dutch *limes* area.

Large yet detailed palaeogeographic reconstruction allows for analyses of archaeological phenomena on an unprecedented scale. Examples include the reconstruction of transport connections (Sect. 12.3; Groenhuijzen and Verhagen 2015; Van Lanen et al. 2016), the modelling of agricultural production (Van Dinter et al. 2014; Chap. 7, Joyce) and site location analysis (Sect. 12.4; Verhagen et al. 2016).

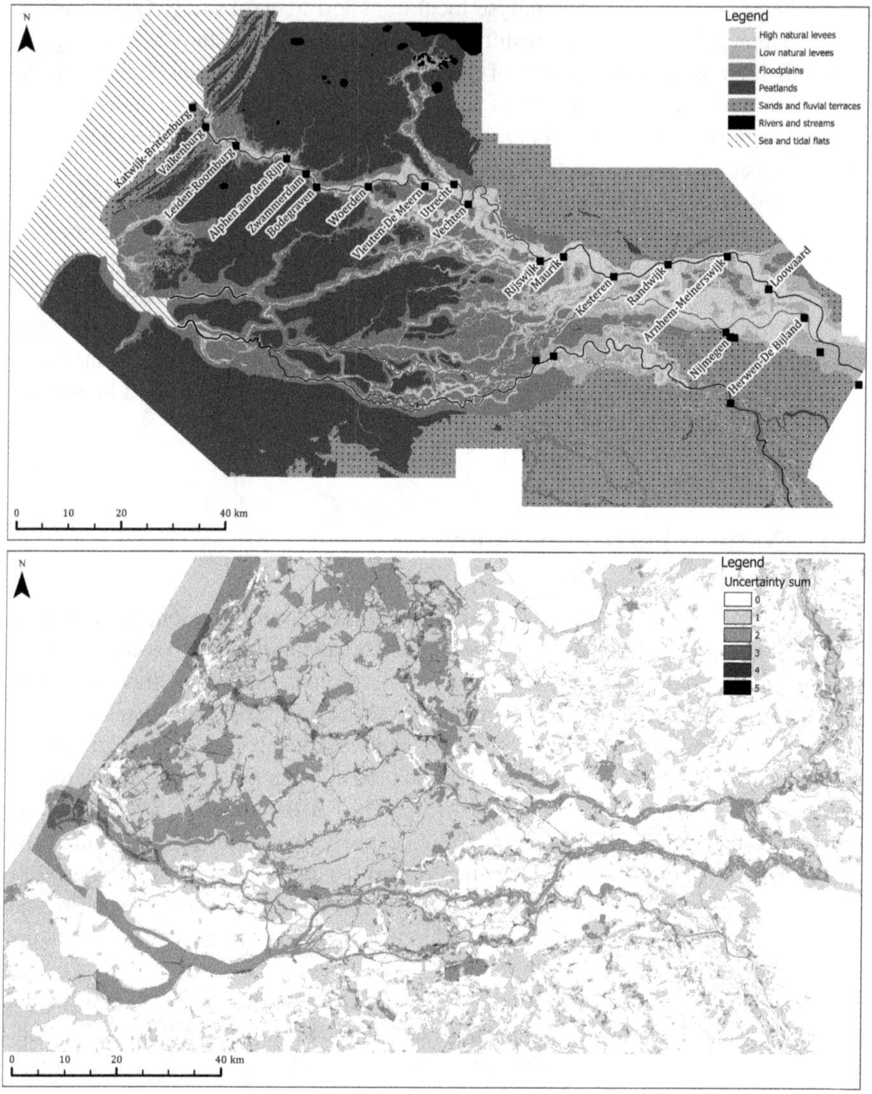

Fig. 12.1 (**a**) Natural palaeogeographic reconstruction (simplified) with diachronic overview of Roman fort locations. (**b**) Cumulative uncertainty map associated with the natural palaeogeographic reconstruction

The value of such reconstructions for archaeological research has become more prominent in the Netherlands in recent years, also outside the 'Finding the limits of the *limes*' project (e.g. Pierik 2017; Van Lanen 2017; De Kleijn et al. 2018).

An additional advantage to performing the detailed palaeogeographic reconstruction in a GIS is the ability to incorporate other information alongside the reconstruction. One important factor which is often overlooked in analyses using reconstructed landscapes is the uncertainty of the reconstruction itself. For the Rhine-Meuse delta, such uncertainty can come from post-Roman fluvial erosion, drift sand activity, peat reclamation or excavation and anthropogenic developments. By mapping the sources of uncertainty, a cumulative uncertainty map can be generated that can be used in further analyses (Fig. 12.1b), for example to filter the site dataset to only include those for which the palaeogeographic information is relatively certain, as has been done for the settlement location analysis (Sect. 12.4).

12.3 Transport Networks

12.3.1 Introduction

The study of mobility and transport in the Roman period has traditionally been focussed on the regional to empire-wide scale and particularly on shipping in the Mediterranean and on the military road networks, including that in the Netherlands (e.g. Scheidel 2014; Van der Heijden 2016). In comparison, fairly little research has been done on transport on the local to intraregional scales, mainly due to the lack of archaeologically visible local road systems.

In order to bridge this gap of knowledge, computational approaches have become increasingly popular, and the basic parameters of movement are rather well understood (Murrieta-Flores 2010; Polla and Verhagen 2014). Most computational approaches apply least-cost path (LCP) modelling, since this method allows for the incorporation of various cost components, for example regarding ancient topography. However, until recently, most applications of LCP modelling in the study of movement have been done to reconstruct single routes or small sets of routes or to identify the factors involved in establishing routes (e.g. Bell and Lock 2000; Llobera 2000; Zakšek et al. (2008); Verhagen 2013). The majority of LCP studies utilises elevation/slope as the main component and only models walking (Herzog 2014), and there are many functions available to do this analysis (Herzog 2013a). Applications that use other cost components are sparse, however (e.g. Livingood 2012; Verhagen 2013), as is the application of LCP modelling on other modes of transport (e.g. Wheatley and Gillings 2002; Verhagen et al. 2014).

Networks have become a common concept in archaeology, and over the last decade the use of network science in computational archaeology has grown in popularity (Brughmans 2013a). The formal study of sets of LCPs as networks however has thus far only been explored in a limited way, even though the application of formal network analysis techniques has shown to offer additional information that cannot be deduced from LCP maps qualitatively (e.g. Verhagen et al. 2013).

12.3.2 Modelling Transport

In order to study transport in the Dutch *limes* area, transport connections between all settlements were modelled in Python using a LCP approach. Since the Rhine-Meuse delta has fairly little topographical relief, the impact of terrain conditions on movement is more important than that of slope. The formula (Eq. 12.1) provided by Pandolf et al. (1977) allows for the calculation of walking speed (V in m/s) while incorporating the walker's weight (W in kg), carried load (L in kg), standard metabolic rate (M in W) and the natural terrain through a terrain coefficient (η), with the coefficients provided by Soule and Goldman (1972). LCPs could thus be modelled using the reconstructed natural palaeogeography, resulting in a more accurate representation of local transport in the Dutch *limes* area (Groenhuijzen and Verhagen 2015).

$$V = \sqrt{\frac{M - 1.5W - 2.0\left(W + L\right)\left(\frac{L}{W}\right)^2}{1.5\eta\left(W + L\right)}} \qquad (12.1)$$

Furthermore, the Pandolf et al. (1977) formula allows for the incorporation of varying weights of the carried load. It was found that this has a significant impact on how people could move through the landscape and particularly the time it takes to move. In general, movement with animal-drawn carts is slower and less forgiving for difficult terrains, which results in different properties of the transport networks that were constructed afterwards (Groenhuijzen and Verhagen 2015).

Besides walking, other modes of transport must also have played a role in the local transport system of the Dutch *limes* area. Animal-drawn carts were modelled using LCPs, with the costs based on functions provided by Raepsaet (2002). The modelled routes tend to avoid the wetter parts of the landscape, with most movement occurring on the higher and drier levees.

Little is known about local-scale transport infrastructure, likely largely due to the immaterial nature of the routes (Willems 1986). However, a comparison with the known infrastructure, namely the military road along the Rhine, is possible. Interestingly enough, a comparison of the modelled routes with an archaeological reconstruction of the road and potential secondary routes in the direct hinterland (Vos 2009) shows that the modelled routes largely concentrate outside the military road, and actually quite closely align with the assumed secondary routes (Fig. 12.2). Based on the LCP analysis performed in this study, the conclusion can be drawn that the military road thus seems to be largely peripheral to the majority of local-scale interactions (Groenhuijzen and Verhagen 2015).

In addition to land-based transport modes, the local and military population also made use of water-based transport options, as has been attested by a number of dugouts and larger river ships that have been found in the research area (e.g. Jansma and Morel 2007). This study has modelled dugouts as the main representative of

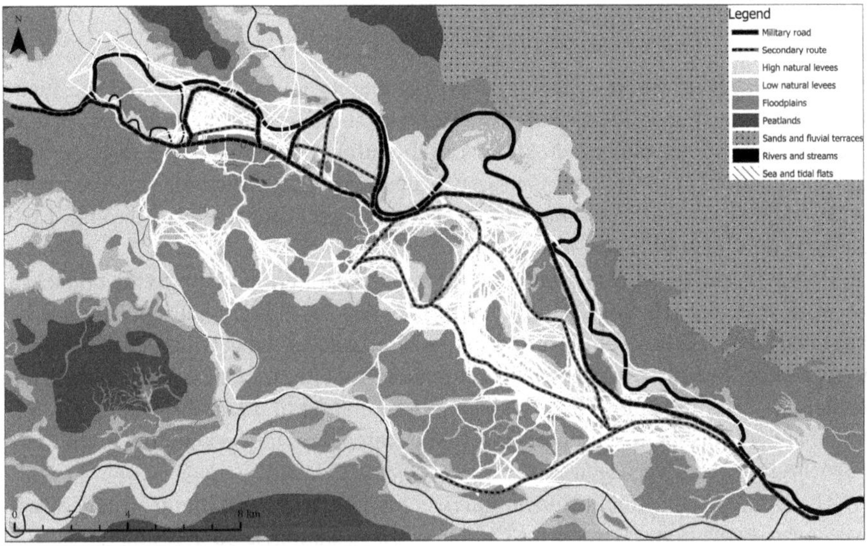

Fig. 12.2 Comparison of ox-cart-based transport connections modelled through LCP analysis (white lines) with the archaeological reconstruction of the military road and possible secondary routes (Vos 2009)

water-based transport on the local scale using experimental data (Gregory 1997). One of the problems when modelling water-based transport using a LCP approach is that in reality it is not possible to easily transfer between land- and water-based modes, and it is probably not possible at every location along a waterway. It is largely unknown where potential transfer places in the Rhine-Meuse delta would be, which means that the routes modelled through LCP analysis may not be the most realistic.

Through modelling multimodal routes between settlements in the research area (combining land- and water-based transport) it was found that some routes preferred waterways over land-based routes, but the majority of movement still followed the levees rather than water. This is likely due to the location of rivers: they are largely peripheral to local scale transport, and flow in an east-west direction, whereas a fair share of movement is south-north directed (or vice versa), particularly when moving from settlements in the hinterland towards the forts along the Rhine.

In general, the modelling of local transport connections through a LCP approach in this PhD study was successful in terms of understanding the interaction between movement and the natural environment. However, the modelling of movement on foot remains more reliable than those of animal-based or water-based transport modes. The former has a stronger tradition in physiological and archaeological research, whereas animal- and water-based transport models have to rely on fewer and less compatible sources to the situation of the Dutch Rhine-Meuse delta (e.g. in terms of terrain factors for carts or the influence of rivers on dugouts). The modelling of alternative means of transport thus remains a valuable avenue for future research.

12.3.3 Constructing Networks

Modelled local transport connections do not readily tell anything about the functioning of transport in the Roman period, for example regarding questions such as the movement of surplus production from the rural settlements to the Roman military population. In order to address such questions, an additional step has to be undertaken to convert the dataset of transport connections modelled through LCP analysis into local transport networks.

However, earlier LCP network studies have given little thought to the choice of network structure (Herzog 2013b, c). Rivers et al. (2013) argue this choice must be based on the suitability for the archaeological record that the network structure aims to represent. To address this, a comparison was made between network construction techniques with the aim to find the best representation of a local provisioning system that connects the rural settlements to the Roman military population in the forts (Groenhuijzen and Verhagen 2017).

The network construction techniques compared were maximum distance networks, proximal point networks, a Delaunay triangulation, a Gabriel graph (Gabriel and Sokal 1969) and efficiency networks (Fulminante et al. 2017). The networks were evaluated on the criteria that all forts have a sufficient amount of settlements connected to it (either directly or indirectly), that the network does not contain too many connections, and that the forts are relatively easily accessible so that provisioning could be carried out relatively efficiently. The latter was measured through 'local' average path length, which is the average path length calculated from a limited number of nearest settlements to each fort. It was found that the Gabriel graph was the best representation of a local transport network functioning as a provisioning system connecting the rural settlements to the forts (Fig. 12.3 and Table 12.1). It had a relatively low 'local' average path length without creating too many connections. It was matched by some proximal point networks, but only for those that had an unrealistically high number of neighbours, and the Delaunay triangulation, which was disregarded on the basis of the inclusion of a number of unrealistic long-distance connections (Groenhuijzen and Verhagen 2017).

Besides finding a network structure that best represents a local transport network for the Dutch *limes* area, this study has confirmed the position of Rivers et al. (2013) that the choice of network construction technique is important and must be consciously based on the archaeological case it aims to represent, and it has presented a strategy through which such a decision can be made (Groenhuijzen and Verhagen 2017).

Additionally, this study has found that the application of LCPs instead of regular geodesic connections to construct networks has a significant impact on the resulting networks and the conclusions that can be drawn from them, for instance with the maximum distance network replacing the proximal point network as the most efficient one in terms of 'local' average path length (Table 12.1). This shows that incorporating the natural terrain, in this case through a LCP approach, can be important

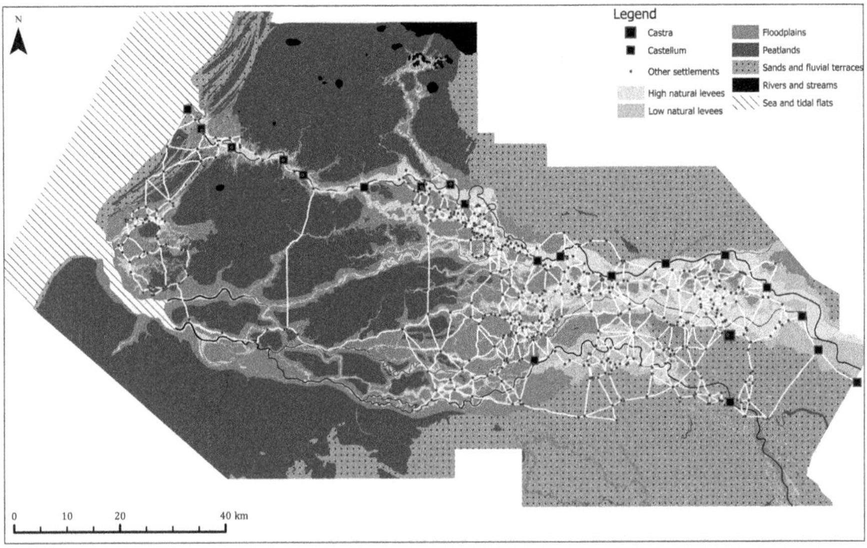

Fig. 12.3 Gabriel graph network of transport connections modelled through LCP analysis (white lines), based on walking while carrying a load of 20 kg in the Middle Roman Period A

Table 12.1 Average of the 'local' average path lengths (in minutes) to the forts from the nearest 25 settlements, shown in a comparison between temporal distances derived from LCPs and geodesic distances

	Temporal distances (derived from LCP)	Geodesic distances	Difference
Max. distance (90 min.)		85.4	
Max. distance (120 min.)	124.5	84.2	+44.0% ±12.4%
Proximal point (3 neighbours)			
Proximal point (5 neighbours)	127.6	92.8	+36.9% ±13.9%
Proximal point (7 neighbours)	120.7	87.0	+37.5% ±6.2%
Delaunay triangulation	121.2	86.7	+39.0% ±6.4%
Gabriel graph	130.0	94.1	+37.6% ±7.3%
Minimum spanning tree	170.1	123.5	+36.6% ±5.4%
Efficiency (10% size increase)	143.5	107.6	+33.4% ±6.1%
Efficiency (25% size increase)	139.7	101.9	+38.1% ±7.1%
Efficiency (50% size increase)	134.0	97.1	+38.1% ±5.7%

LCPs are based on walking while carrying a load of 20 kg. Missing values are the result of forts not being reachable by at least 25 settlements. (Groenhuijzen and Verhagen 2017)

for better understanding how transport worked or, more generally, how space was utilised in the past (Groenhuijzen and Verhagen 2017).

Using the LCP-based networks, archaeological questions can be addressed through formal network approaches. However, the various uncertainties involved in even reaching this step are often overlooked. These uncertainties, for example, may be the result of the chosen software (Gietl et al. 2008), the methods for calculating the costs of movement (Herzog 2013a) or the sources on which these costs are based (Herzog and Posluschny 2011) which have been treated to some extent in the given references. Since the current approach constructs networks on the basis of LCPs between settlements, the settlement dataset itself is another important source of uncertainty. In general, past studies in network analysis of transport in archaeology have paid little attention to the validation of results, even though network measures can become less stable when the data is imperfect (Borgatti et al. 2006) or when sampling the network dataset (Costenbader and Valente 2003). To address this potential problem, a robustness analysis was applied on local network metrics in the constructed network (Groenhuijzen and Verhagen 2016).

The robustness analysis was carried out in a model written in NetLogo (Wilensky 1999), a software package not commonly used for network analysis but useful through its easy accessibility and parallel processing capabilities. In the model, a single network was repeatedly constructed from scratch by iteratively adding sites to the network, and recalculating the local network measure of betweenness centrality. By tracking the development of this measure throughout the iterative construction of the network, a stabilisation point can be established, i.e. the point at which the measure has reached the value it retains until the network is fully constructed. If this happens well before the network is complete, the network measure on this site could thus be considered relatively robust (Groenhuijzen and Verhagen 2016).

The study found that 64% of all sites in the network have a betweenness centrality measure that is relatively robust. This rises to 81% when only considering sites that have a high betweenness centrality, which from an archaeological point of view are often considered to be important sites in the network, as a high betweenness centrality indicates a high amount of control over the network. These results have implications for the application of network analysis on archaeological networks; while a majority of sites is relatively robust (i.e. not susceptible to slight changes in the site dataset) and thus is trustworthy enough to warrant an archaeological interpretation regarding roles in the network, this is not the case for a considerable amount of other sites (Groenhuijzen and Verhagen 2016).

12.3.4 *Applications*

After the construction of a network, the dataset of settlements and modelled transport connections becomes accessible to a more quantitative study in the form of network analysis. In this research, two studies have been carried out in the context of the Dutch *limes* area. Firstly, how were goods moved from the local population to the military population? Secondly, what is the role of stone-built rural settlements, a small subset of the rural settlement dataset, in transport networks? Since the Gabriel graph was found to be the best representation of a local transport network (Groenhuijzen and Verhagen 2017), this network structure was used to model local transport networks from the LCP dataset. The rural settlement dataset was filtered for chronological reliability using the methodology described by Verhagen et al. (2016), resulting in a diachronic dataset of 636 sites (58% of the original size). Per time period, the number of rural settlements ranges between 284 (Late Iron Age) and 587 (Middle Roman Period B).

Regarding the first question, two contrasting hypotheses were posed: one in which all goods flowed from each rural settlement directly to the nearest fort, and an alternative one in which goods were gathered at an intermediary site before moving in bulk to the fort (a dendritic hierarchic system, cf. Willems 1986; Vos 2009). The premise of the latter hypothesis is that the most ideal gathering point is on average 'closer' to the rural settlements than the forts themselves. As potential intermediary sites, a selection was made of towns, *vici*, stone-built rural settlements, large rural settlements and settlements containing *horrea* (warehouses, often granaries, but could also be used for other goods). The hypotheses were tested using the network measure of path length, expressed in minutes of travel time over the links in the network (derived from the LCPs). For the alternative hypothesis to be valid, the sum of the path lengths (L) to reach the intermediary site (i) from a number of settlements (s) in addition to the path length of the intermediary site to the fort (f) should be lower than the sum of the path lengths to reach the fort directly (Eq. 12.2). Since provisioning is more likely to occur from the settlements that are near than ones that are further away, the total path length was calculated for the 25 nearest settlements.

$$\mathrm{TPL}_{\mathrm{intermediary}} < \mathrm{TPL}_{\mathrm{fort}}, \text{where}: \tag{12.2}$$

$$\mathrm{TPL}_{\mathrm{fort}} = \sum_{s} L(s,f)$$

$$\mathrm{TPL}_{\mathrm{intermediary}} = L(i,f) + \sum_{s} L(s,i)$$

The results (Fig. 12.4) shed light on how the provisioning of the Roman army may have worked. Fairly little can be said about the western part of the Dutch *limes* area (corresponding to Katwijk-Brittenburg until Utrecht), since very few sites have been identified as potential intermediary sites. The few ones that are are so distant from the forts that they may have functioned as an intermediary site for more than one fort. In terms of total path length they are more efficient than the forts themselves as gathering sites, making the alternative hypothesis more likely. Additionally, it is possible that the forts themselves functioned as gathering places for their local area. In contrast, a large number of intermediary sites are available in the central part of the Dutch *limes* area (Vechten and Rijswijk). A number of these were found

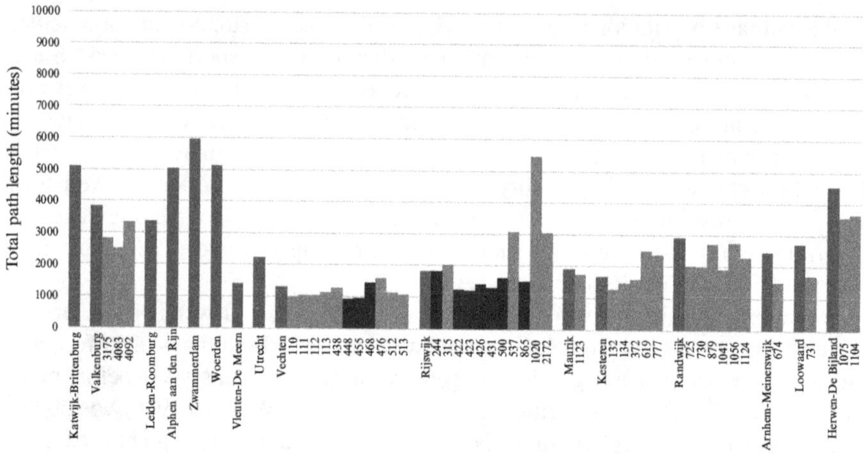

Fig. 12.4 Comparison of the total path length to reach forts against total path length to reach forts via the selected intermediary sites (alternative hypothesis), measured from the 25 nearest settlements in the network of walking while carrying a load of 20 kg. The intermediary sites (light grey colours) are grouped by the nearest fort (dark grey colours), with 'large' rural settlements in the Kromme Rijn region shown through hatching. For locations see Fig. 12.1a

to have a lower total path length than the forts, although this is not true for all sites. Interestingly enough, almost all sites that have been identified as 'large' rural settlements (Vos 2009) have a lower total path length than the forts, whereas *vici* and some stone-built rural settlements do not. In the eastern part of the Dutch *limes* area (from Maurik to Herwen-De Bijland) almost all intermediary sites have a lower total path length than the forts, indicating that the alternative hypothesis is more likely in this area. The difference between the central and eastern parts may be caused by a more diffuse settlement pattern in the eastern part of the Dutch *limes* area; on an average, settlements in the central part are closer to the forts than in the eastern part. This could have resulted in an increased need for intermediary sites in a provisioning system in the eastern part of the Dutch *limes* area.

The second study revolved around the role of stone-built rural settlements in transport networks, more particularly, if the position of these settlements in transport networks may have led them to grow in importance and become stone-built. This was approached using the network measure of betweenness centrality, which represents the amount of control a site has over movement in the network. More explicitly, the question is thus if at any point in time (but especially before becoming stone-built) there is a notable/significant difference in betweenness centrality for the stone-built rural settlements compared to other settlements?

For this analysis, the stone-built settlements were compared to their ten nearest neighbours, since betweenness centrality is also dependent on the location of sites in the network as a whole, and it is more interesting to compare stone-built settlements to their nearest neighbours to see if they hold some remarkable position in the network. If the betweenness centrality was more than one standard deviation away from the mean betweenness centrality of its ten nearest neighbours, it was deemed to have occupied such a notable position in the network (Table 12.2).

For the Late Iron Age-Middle Roman Period B interval, roughly a third of stone-built rural settlements exceed the mean betweenness centrality of the ten nearest settlements by more than one standard deviation. This is more than would be expected, since at any time only 5–7% of all rural settlements are (or would later become) stone-built. A total of 17 out of 33 stone-built rural settlements exceeded the mean by more than one standard deviation at any point in time, and only three did so in the Middle Roman Period at the latest. The other 14 settlements did so already in the Late Iron Age-Early Roman Period B interval. It can thus be interpreted that one of the reasons why these sites became stone-built in the Middle Roman Period is the potential for control that these sites have over movement in transport networks in the preceding time periods. This cannot be the only reason however, since there are 16 stone-built rural settlements that do not stand out from their neighbours, and likewise there are rural settlements that do stand out yet have never become stone-built.

Comparing the results of the second case study to the first one presented in this section, it was found that some stone-built settlements that do not stand out in terms of betweenness centrality were able to potentially fulfil their role as intermediary site in provisioning systems. This shows that a settlement may have become stone-built for more than one reason related to centrality in local transport networks: because it can be easily reached by other settlements, or because it needs to be traversed to reach other settlements.

12.4 Settlement Location Analysis

The location of settlements in the landscape has long been of interest to archaeologists, but many studies do not go much further than incorporating the natural terrain. Less frequently, other components are included, such as social, cultural or historical influences. This study has studied the location of settlements through a multivariate

Table 12.2 Total number of stone-built rural settlements per time period (n), and the numbers and percentage that have a betweenness centrality (C_B) that is more than one standard deviation above the mean betweenness centrality of the ten nearest settlements

	LIA	ERP A	ERP B	MRP A	MRP B	LRP A	LRP B
n	18[a]	20[a]	21[a]	27	32	23	23
n with $C_B \geq \overline{C_{B10nn}} + \sigma_{10nn}$	7	5	8	8	8	5	3
% with $C_B \geq \overline{C_{B10nn}} + \sigma_{10nn}$	38.9	25	38.1	29.6	25	21.7	13.0

LIA Late Iron Age, *ERP* Early Roman Period (A/B), *MRP* Middle Roman Period (A/B), *LRP* Late Roman Period (A/B)

[a]Sites in the LIA-ERP B interval were regular post-built rural settlements, and only become stone-built in the MRP A

approach, taking into account the natural palaeogeography, (distance to) rivers and streams, forts, transport networks (using the Gabriel graph constructed from the LCP dataset), potential intermediary sites in transport networks and the influence of the historical landscape (previously existing settlements). The question that is studied can be put quite simply as: what governed the location settlements in the Dutch Rhine-Meuse delta? However, since the primary interest of this research lies on the relation between the military and the rural population, the question can also be specified as: can the location preferences of rural settlements shed light on the interaction between the local population and the military population?

A binomial logistic regression was applied to investigate the relations between and the individual importance of the aforementioned variables for rural settlement location in the Dutch *limes* area. The dependent variable of the regression model is binary: a rural settlement is either present or absent. For this reason, 10,000 non-site locations were modelled to include in the dataset alongside the settlement locations. The rural settlement dataset itself was filtered for chronological reliability following the methodology outlined by Verhagen et al. (2016) and for spatial uncertainty (Sect. 12.2). This resulted in a diachronic dataset of 450 sites (41% of the original size), mostly focussed on the Central and Eastern River Area.

Most parameters are relatively straightforward to implement, the exceptions being the natural palaeogeography and the historical landscape. A settlement location in the natural landscape is not just decided by the point location but also by what kind of landscape elements are available in its vicinity. To solve this, the natural palaeogeographic composition of each site's vicinity was calculated within a 500 m range, and cluster analysis was applied to create 'landscape types' (Verhagen et al. 2016). For the historical landscape, 'heritage maps' were created using an incremental kernel density approach following the methodology of Nuninger et al. (2016).

The logistic regression was applied with a Monte Carlo method approach for each time period, where in each of the simulation runs, half of the rural settlements during that time period were randomly selected as training dataset to fit the regression model, along with a set of non-sites of equal size. The other half of the rural settlements served as part of the testing dataset, again with an equal-sized set of non-sites. The testing dataset was used to assess the predictive capability of the model.

The logistic regression found that the historical landscape and distance to the transport networks were important factors for settlement location. The former indicates that sites are more likely to appear in areas where other sites are already present. Of course, the distance to transport networks goes hand in hand with the historical landscape; the transport networks are modelled on the basis of the settlements and thus tend to have a higher density in areas where site density is also higher, and thus the heritage factor is stronger. Furthermore, both the settlements and the transport network tend to concentrate on the levees. These variables thus strongly interact with each other and with the natural landscape (specifically the 'levees' category), which is evident also in this analysis. The other considered factors, namely, the distance to rivers and streams, forts and intermediary sites in transport networks, are not found to be important for the location of rural settlements in the Dutch *limes* area. An interpretation that can be attached to this is that the location of rural settlements is governed by landscape suitability and the potential to interact with other rural settlements, but not particularly to interact with the military population or with sites that may have accommodated interaction with the military population.

Furthermore, some interesting shifts were found in settlement location preferences through time. During two intervals within the Early Roman Period and Middle Roman Period there was a shift towards more 'marginal' areas, both in terms of the natural environment as well as the settlement landscape. This may be explained as a result of changing modes of production or as a result of increasing pressure in the core habitation area on the levees. The opposite trend is seen in the Late Roman Period, where new settlements tend to appear within the core habitation area rather than along the margins, perhaps because the lower population density did not necessitate such a move.

12.5 Conclusions

The LCP modelling, network studies and settlement location analysis presented above have provided some new and valuable insights into the properties of movement on the local scale in the Dutch Rhine-Meuse delta, the potential functioning of the Roman military provisioning system, the role of individual sites within these local transport networks and the relation between settlements and their natural and social environment. For example, the case studies applied on the modelled transport networks have found that at least for the eastern and central parts of the study area it is more likely that transport from the local to the military population was carried out through intermediary sites rather than through the forts, supporting the archaeological hypothesis of a dendritic hierarchic settlement system. Furthermore, the role that individual settlements have in these networks of transport could have given rise to the higher-status stone-built settlements, as some of these have been shown to be valuable as potential intermediary sites and/or to be centrally located on routes between other settlements. The settlement location analysis has found that settlements tend to concentrate on the levees in areas where settlements already existed previously and close proximity to transport networks. Other factors were less important, showing that the location of new settlements is mostly governed by landscape suitability and the potential to interact with other rural settlements and not particularly to interact with the military population. The findings stated above are valuable for archaeologists to further their thought on interactions between the local and military population of the Dutch *limes* area.

Of similar importance are the methods through which these results are achieved. By formulating the archaeological questions in such a way that they can be addressed by the computational approaches, these studies can provide new insights that were not readily extractable from the archaeological data beforehand. In contrast to tailoring an archaeological problem to the computational approach, which is sometimes offered as a criticism in some computational studies (e.g. Brughmans 2013b; Herzog 2014), formulating a question- or hypothesis-based approach and tailoring the computational approaches to that topic can add value to the application of computational approaches in archaeology.

More specifically tailored to the approaches applied in this research, the application of LCP analysis to model local transport connections has proven valuable, as it allows for the inclusion of the natural terrain, and this was found to have significant impacts on the following analyses. The application of network analysis on problems that are specifically suitable to be addressed as networks (such as questions on the Roman provisioning system) has proven to be valuable and lead to interesting archaeological conclusions, and the results of this research thus encourages similar future problems around transport to be addressed as networks as well.

Important in the application of computational approaches is the need to account for uncertainty in the data and methods and for the validation of the results. Wherever possible, in this research, it was attempted to take uncertainty into account, such as the spatial uncertainty of the natural palaeogeographic reconstruction (Sect. 12.2) and the chronological uncertainty in the site dataset (Verhagen et al. 2016). The results of the network analysis were subjected to a robustness analysis (Sect. 12.3.3; Groenhuijzen and Verhagen 2016), in order to make the interpretations drawn from these results more reliable. However, there is still more work to do in this area. Archaeological data is inherently uncertain and incomplete, and quantitative approaches thus remain susceptible to such data problems; this research only shows some ways in which these uncertainties can be incorporated into the research to strengthen the output.

References

Bell T, Lock G (2000) Topographic and cultural influences on walking the ridgeway in later prehistoric times. In: Lock G (ed) Beyond the map. Archaeology and spatial technologies. IOS Press, Amsterdam, pp 85–100

Borgatti SP, Carley KM, Krackhardt D (2006) On the robustness of centrality measures under conditions of imperfect data. Soc Networks 28:124–136. https://doi.org/10.1016/j.socnet.2005.05.001

Brandt R, Groenewoudt BJ, Kvamme KL (1992) An experiment in archaeological site location: modeling in the Netherlands using GIS techniques. World Archaeol 24:268–282. https://doi.org/10.1080/00438243.1992.9980207

Brughmans T (2013a) Networks of networks: a citation network analysis of the adoption, use, and adaptation of formal network techniques in archaeology. Lit Linguist Comput 28:538–562. https://doi.org/10.1093/llc/fqt048

Brughmans T (2013b) Thinking through networks: a review of formal network methods in archaeology. J Archaeol Method Theory 20:623–662. https://doi.org/10.1007/s10816-012-9133-8

Cohen KM, Stouthamer E, Hoek WZ, Berendsen HJA, Kempen HFJ (2009) Zand in banen. Zanddiefptekaarten van het Rivierengebied en het IJsseldal in de provincies Gelderland en Overijssel, 3rd edn. Provincie Gelderland, Arnhem

Cohen KM, Stouthamer E, Pierik HJ, Geurts AH (2012) Rhine-Meuse delta studies' digital basemap for delta evolution and palaeogeography. Dept. Physical geography, Utrecht University, Utrecht

Costenbader E, Valente TW (2003) The stability of centrality measures when networks are sampled. Soc Networks 25:283–307. https://doi.org/10.1016/S0378-8733(03)00012-1

De Kleijn M, Beijaard F, Koomen E, Van Lanen RJ (2018) Simulating past land use patterns; the impact of Romans on the Lower Rhine delta in the first century AD. In: De Kleijn M (ed) Innovating landscape research through geographic information science. Implications and opportunities of the digital revolution in science for the research of the archaeology, history and heritage of the landscape from a GIScience perspective. Vrije Universiteit Amsterdam, Amsterdam, pp 125–148. Available at http://dare.ubvu.vu.nl/handle/1871/55517. Accessed on 7 June 2018

Fernandes R, Geeven G, Soetens S, Klontza-Jaklova V (2011) Deletion/substitution/addition (DSA) model selection algorithm applied to the study of archaeological settlement patterning. J Archaeol Sci 38:2293–2300. https://doi.org/10.1016/j.jas.2011.03.035

Fulminante F, Prignano L, Morer I, Lozano S (2017) Coordinated decisions and unbalanced power. How latin cities shaped their terrestrial transportation network. Front Digit Humanit 4. https://doi.org/10.3389/fdigh.2017.00004

Gabriel KR, Sokal RR (1969) A new statistical approach to geographic variation analysis. Syst Zool 18:259–270. https://doi.org/10.2307/2412323

Gietl R, Doneus M, Fera M (2008) Cost distance analysis in an alpine environment: comparison of different cost surface modules. In Posluschny A, Lambers K, Herzog I (eds) Layers of perception: Proceedings of the 35th international conference on computer applications and quantitative methods in archaeology (CAA). Berlin, Germany, April 2–6, 2007, Dr Rudolf Habelt GmbH, Bonn, pp 316–321

Gregory NTN (1997) A comparative study of Irish and Scottish Logboats. University of Edinburgh, Edinburgh

Groenhuijzen MR (2018) Palaeogeographic analysis of the Dutch part of the Roman limes. Vrije Universiteit Amsterdam, Amsterdam

Groenhuijzen MR, Verhagen P (2015) Exploring the dynamics of transport in the Dutch limes. eTopoi J Anc Stud Spec 4:25–47. Available at http://journal.topoi.org/index.php/etopoi/article/view/203/227. Accessed on 10 May 2018

Groenhuijzen MR, Verhagen P (2016) Testing the robustness of local network metrics in research on archeological local transport networks. Front Digit Humanit 3. https://doi.org/10.3389/fdigh.2016.00006

Groenhuijzen MR, Verhagen P (2017) Comparing network construction techniques in the context of local transport networks in the Dutch part of the Roman limes. J Archaeol Sci Rep 15:235–251. https://doi.org/10.1016/j.jasrep.2017.07.024

Herzog I (2013a) Theory and practice of cost functions. In Contreras F, Farjas M, Melero FJ (eds) Fusion of cultures. Proceedings of the 38th Annual conference on computer applications and quantitative methods in archaeology, Granada, Spain, April 2010. Archaeopress, Oxford, pp 375–382

Herzog I (2013b) Least-cost networks. In Earl G, Sly T, Chrysanthi A, Murrieta-Flores P, Papadopoulos C, Romanowska I, Wheatley D (eds) CAA2012. Proceedings of the 40th conference in computer applications and quantitative methods in archaeology, Southampton, United Kingdom, 26–30 March 2012. Pallas Publications, Amsterdam, pp 240–251

Herzog I (2013c) Review of least cost analysis of social landscapes. Archaeological case studies. Internet Archaeol 34. https://doi.org/10.11141/ia.34.7

Herzog I (2014) A review of case studies in archaeological least-cost analysis. Archeologia e Calcolatori 25:223–239. Available at http://www.archcalc.cnr.it/indice/PDF25/12_Herzog.pdf. Accessed on 10 May 2018

Herzog I, Posluschny A (2011) Tilt – slope-dependent least cost path calculations revisited. In: Jerem E, Redő F, Szeverényi V (eds) On the road to reconstructing the past. Computer applications and quantitative methods in archaeology (CAA). Proceedings of the 36th international conference. Budapest, April 2–6, 2008. Archaeolingua, Budapest, pp 212–218, Available at https://proceedings.caaconference.org/paper/cd31_herzog_posluschny_caa2008. Accessed on 26 July 2018

Jansma E, Morel JMAW (2007) Een Romeinse Rijnaak, gevonden in Utrecht-De Meern. Resultaten van het onderzoek naar de platbodem 'De Meern 1'. Rijksdienst voor Archeologie, Cultuurlandschap en Monumenten, Amersfoort

Livingood P (2012) No crows made mounds. In: White DA, Surface-Evans S (eds) Least cost analysis of social landscapes. Archaeological case studies. The University of Utah Press, Salt Lake City, pp 174–187

Llobera M (2000) Understanding movement: a pilot model towards the sociology of movement. In: Lock G (ed) Beyond the map. Archaeology and spatial technologies. IOS Press, Amsterdam, pp 64–84

Murrieta-Flores PA (2010) Traveling in a prehistoric landscape: exploring the influences that shaped human movement. In Frischer B, Webb Crawford J, Koller D (eds) Making history interactive. Computer applications and quantitative methods in archaeology (CAA). Proceedings of the 37th international conference, Williamsburg, Virginia, USA, March 22–26, 2009. Archaeopress, Oxford, pp 249–267. Available at https://proceedings.caaconference.org/paper/31_Murrieta-Flores_CAA2009. Accessed on 26 July 2018

Nuninger L, Verhagen P, Bertoncello F, Castrorao Barba A (2016) Estimating 'land use heritage' to model changes in archaeological settlement patterns. In: Multi-, inter- and transdisciplinary research in landscape archaeology. Proceedings of LAC 2014 conference, Rome, 19–20 September 2014. Vrije Universiteit Amsterdam, Amsterdam. https://doi.org/10.5463/lac.2014.60

Pandolf KB, Givoni B, Goldman RF (1977) Predicting energy expenditure with loads while standing or walking very slowly. J Appl Physiol 43:577–581. https://doi.org/10.1152/jappl.1977.43.4.577

Pierik HJ (2017) Past human-landscape interactions in the Netherlands: reconstructions from sand belt to coastal-delta plain for the first millennium AD. Utrecht University, Utrecht

Polla S, Verhagen P (eds) (2014) Computational approaches to the study of movement in archaeology. De Gruyter, Berlin. https://doi.org/10.1515/9783110288384

Raepsaet G (2002) Attelages et Techniques de Transport Dans Le Monde Gréco-Romaine. Le Livre Timperman, Brussels

Rivers R, Knappett C, Evans T (2013) What makes a site important? Centrality, gateways and gravity. In: Knappett C (ed) Network analysis in archaeology: new approaches to regional interaction. Oxford University Press, Oxford, pp 125–150. https://doi.org/10.1093/acprof:oso/9780199697090.003.0006

Scheidel W (2014) The shape of the Roman world: modelling Imperial connectivity. J Roman Archaeol 27:7–32. https://doi.org/10.1017/S1047759414001147

Soule RG, Goldman RF (1972) Terrain coefficients for energy cost prediction. J Appl Physiol 32:706–708. https://doi.org/10.1152/jappl.1972.32.5.706

Stančič Z, Veljanovski T (2000) Understanding Roman settlement patterns through multivariate statistics and predictive modelling. In: Lock G (ed) Beyond the map. Archaeology and spatial technologies. IOS Press, Amsterdam, pp 147–156

Van der Heijden P (2016) Romeinse wegen in Nederland. Matrijs, Utrecht

Van Dinter M (2013) The Roman limes in the Netherlands: how a delta landscape determined the location of the military structures. Neth J Geosci 92:11–32. https://doi.org/10.1017/S0016774600000251

Van Dinter M, Kooistra LI, Dütting MK, Van Rijn P, Cavallo C (2014) Could the local population of the lower rhine delta supply the Roman army? Part 2: modelling the carrying capacity using archaeological, palaeo-ecological and geomorphological data. J Archaeol Low Ctries 5:5–50

Van Lanen RJ (2017) Changing ways. Patterns of connectivity, habitation and persistence in Northwest European lowlands during the first millennium AD. Utrecht University, Utrecht

Van Lanen RJ, Groenewoudt BJ, Spek T, Jansma E (2016) Route persistence. Modelling and quantifying historical route-network stability from the Roman period to early-modern times (AD 100–1600): a case study from the Netherlands. Archaeol Anthropol Sci 8. https://doi.org/10.1007/s12520-016-0431-z

Verhagen P (2007) Case studies in archaeological predictive modelling. Leiden University Press, Leiden. https://doi.org/10.5117/9789087280079

Verhagen P (2013) On the road to nowhere? Least cost paths, accessibility and the predictive modelling perspective. In Contreras F, Farjas M, Melero FJ (eds) Fusion of cultures. Proceedings of the 38th annual conference on computer applications and quantitative methods in archaeology, Granada, Spain, April 2010. Archaeopress, Oxford, pp 383–389

Verhagen P, Brughmans T, Nuninger L, Bertoncello F (2013) The long and winding road: combining least cost paths and network analysis techniques for settlement location analysis and predictive modelling. In Earl G, Sly T, Chrysanthi A, Murrieta-Flores P, Papadopoulos C, Romanowska I, Wheatley D (eds) CAA2012. Proceedings of the 40th conference in computer applications and quantitative methods in archaeology, Southampton, United Kingdom, 26–30 March 2012. Pallas Publications, Amsterdam, pp 357–366

Verhagen P, Polla S, Frommer I (2014) Finding Byzantine junctions with Steiner trees. In: Polla S, Verhagen P (eds) Computational approaches to the study of movement in archaeology. De Gruyter, Berlin, pp 73–97. https://doi.org/10.1515/9783110288384.73

Verhagen P, Vossen I, Groenhuijzen MR, Joyce JA (2016) Now you see them, now you don't: defining and using a flexible chronology of sites for spatial analysis of Roman settlement in the Dutch river area. J Archaeol Sci Rep 10:309–321. https://doi.org/10.1016/j.jasrep.2016.10.006

Vos PC (2015) Origin of the Dutch coastal landscape. Long-term landscape evolution of the Netherlands during the Holocene, Described and visualized in national, regional and local palaeogeographic map series. Barkhuis, Groningen. https://doi.org/10.2307/j.ctt2204s8d

Vos PC, De Vries S (2013) 2e generatie paleogeografische kaarten van Nederland (versie 2.0). Deltares, Utrecht

Vos PC, Gerrets DA (2005) Archaeology: a major tool in the reconstruction of the coastal evolution of Westergo (Northern Netherlands). Quat Int 133–134:61–75. https://doi.org/10.1016/j.quaint.2004.10.008

Vos WK (2009) Bataafs platteland. Het Romeinse nederzettingslandschap in het Nederlandse Kromme-Rijn gebied. Rijksdienst voor het Cultureel Erfgoed, Amersfoort

Wheatley D, Gillings M (2002) Spatial technology and archaeology. The archaeological application of GIS. CRC Press, London. https://doi.org/10.4324/9780203302392

Wilensky U (1999) NetLogo (and NetLogo user manual). Northwestern University, Evanston (IL)

Willems WJH (1986) Romans and Batavians. A regional study in the Dutch eastern river area. University of Amsterdam, Amsterdam

Zakšek K, Fovet E, Nuninger L, Podobnikar T (2008) Path modelling and settlement pattern. In Posluschny A, Lambers K, Herzog I (eds) Layers of perception: Proceedings of the 35th international conference on computer applications and quantitative methods in archaeology (CAA). Berlin, Germany, April 2–6, 2007. Dr. Rudolf Habelt GmbH, Bonn, pp 309–315

Chapter 13
Network Analysis to Model and Analyse Roman Transport and Mobility

Pau de Soto

Abstract The analysis of Roman infrastructures, which helps to understand the transport costs, the commercial routes and the territorial configuration, is an indispensable way to know the benefits and shortcomings of the transportation system created in Roman times. It is well known that the Roman Empire built the first big transport network in Western Europe, parts of Eastern Europe, the Middle East and Northern Africa. In this paper, we show our attempt to reconstruct the Roman transport conditions in Hispania by valuating its connectivity and by modelling the travel costs and times. All of these calculations have been made based in a highly digitized transport network and Network Science applications. The results of such methodologies provide us with new information to understand the Iberian territorial organisation, the distribution of commodities, product competition and problems of stagnation in ancient economies such as that of Ancient Rome.

Keywords Roman transport · Roman commerce · Network analysis · Archaeology · Trade

13.1 Introduction

Analysing and understanding the distribution systems of goods in antiquity has not been (nor is it) a simple task. There are many elements that must be taken into account such as infrastructures, means of transport, goods, geological conditions and so on. Traditionally, scholars have used different material testimonies (*amphorae*, ceramics, marbles, etc.) or written sources to interpret the movement of goods. Until now, scholars have made different methodological approaches to define the

This project has received funding from the European Union's Horizon 2020 research and innovation programme under the Marie Skłodowska Curie grant agreement No 706260

P. de Soto (✉)
Instituto de História Contemporânea, Faculdade de Ciências Sociais e Humanas, Universidade Nova de Lisboa, Lisbon, Portugal

P. Verhagen et al. (eds.), *Finding the Limits of the Limes*, Computational Social Sciences, https://doi.org/10.1007/978-3-030-04576-0_13

performance of historical transport networks. The study of Ancient sources and archaeological materials and their dissemination have been used as a proof of commerce and as a main element to determine the existence and morphology of transport routes. But, both kinds of sources uniquely give testimony of the relationship between places (mostly origin and destination of goods), and we still miss a lot of information about the possible routes and the economic impact of them. For that reason, recently there has been a growing interest in creating new ways of quantifying the historical economy and trade (Adams 2007; Bowman and Wilson 2009; De Callataÿ 2014; Meijer and Van Nijf 1992).

The communication and transport infrastructures of each historical period were built and maintained based on their multiple functions within each territory. Roads enabled the export of the goods produced as well as the import of the products that were needed. For this reason, the geographical situation of each urban settlement greatly conditioned their economic possibilities, while the construction of certain infrastructures could sensibly give rise to the alleviation of certain adversities. This issue was highlighted for example by Pliny the Younger in his letter addressed to the emperor Augustus (Ep. X, 46):

> *Bordering upon the territories of the city of Nicomedia is a most extensive lake; over which marbles, fruits, woods, and all kinds of materials, the commodities of the country, are brought over in boats up to the highroad, at little trouble and expense, but from thence are conveyed in carriages to the seaside, at a much greater charge and with great labour.*[1]

Moreover, the construction of new infrastructures, especially in Roman times, clearly served as a propaganda showing the benefits of the Roman domination of the territories. Each great road was marked with milestones providing information to the travellers about which emperor had defrayed the costs of its construction or remodelling. Likewise, triumphal arches, bridges or ports would serve the same purpose. In addition, the improvement in the communications (thanks to the construction of roads that allowed a faster and safer circulation) favoured the connections between territories and the circulation of news and political orders. The construction of these roads also allowed the movement of people, an indispensable element for the dissemination of ideas and religious currents. A paradigmatic case was, for example, the expansion of Mithraism from the East, which was mainly exported by Roman soldiers in places as far away as Rome, Mauritania, Hispania or Britannia.

The development of new technologies, such as GIS, or the application of new methodologies in archaeology such as Network Analysis has allowed us to go a step further and try to model trade and transport in ancient times in different ways.

The Mercator-e project, financed by an IF Marie Curie grant (Project 706260-MSCA | H2020), is focused on the comparative analysis of transport infrastructures in the Iberian Peninsula over a long period of time which is from the Roman times

[1]Pliny the Younger (1909–1914/2001). Letters. Translated by W Melmoth, revised by FCT Bosanquet. P.F. Collier & Son/Bartleby.com, New York. Available at http://www.bartleby.com/9/4/. Accessed on 15 December 2017.

until the mid-nineteenth century.[2] The chosen territory stands out for representing an almost closed geography, which allows to carry out studies in itself.

The studies carried out are focused on the analysis of the morphology of Roman transport networks, that is, how the territory was configured and ordered from the construction of infrastructures (more connected areas vs. more isolated areas). In addition, a study on the functionality of these transport networks has also been developed to complete the knowledge on transport. This second study is based on the calculation of transport costs and times.

13.2 The Iberian Transport Networks

The Iberian Peninsula is an enormously diverse geographical environment where large and wide plains, fertile river valleys, long maritime coasts and rugged mountain systems are combined. The adaptation of a territorial organization to this large and diverse territory, whose main architect is considered to be Agrippa (Rodà 1998), required a great effort of design. The progressive conquest of the Iberian territories by Rome, in a process that lasted around two centuries (218 BCE–219 BCE), caused the existence of a complex communication network, which combined military, political, social and economic motivations.

The construction of the communication system in Hispania must be understood, therefore, from the perspective of the military evolution that took place in these territories, with the subsequent adaptations that were carried out to economically exploit the most fertile areas. There are different kinds of sources that allow us to reconstruct the Iberian land road networks. Classical authors like Titus Livius, Strabo or Julius Caesar, ancient sources like the Antonine Itinerary, the Vicarello Cups or the Tabula Peutingeriana and archaeological features like milestones and road fragments, allowed the researchers to establish the paths of these tracks (Carreras and De Soto 2010, 19–24). The North-East of the Iberian Peninsula was the epicentre of Roman communications during the arrival of Rome and maintained its main role during all the following centuries. The capital of the *Hispania Citerior* province (called later Hispania *Tarraconensis*) was established in Tarraco. The territories of the NE were the closest to Rome (both by sea and by land) of the entire Iberian Peninsula. This gave them a consideration as that of a gateway to the entire province.

Across the Eastern Pyrenees, the continuation in *Hispania* of the Gaul's road known as Via *Domitia* took the name of Via *Augusta*. This route crossed the entire Mediterranean coast to go towards the south of the Iberian Peninsula, passing through *Hispalis* and reaching *Gades*. There was also an important deviation from

[2] The objective of the Mercator-e project (http://fabricadesites.fcsh.unl.pt/mercator-e) is to analyse the evolution of transport networks from the Roman Era to the nineteenth Century. Consequently, it is also possible to visualise the medieval communications and the seventeenth and nineteenth century transport networks, in addition to the Roman roads.

Tarraco that was directed towards the Northwest. This horizontal axis (E-O), which linked together the two sides of the Iberian Peninsula, has historically been configured as a very important communication axis. During the conquest of Hispania, this axis was required to supply the Roman armies in the different military campaigns of the north (*Numantia*, Cantabrian Wars), and it was a hub of communications with the rich gold mines (Las Médulas). Some centuries later, in the medieval ages, the importance of this axis survived being fossilized as the well-known *Camino de Santiago*.

Other important roads were built in the Roman era in the peninsula such as the axis which, from *Caesaraugusta*, headed towards *Emerita Augusta* crossing the whole peninsula from the Northeast to the Southwest. Finally, it is important to highlight two other axes that linked the north and south of the Iberian Peninsula. The first one crossed the entire Atlantic façade on a route that was very close to the coast; it is known as the Via *Atlantica* and connected cities such as *Osonoba* on the south coast with *Olisipo*, *Conimbriga* and *Bracara Augusta* reaching *Brigantium*. Following the same direction, there was another route that headed towards *Emerita Augusta, in* order to go to the North, from *Hispalis* to the Cantabrian area passing through *Salmantica* and arriving at *Asturica Augusta*.

But the Roman transport system in the Iberian Peninsula was not only based on the construction of road infrastructures. Romans took advantage of the benefits offered by the different waterways. The Iberian Peninsula has an important group of rivers and lagoons that drain into three different drainage basins.

The rivers of each of these drainage basins are very different and offered very diverse transportation options. Due to the proximity to the Cantabrian mountain range, the rivers of this basin and its courses are very numerous of abundant waters, short and pronounced. These rivers offered few possibilities of transport use in Roman times. The rivers of the Atlantic basin are very extensive, some born near the Mediterranean, but due to the inclination of the Meseta they end up flowing into the Atlantic Ocean. Due to the climatology, they are irregular, especially in summer. But the numerous tributaries allowed a deep inland navigation in Roman times. Finally, the rivers of the Mediterranean basin stand out for being short and very seasonal, completely disappearing in dry summers. The exception in this aspect is the Ebro River, the largest river in the Iberian Peninsula. The Ebro River was used as a transport route from the Roman era to the Modern Age. Classical authors like Pliny or Strabo offered information about the navigability of some of the Iberian rivers (Parodi 2001; Carreras and De Soto 2010).

Last, but not least, we defined the maritime transport network. The use of the sea for commercial purposes in Roman times was very important as has been demonstrated by the ancient sources, the artistic representations and the numerous discovered wrecks. In the Iberian Peninsula, various cities benefited from the construction of port infrastructures like *Tarraco*, *Dertosa*, *Valentia*, *Carthago Nova*, *Hispalis*, *Olisipo* and many others were connected with Rome and with many other cities thanks to the circulation of large ships. In the north of the peninsula, several lighthouses helped navigation to avoid accidents in the dangerous waters of the Cantabrian Sea. Thanks to the archaeological information, it is possible to establish the sea connectivity of the Iberian coastal cities in conjunction with references in ancient sources.

13.2.1 Digitization of Transport Networks

In previous projects, it was possible to apply the methodological concepts and analysis to a transport network that included the main and secondary roads of the Iberian Peninsula (Carreras and De Soto 2010, 2013; De Soto 2010b, 2011, 2013). However, the current project intends to go a step further using a highly detailed digitized transport network as a base. Thus, from the beginning of Mercator-e, the digitization of all the roads was planned with as much detail as possible. To achieve this goal, the most detailed archaeological published studies were used as well as contacts made with the road researchers to obtain permission to use their digitized data. Diverse recent works have been published on transport networks in Roman Hispania (De Soto 2010a; Moreno 2011; Argüelles Álvarez 2015; Almeida 2017; Fonte et al. 2017). Among them, some used for their projects Geographical Information Systems, so thanks to their willingness to share their data, it was finally possible to include their data into the project database. For the rest of the information, both the published maps and the information and descriptions provided in their texts were counted and digitized. Thanks to this collaboration, the Mercator-e Project is becoming a great open repository, where we can find all the information about historical transport networks of the Iberian Peninsula.[3]

The result of this digitization work has been enormous (Fig. 13.1) if we take into account the size of the geography of the Iberian Peninsula and the number of Roman roads. The means of communication have been catalogued in four different categories depending on the means of transport they represent and their category. Thus, we can find maritime routes, waterways and main and secondary roads. In total, 41,781 km of terrestrial communication roads were digitized, 2868 km of navigable rivers and 4759 km of maritime connections. All this network of Roman infrastructures digitized with high detail represents the largest compilation of routes and routes of the Iberian Peninsula carried out until today.[4] Nowadays, it is possible to visualise all the digitized networks with high precision in the project webpage (http://fabricadesites.fcsh.unl.pt/mercator-e/), but following the Horizons 2020 Open Data policy, it is also possible to observe the Mercator-e's Roman Networks in other Linked Open Data online platforms related to antiquity as the Digital Atlas of the Roman Empire from the Pelagios Commons project (http://dare.ht.lu.se/). In order to create a more dynamic project, all the Mercator-e's networks will be openly accessible to downloads in the near future to let scholars use them in their own projects.

The base used to digitize the different routes has depended on the digital data available in each country. Consequently, in Spain, it has been possible to use the municipal topographic base (1:5000), whereas in Portugal, the database used has been noticeably less detailed, but it has been compensated with the digitization of

[3] Up to now, eight different projects and researchers have shared their digitized data with the Mercator-e Project. At the same time, five research projects have been interested in using the Mercator-e networks.

[4] Until now, the most important collection on the Roman roads in the Iberian Peninsula has been made by Arias (2004), compiling all the data collected between the years 1963–2006.

Fig. 13.1 Map of Roman roads digitised in the Mercator-e project

different topographic maps a little bit older, which are from the early twentieth century. Because the objectives of the Mercator-e project include the diachronic study of the Iberian Peninsula, it has also been possible to compare the routes of the Roman roads with the medieval, modern and contemporary routes.

13.3 Methodology

13.3.1 Network Analysis Applied to Historical Transport Roads

The use of Network Analysis is currently widespread throughout our society. From genealogical trees or subway maps to many other applications such as social networks or online road maps, they use some of the concepts developed in Network Analysis in one way or another. The conceptual basis of Network Analysis is the Graph Theory. This theory, widely used today, has its origin in the eighteenth century. In 1736, Leonhard Euler, a renowned mathematician confronted a problem, raised by the city of Königsberg, about the possibility of crossing its seven bridges without repeating any. Despite the fact that Euler found it impossible to solve that problem, his procedures to find a solution was a key factor for the Graph Theory's future. He converted each land area into a node (point) and each bridge into an edge (line). The ability to translate a real (or imaginary) concept into a scheme formed by points and lines became the base of Graph Theory. Since 1736, many other researchers from many different science fields have used this methodology: in 1847 Kirchhoff in order to work on electrical systems, in 1857 Cayley and the isomers of an organic compound, in 1859 Hamilton devised some journeys in dodecahedrons or Jordan and in 1869 studied abstract tree forms among others.

In the Mercator-e project, the Graph Theory is applied to the analysis of transport infrastructures. The basis of the project is to identify cities and urban settlements as nodes while the road sections that connect them are identified as edges. This methodology is not new and has been applied before in various archaeological studies on transport and archaeology (Graham 2006; De Soto and Carreras 2008; Isaksen 2008; Brughmans 2013; Preiser-Kapeller and Werther 2016). The conversion of real historical transports into structures formed by graphs offers a large number of options to perform calculations and interpret the roles of the different urban centres, in this case within the Roman transport network in the Iberian Peninsula.

13.3.2 Connectivity

Thanks to the evolution in Social Network Analysis studies, there are different methods and calculations to evaluate the position and role of the different nodes within a network. Freeman (1979) already clarified the mathematical principles of some of these calculations such as centrality, closeness and betweenness degree for use in social sciences. Much has been written about its application in other disciplines, including archaeology (Mills 2017). In recent decades, its use in archaeology has increased exponentially (Brughmans 2010, Collar et al. 2015), allowing us to analyse very diverse elements and relationships in this field.

The centrality calculations allow scholars and researchers to analyse on key elements of the configuration and integration of territories. Historical connectivity of the Mediterranean has been fully developed with wide acceptation in the work of Horden and Purcell (2000) although with some criticism about its quantification models or the difficulty to explain the evolution of the connectivity during the different Roman highly urbanised phases (Tacoma and Lo Cascio 2016, 14). In this project, we understand the connectivity as the capacity of the different urban settlements to allow the circulation of people and goods. This connectivity could also be understood as accessibility. The basis for this analysis is the belief that in historical times there was a direct relationship between the quality and quantity of infrastructures and the economic, political and social significance of each settlement. Important cities and provincial capitals benefited from the construction of important transport routes, large roads, fluvial and/or maritime ports that allowed them to nourish with all the goods they needed, as well as facilitated the arrival and departure of citizens. In this way, a simple and direct methodology of visualizing the significance of an establishment through the quantification of its accessibility has been configured.

Table 13.1 Centrality values of each edge type

Means of transport	Capacity	Speed	Cost	Edge Value
Sea transport	92 T	4.25 km/h	0.097 kg wheat T/km	4
River transport	5,5 T	2.51–0.62 km/h	0.33–0.66 kg w. T/km	3
Land (main road)	0.4 T	2.1 km/h	4.92 kg wheat T/km	2
Land (secondary road)	0.1 T	3 km/h	4.92 kg wheat T/km	1

Adapted from De Soto 2010a

The Mercator-e project is based on a methodology that has been developing in recent years to quantify accessibility from transport infrastructures (De Soto and Carreras 2008; De Soto 2011; Carreras and De Soto 2012). The calculation of the centrality degree is used as a methodological basis, that is, the value of each node corresponds to the sum of the total number of edges that are connected to it. The main methodological novelty of this calculation lies in the different weights given to each edge in relation to the means of transport that they represent, creating a weighted network (Barrat et al. 2004). According to this method, the edges of a network are tested not only if they are absent or not (binary calculation), but they can have different values and, therefore, the weight of a node is calculated from the sum of the different values of the edges that are communicated. For non-social networks, the weight often represents the capacities of the ties, for example, the airports' connections (e.g., the number of seats among airports, Colizza et al. 2007, Opsahl et al. 2008). In this way, the weight of the edges depends on the importance of the road that they represent and the characteristics of the means of communication used. For this project, four different types of edges have been catalogued depending on whether they represented a maritime communication, a fluvial communication, a main road or a secondary road.

As can be seen in the previous table (Table 13.1), the edges that represent maritime communications are given the highest value (4). This is due to the importance of maritime transport in antiquity, which allowed the distribution of large quantities of goods at the highest speeds compared with other means of transport. Therefore, as the classical sources have reflected, the availability of a port was very appreciated by its inhabitants. A clear example of this can be shown through the words of Gregory Nazianzes (Orationes 43):

> *For maritime cities are able to bear such times of need without difficulty, by an exchange of their own products for what is imported: but an inland city like ours can neither turn its superfluity to profit, nor supply its need, by either disposing of what we have, or importing what we have not...*[5]

In the next place, the edges that offer a higher value of centrality, but less than those representing the maritime connections, are those that represent a fluvial transport. The cities that were built in the vicinity of a navigable river were also favoured by

[5] Gregory Nazianzes (1894) Orations. Translated by CG Browne and JE Swallow. In: Schaff P, Wace H (eds) Nicene and Post-Nicene Fathers, Second Series, Vol. 7. Christian Literature Publishing Co., Buffalo (NY). Revised and edited by K Knight. Available at http://www.newadvent.org/fathers/310243.htm. Accessed on 12 May 2018.

the possibilities which these fluvial courses offered for the transport of merchandises. Although much more limited than shipping, river transport had good transport characteristics downstream, while it has much less favourable condition in the opposite direction (upstream).

Finally, the last two categories of edges correspond to means of land transport. The differentiation between both types of edges is based not on the characteristics of the means of communication that circulated through them but on the category of the roads. As discussed in Sect. 13.2, on the one hand, it has been considered opportune to identify the routes depending on their role in the communications of the territories, as main roads have been considered those that were collected in itineraries and ancient sources due to their importance. Some examples in the Iberian Peninsula could be the Via Augusta or the Via Atlantica. And at the same time, those roads with archaeological data without having the same importance as the main roads have also been collected as secondary roads. These roads have been considered secondary, due to their morphology and their position within the transport network.

As a result of the application of this methodology to value the different types of edges, we have obtained a weighted Network where a node with few connections has a higher value than other nodes with a greater number of edges, because the final centralidy degree will depend on the value of the edges. It could be interpreted that the final value of the centrality in this project is not only a quantitative value but also a qualitative one (Fig. 13.2).

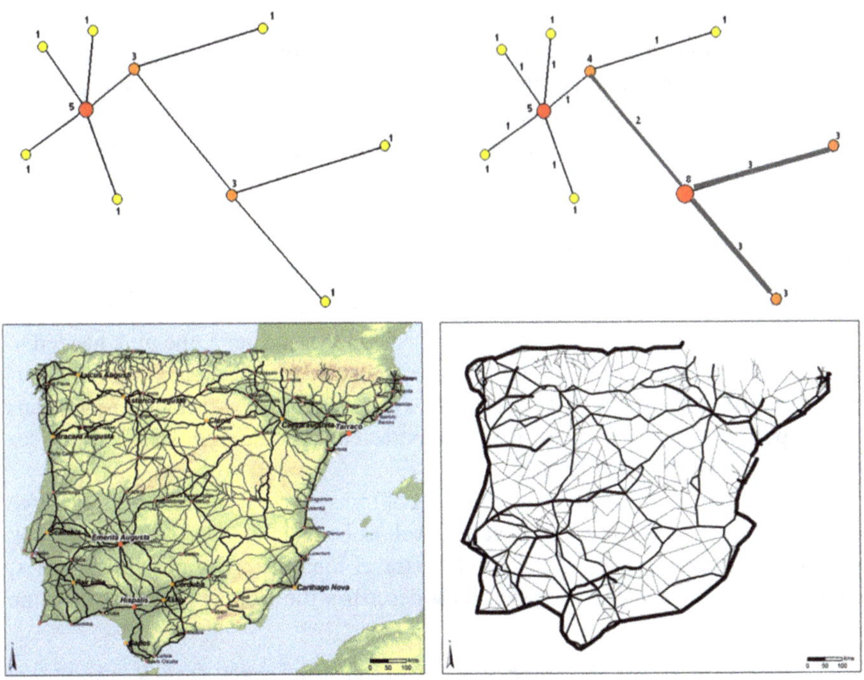

Fig. 13.2 Scheme on the change of the value system of the edges (above) and the result of its application in the Roman transport network in the Iberian Peninsula (below)

13.3.3 Transport Time Costs and Financial Expenses

Another element analysed in this project focuses on the analysis of the functionality offered by the Roman transport network. This aspect evaluates the situation of each territory of the Iberian Peninsula in relation to the transport costs (in money and time) that is needed to transport goods to the rest of the network. The data generated creates a clear visualization of the position of the different cities and territories to favour an active commercial economy.

It is important to remark that these calculations do not attempt to determine the exact cost of transporting a commodity in a given path but rather to establish dispersion or distribution models in relation to estimated costs. Today, with the data and knowledge available, it is still very difficult to try to establish an exact cost for the transport of merchandises in the Roman period. In fact, the only accurate information that has survived has been from some small references of costs in written sources and some legal price lists.

The functionalities offered by Geographic Information Systems and Network Analysis have been used to computerize and simulate the theoretical time cost and financial expense of transport through Iberian transport networks in the Roman period. The methodological basis for carrying out these calculations is based on the use of cost and speed transport values per kilometre travelled that are applied to previously digitized transport networks in a GIS environment. In this way, the more detailed the digitized network is, the more detailed and precise the results obtained can be.

For this reason, due to the search for the most approximate results and possible de-carvings, the digitization of the networks of the different means of transport has been digitized with the greatest possible detail. Thus, all the terrestrial roads respect the geographical features and the different characteristics of the orography through which they pass.

One of the most transcendental elements of this project has been the establishment of the values for the calculation of transport costs and times. So far, data obtained in previous projects have been used (De Soto 2010a; Carreras and De Soto 2010). To perform the calculations on the functionality of the transport network, two different types of values are distinguished. On the one hand, the time needed to distribute goods from one point to the rest of the network is evaluated. For this purpose, it has been necessary to determine the average speeds for each different means of transport. The analysed data have been extracted from different classical sources as well as from ethnographic data.

Maritime transport was the fastest means of transport in Roman times. The large vessels that crossed the Mediterranean as well as boats of smaller dimensions took advantage of the currents and the winds to travel long distances in reduced times. Pliny the Elder (NH XIX, 3–4) perfectly describes the Roman view of maritime circulation:

> *...and in what production of the earth are there greater marvels revealed to us than in this? To think that here is a plant which brings Egypt in close proximity to Italy!—so much so, in*

> *fact, that Galerius and Balbillus, both of them prefects of Egypt, made the passage to Alexandria from the Straits of Sicily, the one in six days, the other in five! It was only this very last summer, that Valerius Marianus, a senator of prætorian rank, reached Alexandria from Puteoli in eight days, and that, too, with a very moderate breeze all the time! To think that here is a plant which brings Gades, situate near the Pillars of Hercules, within six days of Ostia, Nearer Spain within three, the province of Gallia Narbonensis within two, and Africa within one!—this last passage having been made by C. Flavius, when legatus of Vibius Crispus, the proconsul, and that, too, with but little or no wind to favour his passage!*[6]

The main propulsion of these boats were the sails, supported with oars in their approaches to the ports and complicated zones. The speeds of the Roman ships have already been studied before, with Lionel Casson being one of its most important researchers. According to this author (Casson 1985), after collecting some classic sources, he determined that there were two different speeds: 6.75 knots in favourable conditions and 3 knots in unfavourable wind conditions (16 h of navigation per day). More recently, other authors have analysed this question again (Arnaud 2005; Lawton 2004; Scheidel 2013), modifying and incorporating some data. Cabotage navigation, the most used to redistribute goods from the large ports that connected different provinces to the rest of the maritime settlements of the transport network, had limited the speeds because the proximity of the coast reduced the existence of winds and the navigable conditions (McGrail 1983). With all the data provided, an average speed (favourable/unfavourable winds) was established for maritime transport of 2.3 knots (4.26 km/h).

In Roman times, other much used means of communication were the different waterways. In certain territories, the rivers represented true arteries of penetration inside the territories. In the case of the Iberian Peninsula, it is well known that the main rivers were used as transport paths. Fluvial ports are known, and data have been preserved in written sources about the use of Iberian rivers as means of transport (Parodi 2001). But determining the speeds of river boats in Roman times has been a difficult task, mainly due to the lack of data on these fluvial media in the written sources. In river navigation, two situations are clearly distinguished and differentiated: downstream and upstream navigation. The first represented the simplest form of transportation. It required very little crew, and depended on the speed of the river waters. In the second case, for the upstream navigation, the help of human or animal traction from the shore was necessary to overcome the unevenness. It was also necessary to build certain infrastructures on the banks such as towpaths. Pliny the Elder (NH VI, 102) documented a trip across the Nile River upstream between the Delta and Coptos that lasted 12 days, although the case of the Nile is not exactly comparable to the rivers of the Iberian Peninsula. These data together with other ethnographic information (Carreras 1994; Carreras and De Soto 2010) allowed to establish a speed of 2.51 km/h for the transport of merchandise by river downstream, while a speed of 0.62 km/h has been established for the upstream transport. In order to improve the final calculations on river speeds, other recent bibliographical sources will be taken into account (Cooper 2014; Malmberg 2015).

[6] Pliny the Elder (1855). The Natural History. Translated by J Bostock and HT Riley. Taylor and Francis, London. Available at http://www.perseus.tufts.edu/. Accessed on 12 May 2018.

Table 13.2 Speeds determined by this project divided by means of transport

Means of transport	Speed
Sea transport	4.26 km/h
River transport (downstream)	2.51 km/h
River transport (upstream)	0.62 km/h
Land transport	2.5 km/h

Finally, the speed of land transport has also been determined. For this type of transport, we have more information. There are several authors who have reflected the transport of goods and the time needed to carry out the journeys. The average speed of a cart drawn by oxen was about 25–30 miles per day, which could mean 1.5 miles per hour (2.1 km/h) counting rest stops (Casson 1974). Similar results were determined by Landels (1978) for the transport of carts with heavy load. These vehicles needed wide roads with little inclination. In mountainous areas, where narrower and more sinuous roads were created, caravans of pack animals were used, such as donkeys and mules. Their speeds were slightly higher, because they were easier to move. According to historical and ethnographic data, caravans of animals could travel up to 50 kilometres per day, which means a speed of 3 km/h with a daily rest of 8 h. For this project, a single speed for land transport has been established because if both values were used, there would always be a predilection for mountain transport (without taking into account the load capacity or the orography of the road used). For this reason, an average land transport speed of 2.5 km/h has been established (Table 13.2).

The second aspect analysed on the performance of the transport network focuses on transport costs. As in the previous case, the methodology used to perform these calculations is based on the establishment of cost values for each means of transport. However, determining these transport costs is more complicated than knowing their speeds. In fact, very few sources have been conserved that made reference to transport costs in Roman times. For example, there are some well-known citations, such as Cato (De Agricultura 22.3), which narrates the transportation of an oil mill (circa 400 Kg) from Suessa to Venafro (60 km) in a mountainous region:

> *A mill is bought near Suessa for 400 sesterces and fifty pounds of oil. The cost of assembling is 60 sesterces, and the charge for transportation by oxen, with six days' wages of six men, drivers included, is 72 sesterces. The bar complete costs 72 sesterces, and there is a charge of 25 sesterces for oil; the total cost is 629 sesterces. At Pompeii one is bought complete for 384 sesterces, freight 280 sesterces. It is better to assemble and adjust on the ground, and this will cost 60 sesterces, making a total cost of 724 sesterces.*[7]

Perhaps the most important source where transportation costs were collected from Roman times is the Edict of Diocletian, promulgated in 301 CE. (Lauffer 1971; Giacchero 1974; Roueché 1989). This legal text elaborated to establish fixed prices for certain products and economic activities offers very valuable information for

[7]Cato, Varro (1934). On Agriculture. Translated by WD Hooper and HB Ash. Harvard University Press, Cambridge (MA).

Table 13.3 Transport characteristics, costs and ratios between them

Means of transport	Speed	Capacity	Cost	Ratio
Sea transport	4.26 km/h	92 T	0.097 kg wheat T/km	1
River transport (downstream)	2.51 km/h	5.5 T	0.33 kg wheat T/km	3.4
River transport (upstream)	0.62 km/h	0.4 T	0.66 kg wheat T/km	6.8
Land transport	2.5 km/h	0.1 T	4.92 kg wheat T/km	50.72

this project. Up to this point, we have used the interpretation and calculations made in previous projects (De Soto 2010a, 2010b; Carreras and De Soto 2010). The analyses carried out have established transport costs in kilograms of wheat per ton transported and kilometre travelled for each means of transport (Table 13.3):

The relationships between the costs of each means of transport are similar to other works published by other researchers like Duncan-Jones (1974): 1–4.9–56, Künow (1980): 1–5.9–62.5, Deman (1987): 1–5.8–39 or much more recently, Scheidel (2014): 1–5/10–52. In all of them, the great differences in transportation costs that would exist in Roman times, mainly between maritime transport and land transport, seem to be demonstrated.

13.4 Results

Up to now, the main results obtained in this project have been the creation of a new transport network of the Iberian Peninsula in Roman times. The highly detailed and as accurate as possible digitization of all communication routes (maritime, fluvial and terrestrial) has required the dedication of many efforts, as well as the preparation of a new database with all the available information. As mentioned above, 1341 sections of roads have been digitized by all means of communication that sum up to 49,408 kilometres.

The next phase of the project is to focus on the study of centrality of this new digitized transport network. Based on the results of previous projects carried out from networks that are not as complete or detailed, we have some preliminary results that allow us to advance provisional results. The expected results will allow us to interpret how the Roman transport network in the Iberian Peninsula was organized (Fig. 13.3).

From previous and less detailed projects, it could already be seen how the configuration of communications in the Iberian Peninsula responded to three main axes. On the one hand, it highlighted the route linking the northeast of the peninsula with the northwest. This great axis will be fossilized in Iberian communications on the well-known Camino de Santiago during the Middle Ages. It was an important road, connecting the oldest conquered territories with the last areas to be conquered. This must have been the route used to export the minerals and gold exploited in the northwest, with mines such as Las Médulas. This route took advantage of the facilities of passage of the Ebro valley, one of the most important productive areas

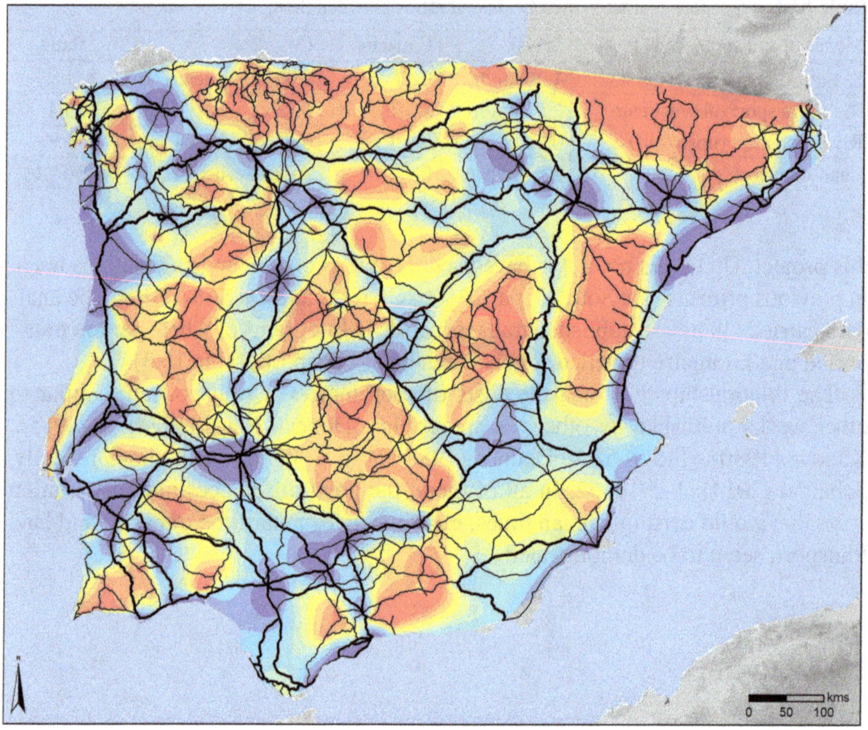

Fig. 13.3 Map of the accessibility of the Iberian Peninsula (De Soto and Carreras 2015)

of the Iberian Peninsula. Also, the whole area of the Mediterranean coast was well connected. The existence of the Via Augusta, which connected the south of the peninsula with Gaul, favoured the movement and circulation of people and goods. On this route, another river route exerted a great attraction for the development of communications, in this case the Guadalquivir River. Finally, there was another great route that communicated the south and north of Hispania. This route started from *Hispalis* and headed north, passing through towns such as *Emerita Augusta*, *Salmantica* or *Asturica Augusta* to finally reach the north-western territories of the peninsula. Conversely, large poorly communicated areas can also be seen in this first map, of which mainly were mountainous areas such as the Pyrenees, the Cantabrian Mountains, Sierra Morena or the Baetic Mountains.

As regards transportation costs, the results obtained should complement in more detail those recently obtained (De Soto and Carreras 2015) where the strong dependence of distribution on maritime and fluvial communications can be observed. Analysing the transport costs from a coastal city allows us to visualize the isolation of the inner territories of the Iberian Peninsula, and helps to explain the organization of this territory. In this case, large cities such as provincial capitals were located in easily accessible locations from the outside. All these cities were situated on the coast or in the navigable valleys of large rivers. These territories, well communicated and with reduced transport costs, were the most economically exploited territories, where more efforts were devoted to the production of oil and wine.

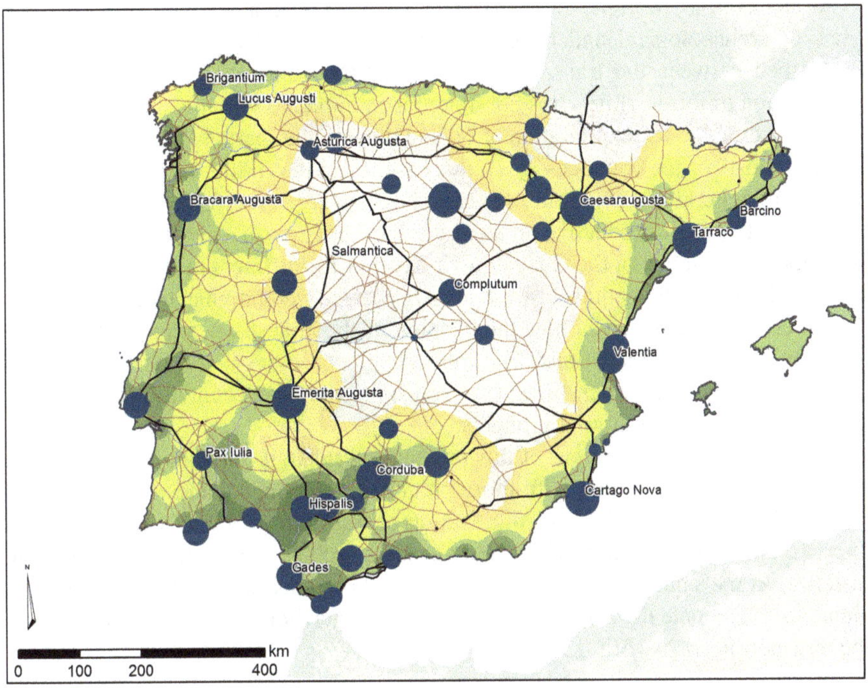

Fig. 13.4 Transportation costs from *Hispalis* (Seville) and measurement of the main cities of the Iberian Peninsula

From the previously obtained data, it can be seen how the most economically exploited areas were those where it was cheaper to export their goods abroad, mainly to Rome by waterways and maritime routes. These better communicated areas were the fertile valley of the Ebro River, rich in cereal production, the coastal area of the Northeast, known for its production of wine, the valley of the Guadalquivir River, famous for its enormous production of olive oil or the southwest and northwest extremes with its production of minerals and precious metals. All these areas represented the main source of wealth that Rome exploited from the Iberian Peninsula (Fig. 13.4).

13.5 Conclusions

The study of the configuration of transport networks allows us to visualize how a territory was organized in the past. This methodology offers quantified results on the configuration of transport routes and commercial distribution that can only be calculated with this type of analysis. Through its connectivity and transport costs, the characteristics (benefits and disadvantages) of the geographical situation of each city and territory can be understood. With this information, some economic, political and social dynamics can be explained with more quantified data.

As an example, from the comparison between the results obtained with different types of archaeological and historical data, patterns and relationships could be established between the transport network and the political, economic or social organization of this territory. It is possible, for example, to visualize the distribution of sites destined to the exploitation of oil and wine in the Iberian Peninsula with the transport costs or the connectivity. In this case, from the results extracted from the analysis of generalized networks, it is clear how the greatest efforts of Rome served to connect the most productive areas of the Iberian Peninsula. The eastern coastal zone, the fertile valley of the Guadalquivir River or the different mining areas of the south and west of the peninsula were always perfectly communicated. In the same way, it can also be observed how the location of the largest cities responds mainly to the best connected locations. The most developed cities were located in well-connected areas, with several means of transport and with economic facilities for the importation/exportation of products.

Definitely, the development of this project will make it possible to improve the analyses carried out to date with more precise measurements and more complete methodologies. The detail in the digitization of transport networks will offer more approximate results, taking into account aspects such as orography or a more real distance. At the same time, new analyses in centrality measurements will offer new elements to evaluate the role of different cities and territories in the construction of the transport network (Fig. 13.5).

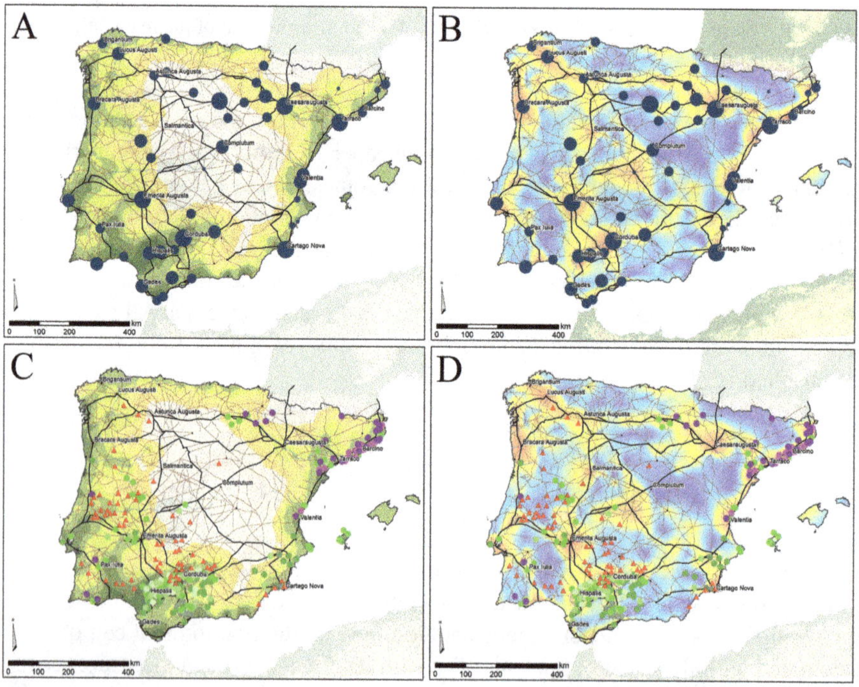

Fig. 13.5 Map with transport costs (left) and connectivity (right) in relation to the measurement of the cities (above) and the production areas (below) of oil (green), wine (purple) and mining (red)

Acknowledgements This project has received funding from the European Union's Horizon 2020 research and innovation programme under the Marie Skłodowska-Curie grant agreement No 706260.

References

Adams C (2007) Land transport in Roman Egypt: a study of economics and administration in a Roman province. Oxford University Press, Oxford. https://doi.org/10.1093/acprof:oso/9780199203970.001.0001

Arias G (2004) Repertorio de caminos de la Hispania Romana. Malaga

A. Barrat, M. Barthelemy, R. Pastor-Satorras, A. Vespignani, (2004) The architecture of complex weighted networks. Proceedings of the National Academy of Sciences 101 (11):3747–3752

Almeida MJ (2017) De Emerita Augusta a Olisipo por Ebora: una leitura do território a partir da rede viaria. Universidade Nova de Lisboa, Lisbon. Available at https://repositorio.ul.pt/bitstream/10451/29682/1/ulfl238842_td.pdf. Accessed on 12 May 2018

Argüelles Álvarez PA (2015) Roman exploitation and new road infrastructures in Asturia Transmontana (Asturias, Spain). In: Roselaar S (ed) Processes of cultural change and integration in the Roman world. Brill, Leiden, pp 191–200. https://doi.org/10.1163/9789004294554_012

Arnaud P (2005) Les routes de la navigation antique. Itinéraires en Méditerranée. Éditions Errance, Paris

Bowman AS, Wilson A (2009) Quantifying the Roman economy. Methods and problems. Oxford University Press, Oxford. https://doi.org/10.1093/acprof:oso/9780199562596.001.0001

Brughmans T (2010) Connecting the dots: towards archaeological network analysis. Oxf J Archaeol 29(3):277–303. https://doi.org/10.1111/j.1468-0092.2010.00349.x

Brughmans T (2013) Thinking through networks: a review of formal network methods in archaeology. J Archaeol Method Theory 20:623–662. https://doi.org/10.1007/s10816-012-9133-8

Carreras C (1994) Una reconstrucción del comercio en cerámicas: la red de transportes en Britannia. Edicions Servei del Llibre l'Estiquarot, Barcelona

Carreras C, De Soto P (2010) Historia de la movilidad en la Península Ibérica. Redes de transporte en SIG. Editorial UOC, Barcelona

Carreras C, De Soto P (2012) La red de comunicaciones romana en cataluña: actualización y metodología. ANAS 21–22:319–340

Carreras C, De Soto P (2013) The roman transport network: a precedent for the integration of the european mobility. Hist Methods: J Quant Interdiscip Hist 46(3):117–133. https://doi.org/10.1080/01615440.2013.803403

Casson L (1974). Travel in the ancient world. London

Casson L (1985) Ships and seamanship in the ancient world. Princeton University Press, Princeton

Collar A, Coward F, Brughmans T, Mills BJ (2015) Networks in archaeology: phenomena, abstraction, representation. J Archaeol Method Theory 22(1):1–32. https://doi.org/10.1007/s10816-014-9235-6

Colizza V, Pastor-Satorras R, Vespignani A (2007) Reaction–diffusion processes and metapopulation models in heterogeneous networks. Nature Physics 3:276–282. https://doi.org/10.1038/nphys560

Cooper JP (2014) The Medieval Nile: route, navigation, and landscape in Islamic Egypt. The American University in Cairo Press, Cairo

De Callataÿ F (ed) (2014) Quantifying the Greco-Roman economy and beyond. Edipuglia, Bari

De Soto P (2010a) Anàlisi de la xarxa de comunicacions i de transport a la Catalunya romana. Estudis de distribució i mobilitat. Universitat Autònoma de Barcelona, Barcelona. Available at https://www.tdx.cat/handle/10803/5560. Accessed on 12 May 2018

De Soto P (2010b) Transportation costs in NW Hispania. In: Morais R, Carreras C (eds) The Western Roman Atlantic Façade: a study of economy and trade in the Mar Exterior. From the Republic to the Principate, Archaeopress, Oxford, pp 31–46

De Soto P (2011) SIG y Network Analysis en el estudio de las redes de comunicación de la Cataluña. In: Mayoral C, Celestino S (eds) Tecnologías de Información Geográfica y análisis arqueológico del territorio. Actas del V Simposio Internacional de Arqueología de Mérida. Anejos de Archivo Español de Arqueología LIX:651–665

De Soto P (2013) El sistema de transportes del suroeste peninsular en época romana. Análisis desde el funcionamiento de sus infraestructuras. In: Jiménez Ávila J, Bustamante Álvarez M, García Cabezas M (eds) Actas del VI Encuentro de Arqueología del Suroeste Peninsular. Ayuntamiento de Villafranca de los Barros, Mérida, pp 1551–1576. Available at https://digital.csic.es/handle/10261/138498. Accessed on 12 May 2018

De Soto P, Carreras C (2008) Anàlisi de la xarxa de transport a la Catalunya romana: alguns apunts. Revista d'Arqueologia de Ponent 16–17, pp 177–192. Available at https://www.recercat.cat/handle/2072/257365. Accessed on 12 May 2018

De Soto P, Carreras C (2015) GIS and Network analysis applied to the study of the transport in the Roman Hispania. In: Álvarez Martínez JM, Nogales Basarrate T, Rodà I (eds) Centre and Periphery in the Ancient World. XVIIIth Inter-national Congress of Classical Archaeology. Museo Nacional de Arte Romano, Mérida, pp 733–738

Deman A (1987) "Réflexions sur la navigation fluviale dans l'antiquité romaine". T. Hackens; P. Marchetti (eds.) Histoire economique de l'antiquité. Louvain. 79–106.

Duncan-Jones RP (1974) The Economy of the Roman Empire: Quantitative Studies. Cambridge.

Fonte J, Parcero-Oubiña C, Costa-García JM (2017) A GIS-based analysis of the rationale behind Roman roads. The case of the so-called via XVII (NW Iberian Peninsula). Mediterr Archaeol Archaeometry 17(3):163–189

Freeman LC (1979) Centrality in social networks. Conceptual classification. Soc Networks 1(3):215–239. https://doi.org/10.1016/0378-8733(78)90021-7

Giacchero M (1974) Edictum Diocletiani et Collegarum de Pretiis rerum venalium. Istituto di storia antica e scienze ausiliarie dell'Universitá di Genova, Genoa

Graham S (2006) Networks, agent-based models and the Antonine itineraries: implications for Roman archaeology. J Mediterr Archaeol 19(1):45–64. https://doi.org/10.1558/jmea.2006.19.1.45

Horden P, Purcell N (2000) The Corrupting Sea. A study of Mediterranean history. Wiley-Blackwell, Oxford

Isaksen L (2008) The application of network analysis to ancient transport geography: a case study of Roman Baetica. Digit Medievalist 4. https://doi.org/10.16995/dm.20

Künow J (1980) Negotiator et ventura: Händler und transport im freiem Germanien. Marburg.

Landels JG (1978) Engineering in the Roman world. Berkeley.

Lawton B (2004) Various and ingenious machines. Power generation and transport, vol 1. Brill, Leiden

Lauffer S (1971) Diokletian's Preisedikt. DeGruyter, Berlin. https://doi.org/10.1515/9783110825398

Malmberg S (2015) 'Ships are seen gliding swiftly along the sacred tiber': The river as an artery of urban movement and development. In Östenberg I, Malmberg S, Bjørnebye J (eds) The moving city: processions, passages and promenades in ancient Rome. Bloomsbury Academic, London, pp 187–201, 307–312

McGrail S (1983) Cross-channel seamanship and navigation in the late 1st millennium BC. Oxf J Archaeol 2:299–337. https://doi.org/10.1111/j.1468-0092.1983.tb00345.x

Meijer F, Van Nijf O (1992) Trade, transport and society in the ancient world: a sourcebook. Routledge, London

Mills BJ (2017) Social network analysis in archaeology. Annu Rev Anthropol 46:379–397. https://doi.org/10.1146/annurev-anthro-102116-041423

Moreno I (2011) Vías Romanas en Castilla y León. Available at http://www.viasromanas.net/. Accessed on 12 May 2018

Parodi MJ (2001) Ríos y lagunas de Hispania como vías de comunicación. La navegación interior en la Hispania romana. Gráficas Sol, Écija

Preiser-Kapeller J, Werther L (2016) Connecting Harbours. A comparison of traffic networks across ancient and medieval Europe. In: Harbours as objects of interdisciplinary research –

Archaeology + History + Geoscience. RGMZ Tagungen 34/Interdisziplinäre Forschungen zu Häfen von der Römischen Kaiserzeit bis zum Mittelalter 5, pp 7–39. Available at https://arxiv.org/abs/1611.09516. Accessed on 12 May 2018

Rodà I (1998) El papel de Agripa en la trama urbana de la Hispania Augustea. In: Rodríguez Colmenero A (ed) Los orígenes de la ciudad en el noroeste hispánico. Actas del Congreso Internacional (Lugo 1996). Diputación Provincial de Lugo, Lugo, pp 275–293

Roueché C (1989) Aphrodisias in late antiquity. The late Roman and byzantine inscriptions. Society for the Promotion of Roman Studies, London

Scheidel W (2013) Explaining the maritime freight charges in Diocletian's Prices Edict. J Roman Archaeol 26:464–468. https://doi.org/10.1017/S1047759413000263

Scheidel W (2014) The shape of the Roman world: modelling imperial connectivity. J Roman Archaeol 27:7–32. https://doi.org/10.1017/S1047759414001147

Tacoma LE, Lo Cascio E (2016) Writing migration. In: Lo Cascio E, Tacoma LE (eds) The impact of mobility and migration in the Roman empire: proceedings of the twelfth workshop of the international network impact of empire (Rome, June 17–19, 2015). Brill, Leiden, pp 1–24

Opsahl T, Colizza V, Panzarasa P, Ramasco JJ (2008) Prominence and Control: The Weighted Rich-Club Effect. Physical Review Letters 101, 168702. https://doi.org/10.1103/PhysRevLett.101.168702

Chapter 14
Footprints and Cartwheels on a Pixel Road: On the Applicability of GIS for the Modelling of Ancient (Roman) Routes

César Parcero-Oubiña, Alejandro Güimil-Fariña, João Fonte, and José Manuel Costa-García

Abstract GIS-based digital modelling tools, such as the well-known least cost paths (LCP), have been widely used in archaeology in recent years as ways of approaching forms of mobility in the past. Roman roads are among the best-known examples of ancient networks of paths and have been widely studied using such approaches. In this paper, we shall make a general reflection on the applicability of those tools for the modelling and analysis of ancient routes, with a special focus on Roman roads. Drawing from a case study in the NW Iberian Peninsula, we shall discuss certain aspects related to the potential and limits of Cumulative Costs, LCP and other related tools for the modelling and analysis of ancient roads. We will illustrate how the use of tools which explore potential mobility in less restricted ways can help to overcome some of the limitations of LCP.

Keywords Roman roads · Mobility · Multiple least cost paths · GIS · NW Iberian Peninsula

C. Parcero-Oubiña (✉)
Institute of Heritage Sciences (Incipit), Spanish National Research Council (CSIC), Santiago de Compostela, Spain
e-mail: cesar.parcero-oubina@incipit.csic.es

A. Güimil-Fariña
Dimenso S.L./Institute of Heritage Sciences (Incipit), Spanish National Research Council (CSIC), Santiago de Compostela, Spain

J. Fonte
Institute of Heritage Sciences (Incipit), Spanish National Research Council (CSIC), Santiago de Compostela, Spain

Department of Archaeology, University of Exeter, Exeter, UK
e-mail: joao.fonte@incipit.csic.es

J. M. Costa-García
University of Santiago de Compostela, Santiago de Compostela, Spain
e-mail: josemanuel.costa@usc.es

P. Verhagen et al. (eds.), *Finding the Limits of the Limes*, Computational Social Sciences, https://doi.org/10.1007/978-3-030-04576-0_14

14.1 Introduction: Tradition and Innovation in the Analysis of Roman Roads

The Roman road system is one of the largest and most widely studied (in archaeological terms) networks of ancient roads in the world. They were an essential tool for the expansion of the Empire and the administration and control of its territory. It has been argued that the network of roads reached a remarkable extension of 120,000 km at its height (Fasolo 2014, 3875), consisting of a vast range of different pathways, from long-distance roads to short-range, local paths. As is to be expected, knowledge of these routes is rather uneven, with most archaeological research focusing on the main, long-distance routes, for which abundant epigraphic and textual documentation exists. A brief account of the case of the NW Iberian Peninsula may be representative of research trends elsewhere.

The study of Roman roads in Iberia has, for a long time, attracted the attention of a heterogeneous group of scholars. Unlike other specialized topics, archaeologists have traditionally occupied a secondary position in this debate. While historians have mainly focused on the analysis of epigraphic (e.g. milestones) and ancient literary sources (*itinera*) (Roldán Hervás 1975; Rabanal Alonso 2006; Fernández Ochoa et al. 2012; Roldán Hervás and Caballero Casado 2014), engineers and other professionals have paid more attention to historical cartography, to the technical problems relating to the construction of the roads and to other elements linked to the latter, such as bridges (Moreno Gallo 2006, 2011a; Vicente González 2013; Alonso Trigueros 2014).

The landscape of the north-western area of the Iberian Peninsula is characterized by its heterogeneity. This aspect has naturally had a strong impact on the degree of preservation of ancient roads and, therefore, on the information we currently have about them. In densely populated areas or in regions where smallholdings are predominant, the conservation of archaeological remains tends to be worse. For instance, the lack of reliable archaeological data and certain scholarly traditions have shaped an intense historiographical debate about the original route of Roman roads in some areas (Estefanía Álvarez 1960; Sáez Taboada 1999; Franco Maside 2000, 2001; Rodríguez Colmenero et al. 2004; Gómez Vila 2005). On the contrary, the local topography in mountainous areas led to the recurrent use of certain natural passages from prehistoric times to our days, thus making the general outline of these routes more easily detectable or, it could be said, less debatable (González Álvarez 2011).

To a great extent, ancient infrastructures are still recognizable on the open fields of the northern Spanish plateau. Where they are no longer in use as modern roads, they may still be detectable as abandoned hollow tracks or via place names. This situation has also made them prone to detection via the use of more comprehensive approaches, such as aerial surveying (Del Olmo Martín 2006). This is the reason why the reconstruction of old itineraries has become more consistent over time, albeit, in general, with small changes when compared to the work of the pioneers on the subject (Loewinsohn 1965; Moreno Gallo 2011b).

In fact, when we are deprived of the (occasionally biased) contribution of ancient written sources, the differences between most ancient routes, either Roman or later, are very small in terms of materiality. The dating and characterization of these paths as Roman roads is, therefore, a significant issue. Moreno Gallo (2006) has argued that "archaeology does not have enough resources to deal with this problem" (p. 186) and that the stratigraphic methodology traditionally used for their study has actually been "par excellence destructive" (p. 223). Far from being an incendiary statement, what this author stresses is the lack of multidisciplinary, holistic approaches for the study of these structures and the general lack of awareness of archaeologists regarding certain basic notions of Roman engineering. Being an engineer himself, his criticism is quite understandable and it is, actually, extremely similar to what an archaeologist might say about those scholars who overuse ancient sources. Regardless of its certitude, the assertion is not entirely original, since the problem had already been pointed out by certain archaeologists (Abásolo Álvarez 1990).

In recent times, the extensive use of new resources and techniques, such as geophysical surveying or airborne LiDAR technology, is slowly transforming the study of Roman roads through the development of more systematic multi-disciplinary surveys (Gethin and Toller 2014; Small 2016). Among these new approaches, digital modelling has contributed to a renewed analysis of Roman roads in different ways, in Spain as well as elsewhere in Europe. The digital modelling of human movement with GIS, based on the use of tools and concepts such as friction, cumulative cost or least cost paths (LCPs onwards), has been one of the most significant contributions. In the following paragraphs, we shall briefly outline some of these recent approaches.

14.2 GIS-Based Modelling of Roman Roads

GIS-based digital modelling tools, such as the well-known LCPs, among others, have been widely used in archaeology in recent years as ways of understanding forms of mobility in the past. A growing body of literature exists presenting both theoretical and methodological proposals, as well as multiple examples of application in different geographical and archaeological contexts (e.g. White and Surface-Evans 2012; Herzog 2013, 2014; Polla and Verhagen 2014; Howey and Brouwer Burg 2017; Supernant 2017, among many others). The analysis of Roman roads is just one of the fields to which those approaches have contributed significantly.

To put it quite simplistically, most of these contributions can be classified either as predictive or "postdictive" approaches. In other words, the former are aimed at reconstructing the layout of ancient networks of paths, while the latter focus on understanding the logic behind the layout of an existing road network. Obviously, there is no sharp division between them, but rather a different emphasis. A review of some examples can help in understanding this difference.

Most GIS-based models of ancient mobility apply slope-dependent cost functions, whereby costs for movement are basically, or exclusively, computed according to the influence of variations in terrain gradient on human mobility. A number of functions exist to compute costs (measured either in energy, changes in speed or any other currency) from slope changes (usually represented in a GIS environment as a slope map). However, other cost factors have also been considered in some cases. The work of Verhagen and Jeneson (2012) is a good example of an explicitly predictive approach whereby other cost factors beyond terrain slope are considered. Their work is based on the explicitly predictive objective of finding plausible hypotheses for the original route of a given Roman road, on a detailed geographical scale:

> *Given the uncertainties regarding the way in which Roman engineers chose routes through difficult terrain, it seems logical to apply least cost path (LCP) models to try to find the most plausible ones.* (Verhagen and Jeneson 2012, 125)

Taking as a starting point a series of locations where the existence of the road is known, LCP is the mechanism used to predict the most probable routes to link them and, consequently, to "join the dots" and predict the probable route of the road in its entirety. In contrast with other approaches, Verhagen and Jeneson consider other factors besides movement costs. In particular, they include visual control over the surrounding landscape as a possible additional factor influencing the layout of the road, considering that this Via Belgica was originally a military route. The different combinations of these factors (anisotropic costs and visual control measured in different ways) produce a range of LCPs, which aid in the validation of the different existing proposals regarding the actual route of the road and provide some plausible hypotheses for ground-truthing in the field.

In a series of recent papers, Van Lanen et al. have developed a detailed predictive model for the identification of Roman and Medieval routes in the Netherlands (Van Lanen et al. 2015a, b, 2016). Within a mostly flat geographical region, with little topographical variation, their proposal stands out for not relying on the use of cost surfaces but on what they call "network friction":

> *Traditional GIS modelling of past routes has largely focussed on correctly defining cost-surface modules [...]. In low-lying regions such as the Netherlands these approaches are less useful when modelling route networks. In these regions, other landscape factors greatly will have determined route networks and local translocation conditions (e.g. the presence of mires, peat bogs, rivers). Network friction calculates regional accessibility conditions based on environmental data and locates transport obstacles and corridors, and therefore can be used to model historical route networks.* (Van Lanen et al. 2015b, 145)

It could be argued that these factors can also be quantified in terms of costs and that they are, actually, producing and using cost surfaces (albeit based not on topographical costs and using relative measurements of friction). Nevertheless, their proposal is a detailed approach to detect the most probable routes (rather than specific roads) connecting a known distribution of Roman and Medieval settlements (High Density Settlement Clusters), considering the likely influence of secondary settlements (Isolated Settlements) in the layout of those routes. Theoretical routes are calculated with two different friction surfaces (terrestrial and maritime) but using direct connections between pairs of points as LCPs do; that is, given certain friction values, the single best connection between points is calculated. The results are tested with archaeological data related to the location of "infrastructural" and "isolated finds" from the Roman period which are used as the ground evidence to measure (with good results) the likelihood of the routes obtained through the modelling analysis.

Equally predictive is the recent proposal by Verbrugghe et al. (2017) in Flanders:

> *Despite this long research tradition the routes of Roman roads in the Civitas Menapiorum (the Roman region covering what are now the Belgian provinces of West and East Flanders, the French Departement du Nord and the Dutch province of Zealand) are still uncertain.* (Verbrugghe et al. 2017, 76)

Again, they do not rely on the common use of slope-based cost surfaces but on a combination of morphometric and land cover analysis to build their cost surfaces, something that is, once more, justified by the specific conditions of the regional landscape:

> *Since the study area is characterised by a large number of dry ridges and wet depressions, two cost surfaces were created based on an ASCII version of the DTM (cell size five metres) for Flanders (2001 and 2004) and a shapefile version of the Belgian soil map of 2001 (cell size five metres). […] The cost ascribed to the DTM was based on the method used by Wiedemann, Antrop and Vermeulen. They used the raster calculator in ArcGIS to give depressions (negative height values) and higher areas (positive height values) a respective high and low cost, since hilltops and ridges were favoured for routes. […] Subsequently, a cost surface based on the Belgian soil map was created. […] The cost ascribed to the resulting map was based on a division into four soil types. Dry sand, dry soils, moist soils and wet soils were ascribed respectively costs of one, two, three and ten. […] Since no objective data on cost preferences in Roman decision making are available, no weights were ascribed to the calculated cost surfaces when combining them. After multiplying the cost surfaces, the resulting cost surface was calibrated in the same way, on a scale of zero to ten.* (Verbrugghe et al. 2017, 79)

Using that friction surface, they calculate the LCP which would probably have joined the "accepted junctions of supralocal Roman roads in Flanders" (ibid, 79). The use of LCPs leads again to obtaining a network composed of the single best route connecting the points in question. To validate their results, they compare those routes with the known location of Roman settlements, with possible ancient paths identified via aerial prospection and with modern-day road segments with names allegedly referring to a Roman origin. In contrast with the preceding papers, in this case, their results are only partially positive, for which the authors themselves give a plausible reason:

> *The choice of costs is one of the explanations why only little similarity could be observed by comparing the buffers for the calculated least cost paths, the known archaeological sites from the CAI and the crop and soil marks on oblique and vertical photographs.* (Verbrugghe et al. 2017, 84)

This is a good case to illustrate why a predictive approach must always rely on an explicit hypothesis where the measurement of movement costs is based on reliable evidence. As in predictive modelling in general, there are two main ways to build these hypotheses: either inductively or deductively (Verhagen and Whitley 2012). In the case of ancient roads in general, and Roman roads in particular, we have seen how most authors agree that one of the main things which remain to be explored is precisely what criteria guided cost preferences in Roman decision making. This has encouraged some authors to take an inductive approach and model Roman roads from a 'postdictive' point of view: taking some cases in which a substantial amount of evidence remains about the actual route of roads in the past. These approaches aim not to reconstruct the routes, but to understand the pieces of evidence which inform us about them. In other words, their objective is:

> *to understand the rationale behind the layout of a Roman road [...] to understand, via the use of a modelling process, the criteria and factors which were taken into account when choosing a particular route for this road.* (Fonte et al. 2017, 164)

A good example of this is the recent contribution by Herzog (2017). Although she is not dealing with Roman roads, she provides an interesting example of a combination of predictive and "postdictive" modelling. She starts with a collection of maps representing ancient roads, which are carefully transferred into their actual geographical position. In parallel, she uses LCPs to calculate the most likely routes to join the places depicted in the historical maps. A comparison between them allows her to further refine the cost factors considered in order to achieve the theoretical LCP which best match the known historical roads (what we would call a "postdictive" approach). This implies unveiling the factors considered in the development of those roads, which in this case were avoiding wet soils and terrains with a critical slope of 12% and giving preference to certain fords which were historically documented. Having refined the model of cost, she was able to obtain a map of the route of those ancient roads on a very detailed scale (a predictive approach), which can be used to guide a prospection based on the identification of hollow tracks in high-resolution airborne LiDAR data.

In summary, these (and other) recent contributions have proved the potential of GIS-based modelling to improve our understanding of Roman roads. Firstly, they illustrate how a reliable prediction must always be based on a previous understanding of the factors which might have influenced their layout and on accurate modelling of them in a digital environment. Secondly, when compared to each other, they show that the relative importance of the factors influencing the layout of Roman roads seems to have been different depending both on the regional geography and on the historical context of their development. Although slope-dependent cost functions have proved to be useful in many cases (e.g. Herzog 2017), their relevance should not be universally taken for granted (a recent good example is Supernant 2017). Again, a deep understanding of the cost factors involved in each specific context is needed. Thirdly, these papers are also informative of both the potential and limits of the widely used LCPs: despite being extremely useful tools, they provide a somehow restricted illustration of mobility, limited to the single best possible connection between points.

In the following sections, we shall attempt to explore some of these issues in more detail, elaborating on our previous work on the analysis of Roman roads in the north-western Iberian Peninsula (Güimil-Fariña and Parcero-Oubiña 2015; Fonte et al. 2017).

14.3 The Case Study: Approaches to Roman Roads in the NW Iberian Peninsula

Our recent approaches to the digital modelling of Roman roads in the north-western Iberian Peninsula have been based on an explicitly "postdictive" perspective aimed at exploring which cost factors best explain the route of some of the main roads which are known in sufficient detail. As the north-west of the Iberian Peninsula is a region with a rugged topography, we relied on the calculation of LCP based on slope-dependent cost functions to approach the rationale behind the layout of the best-known sections of the Roman roads in the region.

An initial paper (Güimil-Fariña and Parcero-Oubiña 2015) enabled us to understand some of the basic factors behind the road network on a general scale and from a pedestrian perspective. We found that, in most cases, the distribution of material indicators related with the Roman roads (essentially milestones, which are reasonably abundant in this region) was highly coincident with the route of the LCPs calculated for pedestrian movement, in which changes in slope were the only influence. Besides slope-dependent friction, we only added an extra cost to river courses, which in this region have gentler slopes than most of the surrounding terrain, to prevent the software from considering them as theoretically good areas for movement and producing LCPs running through rivers. Although good results were obtained for some of the roads, others proved to be dependent on different factors which we were not able to identify at that point.

A second paper (Fonte et al. 2017) focused on a more detailed analysis of a specific road: the so-called Via XVII from the Antonine Itinerary¸ connecting Bracara Augusta (Braga, Portugal) and Asturica Augusta (Astorga, Spain). This analysis provided further arguments to understand the influence of some other physical factors in the layout of the roads. In particular, we focused on the modelling of the movement of animal-drawn wheeled vehicles, finding that the known layout of the road analysed showed a very good coincidence with the theoretical LCP which, besides considering the effect of the slope on pedestrian movement, avoids higher altitudes and prioritizes terrain below a given critical slope. In our case, dealing with a succession of regions of sharp topographical contrast, between hilly terrain and open flat land, the threshold for the critical slope was found to occur between 8 and 16%, depending on the sector. Table 14.1 summarizes the model of friction which we found useful in understanding the layout of the Via XVII road.

This approach allowed us to acquire a good understanding of the rationale behind the Via XVII and, to our view, provided a perspective which was complementary to the more traditional approaches aimed at the reconstruction of the route of the road based on what we call a "joining the dots" approach (for this particular road, Lemos 2000; Rodríguez Colmenero et al. 2004; Maciel and Maciel 2004; Moreno Gallo 2011a; Fontes and Andrade 2012). In a way, drawing from the proposals of Limp and Opitz regarding the impact of digital measurement tools in archaeology (Opitz and Limp 2015; Limp 2016), our results could be seen as an "independent measure", against which the likelihood of the existing archaeological interpretations can be tested.

Table 14.1 Cost factors used to model the route of the Roman road between Bracara Augusta and Asturica Augusta (NW Iberian Peninsula) by Fonte et al. (2017)

Cost factor	Ascribed cost
Slope-based pedestrian cost (Llobera and Sluckin 2007)	$MS_w = 2.635+17.73\ S_w+42.37\ Sw^2 - 21.43\ Sw^3+14.93\ Sw^4$
Extra cost to avert slopes unsuited for wheeled vehicles (8–16%, depending on the sector)	2x
Extra cost to block high altitude areas (950–1050 m, depending on the sector)	10x
Extra cost to block river beds	10x

MS_w = energetic expenditure (Kj/m), S_w = terrain gradient

However, these results opened up a number of new questions and/or avenues for further research. One obvious possibility would be to use the more refined results of this second analysis to fuel a predictive approach in order to find the most plausible routes of the roads, or sections of roads, for which a greater degree of uncertainty exists. Although we have already begun exploring this approach, it extends beyond the limits available for this publication. In this case, we shall focus on certain parts of the Via XVII in an attempt to explore the utility of certain tools which allow movement to be modelled less restrictively than is the case with LCPs.

14.4 Beyond Least Cost Paths: Finding Multiple Optimal Routes Between Points

14.4.1 Combining Optimal Routes for Different Friction Models

One of the main limitations of LCP-based approaches is that, given a specific model of friction, it is possible to find only the first optimal connection between points. One simple way to overcome this limitation is to use multiple models of friction, as some authors have done to obtain and compare, for instance, optimal terrestrial and maritime routes (Howey 2007; Van Lanen et al. 2015b) or to calculate various potential optimal paths based on different factors (Verhagen and Jeneson 2012; Surface-Evans 2012; De Gruchy 2016). However, even in those cases, for each single friction model, the results are always limited to the first single optimal connection between points. Therefore, the outcome is a collection of multiple single optimal connections, based on different criteria.

Although this is not necessarily a problem in many cases, in others it might be relevant to explore the possibility of multiple potential pathways to connect a network of points (Howey 2011). This can also occur in the case of highly formalized road networks such as the main Roman roads where different branches are some-

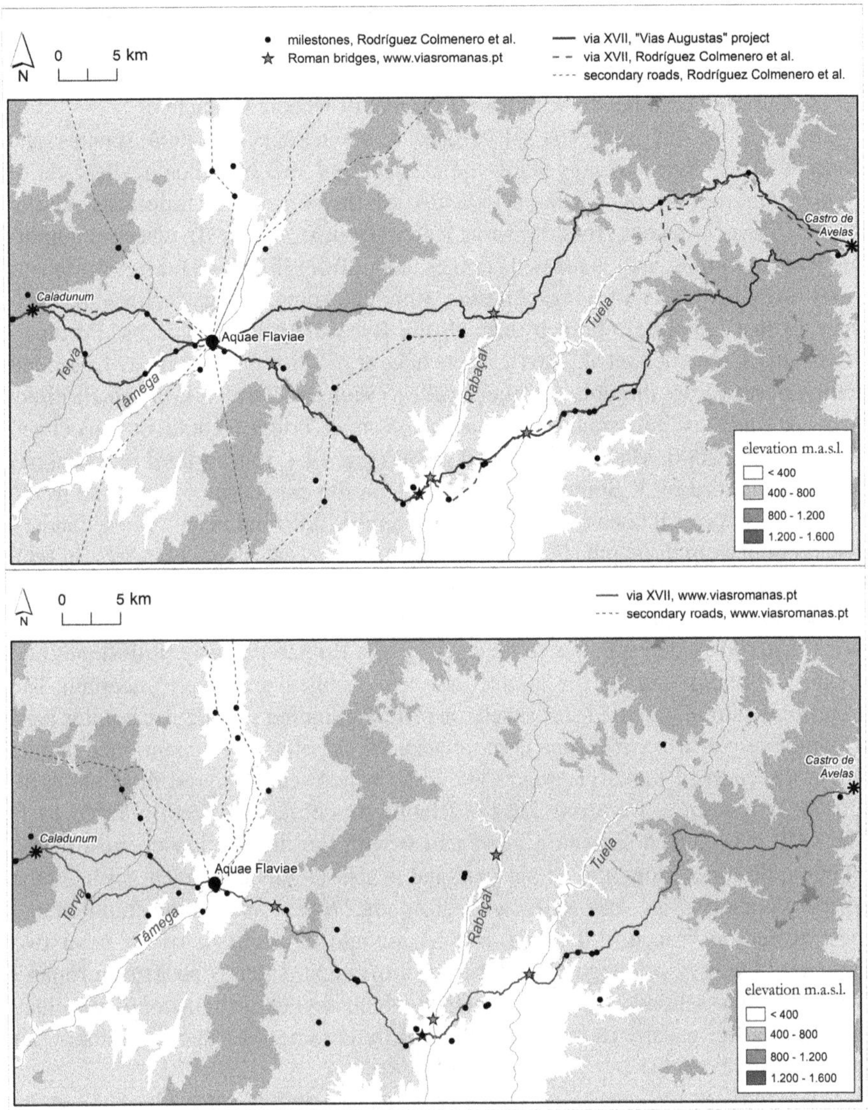

Fig. 14.1 Roman roads around *Aquae Flauiae*: direct remains of the roads and main existing reconstructive proposals. The main road (Via *XVII*) and the secondary roads, as have been proposed, are shown in different symbology

times supposed to have connected two points. A section of the Via *XVII* around *Aquae Flauiae* (Chaves, Portugal) which we previously analysed in Fonte et al. (2017) provides a good case in point (Fig. 14.1).

As was observed in our previous paper, it seems that *Aquae Flauiae* acted as a primary node in the layout of this road, something which is in accordance with its importance as a central place of secondary level in Roman times. The topography around *Aquae Flauiae* is especially rugged, which must have implied some limitations to mobility in the past: less than 50% of the area represented in Fig. 14.1 has a slope below 16%, and only 22.5% below 8%, referring to the range of slopes which is usually assumed to limit the movement of wheeled vehicles.

The most recent proposals (Rodríguez Colmenero et al. 2004; Fontes and Andrade 2012) agree in suggesting the existence of two branches to the west of *Aquae Flauiae*, both of which are indicated by the presence of milestones and/or bridges. These branches cross the Terva valley (Boticas, Portugal), where an important Roman mining area is located (Fontes et al. 2011) (Fig. 14.1). Less consensus exists towards the east of *Aquae Flauiae*. Although some authors propose the existence of just one single branch through the Rabaçal valley (Valpaços, Portugal) (Rodríguez Colmenero et al. 2004), others have argued for the existence of a second branch northwards, through the Tuela valley (Vinhais, Portugal), to which direct evidence such as milestones and possible Roman bridges could be associated (Lemos 1993, 2000; Maciel and Maciel 2004) (Fig. 14.1, top). A third proposal has been put forward by P. Soutinho, who agrees on the existence of that route to the north but interprets it not as a branch of the main Via *XVII* but as part of a secondary road coming from the south (Fig. 14.1, bottom).[1] In any case, both branches, or both roads, would have come together around Castro de Avelãs (Bragança, Portugal).

The context is open to different interpretations. There are some locations where direct material evidence points to the passing of a Roman pathway (milestones and bridges), although some of the connections between them are largely uncertain. The proposals summarized in Fig. 14.1 rely on different, indirect, evidence, but it is hard to definitively affirm which one is more accurate or reliable. As mentioned above, this is a section of the larger road (Via *XVII*) which was analysed in Fonte et al. (2017). In that case, we arrived at the friction model summarized in Table 14.1. The LCP it produced showed a good match with the distribution of most of the known milestones along the whole road and is also largely coincident with (1) the northern branch of the road to the west of *Aquae Flauiae* and (2) the southern and most agreed-on branch to the east. But what could be the logic of the other two branches? Do they privilege other types of movement, such as pedestrian routes? Do they lead to secondary places of interest which deviate from the optimal route? Are they earlier or later routes, suitable for different criteria and cost factors? Are they seasonal branches?

If we limit our analysis to the use of LCP, we can only test those hypotheses by designing alternative friction models and checking their coincidence with the available evidence. For other sections of this same road, the possible existence of changes in time has been already suggested (Fernández Ochoa et al. 2012): a road initially developed in a context of military conquest was later turned into an administrative and commercial route, which would have implied some redesign. This is an idea worth exploring, with a possible hypothesis being that any of the branches could

[1] This proposal is developed on the website http://ww.viasromanas.pt, which includes a detailed mapping of the proposed routes and the location of a large number of material remains related to Roman roads in Portugal.

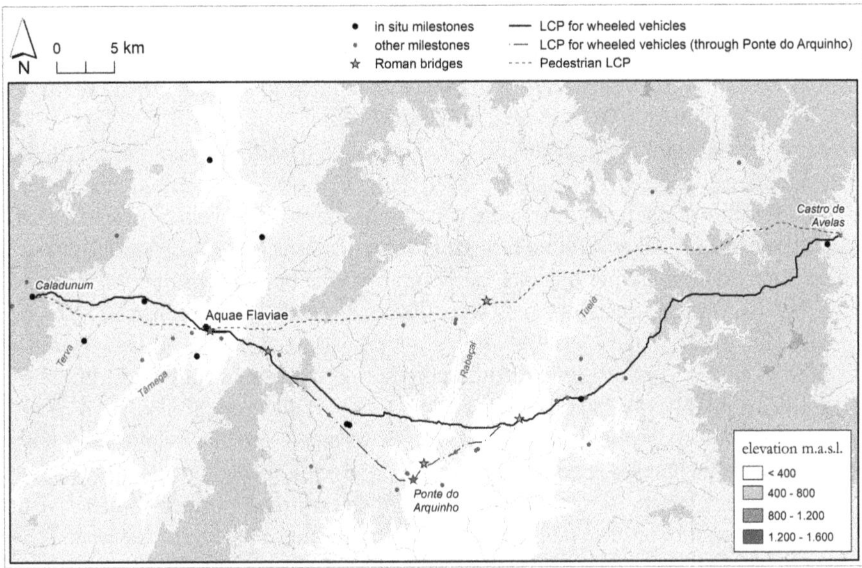

Fig. 14.2 LCP between *Caladunum*, *Aquae Flauiae*, and Castro de Avelãs, for both pedestrian and wheeled movement and with the inclusion of the bridge at Ponte do Arquinho as an extra node

correspond to optimal pedestrian paths which were later replaced, or complemented, by more adequate routes for wheeled vehicles (Fig. 14.2).

To test this possibility, we returned to the area around *Aquae Flauiae* in order to carry out further analyses. In this case, we used a higher definition DEM, with a spatial resolution of 10 m, built using the elevation data (contours and height points) of the Portuguese Army Geographical Institute (IGeoE) 1:25,000 cartography.

Our first step was to calculate the LCP for pedestrian movement between three nodes which are assumed to have been located along the road in this sector: *Aquae Flauiae* (without a doubt a central node of the road), Castro de Avelãs (whose Roman name is uncertain but its relationship to the road seems clear) and the supposed location of the *mansio Caladunum* (the site is unknown, but there is general agreement that the road ran through the place we have chosen and direct evidence for this theory). We also re-calculated the LCP for wheeled vehicles, using the same parameters as in our previous work, but with the more detailed DEM now available.

None of the results were satisfactory. On the one hand, on this more detailed scale, the LCP designed for wheeled vehicles provides only a partial coincidence with the assumed main route of the road, especially to the east of *Aquae Flauiae*. This deviation, which was not noticeable in our previous analysis on a more general scale, might suggest that the selection of a specific point to cross the River Rabaçal must have also had a local influence on the route of the road (as seems to occur, on a more general scale, with other bridges (Güimil-Fariña and Parcero-Oubiña 2015). For this reason, we have included the Ponte do Arquinho bridge as a fourth node in our calculation of the wheeled LCP. In this case, the match is very good, and the LCP aligns well with the milestones and bridges located there. Although this looks like a good solution, we shall return to this issue later on to see whether there might be a subtler explanation for this particular question.

On the other hand, the pedestrian LCP shows only a partial coincidence with the known evidence about the branches. Towards the west of *Aquae Flauiae*, the pedestrian LCP follows practically the same corridor as the LCP for vehicles. To the east, the pedestrian LCP takes a rather straighter route towards Castro de Avelãs, a route which aligns with a couple of milestones and a bridge before crossing the Rabaçal river, but which runs far from the two milestones to the northwest of Castro de Avelãs. This might make it possible to argue that part of the northern branch of the road to the east of *Aquae Flauiae* could correspond to optimal routes for other criteria. Unfortunately, we have had no chance to test if they could also have corresponded to the second or third best routes for wheeled vehicles which may have been in use for whatever reason. Besides this, and even if we consider that pedestrian movement can help to understand part of the northern branch to the east of *Aquae Flauiae*, it is of little help in clarifying the southern branch to the west.

14.4.2 Overcoming the Limitations of the Single Least-Cost Path Model

This is where the use of LCPs can take us. If we wish to explore further the possible logic of these branches, we need to resort to other methodological tools which reach beyond the restrictions of LCPs. These restrictions have recently been discussed, and some alternate methods have been proposed, such as "circuit theory" (Howey and Brouwer Burg 2017) or the exploration of potential movement in terms of "flows" or as "topographies of movement" (Fábrega-Álvarez 2006; Frachetti 2006; Llobera et al. 2011; Mlekuž 2014; Frachetti et al. 2017). We decided to use Focal Mobility Networks, or MADO in its Spanish acronym (Llobera et al. 2011), for two main reasons. Firstly, because we are more familiar with its operation, as one of us (C.P-O) was one of the authors who developed it, and we have previous experience in applying it. Secondly, because MADOs can be calculated using any desktop GIS software, thus simplifying our analysis, since we could limit ourselves to using one single piece of software (ArcGIS in our case).

MADO has been defined as "the network of most likely paths towards a given destination". It is based on the application of hydrological tools (flow direction and accumulation) to cumulative cost surfaces. The final result, a raster image of "cumulative probability of movement", can be reclassified into a network of potential paths towards the destination of choice (Llobera et al. 2011; an example of a similar approach in Fábrega-Álvarez et al. 2011).

Applying this approach to our case study, we calculated the MADO towards the three nodes on which the Roman roads in our area are based (*Aquae Flauiae*, Castro

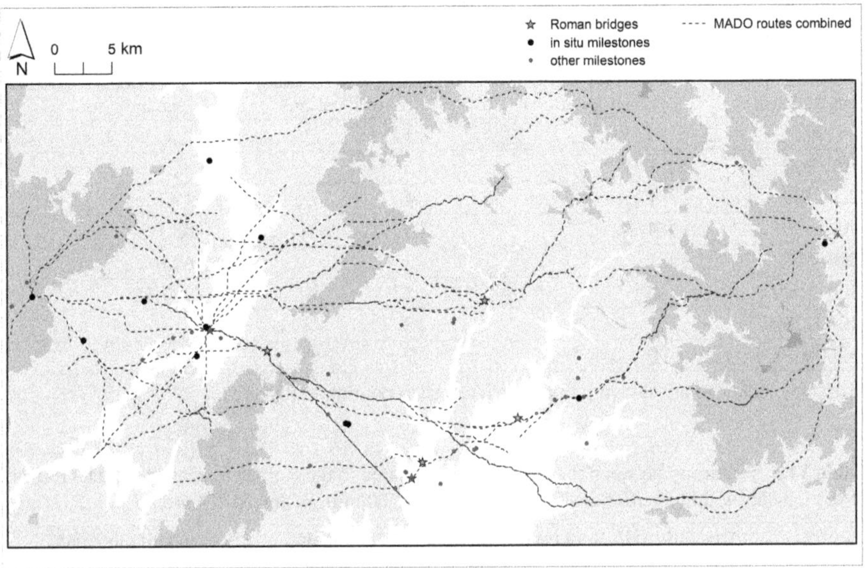

Fig. 14.3 An overlay of the MADO routes leading towards *Caladunum*, *Aquae Flauiae* and Castro de Avelãs

de Avelãs and *Caladunum*) and obtained a map of the potential natural corridors heading towards any of the three destinations (Fig. 14.3).[2] Even though, according to the LCP analysis, Ponte do Arquinho also seemed to be a primary node in the area, we intentionally decided to leave it out in this case so as to double check the preliminary idea.

This led to an initial interpretation of the most probable corridors of mobility towards the four destinations we have chosen. A measure of the reliability of these corridors with respect to mobility in Roman times can be obtained by quantifying their proximity to the material elements related with Roman roads (milestones and bridges). In the area of interest for our analysis, six bridges with a Roman origin have been documented and a total of 73 milestones are known (Rodríguez Colmenero et al. 2004). Since some of them are clustered in one single location, the actual number of milestone locations is 53. While bridges are obviously in situ elements, most of the milestones known in the area are found today in secondary locations. The exact place of origin is known only for a few of them (12) and, although most of the remaining ones are thought to be placed near their original location, we have considered them separately for our purpose here.

Table 14.2 summarizes the results of this measurement, showing a relatively high proximity between all the in situ elements and the closest MADO route: only one in

[2] The threshold to extract the lines visible in Fig. 14.3 was set at 600,000 cells (60 km^2 of "mobility basin" at this resolution). For further details, see Llobera et al. (2011).

Table 14.2 Linear distance of material elements related to the Roman roads and the closest MADO route

	In situ milestones	All milestones	Bridges
Distance (m)	N° of locations	N° of locations	Distance (m)
0–100	4	14	0.5
100–200	1	5	8.3
200–300	1	4	19.1
300–400	4	6	45.1
400–500	1	2	69.0
500–1000	0	12	259.3
1000–2000	1	8	
>2000	0	2	

Milestone locations are shown grouped in intervals according to distance

Table 14.3 Proximity between material elements related to the Roman roads and MADO routes: % of elements within a buffer distance of 250 m and 500 m from any MADO route

Buffer distance	Area covered (km^2)	% of total area	% of material elements within Buffer distance	% of in situ elements within Buffer distance
250	404.3	12.94	44.06	61.11
500	732.3	23.44	62.71	83.33

situ milestone location is more than 500 m far from any MADO route. A complementary quantification, taking into account the density of MADO routes in the area, is shown in Table 14.3. Almost all the in situ elements are located within a buffer distance of 500 m of the MADO lines depicted in Fig. 14.3, which represents around 23% of the total area under analysis.

14.4.3 From MADO Meshes to Multiple Discrete Optimal Connections

All the above seems to indicate that the potential routes modelled with our MADO analysis show a high degree of coincidence with the actual routes used by Roman mobility in the area. In turn, this reinforces the conclusions of Fonte et al. (2017) in relation to the suitability of the friction model developed for modelling Roman mobility in this region. However, if we want this MADO analysis to be more useful in understanding the logic behind the different branches of the Via *XVII* which seem to have existed here, we still need to simplify the extremely dense network of potential routes shown in Fig. 14.3. In fact, MADO analysis does not by definition provide connections between points, but rather potential paths with no specific origin. This is clearly obvious in some routes in Fig. 14.3 which “lead to nowhere”, while some others are prolonged across the whole area and do indeed connect the destination points of choice. This happens when MADO lines leading to one location (for instance, *Aquae Flauiae*) overlap at some point with MADO lines leading to any other of the two given positions (Castro de Avelãs or *Caladunum*). Thus, there is an intrinsic network of multiple LCPs hidden behind the larger complete mesh of MADO lines.

In order to extract the network of multiple LCP, we followed the proposal of Lynch and Parcero-Oubiña (2017): simply selecting the overlapping segments of the lines obtained from all sites independently and merging them into one single path connecting the three nodes. Prior to this, we calculated a line density map in order to see which corridors had a higher concentration of potential mobility. This, together with the elimination of the lines with a centrifugal direction, ended up in the multiple LCP shown in Fig. 14.4.

This network of multiple optimal connections can also be organized in a hierarchy using different criteria, which might help us to further understand why some of them seem to correspond better than others with the distribution of material indicators of the Roman roads. Cost distance measurements are a combination of linear distance and terrain friction, two factors which can be explored separately in order to obtain two complementary path hierarchies. Firstly, we can look at the length of each path. Figure 14.4, top, shows that line width is proportional to the length of each path with the labels quantifying the relative length of each one, with 1 being the shortest in each direction (to the west and east of *Aquae Flauiae,* respectively). To the west, the shortest path is also the LCP in terms of cost (see Fig. 14.2). However, the most remarkable result is the extremely good coincidence of the second shortest path with the distribution of milestones marking the supposed route of the southern branch (compare with Fig. 14.1). The third potential path takes a substantial detour and is almost 40% longer than the shortest one.

Between *Aquae Flauiae* and Castro de Avelãs, the network of potential paths is denser. In this case, the LCP obtained in Fig. 14.2 is not the shortest one, but only the fourth in length: three shorter routes exist northwards, which converge in crossing the Rabaçal river around Ponte de Picões and, when combined, are not too different from some of the reconstructions proposed for the northern branch of the Via *XVII* in this area. One of them is also rather similar to the pedestrian LCP, as shown in Fig. 14.2. Among the options to the south, and with respect to the LCP represented in Fig. 14.2, this analysis shows how the connection via the bridge of Ponte do Arquinho is, actually, one of the optimal choices to travel between *Aquae Flauiae* and Castro de Avelãs, even if the path is not obliged to go over that bridge. Finally, there is one more optimal path with a significantly longer route which implies an extra 12–16 km.

A complementary, and perhaps more illuminating, hierarchy emerges if we quantify the total friction of the terrain crossed by each path. This quantification is made by adding the friction values of all the cells that each path goes across. To ease comparison, we have also represented these values in relative magnitudes, with 1 being the sum of frictions of the less costly path in each direction independently (to the west and east of *Aquae Flauiae,* respectively).

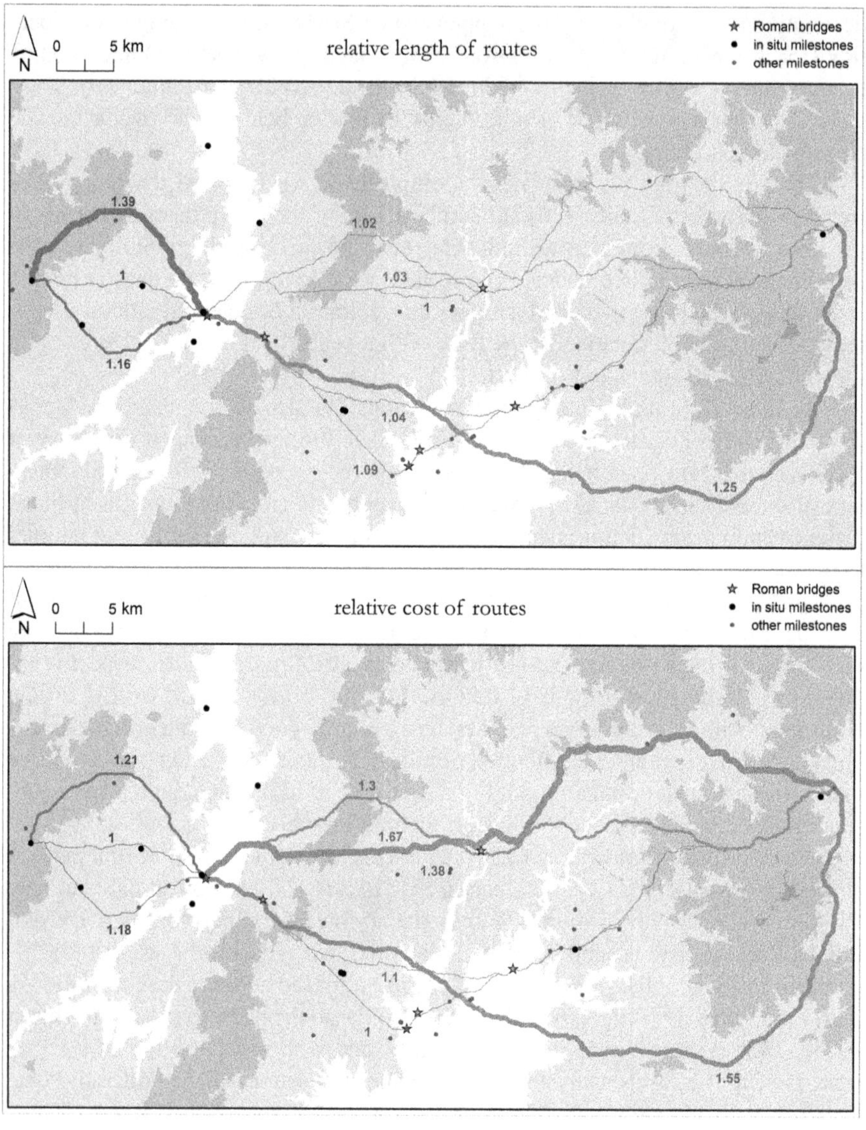

Fig. 14.4 The most probable routes between the different nodes considered, compared in relative terms of length and cost. Top: line thickness is proportional to length (longest routes correspond to thicker lines); labels indicate how much longer each route is with respect to the shortest one. Bottom: line thickness is proportional to accumulated friction crossed (higher frictions correspond to thicker lines); labels indicate, in relative terms, how much more accumulated friction each route implies with respect to the least cost one. An independent relative scale is used, respectively, for the routes to the east and west of *Aquae Flauiae*

To the west of *Aquae Flauiae*, this friction-based hierarchy, once more, defines the first LCP as the optimal one (as should be expected). The second shortest path is also in second place in terms of friction travelled. The longer detour to the north also implies a higher cost and, although the differences are not very high, when combined with length, it is clear that this is the least optimal of the three most probable routes. Again, it must be highlighted that the two first optimal paths are those which coincide well with the distribution of milestones in this sector.

To the east of *Aquae Flauiae,* the situation is somewhat more complicated and interesting. Quite surprisingly, the LCP though Ponte do Arquinho is now the best option (i.e. the pathway which implies crossing a terrain with a lower degree of overall friction), and it is only due to the fact that it is slightly longer (2 more km) that it does not come out as the optimal connection between *Aquae Flauiae* and Castro de Avelãs when a LCP approach is used. This is an interesting result which also helps to qualify the true influence of Ponte do Arquinho as a node in this section: rather than it being a direct conditioning factor for the layout of the road, it could be interpreted as the crossing point coinciding with one of the best "natural corridors" across the area.[3] The extra distance implied by this route with respect to the first optimal choice (ca. 2 km), as calculated by the LCP analysis, seems to have been less relevant in Roman times than the lower overall friction that it offered.

As far as the northern routes, which were shorter in length, are concerned, they now imply a more substantial extra friction of 30–67% when compared to the two southern routes. In this case, the existence of a possible branch of the road in this area would not be fully explained merely in terms of an alternative optimal route for wheeled vehicles. It seems clear that certain other factors must have come into play.

14.5 Final Comments

The results of our analysis seem to imply that a balance between terrain friction and distance lay behind the apparent selection of the routes that were followed at some point to travel across this region in Roman times. Between *Aquae Flauiae* and *Caladunum,* the shortest and least costly path was complemented by the second-best choice in terms of both cost and length, facilitating the access to a southern area of the Terva valley which, at some point in time, became important for the mines located nearby. What our analysis shows is that the route across this part of the valley was chosen following the same criteria which lay behind the selection of the first route northwards: the preference for terrain suitable for wheeled vehicles, according to the friction model summarized in Table 14.1.

Between *Aquae Flauiae* and Castro de Avelãs, the situation is a little more complex, since the hierarchy of best routes changes depending on how it is measured: in

[3] Rather than being the only, or best, possible way to cross the Rabaçal river, as seems to have been the case with other bridges in the region, such as Ponte Bibei on a nearby road (Güimil-Fariña and Parcero-Oubiña 2015).

terms of length or travelled friction. The analysis based on the use of MADO for the calculation of multiple LCP shows that a single LCP analysis may imply an over-simplification of a subtler case. Although the path that best matches the distribution of known milestones and bridges is not the first LCP between *Aquae Flauiae* and Castro de Avelãs, it is, however, among the optimal choices available. Indeed, it is the path which implies travelling over terrain with a lower degree of friction, despite being slightly longer. The MADO-based calculation of multiple LCP has allowed us to better understand that the rationale behind this section of the road is no different from what was proposed for the road as a whole. The apparent influence of Ponte do Arquinho as a primary node is also lessened by this analysis.

The location of the elements signalling the supposed northern branch of the road in this sector shows, in general, a rather good coincidence with other potentially optimal routes, which would have implied higher costs to traverse, despite being shorter. It should be noted that a large section of these routes is coincident with the pedestrian LCP calculated for this area, and the combination of these two factors may provide an argument to help understand the logic of this branch: a shorter connection for pedestrian travel, allowing access to a different portion of the territory which, although it is only a secondary option for wheeled movement, is also among the "natural corridors" to cross the area in those circumstances.

The analysis we have summarized here offers just a brief example of the potential of using tools other than LCP to digitally explore and predict the possible routes of ancient roads. Undoubtedly, a more refined approach is needed than that shown here, but hopefully this example will illustrate the benefits of using tools, such as MADO, to explore potential mobility in less restrictive ways.

References

Abásolo Álvarez JA (1990) El conocimiento de las vías romanas. Un problema arqueológico. In: Simposio sobre la red viaria en la Hispania romana. Institución Fernando el Católico, Zaragoza, pp 7–20

Alonso Trigueros JM (2014) Modelo gráfico para la datación de las vías romanas empedradas a partir del estudio de sus estados de frecuentación y del análisis superficial de roderas. Universidad Politécnica de Madrid, Madrid. Available at http://oa.upm.es/32697/. Accessed on 12 May 2018

De Gruchy MW (2016) Beyond replication: the quantification of route models in the North Jazira, Iraq. J Archaeol Method Theory 23(2):427–447. https://doi.org/10.1007/s10816-015-9247-x

Del Olmo Martín J (2006) Arqueología Aérea de las Ciudades Romanas en la Meseta Norte. Algunos ejemplos de urbanismo de la primera Edad del Hierro, segunda Edad del Hierro y Romanización. In: Moreno Gallo I (ed) Nuevos Elementos de Ingeniería Romana, III Congreso de las Obras Públicas Romanas. Junta de Castilla y León / Colegio de Ingenieros Técnicos de Obras Públicas, Astorga, pp 313–340, Available at http://www.traianvs.net/pdfs/2006_12olmo.pdf. Accessed on 12 May 2018

Estefanía Álvarez D (1960) Vías romanas de Galicia. Zephyrus 11:5–104

Fábrega-Álvarez P (2006) Moving without destination. A theoretical GIS–based determination of movement from a given origin. Archaeol Comput Newsl 64:7–11. Available from http://digital.csic.es/handle/10261/15993. Accessed on 12 May 2018.

Fábrega-Álvarez P, Fonte J, González García FJ (2011) Las sendas de la memoria. Sentido, espacio y reutilización de las estatuas-menhir en el noroeste de la Península Ibérica. Trab Prehist 68(2):313–330. https://doi.org/10.3989/tp.2011.11072

Fasolo M (2014) Infrastructure in the Roman world: roads and aqueducts. In: Smith C (ed) Encyclopedia of global archaeology. Springer, New York, pp 3873–3882. https://doi.org/10.1007/978-1-4419-0465-2_1458

Fernández Ochoa C, Morillo Cerdán Á, Gil Sendino F (2012) El «Itinerario de Barro». Cuestiones de autenticidad y lectura. Zephyrus 70:151–179

Fonte J, Parcero-Oubiña C, Costa-García JM (2017) A GIS-based analysis of the rationale behind Roman roads. The case of the so-called via XVII (NW Iberian Peninsula). Mediterr Archaeol Archaeometry 17(3):163–189. https://doi.org/10.5281/zenodo.1005562

Fontes L, Alves M, Martins CMB, Delfim B, Loureiro E (2011) Paisagem, povoamento e mineração antigas no vale alto do rio Terva, Boticas. In: CMB M, AMS B, Martins JIFP, Carvalho J (eds) Povoamento e Exploração dos Recursos Mineiros na Europa Atlântica Ocidental. CITCEM/APEQ, Braga, pp 203–219

Fontes, LFO, Andrade F (2012) O traçado da via romana Bracara-Asturica, por Aguae Flaviae, no concelho de Boticas. Unidade de Arquelogia, Universidade do Minho, Braga. Available at http://repositorium.sdum.uminho.pt/handle/1822/16561. Accessed on 12 May 2018

Frachetti MD (2006) Digital archaeology and the scalar structure of pastoral landscapes. In: Evans TL, Daly P (eds) Digital archaeology: bridging method and theory. Routledge, London, pp 128–147

Frachetti MD, Smith CE, Traub CM, Williams T (2017) Nomadic ecology shaped the highland geography of Asia's Silk Roads. Nature 543(7644):193–198. https://doi.org/10.1038/nature21696

Franco Maside RM (2000) Rutas naturais e vías romanas na provincia de A Coruña. Gallaecia 19:162–166. Available at https://dialnet.unirioja.es/servlet/articulo?codigo=83901. Accessed on 12 May 2018

Franco Maside RM (2001) La vía per loca maritima: un estudio sobre vías romanas en la mitad Norocidental de Galicia. Gallaecia 20:224–229. Available at https://dialnet.unirioja.es/servlet/articulo?codigo=83925. Accessed on 12 May 2018

Gethin B, Toller H (2014) The Roman marching camp and road at Loups Fell, Tebay. Britannia 45:1–10. https://doi.org/10.1017/S0068113X13000548

Gómez Vila J (2005) Vías romanas de la actual provincia de Lugo. University of Santiago de Compostela, Santiago de Compostela. Available at https://minerva.usc.es/xmlui/handle/10347/9615. Accessed on 12 May 2018

González Álvarez D (2011) Vías romanas de montaña entre Asturias y León: La integración de la «Asturia transmontana» en la red viaria de Hispania. Zephyrus 67:171–192

Güimil-Fariña A, Parcero-Oubiña C (2015) "Dotting the joins": a non-reconstructive use of Least Cost Paths to approach ancient roads. The case of the Roman roads in the NW Iberian Peninsula. J Archaeol Sci 54:31–44. https://doi.org/10.1016/j.jas.2014.11.030

Herzog I (2013) The potential and limits of optimal path analysis. In: Bevan A, Lake M (eds) Computational approaches to archaeological spaces. Left Coast Press, Walnut Creek (CA), pp 179–211

Herzog I (2014) A review of case studies in archaeological least cost analysis. Archeologia e Calcolatori 25:223–239. Available at http://www.archcalc.cnr.it/indice/PDF25/12_Herzog.pdf. Accessed on 12 May 2018

Herzog I (2017) Reconstructing pre-industrial long distance roads in a hilly region in Germany, based on historical and archaeological data. Stud Digit Herit 1(2):642–660. https://doi.org/10.14434/sdh.v1i2.23283

Howey MCL (2007) Using multi-criteria cost surface analysis to explore past regional landscapes: a case study of ritual activity and social interaction in Michigan, AD 1200–1600. J Archaeol Sci 34(11):1830–1846. https://doi.org/10.1016/j.jas.2007.01.002

Howey MCL (2011) Multiple pathways across past landscapes: circuit theory as a complementary geospatial method to least cost path for modeling past movement. J Archaeol Sci 38(10):2523–2535. https://doi.org/10.1016/j.jas.2011.03.024
Howey MCL, Brouwer Burg M (2017) Assessing the state of archaeological GIS research: unbinding analyses of past landscapes. J Archaeol Sci 84:1–9. https://doi.org/10.1016/j.jas.2017.05.002
Lemos FS (1993) Povoamento romano de Trás-os-Montes Oriental. Universidade do Minho, Braga
Lemos FS (2000) A Via Romana entre Bracara Augusta e Asturica Augusta, por Aquae Flaviae. Revista de Guimarães 110:15–51
Limp WF (2016) Measuring the face of the past and facing the measurement. In: Forte M, Campana S (eds) Digital methods and remote sensing in archaeology. Springer, Cham, pp 349–369. https://doi.org/10.1007/978-3-319-40658-9_16
Llobera M, Fábrega-Álvarez P, Parcero-Oubina C (2011) Order in movement: a GIS approach to accessibility. J Archaeol Sci 38(4):843–851. https://doi.org/10.1016/j.jas.2010.11.006
Llobera M, Sluckin TJ (2007) Zigzagging: theoretical insights on climbing strategies. J Theor Biol 249:206–217. https://doi.org/10.1016/j.jtbi.2007.07.020
Loewinsohn E (1965) Una calzada y dos campamentos romanos del conuentus asturum. Arch Esp Arqueol 38:26–43
Lynch J, Parcero-Oubiña C (2017) Under the eye of the Apu. Paths and mountains in the Inka settlement of the Hualfín and Quimivil valleys, NW Argentina. J Archaeol Sci Rep 16:44–56. https://doi.org/10.1016/j.jasrep.2017.09.019
Maciel T, Maciel MJ (2004) Estradas romanas no território de Vinhais: a antiga rede viária e as suas pontes. Câmara Municipal de Vinhais, Vinhais
Mlekuž D (2014) Exploring the topography of movement. In: Polla S, Verhagen P (eds) Computational approaches to movement in archaeology. Theory, practice and interpretation of factors and effects of long term landscape formation and transformation. De Gruyter, Berlin, pp 5–22. https://doi.org/10.1515/9783110288384.5
Moreno Gallo I (2006) Vías romanas. Ingeniería y técnica constructiva. CEHOPU/Ministerio de Fomento, Madrid
Moreno Gallo I (2011a) Identificación y descripción de la vía de Astorga a Braga por Chaves. De Asturica a Veniata. In: Vías romanas en Castilla y León. Junta de Castilla y León, Valladolid, pp 2–38. Available at http://www.viasromanas.net/pdf/00_Vias_romanas_en_Castilla_y_Leon.pdf. Accessed on 12 May 2018
Moreno Gallo I (2011b) Vías romanas en Castilla y León. Available at http://www.viasromanas.net/. Accessed on 12 May 2018
Opitz R, Limp F (2015) Recent developments in high-density survey and measurement (HDSM) for archaeology: implications for practice and theory. Annu Rev Anthropol 44(1):347–364. https://doi.org/10.1146/annurev-anthro-102214-013845
Polla S, Verhagen P (eds) (2014) Computational approaches to the study of movement in archaeology, theory, practice and interpretation of factors and effects of long term landscape formation and transformation. De Gruyter, Berlin. https://doi.org/10.1515/9783110288384
Rabanal Alonso MA (2006) Las vías romanas en las provincias de Zamora y León. Instituto de Estudios Zamoranos "Florian de Ocampo"/Diputación de Zamora/UNED, Zamora
Rodríguez Colmenero A, Ferrer Sierra S, Álvarez Asorey R (2004) Miliarios e outras inscricións viarias romanas no Noroeste Hispánico (conventus Bracarense, Lucense y Asturicense). Consello da Cultura Galega, Santiago de Compostela. Available at http://consellodacultura.gal/mediateca/extras/CCG_2004_Miliarios-e-outras-inscricions-viarias-romanas-do-noroeste-hispanico-conventos-bracarense-lucense-e-asturicense.pdf. Accessed on 12 May 2018
Roldán Hervás JM (1975) Itineraria Hispana. Fuentes antiguas para el estudio de las vías romanas en la península ibérica. Universidad de Valladolid, Valladolid
Roldán Hervás JM, Caballero Casado C (2014) Itineraria Hispana. Estudio de las vías romanas en Hispania a partir del Itinerario de Antonino, el Anónimo de Rávena y los Vasos de Vicarello. El Nuevo Miliario 17:1–255

Sáez Taboada B (1999) Vías 19 y 20: Trazado y función. University of Sevilla, Sevilla
Small F (2016) The lost Roman road from Chichester to Arundel. Hist Engl Res 4:3–8. Available at https://historicengland.org.uk/images-books/publications/historic-england-research-4. Accessed on 12 May 2018
Supernant K (2017) Modeling Métis mobility? Evaluating least cost paths and indigenous landscapes in the Canadian west. J Archaeol Sci 84:63–73. https://doi.org/10.1016/j.jas.2017.05.006
Surface-Evans S (2012) Cost catchments: a least cost application for modeling hunter-gatherer land use. In: White DA, Surface-Evans SL (eds) Least cost analysis of social landscapes: Archaeological case studies. University of Utah Press, Salt Lake City, pp 128–151
Van Lanen RJ, Jansma E, Van Doesburg J, Groenewoudt BJ (2016) Roman and early-medieval long-distance transport routes in north-western Europe: modelling frequent-travel zones using a dendroarchaeological approach. J Archaeol Sci 73:120–137. https://doi.org/10.1016/j.jas.2016.07.010
Van Lanen RJ, Kosian MC, Groenewoudt BJ, Jansma E (2015a) Finding a way: modeling landscape prerequisites for Roman and early-medieval routes in the Netherlands. Geoarchaeology 30(3):200–222. https://doi.org/10.1002/gea.21510
Van Lanen RJ, Kosian MC, Groenewoudt BJ, Spek T, Jansma E (2015b) Best travel options: modelling Roman and early-medieval routes in the Netherlands using a multi-proxy approach. J Archaeol Sci Rep 3:144–159. https://doi.org/10.1016/j.jasrep.2015.05.024
Verbrugghe G, De Clercq W, Van Eetvelde V (2017) Routes across the Civitas Menapiorum: using least cost paths and GIS to locate the Roman roads of Sandy Flanders. J Hist Geogr 57:76–88. https://doi.org/10.1016/j.jhg.2017.06.006
Verhagen P, Jeneson K (2012) A Roman puzzle. Trying to find the via Belgica with GIS. In: Chrysanthi A, Murrieta Flores P, Papadopoulos C (eds) Thinking beyond the tool. Archaeological computing and the interpretive process. Archaeopress, Oxford, pp 123–130
Verhagen P, Whitley T (2012) Integrating archaeological theory and predictive modeling: a live report from the scene. J Archaeol Method Theory 19:1–52. https://doi.org/10.1007/s10816-011-9102-7
Vicente González JL (2013) Vías romanas del Noroeste Hispano: génesis, trazado y una nueva metodología para su estudio. Revista Mapping 22(160):48–67. Available at http://www.jlvg.es/Publicaciones/2013_05_06_VIAS_ROMANAS_NW_HISPANO_JLVG.pdf. Accessed on 12 May 2018
White DA, Surface-Evans SL (eds) (2012) Least cost analysis of social landscapes. Archaeological case studies. University of Utah Press, Salt Lake City

Chapter 15
Rethinking Approaches for the Study of Urban Movement at Ostia

Katherine A. Crawford

Abstract Despite a range of existing approaches for examining movement within ancient cities, the study of movement intent has received limited attention. This paper begins to address this gap by considering how pedestrian movement can be studied at Ostia, Rome's ancient port, by transitioning focus to what structured movement routes, namely the built environment and social activity. Using the UNA (Urban Network Analysis) Toolbox developed for ArcGIS, betweeness centrality is calculated in relation to different types of buildings. The results, when associated with Ostia's streets, provide a visualization of potential areas of movement specific to certain social activities that occurred within the urban landscape. This provides a novel methodological approach for assessing different forms of directed movement within ancient urban landscapes.

Keywords Urban Network Analysis · GIS · Archaeology · Ostia

15.1 Introduction

The study of movement within ancient Roman cities has seen a growing corpus of scholarship in recent years (Laurence 2008; Laurence and Newsome 2011; Östenberg et al. 2015; Poehler 2017). While the majority of research has followed either literary accounts of ancient movement (Favro 1996; Laurence 2011) or proxy evidence that is indicative of movement (Ellis 2004; Hartnett 2008, 2017; Poehler 2017), an increasing number of studies are beginning to apply computational approaches as a way to study pedestrian movement that is otherwise invisible within the archaeological record (Stöger 2011; Van Nes 2014).

Network science methodologies constitute one of the most frequently used methods for examining pedestrian movement, providing a quantitative approach for studying urban movement patterns that have developed out of modern urban planning techniques (Barthelemy 2011; Porta et al. 2006; Sarkar 2013). In particular, the

K. A. Crawford (✉)
University of Southampton, Southampton, UK
e-mail: k.a.crawford@soton.ac.uk

P. Verhagen et al. (eds.), *Finding the Limits of the Limes*, Computational Social Sciences, https://doi.org/10.1007/978-3-030-04576-0_15

application of space syntax theories and methods, developed by Hillier and Hanson (Hillier and Hanson 1984) for spatial analysis, has been predominantly applied to questioning how ancient street systems structured movement (Kaiser 2011; Stöger 2011). However, such methods do not address questions concerning different types of pedestrian movement or movement with varying intents.

Roman pedestrian research is largely limited to the analysis of random movement patterns that are structured by a city's street network. Studies of movement intent, movement with intended goals, that use computational approaches have received very little attention (Branting 2004; Poehler 2016; Thaler 2005). The majority of pedestrian movement, arguably, would have occurred with pedestrians having intended destinations or varying levels of knowledge of the urban landscape they traversed. And while the topic has received some attention in the context of Roman cities (Macaulay-Lewis 2011), the lack of engagement is largely due to the minimal trace that is left within the archaeological record and the limited written commentary about specific forms of movement. Thereby, any attempt to study pedestrian intent within a specific city is increasingly complicated.

This paper addresses this limitation by introducing a new computational approach for the study of directed urban movement that focuses upon how the built environment, indicative of social activity, may have played a role in structuring movement routes throughout a city. Using Ostia, Rome's ancient port, as a case study, this paper proposes a new way to look at how pedestrian movement can be studied within the late second century CE city. The size of the city and the extent to which it has been excavated make Ostia an ideal case study for applying an integrated computational approach that combines archaeological data, GIS, and urban network analysis (Sevtsuk et al. 2016), enabling the study of possible urban movement patterns.

15.2 Methods

15.2.1 Modelling Movement Intent

Recognizing the difficulties of studying urban movement, a new method needs to be developed that moves beyond studying how a city's streets promoted generic movement patterns. One way to approach this is by questioning how a city's built environment and corresponding social activity played a role in structuring different types of urban movement. Scholars have long recognized the relationship that existed between a city's built form and social activity (Lawrence and Low 1990; Rapoport 1982). Various urban theorists have focused attention upon how people understand and inhabit cities as well as how a city should be structured to promote different forms of social activity (Jacobs 1961; Kostof 1985; Lynch 1960). In terms of Roman studies, these theories have been adapted by scholars such as MacDonald

(1986) to gain a better understanding about how people both interacted with and experienced a city.

Despite the acknowledged correlation between the built environment and social activity, questions of different types of ancient pedestrian movement have yet to be addressed with appropriate methodological rigour. The predominant methodologies for studying Roman pedestrian movement adopt either phenomenological approaches informed by random walks through the city (Favro 1996; Yegül 1994) or apply computational approaches like space syntax that consider movement in terms of a city's street network design (Stöger 2011). In both instances, the pedestrian movement under consideration is random and does not account for other urban dynamics that influenced pedestrian routes. By transitioning focus back towards how a city influences movement patterns, beyond solely its visibility or geometric design, a more nuanced approach can be developed for looking at ancient urban movement.

15.2.2 Ostia's Urban Landscape

In order to question how Ostia's built environment shaped different pedestrian movement patterns, a detailed plan of the second century CE built environment and street network is required. The excavated city represents a palimpsest of periods ranging from the end of the fourth century BCE into the sixth century CE (Pavolini 2006). The present study focuses upon the end of the second century CE because it represents one of the most well-defined periods for Ostia's urban landscape (DeLaine 2005). The extensive number of studies into buildings dating to the second century CE means that the built environment and corresponding streets are relatively well identified (Calza 1953; DeLaine 2002; Mar 2008; Meiggs 1973; Pavolini 2016). The extent to which the city has been excavated and knowledge of its street network provide an excellent opportunity to study pedestrian movement dynamics within the city.

Following a general conception of Roman urban space, buildings are classified within five broadly defined categories of space: commercial, production, residential, public, and religious (Fig. 15.1). These classifications do not negate the complexity of urban space, instead, they serve as an exploratory method to assess how different buildings, associated with specific types of social activity, shaped movement patterns within Ostia's urban landscape. All excavated buildings that compose the late second century CE city were classified into one of these five categories following their general architectural function (Flohr 2013; Heinzelmann 2005; Meiggs 1973; Packer 1971; Russell 2016). There is a certain degree of speculation within these classifications. First, due to how the site was excavated the purpose of many of the buildings has to be inferred through various comparative studies at Ostia and other Roman cities. Second, the majority of structures found at Ostia

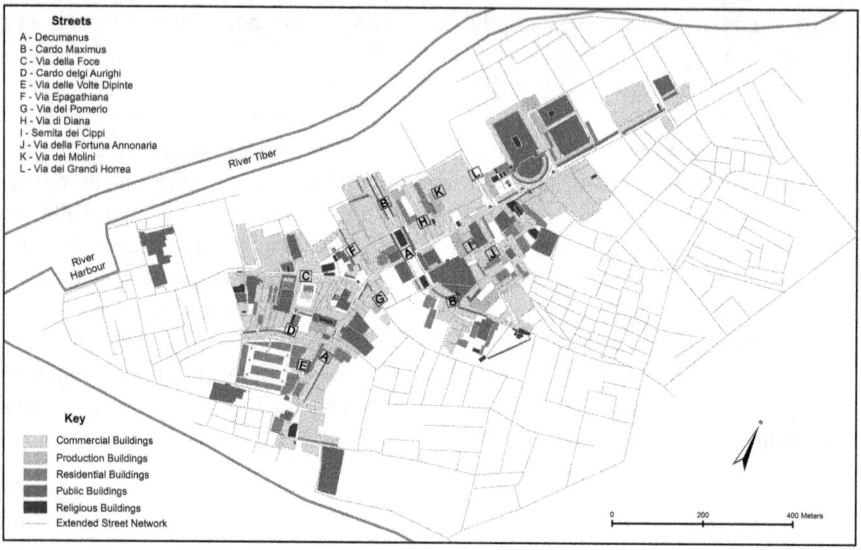

Fig. 15.1 Plan of Ostia at the end of the second century CE showing the building classifications and the main streets. (After Calza 1953; Mannucci 1995)

would not have had only one purpose. Instead, ground floor and upper storey spaces could have accounted for a variety of different activities, such as ground floor shops and storage rooms and upper storey residential spaces (Pirson 2007). For the present study, the classifications are indicative of ground floor spaces that are directly accessible from the street. Furthermore, the limitation of space classifications to five categories enables a workable dataset that begins to question how different aspects of the built environment structured movement patterns throughout Ostia.

The street network used within this study needs additional clarification. Within the excavated city, the streets date to the end of the second century CE (Mar 2008). In order to more accurately study movement patterns, the extended street network is additionally included following preliminary geophysical survey results (Heinzelmann 1998; Martin and Heinzelmann 2000) as well as the space syntax axial graph produced by Stöger (Stöger 2011) based upon these initial survey results. It needs to be noted that portions of the extended street network date to the beginning of the third century CE, thereby slightly postdating the present period of study. However, until the geophysical survey results are fully published it is difficult to know exactly which sections of the street network date to which period. Therefore, the total extended street network is included in order to negate issues of an edge effect, or the creation of an artificial boundary, within the urban network analysis calculations by accounting for the possibility of movement travelling beyond the excavated city. While it needs to be acknowledged that any adjustment to the extended street network design may have some effect upon the network analysis results, the variation is less extreme than if only the excavated streets were used.

15.2.3 Urban Network Analysis

Centrality measurements are one of the predominant network analysis calculations used by modern urban researches to investigate pedestrian movement. Until relatively recently, however, these measures have been used within the context of relational networks rather than accounting for geographical scale (Crucitti et al. 2006; Hillier and Hanson 1984). The concept of centrality is based upon the idea that within a network, certain nodes are more important. In terms of urban movement, centrality provides a way to determine likely areas of movement. Among the possible measurements, the most relevant for the present study is the application of betweenness centrality. Betweenness centrality computes the likelihood that a certain node, or in this case building, will be passed when travelling the shortest distance between two nodes (Brughmans 2010; Brughmans et al. 2016; Isaksen 2013). This enables the subsequent study of individual streets with a high degree of movement potential relative to the built environment. By focusing attention upon through movement, what is passed by pedestrians can be assessed regardless of their destination or origin. In this way, focus remains upon what is being passed regardless of the overall purpose of the journey.

Betweenness centrality graphs are traditionally computed using two network elements, nodes and edges. When applied to pedestrian studies on the scale of a city's street network, this correlates to nodes representing intersections while edges symbolize the streets (Porta et al. 2006). Space syntax, in contrast, inverts this network structure where the edges become nodes, and nodes represent edges (Hillier and Hanson 1984). In both of these types of network analyses, the level of enquiry is focused upon the spatial connection between the nodes and edges. However, within these network graphs, the relationship of the surrounding urban environment or related social activities remains unaccounted for within present movement-centred studies (Sevtsuk and Mekonnen 2012).

The vast majority of archaeological studies use betweenness centrality measures within the context of regional queries, focused upon the structure and connectivity of various sites (Bikoulis 2012; Brughmans 2010; Groenhuijzen and Verhagen 2015). Within these studies, the mobility of objects, people, or ideas within a landscape often becomes the emphasis of study. Despite the predominant applications of centrality to archaeological questions based upon regional scales, this does not limit its application to smaller urban datasets, such as a specific city (Mol and Mans 2013). The only existing example of betweenness centrality applied to an ancient urban street network is Poehler's (Poehler 2016) analysis of movement potential relative to doorways located along Pompeii's street system. While innovative in determining which Pompeiian streets saw the greatest amount of traffic by applying network analysis principals, it considers only generic movement patterns. Other urban factors that may have affected traffic within the city in addition to the network structure are unaccounted for within the present model.

To transition enquiry away from assessing movement in isolation to its surrounding built environment, urban network analysis is used to focus upon how buildings played a role in structuring movement along a street network using an adapted form of network analysis. Betweenness centrality is calculated in relation to the previously specified building classifications using the ArcGIS UNA (Urban Network Analysis) toolbox (Sevtsuk et al. 2016). The toolbox was created by urban planners as a way to question how the presence of buildings affects traditional centrality measurements (betweenness, centrality, reach, etc.) directly within GIS. Whereas standard network analysis is computed using nodes and edges, urban network analysis enables the addition of buildings as a third metric of study, creating a tripartite network. As a result, buildings become the focus of analysis, which are then computed in relation to their position along the street network previously detailed in ArcGIS. The betweenness centrality equation used by the UNA toolbox is adapted from Freeman (Freeman 1977) to highlight which buildings within the urban system saw the greatest potential of having passing movement along a street network. The results indicate the likelihood of a building being passed by through movement regardless of its destination or origin.

An innovative feature of the UNA toolbox and its application to archaeological questions of urban movement concerns the adaptability of the scale of measurement and the ability to attribute buildings with different variables or building weights. In terms of scale, a specific radius can be defined within the betweenness centrality calculations which limits the distance calculated from one building to all other buildings within the cityscape. Within modern cities a 400 m radius traditionally conforms to pedestrian scale movement while a 800 m radius is specific to vehicular traffic (Omer et al. 2015). However, these values do not necessarily directly relate to movement scale within the ancient city.

The best radius relative to pedestrian movement needs to be determined in relation to Ostia's built environment. A specified radius ensures that the centrality calculations of each building are computed only if a building is located within an equal or less geodesic distance from the specified radius from every other building along the street network (Sevtsuk and Mekonnen 2012). Additionally, calculations are computed using a network radius rather than a Euclidian radius to ensure that the results correspond to movement only occurring along the streets, not through buildings. To determine the ideal radius, six different betweenness centrality calculations were run using a 100–600 metre radius (Fig. 15.2). Within each betweenness graph, the buildings included within the highest betweenness centrality category (indicated in black) were then used as nodes to create a delineated area of greatest movement potential. Figure 15.2 shows that the greatest area of high movement potential is illustrated with a 100–300 metre radius; however, in these examples, movement is concentrated within either the western or eastern ends of the city. A 400 or 600 metre radius is more indicative of continuous movement across a larger portion of Ostia's cityscape. To ensure that the measurements correspond to both the excavated cityscape and local-scale pedestrian movement, a 400 metre radius is ultimately chosen.

A second feature of the UNA toolbox that has significant potential for the study of directed movement is the ability to weight buildings with different attributes. This can include variables such as a building's size, number of occupants, or

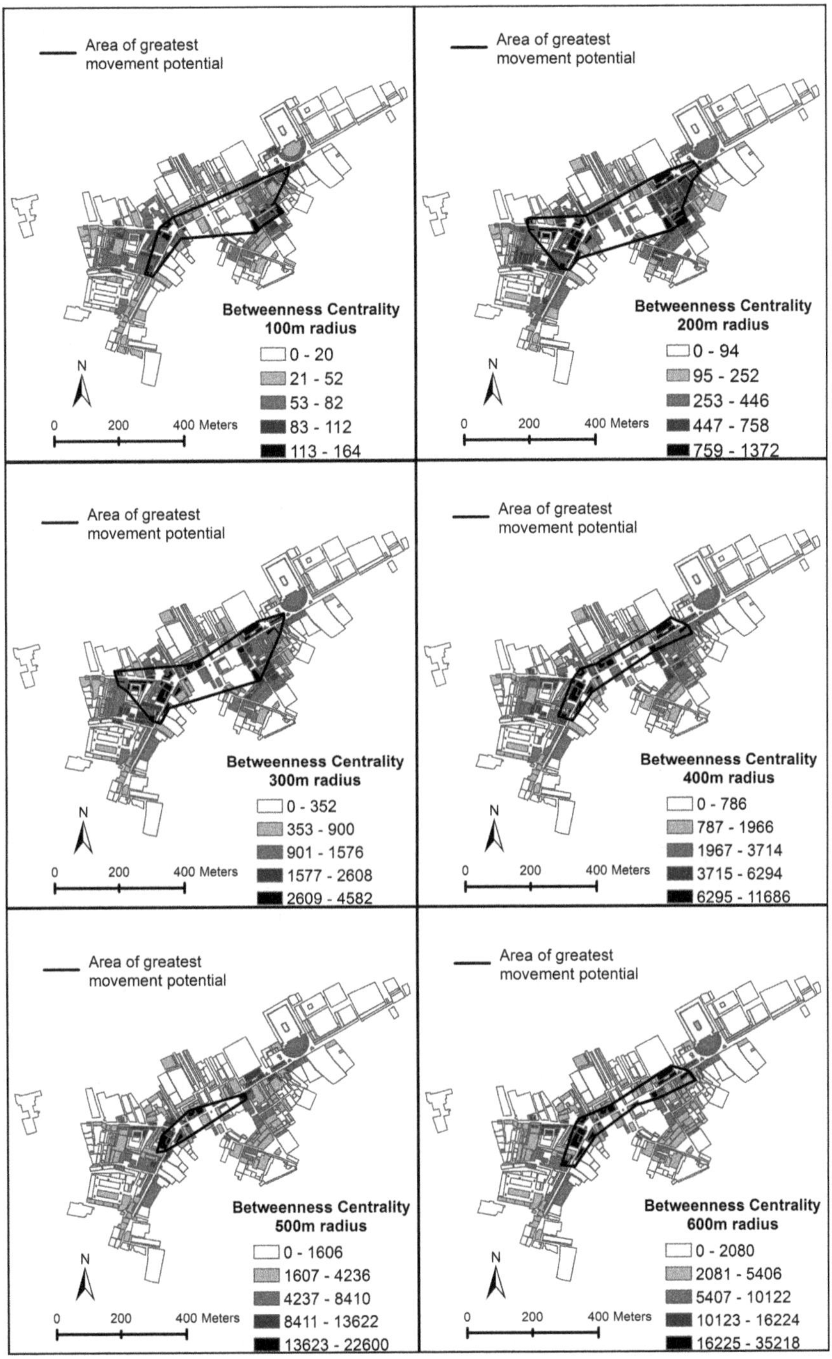

Fig. 15.2 Betweenness centrality measurements using a radius of 100–600 metres. The general areas with the highest betweenness values are detailed

building type. For the present study, weighted values relate to the five different building classification categories and their individual influence upon passing movement. Betweenness centrality was run for each classification category, weighted with a value of 10 to reflect its assumed importance for pedestrian movement. The other four spaces were provided with a value of 1 to ensure that every building within the excavated cityscape is accounted for within the calculations (e.g., commercial spaces, weight 10; other four spaces, weight 1).

The application of betweenness centrality using Ostia's building classifications as the focus of analysis enables the assessment of what buildings were likely passed when weighted according to building type that is indicative of various social activities. The resulting betweenness centrality graphs (Figs. 15.3 and 15.4) present a visualization of the betweenness values relative to each building classification category. To more easily correlate this to possible movement routes, the streets corresponding to the two highest betweenness values are subsequently detailed. This enables a comparison between the different graphs to determine the extent to which the five building classifications affect pedestrian movement along Ostia's streets, ultimately reflecting distinct forms of movement intent.

15.3 Results

The calculation of betweenness centrality weighted by building importance gives some insight into the way in which social activity structured possible movement routes. To assess the degree to which weighted calculations affect the results, an unweighted betweenness centrality graph, applying a 400 m radius, was initially calculated (Fig. 15.3). The results illustrate the areas of the cityscape that saw the greatest potential of use. Ostia's primary street, the *decumanus*, has the highest degree of movement potential which correlates to the highest centrality measures. The areas of movement potential largely reflect how random movement is structured by the design of the built environment and the street network configuration if no other factors are taken into account. While the unweighted graph provides insight into the general configuration of the city for generating movement, weighted calculations begin to address the nuances of how the built environment structures movement depending upon what buildings are significant for passing pedestrian movement.

The calculation of weighted betweenness centrality shows some variation in results (Figs. 15.3 and 15.4), indicating that building importance can play a noticeable role in structuring movement directionality. While the highest betweenness centrality values stay relatively consistent throughout all of the graphs, variation is shown by the second highest betweenness value, represented by the top 40% intensity of street use visualization. This provides a clear indication that building importance has a direct correlation to potential movement routes.

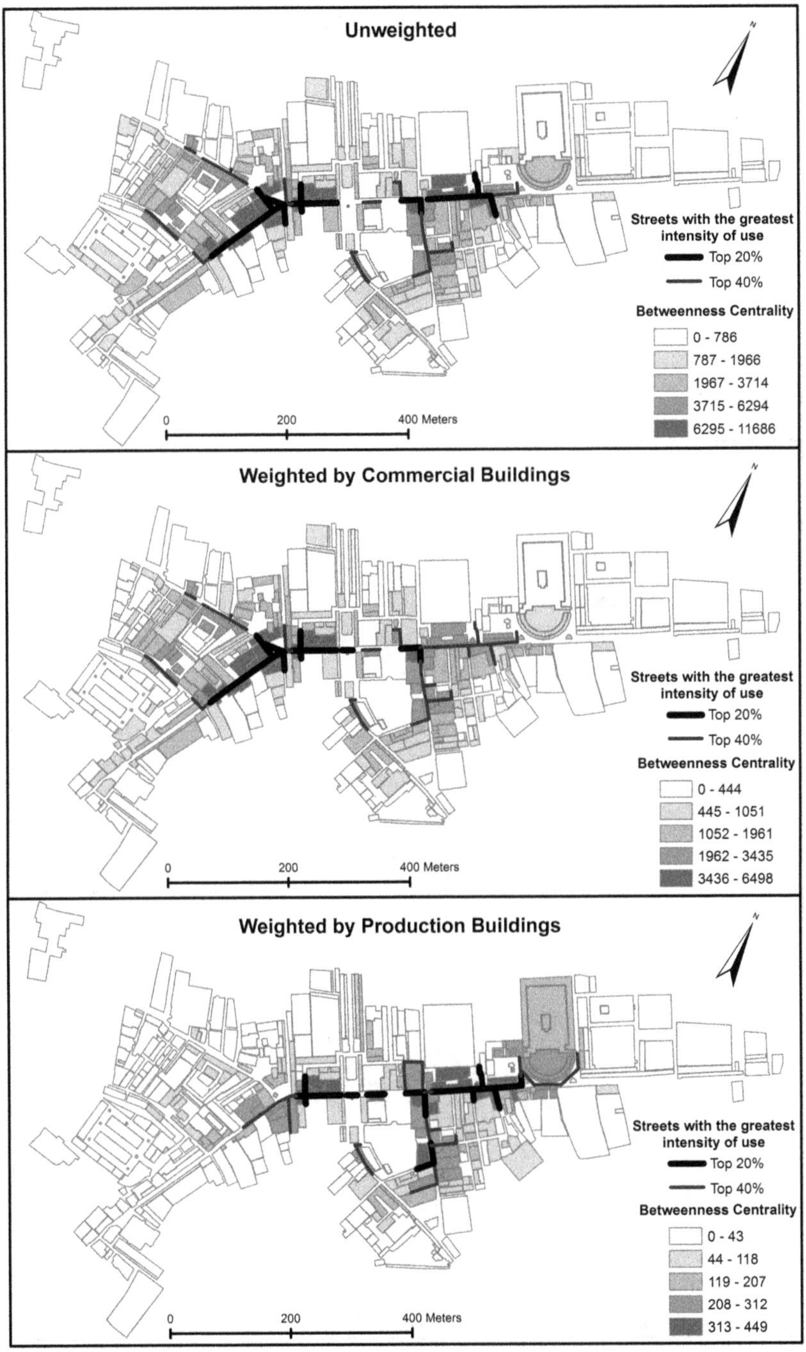

Fig. 15.3 Betweenness centrality measurements following unweighted buildings, commercial weighted buildings, and production weighted buildings and the corresponding streets with the greatest intensity of use (radius, 400 m)

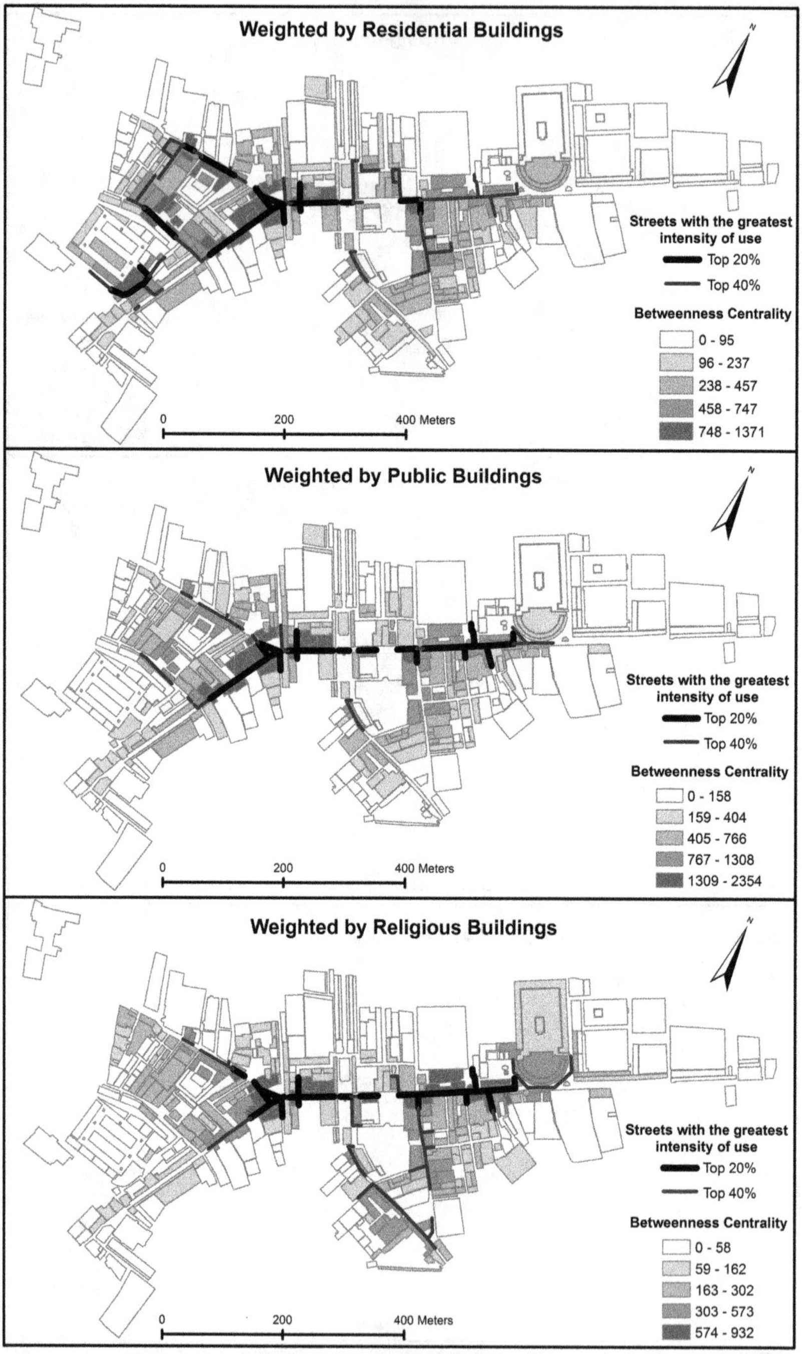

Fig. 15.4 Betweenness centrality measurements following residential weighted buildings, public weighted buildings, and religious weighted buildings and the corresponding streets with the greatest intensity of use (radius, 400 m)

15.4 Discussion

A range of different movement patterns become visible through the calculation of betweenness centrality when applying urban network analysis (Figs. 15.3 and 15.4). The results, when compared to the unweighted calculation of betweenness centrality shown in Fig. 15.3, indicate that building functionality has a notable effect upon areas of movement. While the movement potential along streets can be attributed in part to how various buildings have been classified, the potential of the method for exploring questions of how building type affected areas of urban movement is evident.

Movement along the city's primary street, the *decumanus,* has the greatest movement potential within all of the weighted betweenness calculations. The western portion of the *decumanus* sees predominant use within the commercial and residential weighted calculations. The production and religious weighted graphs show the greatest intensity of movement occurring along the eastern portion of the *decumanus.* When weighted by public buildings, in contrast, the results indicate a relatively even dispersal, which likely corresponds to the number of public buildings that are accessible from this street.

The *Via della Foce*, one of Ostia's secondary streets, sees a substantial amount of likely passage. Residential and religious weighted graphs have the greatest percentage of potential movement along this street, while commercial and public have the second highest probability of use. This street's high degree of movement activity is not surprising considering its connection to the *decumanus* and that it leads to the city's river harbour that is located northwest of the excavated city.

A less consistently used street is the *Cardo degli Aurighi,* which parallels the *Via della Foce.* The residential weighted graph shows that this street has a high degree of use, which is unsurprising considering the concentration of residential spaces located within its vicinity. The other betweenness graphs indicate that it has some degree of movement potential when the calculations are weighted by both commercial and public buildings. In these two examples, the street has the second highest degree of movement potential. Movement along the internal streets connecting both the *Cardo degli Aurighi* and the *Via della Foce* also occurs only when weighted by residential space. This provides an indication that potential movement routes can have noticeable variation depending upon what structures are deemed important for movement travelling throughout the city.

The *Semita dei Cippi*, which extends south off of the eastern *decumanus* has an inconsistent degree of use. All of the betweenness graphs, except for the public weighted measurements, indicate that this street has the second highest probability of use. In terms of Ostia's commercial movement economy, this street likely saw an increased amount of commercial traffic since the street served as a connection between Ostia's southern entrance gate and the Tiber (DeLaine 2005; Mar 2008).

The final street that sees a medium degree of use is the *cardo maximus.* The southern *cardo maximus* consistently has the second highest probability of use. When weighted by religious structures, this area of movement extends to the limits of the excavated portion of the street. The northern *cardo maximus* sees a bit more variation in usage. Production and residential weighted graphs show the greatest probability of movement travelling towards the northern *cardo maximus*. This correlates to the concentration of apartment buildings located within the vicinity of this street as well as a number of production buildings positioned near the Tiber. The other weighted classifications show little potential of movement travelling along Ostia's northern streets. Considering the number of warehouses and storage buildings located along the Tiber's edge, it is unsurprising that movement within parts of the northern city is limited.

The results of these different weighted betweenness centrality graphs all show the degree to which buildings influenced possible areas of movement throughout the second century CE cityscape. When compared to the unweighted betweenness centrality graph (Fig. 15.3), the five weighted calculations (Figs. 15.3 and 15.4) provide a visual representation about how movement directionality can change when study is focused upon what is being passed rather than just the structure of a city's street network.

15.5 Conclusion

This paper has aimed to introduce a new approach for studying directed pedestrian movement by applying urban network analysis to assess how building usage shapes potential movement areas. By moving enquiry beyond traditional approaches that focus upon how the construct of the street network promotes pedestrian movement, the calculation of betweenness centrality using building importance at a weighted scale shows distinct areas of movement potential. The results indicate that there is noticeable variation in possible routes at Ostia depending upon what types of buildings are most influential to pass.

The framework introduced above for studying movement intent can be subsequently tied to more detailed questions concerning Ostia's built environment. This could range from considering how additional building classifications or the occupancy size of buildings effects movement throughout the city. The results provide a heuristic tool for assessing how different aspects of Ostia's built environment impact movement throughout the city, allowing different assumptions to be tested. At present, only one building was weighted, but future analyses can assess how different combined weights of building types affect the betweenness results. This paper has illustrated the possibility of studying how pedestrian movement may have been shaped by different urban factors at Ostia. The application of urban network analysis shows significant potential for enabling new avenues of research to be developed that consider the nuances of urban pedestrian movement.

References

Barthelemy M (2011) Spatial networks. Phys Rep 499:1–101. https://doi.org/10.1016/j.physrep.2010.11.002

Bikoulis P (2012) Revisiting prehistoric sites in the Göksu valley: a GIS and social network approach. Anatol Stud 62:35–59. https://doi.org/10.1017/S0066154612000026

Branting S (2004) Iron age pedestrians at Kerkenes Dağ: an archaeological GIS-T approach to movement and transportation. State University of New York, Buffalo

Brughmans T (2010) Connecting the dots: towards archaeological network analysis. Oxf J Archaeol 29(3):277–303. https://doi.org/10.1111/j.1468-0092.2010.00349.x

Brughmans T, Collar A, Coward F (eds) (2016) The connected past. Challenges to network studies in archaeology and history. Oxford University Press, Oxford

Calza G (ed) (1953) Scavi di Ostia I. Topografia generale. Poligrafico dello Stato, Rome

Crucitti P, Latora V, Porta S (2006) Centrality measures in spatial networks of urban streets. Phys Rev E 73(36125):1–5. https://doi.org/10.1103/PhysRevE.73.036125

DeLaine J (2002) Building activity in Ostia in the second century AD. In: Bruun C, Gallina Zevi A (eds) Ostia e Portus nelle loro relazioni con Roma. Acta Instituti Romani Finlandiae 27:41–101

DeLaine J (2005) The commercial landscape of Ostia. In: MacMahon A, Price J (eds) Roman working lives and urban living. Oxbow, Oxford, pp 29–47

Ellis S (2004) The distribution of bars at Pompeii: archaeological, spatial and viewshed analyses. J Roman Archaeol 17:371–384. https://doi.org/10.1017/S104775940000831X

Favro D (1996) The urban image of Augustan Rome. Cambridge University Press, Cambridge

Flohr M (2013) The world of the fullo: work, economy, and society in Roman Italy. Oxford University Press, Oxford. https://doi.org/10.1093/acprof:oso/9780199659357.001.0001

Freeman L (1977) A set of measures of centrality based on betweenness. Sociometry 40(1):35–41. https://doi.org/10.2307/3033543

Groenhuijzen MR, Verhagen P (2015) Exploring the dynamics of transport in the Dutch limes. eTopoi J Anc Stud Spec Issue 4:25–47. Available at http://journal.topoi.org/index.php/etopoi/article/view/203/227. Accessed on 10 May 2018

Hartnett J (2008) Si quis hic sederit: streetside benches and urban society in Pompeii. Am J Archaeol 112(1):91–119. https://doi.org/10.3764/aja.112.1.91

Hartnett J (2017) The Roman street: urban life and society in Pompeii, Herculaneum, and Rome. Cambridge University Press, New York. https://doi.org/10.1017/9781316226438

Heinzelmann M (1998) Beobachtungen zur suburbanen topographie Ostias. Ein orthogonales strassensystem im bereich der Pianabella. Mitteilungen des Deutschen Archäologischen Instituts. Römische Abteilung 105:175–225

Heinzelmann M (2005) Die vermietete Stadt. In: Neudecker R, Zanker P (eds) Lebenswelten. Bilder und Räume in der römischen Stadt der Kaiserzeit. Reichert, Wiesbaden, pp 113–128

Hillier B, Hanson J (1984) The social logic of space. Cambridge University Press, Cambridge. https://doi.org/10.1017/CBO9780511597237

Isaksen L (2013) 'O what a tangled web we weave' – towards a practice that does not deceive. In: Knappett C (ed) Network analysis in archaeology: new approaches to regional interaction. Oxford University Press, Oxford, pp 43–67. https://doi.org/10.1093/acprof:oso/9780199697090.003.0003

Jacobs J (1961) The death and life of great American cities. Random House, New York

Kaiser A (2011) Roman urban street networks. Routledge, New York

Kostof S (1985) A history of architecture: settings and rituals. Oxford University Press, New York

Laurence R (2008) City traffic and the archaeology of Roman streets from Pompeii to Rome. In: Mertens D (ed) Stadtverkehr in der antiken welt. Reichert, Wiesbaden, pp 87–106

Laurence R (2011) Literature and the spatial turn: movement and space in Martial's Epigrams. In: Laurence R, Newsome D (eds) Rome, Ostia, Pompeii: movement and space. Oxford University Press, Oxford, pp 81–99. https://doi.org/10.1093/acprof:osobl/9780199583126.003.0003

Laurence R, Newsome D (eds) (2011) Rome, Ostia, Pompeii: movement and space. Oxford University Press, Oxford. https://doi.org/10.1093/acprof:osobl/9780199583126.001.0001

Lawrence D, Low S (1990) The built environment and spatial form. Annu Rev Anthropol 19:453–505. https://doi.org/10.1146/annurev.an.19.100190.002321

Lynch K (1960) The image of the city. MIT Press, Cambridge (MA)

Macaulay-Lewis E (2011) The city in motion: walking for transport and leisure in the city of Rome. In: Laurence R, Newsome D (eds) Rome, Ostia, Pompeii: movement and space. Oxford University Press, Oxford, pp 262–289. https://doi.org/10.1093/acprof:osobl/9780199583126.003.0012

MacDonald WL (1986) The architecture of the Roman Empire II: an urban appraisal. Yale University Press, New Haven (CT)/London

Mannucci V (1995) Atlante di Ostia antica. Marsilio, Venice

Mar R (2008) Il traffico viario a Ostia: spazio pubblico e progetto urbano. In: Mertens D (ed) Stadtverkehr in der antiken Welt. Reichert, Wiesbaden, pp 125–144

Martin A, Heinzelmann M (2000) The joint AAR-DAI research project at Ostia: 1998 and 1999 seasons. Mem Am Acad Rome 45:277–283. https://doi.org/10.2307/4238773

Meiggs R (1973) Roman Ostia, 2nd edn. Oxford University Press, Oxford

Mol A, Mans J (2013) Old-boy networks in the indigenous Caribbean. In: Knappett C (ed) Network analysis in archaeology: new approaches to regional interaction. Oxford University Press, Oxford, pp 307–327. https://doi.org/10.1093/acprof:oso/9780199697090.003.0013

Omer I, Rofè Y, Lerman Y (2015) The impact of planning on pedestrian movement: contrasting pedestrian movement models in pre-modern and modern neighborhoods in Israel. Int J Geogr Inf Sci 29(12):2121–2142. https://doi.org/10.1080/13658816.2015.1063638

Östenberg I, Malmberg S, Bjørnebye J (eds) (2015) The moving city: processions, passages and promenades in ancient Rome. Bloomsbury Academic, London

Packer JE (1971) The insulae of imperial Ostia. Mem Am Acad Rome 31:1–217. https://doi.org/10.2307/4238664

Pavolini C (2006) Ostia. GLF Editori Laterza, Rome

Pavolini C (2016) A survey of excavations and studies on Ostia (2004–2014). J Roman Stud 106:199–236. https://doi.org/10.1017/S0075435816001015

Pirson F (2007) Shops and industries. In: Dobbins JJ, Foss PW (eds) The world of Pompeii. Routledge, New York, pp 457–473

Poehler E (2016) Measuring the movement economy: a network analysis of Pompeii. In: Flohr M, Wilson A (eds) The economy of Pompeii. Oxford University Press, Oxford, pp 163–208. https://doi.org/10.1093/acprof:oso/9780198786573.003.0007

Poehler E (2017) The traffic systems of Pompeii. Oxford University Press, Oxford

Porta S, Crucitti P, Latora V (2006) The network analysis of urban streets: a primal approach. Environ Plann B 33:705–725. https://doi.org/10.1068/b32045

Rapoport A (1982) The meaning of the built environment: a nonverbal communication approach. Sage Publications, Beverly Hills (CA)

Russell A (2016) The politics of public space in republican Rome. Cambridge University Press, Cambridge. https://doi.org/10.1017/CBO9781139629041

Sarkar S (2013) Street network analysis for understanding typology in cities. Case study on Sydney CBD and suburbs. In: Ruming K, Randolph B, Gurran N (eds) State of Australian cities conference 2013: refereed proceedings. State of Australian Cities Research Network, Sydney, pp 1–9

Sevtsuk A, Mekonnen M (2012) Urban network analysis toolbox. Int J Geomatics Spat Anal 22(2):287–305. https://doi.org/10.3166/rig.22.287-305

Sevtsuk A, Mekkonen M, Kalvo R (2016) Urban network analysis: toolbox for ArcGIS 10/10.1/10.2. City Form Lab, Harvard University, Cambridge (MA), Available at http://media.voog.com/0000/0036/2451/files/20160120_UNA_help_v1_1.pdf. Accessed on 12 May 2018

Stöger H (2011) Rethinking Ostia: a spatial enquiry into the urban society of Rome's imperial port-town. Leiden University Press, Leiden

Thaler U (2005) Narrative and syntax: new perspectives on the Late Bronze Age palace of Pylos, Greece. In: Van Nes A (ed) Proceedings of the 5th international space syntax symposium. Techne Press, Amsterdam, pp 324–339

Van Nes A (2014) Indicating street vitality in excavated towns. Spatial configurative analyses applied to Pompeii. In: Paliou E, Lieberwirth U, Polla S (eds) Spatial analysis and social spaces: interdisciplinary approaches to the interpretation of prehistoric and historic built environments. De Gruyter, Berlin, pp 277–296. https://doi.org/10.1515/9783110266436.277

Yegül FK (1994) The street experience of ancient Ephesus. In: Çelik Z, Favro D, Ingersoll R (eds) Streets: critical perspectives on public space. University of California Press, Berkeley, pp 95–110

Index

A

Adam Smith´s principle, 154
African Red Slip (ARS), 202
Agency-oriented winegrowing specialization production model, 153–156
Agent-based modelling (ABM), 230
- animal husbandry, 113, 116, 117
- arable extensification and intensification, 115–116
- arable farming, 112–113
- experiments, 114
- initialization, 110–111
- land use in reconstructed landscapes, 118–120
- macro-regional supply network, 119, 121, 122
- micro-regional supply network, 119, 121, 122
- population dynamics, 111–112
- ROMFARMS, 109
- surplus debate, 110
- surplus production, 117, 118
- wood collection, 113, 114

Age specific fertility rate (ASFR), 46
Age-structured populations, 153
Agricultural economy, 110
Agricultural exploitation, 66
Agricultural intensification
- Boserup's model, 152–153

Agricultural populations, 66
Agricultural revolution, 66
Agriculture
- analysis, 123
- land and labour costs, 109
- landscapes reconstruction, 117

Agro-ecological and agro-economic endowments
- palaeoclimatic conditions, 135
- physical environment, 135, 136
- territorial/farming plot scale, 135
- viticulture supply chain, 136
- winegrowing production systems, 134
- yield quantification (*see* Yield quantification)

Agro-economic pattern, 153
Agroecosystem, 150, 152, 153, 158
Alsace Bossue, 84
Alveus/goblet technique, 155
Amphorae, 144
Ancient historians, 95
Ancient viticulture, 130, 133, 134, 151, 152, 157
Animal bones, provincial sites, 102
Animal husbandry, 113
- exploitation strategies, 113
- livestock species, 113
- products, 113
- in randomly-generated landscapes, 116, 117

Antiquity, 96, 130
Antiquity's place, 96
Antonine Plague, 15, 29, 34, 102
Aoristic analysis, 168
Arable extensification and intensification
- cost-effectiveness, 116
- limiting factors, 115

Arable farming, 112–113
ArcGIS Pro 10.2.1, 172
Archaeological excavation
- *vs.* survey data, 82–86

Archaeologists, 63

P. Verhagen et al. (eds.), *Finding the Limits of the Limes*, Computational Social Sciences, https://doi.org/10.1007/978-3-030-04576-0

Archaeology, 1, 8
  affordances and movement potential, 218–219
  algorithms, 238
  calculating routes and movement potential
    LCPs and corridors, 229–230
    movement potential, 230–231
  control, 223
  GIS, 217
  infrastructure, 222–223
  methodological issues
    model complexity, 238–239
    validation, pathway models, 238
  modelling ancient movement
    applications, path modelling, 225
    defining movement capability, 226–227
    DEMs, 227
    GIS-based modelling, 226
    LCPs, 225
    modelling socio-cultural costs, 229
    settlement's environment, 225
    terrain costs, 228
    visibility, movement cost, 228
  movement capability
    energy/speed, 219
    transport modes, 220–221
  movement networks and pathways, 217
  natural environment, 221–222
  navigation, 224–225
  network (re)construction techniques, 234–236
  network analysis techniques, 233, 234, 236–237
  pathways, 233
  safety, 223
  sensitivity analysis and validation, 231–233
  social interpretation, 240
  social network analysis, 233
  software, 237
  technological integration, 240
  theoretical issues
    movement practices, 239
    understanding networks, 240
    value of experimental data, 239
Archaeology Data Service (ADS), 62
Area-floodbasin, 111
Area-levee, 111
Artisan activities, 145, 150
Attractors, 193
Autarchic self-sufficient system, 155
Average cost (AC), 139
Average cost per unit, 138, 139
Average fixed costs (AFC), 140
Average total costs (ATC), 140
Average variable cost (AVC), 140

B

Baseline model, 167
Batavians, 6, 10, 13, 14
Bayesian Inference Procedure, 29
Berry's geographical information matrix, 81
Binomial logistic regression, 264
Birth control
  strategies, 56
Birth rates, 28
Black Death, 100
Bob Allen's analysis, 102
Border populations
  features, 31
  foreigners, 32
  guards, 33
Boserup's model
  population growth and agricultural intensification, 152–153
Boserupian pushing force, 154
Bronze Age, 62, 63, 66, 69

C

Cambridge economic history, 97
Cellae vinariae, 145
Civil settlements, 168
Colonization, 7
Conceptual framework, land and farming system, 134
Consumer expenditure, 103
Contagious diseases, 36
Cost quantification
  AC and MC, 139
  ACT, 140
  AFC, 140
  ATC, 140
  AVC, 140
  average cost per unit, 138, 139
  direct costs, 138
  fixed resources, 139
  indirect costs, 138
  long-term production costs, 140
  principle of economic scarcity, 141
  sestertius, 138
  structure, economic activity, 138
  TC, 140
  TFC, 140
  TVC, 140
Cost-effectiveness, 116
Crop-share leased vineyard, 148

D

Dachstein site, 79
Demography, 97–99
  age-sex distributions, 24
  archaeological, 25
  biological uniformity, 25
  birth control, 45, 47–48
  border populations (*see* Border populations)
  contributions, 26
  data sets, 44–45
  diseases, 56
  environmental crises, 33–35
  faltering recovery, 35, 36
  fertility, 27–28
  geographical and chronological fluctuation, 63–64
  laws, 24
  marriage pool, 47
  migration (*see* Migration)
  military camps, 27
  military landscapes, 65
  mortality, 28–29
  NetLogo environment, 56
  NRR, 45
  parameters, 25
  population dynamics, 45, 47, 56
  population growth rates, 44
  population size and structures, 26, 27
  pre-industrial populations, 24, 29
  province of Britannia, 69
  river valleys, 65
  rural populations, 63
  sex ratio, 32–33
  stopping behaviour, 47
  transition, 28
  urban populations, 63
  z-scores, 65, 70
Depopulation, 51
Differential/kicking element, 193
Digital elevation model (DEMs), 227–228
Dutch limes
  agent-based modelling (*see* Agent-based modelling)
Dutch Roman archeology
  surplus debate in, 110
Dutch territory, 7

E

Early medieval periods, 65
Economic analysis
  antiquity, 96
  antiquity's place, 96
  archaeological data, 97
  demography, 97–99
  estimating population numbers, 97–99
  Greco-Roman society, 95
  methodologically, 96
  neo-Marxist thought, 96
  population growth and wealth, 103, 104
  population increase, 100–103
  post-colonial discourse, 96
  pre-Roman society, 96
  scarce goods and services, 95
  and society of Pompeii, 96
  standard of living, 96
  statistical analysis, 97
  theoretical and methodological, 96
Economic models
  agency-oriented winegrowing specialization production model, 153–156
  Boserup's model, 152–153
  "Roman Villa" system, 149–152
  taxes-and-trade model, 156–157
Economic scarcity principle, 141
Economic theory, 157
Economies of scale, 141, 142
Emigration, 50
Endogenous and exogenous agents, 130
Endogenous and exogenous factors, 144
England
  economy
    and landscape change, 65
    cultivation, 66
    floods and alluviation, 66
    settlement patterns, 66
    villa creation, 66
  EngLaId database
    categories, 62
    coins to weapons, 62
    spatial bins, 62
    spatial scale, 62
  EngLaId periods, 69
  EngLaId project, 63, 68
  EngLaId team
    proxy models, 70
  English landscape, 72, 73
  erosion susceptibility, 67, 68
  GIS, 68
  HE'S, 63
  HER records, 69
  transportation
    A1 road, 70
    Britannia, 70
    Cambridgeshire, 72
    Northamptonshire, 72

Environmental crises
  food shortage, 34
  infectious diseases, 34
  population decrease, 34
  population growth, 34
  volcanic eruptions, 34
Epidemiological transition, 24

F

Fertility reduction, 54
Fertility regime, 55
Field surveys
  advantages, 79
  ancient societies, 82
  application, 85
  building materials, 79
  characteristics, 79
  date of appearance, 79
  date of disappearance, 79
  duration of existence, 79
  and excavation, 79, 80
  history of settlement, 79
  linear signal, 79
  regional settlement, 90
  settlement pattern, 87
  Snap entities, 79
  Span entities, 79
  stratigraphic information, 79
  study of settlement patterns
    analysing sets, 81
    duration of occupation descriptor, 81
    making comparisons and associations, 81
    optimal state, 81
    settlement network, 81
    spatiotemporal analysis, 81
    spatiotemporal dynamics, 80
    temporal dynamics, 80
    three-dimensional cube, 81
    time-consuming, 80
    treating temporal data, 81
    typology, 81
    working quantitatively, 81
Flavian period, 12
Flood-basin, 111
Food consumption trends, 102
Foodstuffs, 147
Forensic medicine, 26
Freedmen, 130

G

Gabriel graph, 258
Gallo-Roman period, 29
Geographical space
  civitates, 2
  fluvial landforms, 3
  limes zone, 2, 3, 12
Geography of vineyards, 144
Geospatial and geoeconomic analysis, 130
Germanic territory, 5
Germanic tribes, 6, 51
Germany, 2
GIS least-cost path algorithm, 206
GIS-based spatial analysis, 199
Greco-Roman society, 95
Gross reproduction rate (GRR), 46

H

Head-trained and spur-pruned training system, 155
Heckscher-Ohlin-Samuelson economic model, 154
Hierarchic levels, 202
Hill's index, 87–89
Hispania Citerior, 150, 273
Historic England (HE), 62, 63
Historic Environment Records (HERs), 62
Hop-o'My-Thumb, 193
Horse-breeding, 117
Human reproduction
  birth control, 53
  kinship relations, 53
  marriage strategies, 52–53
  mortality crises, 53
Human-land ratios, 153
Hydrological processes, 66
Hypotheses, 261

I

Increased efficiency, 101
Independent variables
  landforms, 174
  MP, 174–176, 178–180
  PCA, 174
  PCs, 174
Intensive/specialised winegrowing production processes, *see* Laetanian Roman wine
Intervenient agents, 143
Investigation method, 78
Iron Age, 6, 8, 10, 65, 66, 70

J

Juvenility index, 28

K

Kernel Density Estimate (KDE), 64
Kolmogorov-Smirnov (K-S) test, 172

L

Laetanian Roman wine
  agroecological and agroeconomic endowments (*see* Agro-ecological and agro-economic endowments)
  archaeological dataset, 144–146
  archaeological excavations, 143
  conceptual framework, 134
  connectivity, 147–149
  consumption, 143
  economic models (*see* Economic models)
  endogenous and exogenous agents, 130
  endogenous and exogenous factors, 144
  field-surveys, 143
  food supplies, 143
  geospatial and geoeconomic analysis, 130
  global structure of settlement, 130
  hypothesis
    operative, 133, 134
    working, 133
  intervenient agents, 143
  labour division, 144
  land tenure, 146, 147
  land use, 146, 147
  maintenance and self-consumption, 142
  ownership management, 146, 147
  population growth, 130
  population mobility, 130
  production, 130
  quantitative and qualitative analyses, 142
  Roman agronomists, 143
  taxation, 147–149
  territorial scope, 131, 132
  transport infrastructures, 147–149
  typology of rural settlements, 143
  urban and rural world, 142
  viticulture, 130
  workforce availability, 144
Land-based transport modes, 256
Land/labour ratio, 101
Land use
  in reconstructed landscapes, 118–120
Landform classification system, 170
Landforms, 174
Landscape archaeology
  models, 64
Landscape-type, 111
Large establishments, 145
Least-cost path (LCP) modelling, 225, 255
Life expectancy, 27, 28, 50
Linear signal, 79, 80
Living standards, 96, 100–104
Local-scale transport infrastructure, 256
Location analysis, 166, 167, 184
Logistic regression, 264
Logistic regression analysis, 172, 173, 183
Logistic regression models, 178
Lower Rhine frontier, 166, 167, 184

M

Macro-regional supply network, 119, 121, 122
MADO, 302, 303
Marginal cost (MC), 139, 140
Marital fertility, 46
Market exchange, 166
Market potential (MP), 172, 174–176, 178–181
Market production, 167
Marriage migrations, 33
Marriage strategies
  age, 54
  first marriage, 52, 53
  restrictions, 56
  Swedish, 54
  Taiwanese, 54
  time span, 54
Medieval periods, 2, 66, 70, 72
Medieval successors, 63
Medium establishments, 145
Mercator-e project, 278
Micro-regional supply network, 119, 121, 122
Micro-regions, Plateau Lorrain, 82–83
Midden-Delfland landscape, 13, 15
Middle Ages, 2
Migration, 25
  behaviours, 36
  conquest, 30
  deportation, 30
  destruction of harvests, 30
  forced migration, 30
  infiltration, 30
  mass migration, 30
  mobility, 30
  permanent residence, 30
  poor cousin, 29
Military garrisons, 33
Modelling
  settlement networks, 81
  spatial dynamics, 90
Modern period, 2
Monte Carlo method approach, 264
Monte Carlo simulation, 168

Mortality
  empirical data, 44
  epidemics, 48
  fertility schedule, 46
  life tables, 45
  patterns, 44
  true fertility, 46
  warfare, 49
  Woods South 25, 55
Multi-criteria analysis (MCA), 229
Multivariate analysis
  rural marketing
    dependent variable, 173
    independent variables (*see* Independent variables)
    Late Iron Age, 178
    logistic regression analysis, 172
    logistic regression models, 178
    MP, 172
    postdictive, baseline model, 172
    RMSEs, 173, 178, 179
Multivariate approach, 263–264
Multivariate logistic regression model, 167

N
Neolithic period, 66
The Netherlands
  geographical space (*see* Geographical space)
  research history (*see* Research history)
Net reproduction rate (NRR), 45, 46
NetLogo's inbuilt BehaviourSpace function, 114
Network analysis, 205–208
  ancient sources and archaeological materials, 272
  communication and transport infrastructures, 272
  development, technologies, 272
  elements, 271
  infrastructures, 272
  Mercator-e project, 272
  methodological approaches, 271
  methodology
    connectivity, 277–279
    historical transport roads, 276
  Roman transport networks, 273
  trade, 272
  transport time costs and financial expenses
    Geographic Information Systems and Network Analysis, 280
    Guadalquivir River, 284, 285
    Iberian Peninsula, 281, 283, 285
    land transport, 282
    maritime transport, 280
    performance of, 282
    Pyrenees, 284
    Roman transport network, 280, 283
    transcendental elements, 280
    transport characteristics, 283
    transportation costs, 282, 284, 285
Network science, 252, 255

O
Ombrone System
  analysis, 201
  ARS, 202
  distribution, 203
  economic, 202
  navigability, 202, 203
  pottery imports, 203–205
  production waste, 202
  quantitative data, 201
Ombrone valley, 205, 206, 208

P
Palaeoclimatic conditions, 135
Palaeogeographic analysis approaches
  archaeological data, 266
  computational approaches, 266
  Dutch *limes*, 251–253
  higher-status stone-built settlements, 265
  natural and social environment, 265
  natural palaeogeography, 253–255
  network analysis, 266
  Roman *limes*, 251
  transport networks and settlement location, 252
Palaeogeographic reconstruction, 118
Palaeogeography, 168
Patrol route, 31
Physical environment, 135, 136
Pompeii society, 96
Population dynamics, 23, 25, 111–112
Population growth, 130
  Boserup's model, 152–153
Population increase, 100–103
Population mobility, 130
Population pressure, 100, 152, 153
Population pyramid, 24, 27
Portable Antiquities Scheme (PAS), 62
Post-depositional processes, 78
Postdictive, baseline model, 172
Prehistoric populations, 44
Premodern period, 44
Principal component analysis (PCA), 174
Principal components (PCs), 174

Q

Quantitative data, 88
Quantitative methods, 130

R

Rainfall erosivity, 68
Rank-size classification, 192
Reproductive behaviours, 27
Research history
  Cananefatian area, 4
  coins, 8
  colonization, 7
  end of the Dutch *limes*, 8
  extensive excavations, 4
  frontier zone, 6
  Roman *castellum*, 4
  Roman Empire integration, 7
  Roman involvement, 5
  shipwrecks, 4
  substantial erosion, 4
  Vecht River, 5
Roman agronomists, 143
Roman archaeology, 72
Roman demography, *see* Demography
Roman Empire, 97, 98, 101, 103
Roman monetary unit, 138
Roman period
  demography (*see* Demography)
Roman pottery, 193, 202–205, 208–210
Roman road system
  ancient infrastructures, 292
  ancient mobility, 294
  ancient routes, 293
  cost factors, 296
  digital environment, 296
  friction models
    Aquae Flauiae, 300, 301
    interpretations, 300
    LCP-based approaches, 298
    mansio Caladunum, 301
    multiple potential pathways, 298
  friction surface, 295
  geographical and archaeological contexts, 293
  GIS-based digital modelling tools, 293
  heterogeneity, 292
  human movement, 293
  hypotheses, 295
  Iberia, 292
  LiDAR technology, 293
  MADO, 304–307
  multiple discrete optimal connections, 304
  network friction, 294
  NW Iberian Peninsula, 297–298
  predictive and postdictive modelling, 296
  predictive/postdictive approaches, 293
  regional landscape, 295
  Roman and Medieval routes, 294
  Roman and Medieval settlements, 294
  single least-cost path model, 302–304
"Roman Villa" system, 149–152
ROMFARMS, 57
  animal husbandry, 113, 116, 117
  arable farming, 112–113
  experiments, 114
  initialization, 110–111
  land use in reconstructed landscapes, 118–120
  macro-regional supply network, 119, 121, 122
  micro-regional supply network, 119, 121, 122
  population dynamics, 111–112
  surplus production, 117, 118
  wood collection, 113, 114
Root mean square errors (RMSE), 173, 179
Rural economy
  boom and bust, 14
  castella, 15
  municipium, 13, 14
  non-military inhabitants, 10
  periodization, 8
  population sizes, 10, 11
  surplus production, 12
  surplus question, 11–12
  taxation and landownership, 12–14
  urban population, 10
Rural marketing, Lower Rhine
  baseline model, 167
  data, 168, 169, 171
  economic relationship, 166
  environmental factors, 167
  historical implications, 181–183
  location analysis, 166, 167
  market exchange, 166
  market production, 167
  marketing behaviour, 169
  modelling results, 180, 181
  multivariate analysis (*see* Multivariate analysis)
  network analysis, 166
  productive capacity, 169
  scaffolding model, 168
  settlement territories, 169, 170
  sharp relief, 166
  small-scale producers, 167
  study areas, 170

Rural marketing, Lower Rhine (*cont.*)
transportation costs, 166, 167
univariate analysis
(*see* Univariate analysis)
Rural population growth, 50

S
Scaffolding model, 168
Secondary settlements
economic and commercial, 210
framework, 209
long-term trade, 210
macro-economic perspectives, 209
network analysis, 205, 206, 208
Ombrone System (*see* Ombrone System)
quantitative approaches
bibliographic inventory, 194
data mining, 194
descriptive statistics, diachronic trends, 196, 199
long-term historical trends, 194
proportions, collected sites per region, 196
spatial statistics, 199, 200
reviewed sites, 208
theory and method, 192–194
transformations, 208
Settlement evidence
burial evidence, 50
historical evidence, 50
inventories, 49
population sizes, 49, 50
pre-industrial societies, 50
productivity and urbanisation, 50
Settlement population dynamics, 110
Settlement study
archaeological excavations
(*see* Archaeological excavations)
composition and evolution, 86–89
function, 78
method of investigation, 78
qualify and improve, 78
structuring and spatial evolution, 89, 90
survey data quality, 78
survey data *vs.* excavation, 82–86
temporal dimension, 78–82
Sex ratio
epidemiological shock, 32
psychological shock, 32
urbanization, 32
Shannon index, 88, 89
Short-term costs, 139
Simpson index, 88, 89
Slave-based *villae*, 150
Small establishments, 145
Small-scale producers, 167
Smithian market, 154
Snap entities, 79
Social Network Analysis (SNA), 277, 279
Social relationships, 153
Socioeconomic phenomenon, 130
Span entities, 79
Statistics, 194
descriptive, 195–199
fundamental, 206
spatial, 199, 200
Surplus debate in Dutch Roman archeology, 110
Surplus production
in Dutch Roman archaeology, 110
grain and animal products, 110
mechanism, 116
in randomly-generated and reconstructed landscapes, 114
in reconstructed landscapes, 117, 118
in ROMFARMS, 123
Survey data quality, 78
Survey data *vs.* excavation
ancient societies, 82
characteristics, 82
conditions and modalities, 83, 84
evolution of settlements, 82
internal dynamics, 82
micro-regions, Plateau Lorrain, 82–83
model of evolution, 85, 86
trajectories of settlements, 84, 85

T
Taxes-and-trade model, 156
Temporal dimension
field surveys, 78–82
Territorial scope, Laetanian Roman wine, 131, 132
Thames Basin, 68, 69
Thames River basin, 67
Three-dimensional cube, 81
Topography, 221
Total costs (TC), 140
Total fixed costs (TFC), 140
Total variable costs (TVC), 140
Trajectories of settlements, 84, 85
Transport networks
applications, 260–263
Caesaraugusta, 274
communication system, 273
constructing networks, 258–260
digitization, 275–276

Iberian Peninsula, 273–274
mobility, 255
modelling transport, 256–257
networks, 255
settlement location analysis, 263–265
Transportation costs, 166, 167

U
Univariate analysis
rural marketing
diachronic trends, 177
eastern zone, 178
floodplain cluster, 178
Focal Statistics tool, 172
K-S test, 172
landform classification system, 170
Mid-Roman periods, 176
simplified classification, 171, 172
territorial radii, 176
time period, 176
zone and territory size, 176
Urban network analysis, Ostia
archaeological studies, 317
betweenness centrality, 320, 322, 324
cardo maximus, 324
centrality graphs, 317
centrality measurements, 317
decumanus, 323
integrated computational approach, 314
modelling movement intent, 314
network science methodologies, 313
Ostia's Urban Landscape, 315–316
pedestrian movement, 314
radius, 319
Roman pedestrian research, 314
Semita dei Cippi, 323
social activity, 314
study of movement, 313
toolbox, 318
transition enquiry, 317
tripartite network, 318
Via della Foce, 323

V
Villa system, 133
Villae rusticae, 146
Vine-growing specialization, 154
Vineyard yields
harvesting, 137
per strain, 136
productivity, processing machinery, 137
winery, 137
Viticulture supply chain, 136

W
Wages (in wheat) in Roman Egypt, 101
Watermills, 101
Welfare ratios, 100
Wood collection, 113, 114

Y
Yield quantification, agro-ecological and agro-economic endowments
cost quantification, 138–141
economies of scale, 141, 142
vineyard yields, 136–137

CPSIA information can be obtained
at www.ICGtesting.com
Printed in the USA
LVHW051223240623
750703LV00005B/78

9 783030 045753